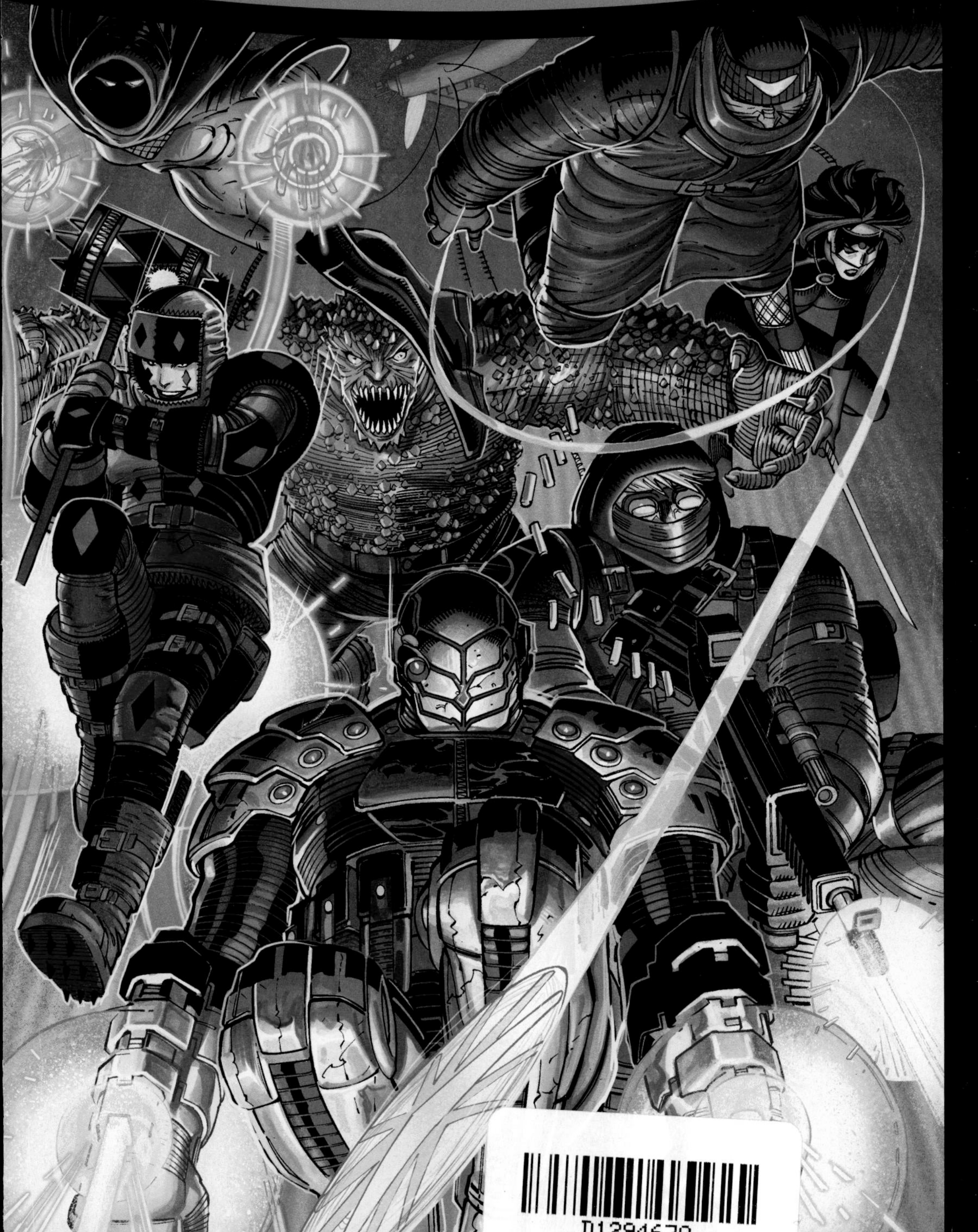

SUICIDE SQUAD

VOL.3 BURNING DOWN THE HOUSE

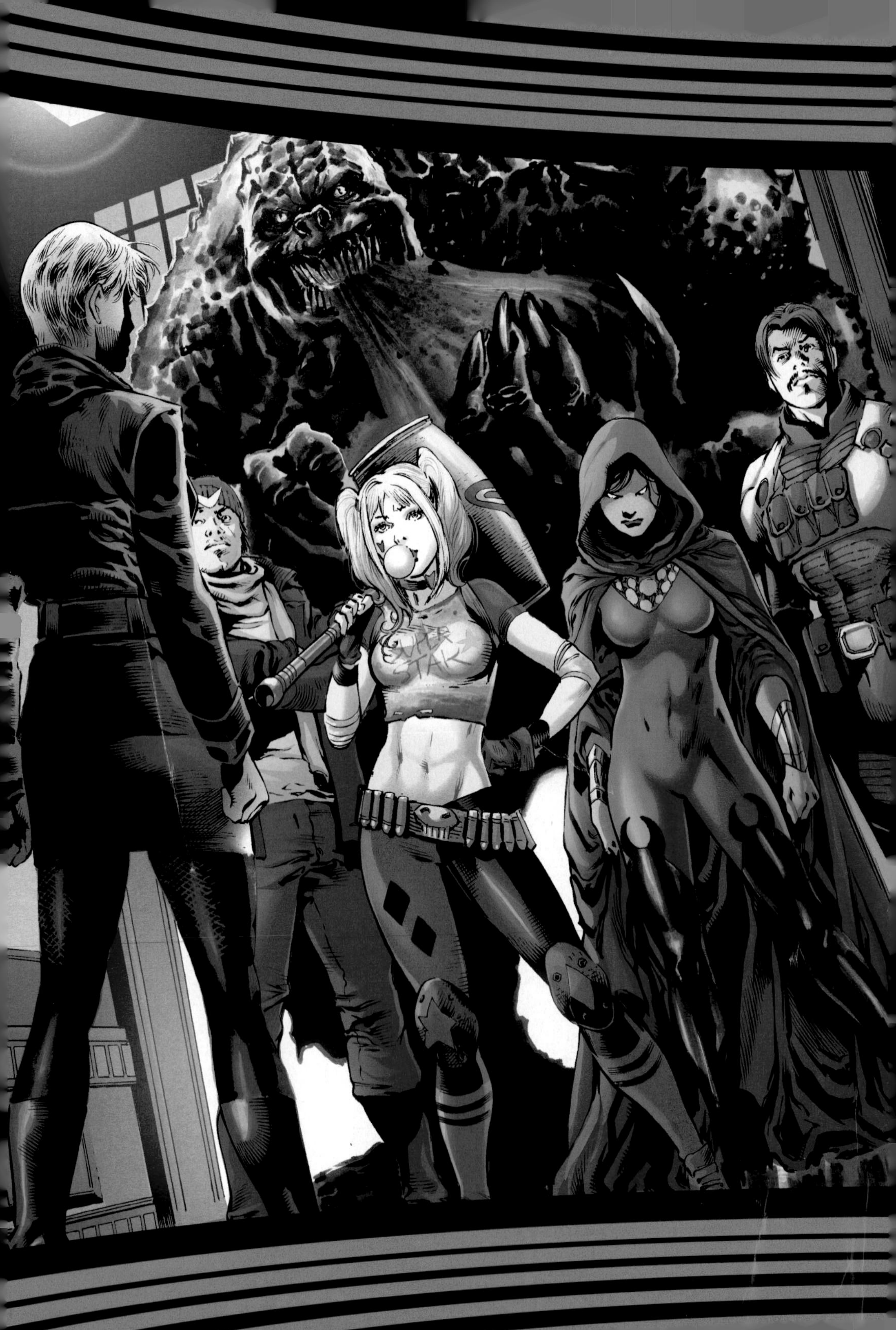

SUICIDE SQUAD
VOL.3 BURNING DOWN THE HOUSE

ROB WILLIAMS * JOHN OSTRANDER
writers

JOHN ROMITA JR. * RICHARD FRIEND
EDDY BARROWS * EBER FERREIRA
GUS VAZQUEZ * CARLOS RODRIGUEZ
artists

DEAN WHITE * ADRIANO LUCAS
GABE ELTAEB * JEREMIAH SKIPPER
colorists

PAT BROSSEAU * NATE PIEKOS
CARLOS M. MANGUAL
letterers

JOHN ROMITA JR., RICHARD FRIEND & DEAN WHITE
collection cover art

JOHN ROMITA JR., RICHARD FRIEND & DEAN WHITE
JUAN FERREYRA
original series covers

AMANDA WALLER created by JOHN OSTRANDER and JOHN BYRNE

ANDY KHOURI Editor - Original Series * **HARVEY RICHARDS** Associate Editor - Original Series
JEB WOODARD Group Editor - Collected Editions * **SCOTT NYBAKKEN** Editor - Collected Edition
STEVE COOK Design Director - Books * **MONIQUE GRUSPE** Publication Design

BOB HARRAS Senior VP - Editor-in-Chief, DC Comics

DIANE NELSON President * **DAN DiDIO** Publisher * **JIM LEE** Publisher * **GEOFF JOHNS** President & Chief Creative Officer
AMIT DESAI Executive VP - Business & Marketing Strategy, Direct to Consumer & Global Franchise Management
SAM ADES Senior VP - Direct to Consumer * **BOBBIE CHASE** VP - Talent Development
MARK CHIARELLO Senior VP - Art, Design & Collected Editions * **JOHN CUNNINGHAM** Senior VP - Sales & Trade Marketing
ANNE DePIES Senior VP - Business Strategy, Finance & Administration * **DON FALLETTI** VP - Manufacturing Operations
LAWRENCE GANEM VP - Editorial Administration & Talent Relations * **ALISON GILL** Senior VP - Manufacturing & Operations
HANK KANALZ Senior VP - Editorial Strategy & Administration * **JAY KOGAN** VP - Legal Affairs
THOMAS LOFTUS VP - Business Affairs * **JACK MAHAN** VP - Business Affairs
NICK J. NAPOLITANO VP - Manufacturing Administration * **EDDIE SCANNELL** VP - Consumer Marketing
COURTNEY SIMMONS Senior VP - Publicity & Communications
JIM (SKI) SOKOLOWSKI VP - Comic Book Specialty Sales & Trade Marketing
NANCY SPEARS VP - Mass, Book, Digital Sales & Trade Marketing

SUICIDE SQUAD VOL.3: BURNING DOWN THE HOUSE

Published by DC Comics. Compilation and all new material Copyright © 2017 DC Comics. All Rights Reserved.
Originally published in single magazine form in SUICIDE SQUAD SPECIAL: WAR CRIMES 1 and SUICIDE SQUAD 11-15. Copyright © 2016, 2017 DC Comics.
All Rights Reserved. All characters, their distinctive likenesses and related elements featured in this publication are trademarks of DC Comics.
The stories, characters and incidents featured in this publication are entirely fictional.
DC Comics does not read or accept unsolicited submissions of ideas, stories or artwork.

DC Comics, 2900 West Alameda Ave., Burbank, CA 91505
Printed by LSC Communications, Kendallville, IN, USA. 8/4/17. First Printing.
ISBN: 978-1-4012-7422-1

Library of Congress Cataloging-in-Publication Data is available.

PEFC Certified
Printed on paper from
sustainably managed
forests, controlled
sources
PEFC/29-31-337   www.pefc.org

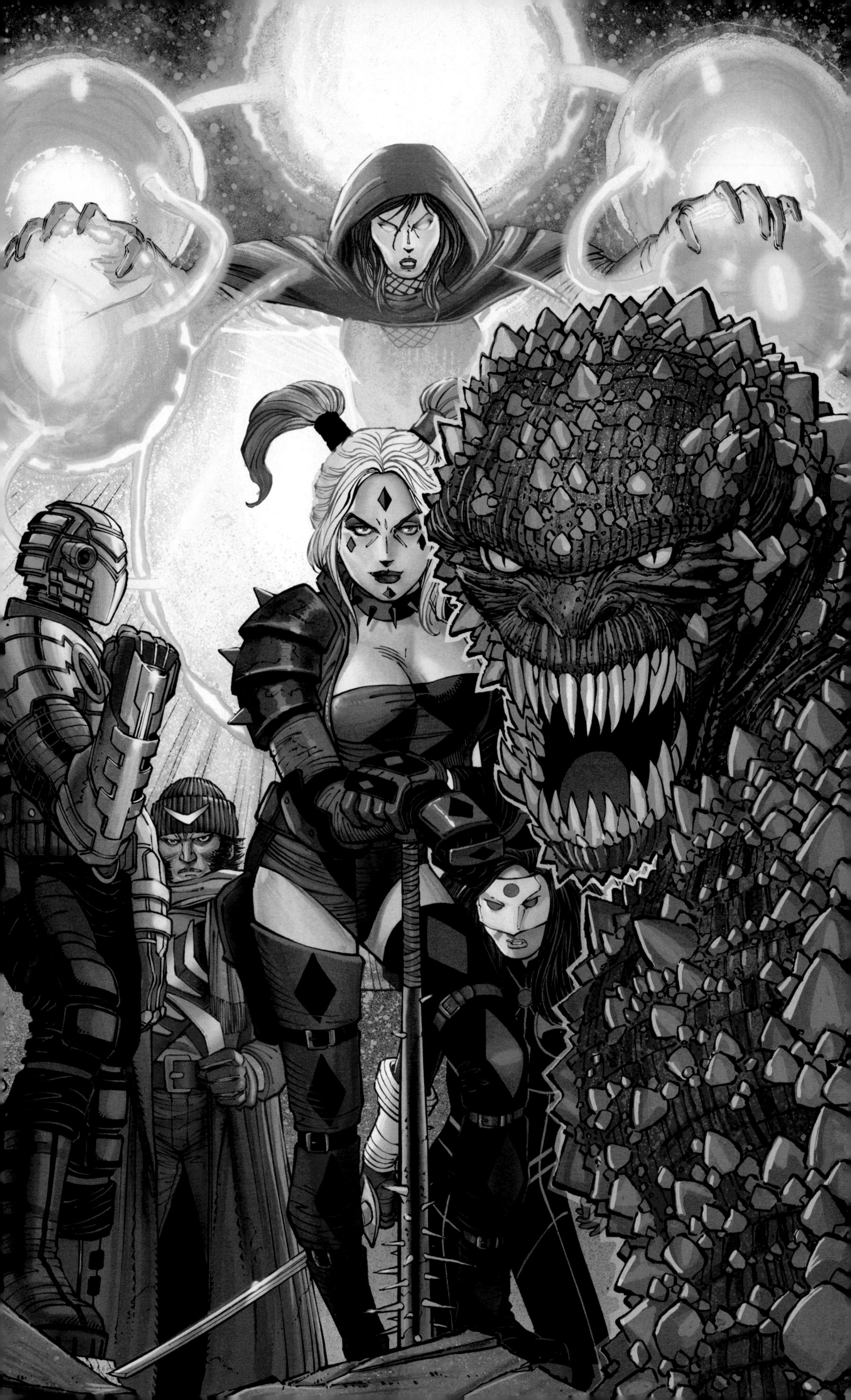

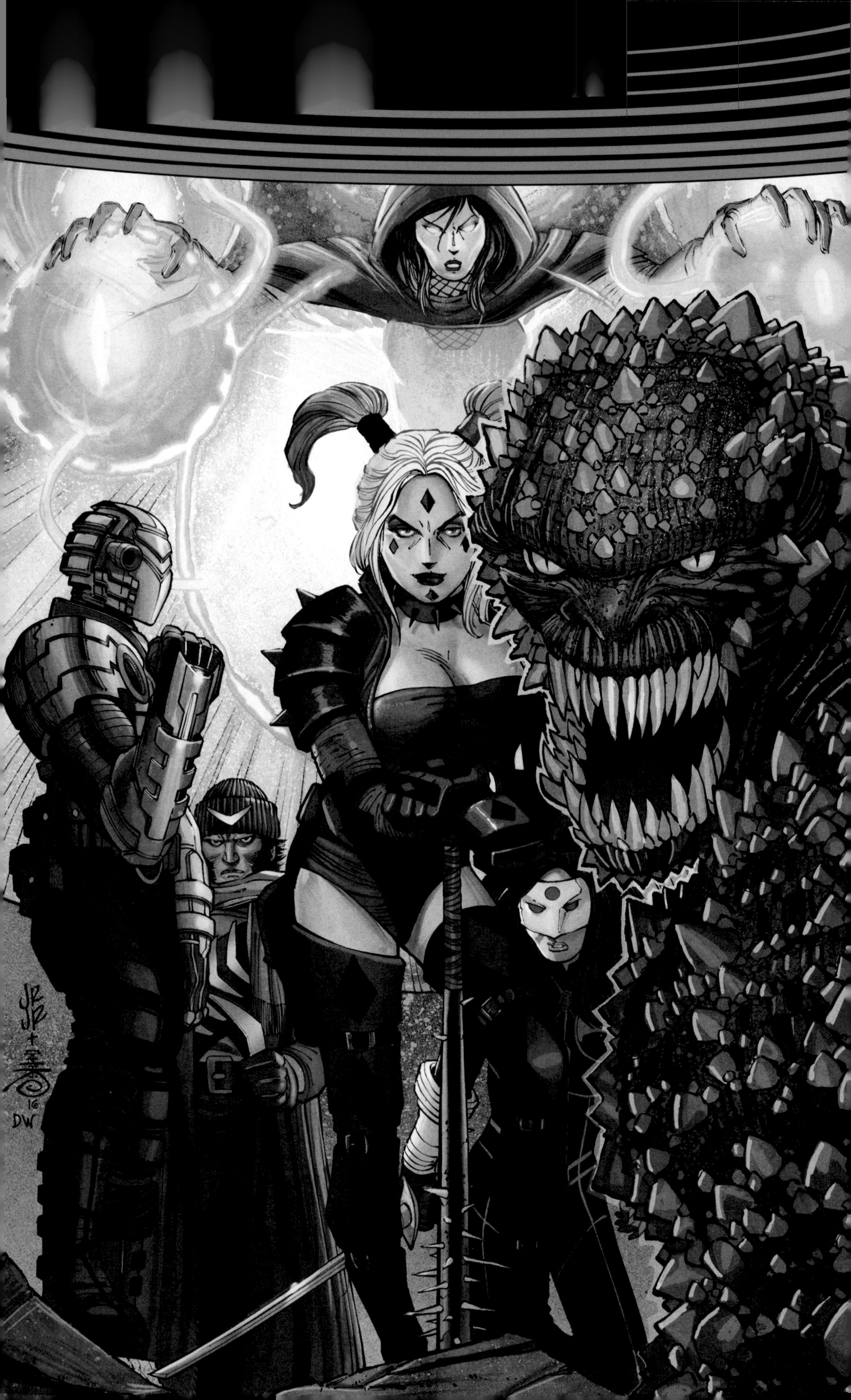

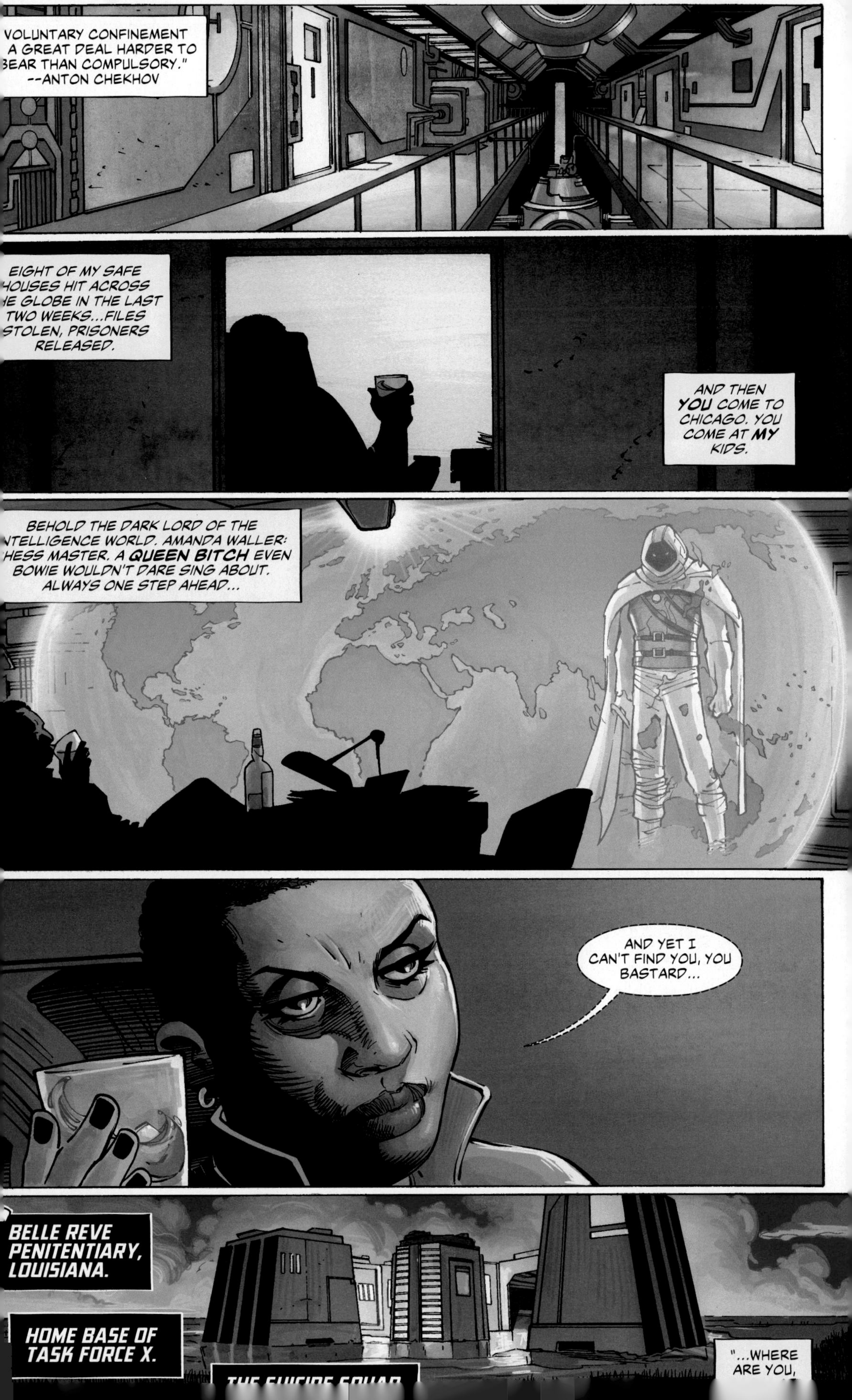

VOLUNTARY CONFINEMENT A GREAT DEAL HARDER TO BEAR THAN COMPULSORY." --ANTON CHEKHOV
EIGHT OF MY SAFE HOUSES HIT ACROSS THE GLOBE IN THE LAST TWO WEEKS...FILES STOLEN, PRISONERS RELEASED.
AND THEN YOU COME TO CHICAGO. YOU COME AT MY KIDS.
BEHOLD THE DARK LORD OF THE INTELLIGENCE WORLD. AMANDA WALLER: CHESS MASTER. A QUEEN BITCH EVEN BOWIE WOULDN'T DARE SING ABOUT. ALWAYS ONE STEP AHEAD...
AND YET I CAN'T FIND YOU, YOU BASTARD...
BELLE REVE PENITENTIARY, LOUISIANA.
HOME BASE OF TASK FORCE X.
"...WHERE ARE YOU,

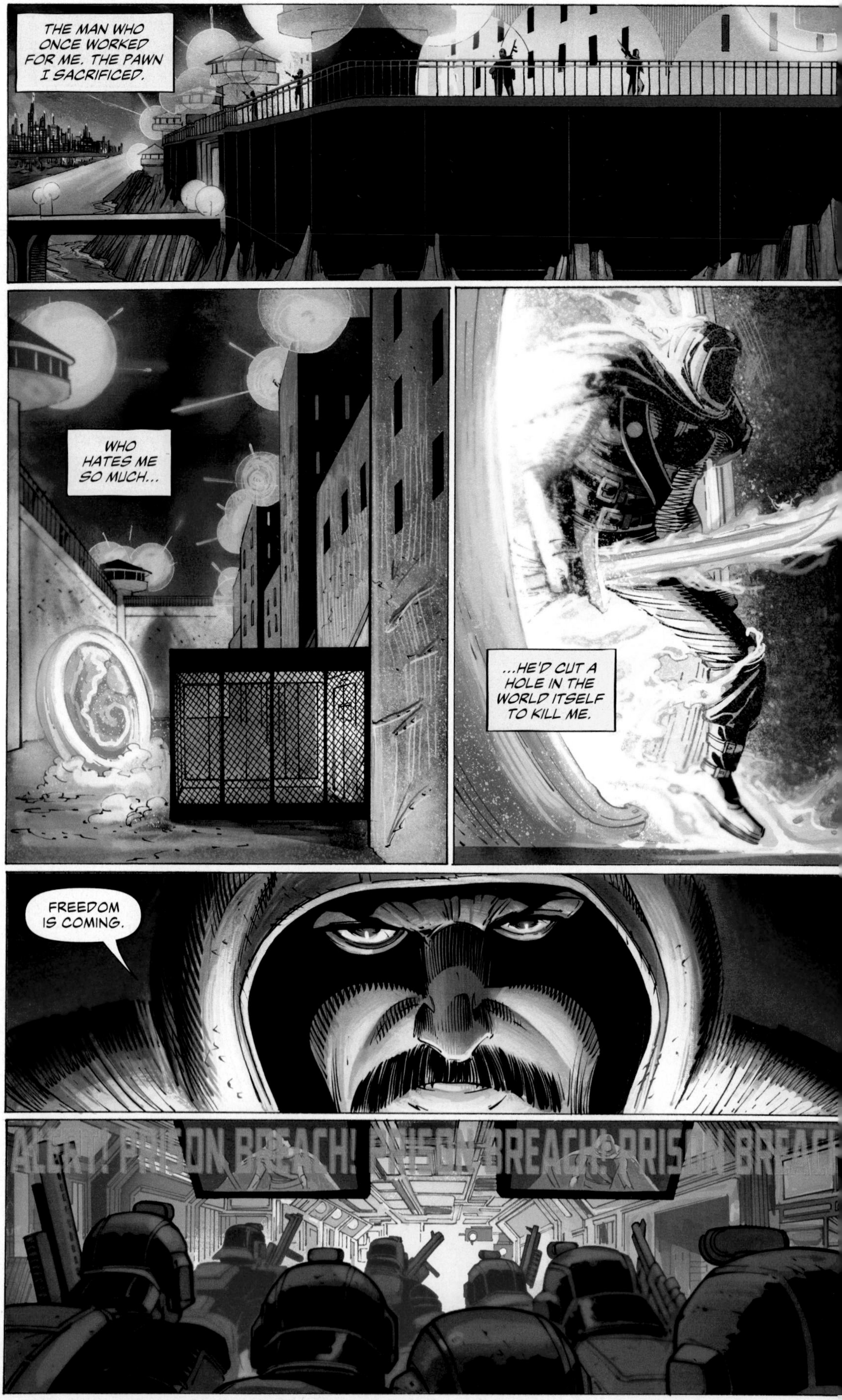
THE MAN WHO ONCE WORKED FOR ME. THE PAWN I SACRIFICED.
WHO HATES ME SO MUCH...
...HE'D CUT A HOLE IN THE WORLD ITSELF TO KILL ME.
FREEDOM IS COMING.
ALERT! PRISON BREACH! PRISON BREACH!

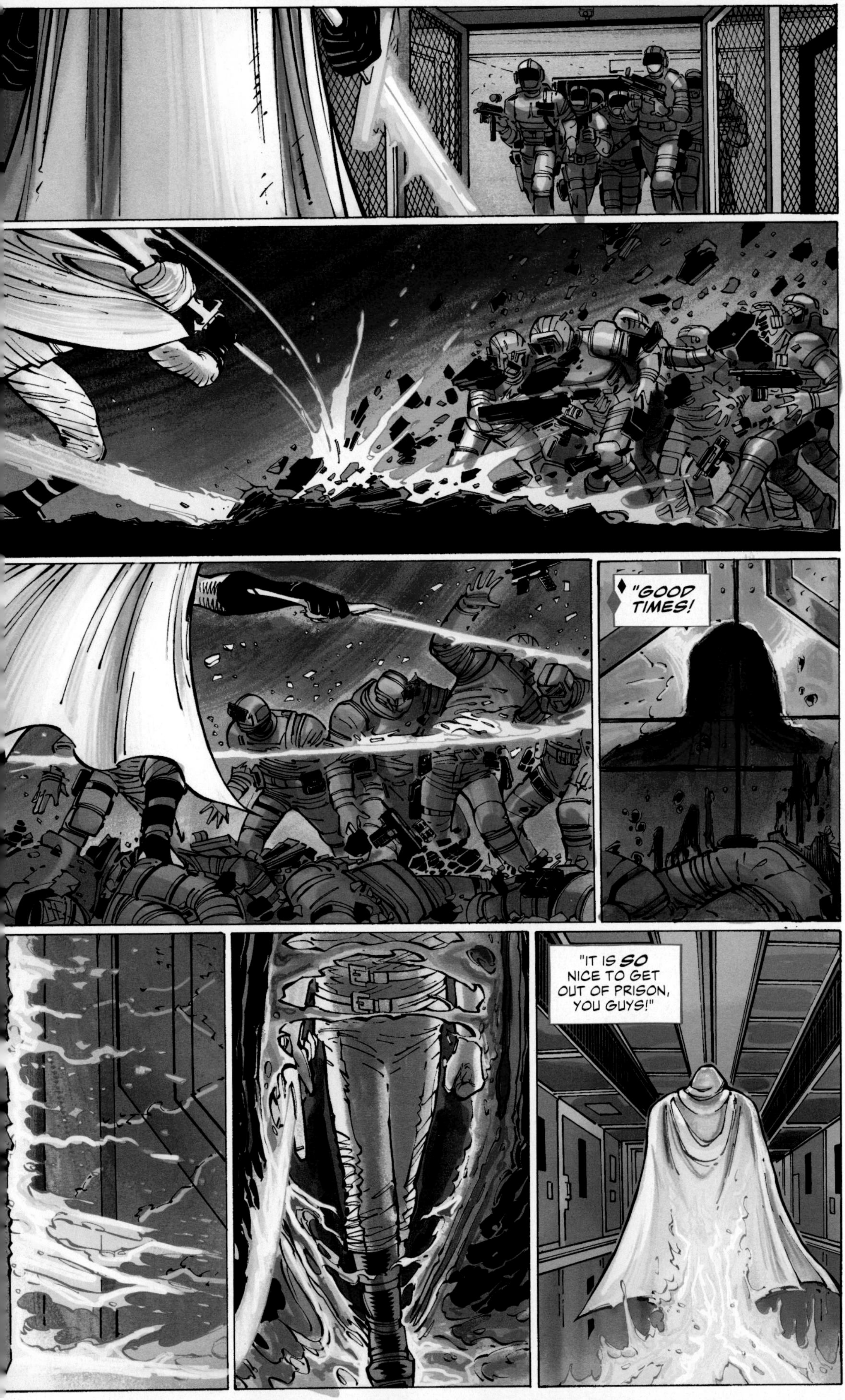
"GOOD TIMES!
"IT IS SO NICE TO GET OUT OF PRISON, YOU GUYS!"

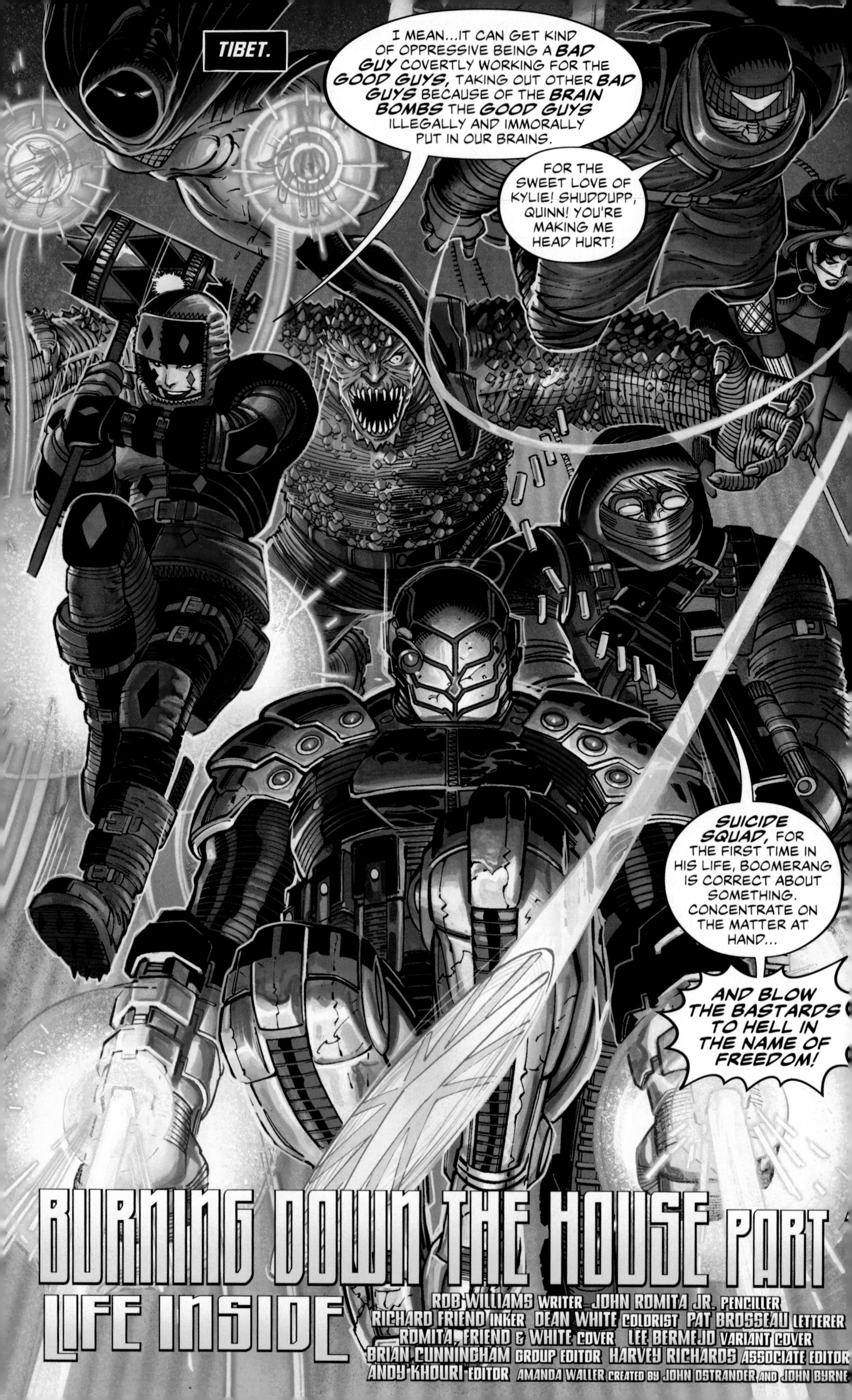
TIBET.
I MEAN...IT CAN GET KIND OF OPPRESSIVE BEING A BAD GUY COVERTLY WORKING FOR THE GOOD GUYS, TAKING OUT OTHER BAD GUYS BECAUSE OF THE BRAIN BOMBS THE GOOD GUYS ILLEGALLY AND IMMORALLY PUT IN OUR BRAINS.
FOR THE SWEET LOVE OF KYLIE! SHUDDUPP, QUINN! YOU'RE MAKING ME HEAD HURT!
SUICIDE SQUAD, FOR THE FIRST TIME IN HIS LIFE, BOOMERANG IS CORRECT ABOUT SOMETHING. CONCENTRATE ON THE MATTER AT HAND...
AND BLOW THE BASTARDS TO HELL IN THE NAME OF FREEDOM!
BURNING DOWN THE HOUSE PART
LIFE INSIDE
ROB WILLIAMS WRITER JOHN ROMITA JR. PENCILLER
RICHARD FRIEND INKER DEAN WHITE COLORIST PAT BROSSEAU LETTERER
ROMITA, FRIEND & WHITE COVER LEE BERMEJO VARIANT COVER
BRIAN CUNNINGHAM GROUP EDITOR HARVEY RICHARDS ASSOCIATE EDITOR
ANDY KHOURI EDITOR AMANDA WALLER CREATED BY JOHN OSTRANDER AND JOHN BYRNE

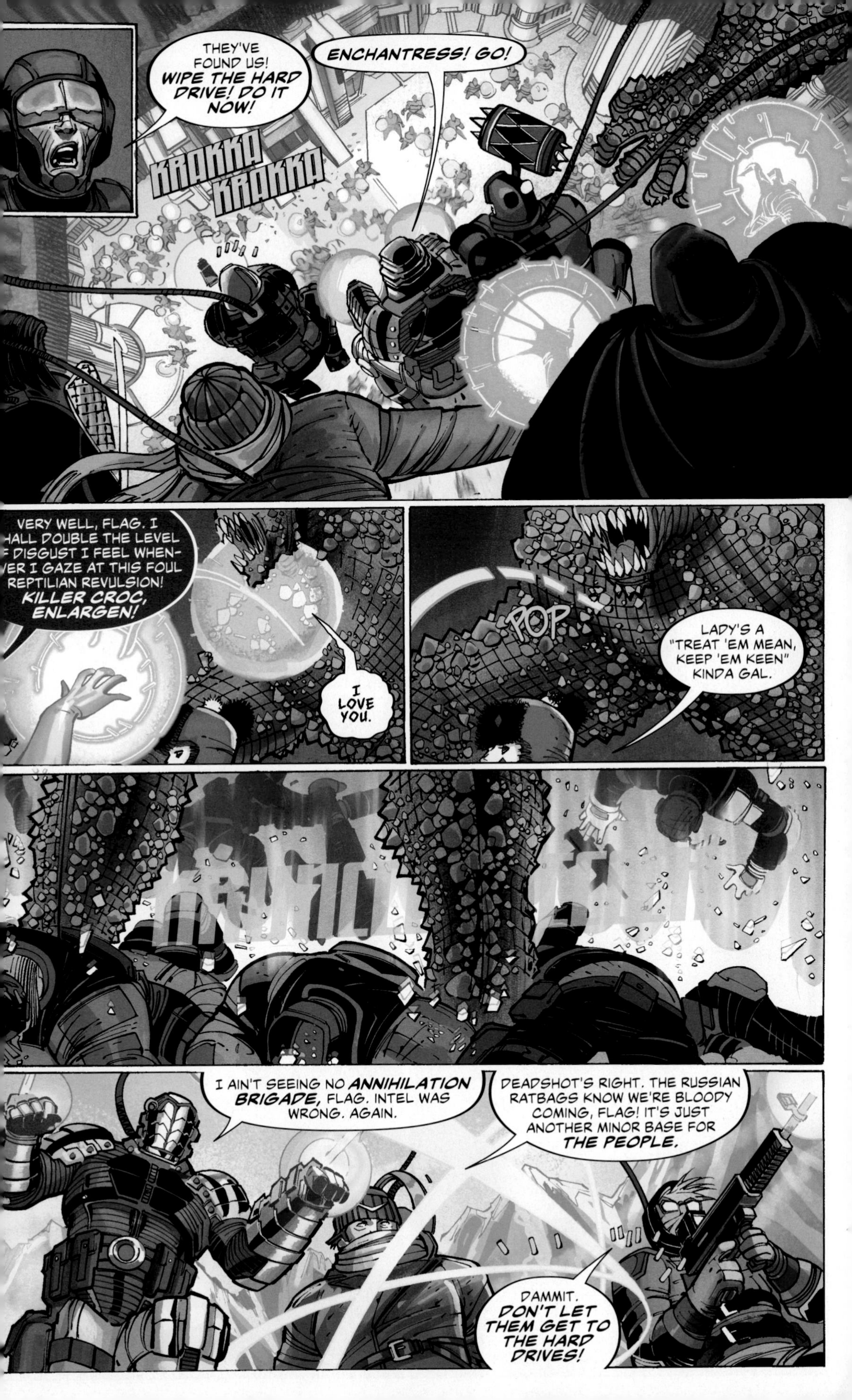
THEY'VE FOUND US! WIPE THE HARD DRIVE! DO IT NOW!
ENCHANTRESS! GO!
KRAKKA KRAKKA
VERY WELL, FLAG. I SHALL DOUBLE THE LEVEL OF DISGUST I FEEL WHENEVER I GAZE AT THIS FOUL REPTILIAN REVULSION! KILLER CROC, ENLARGEN!
I LOVE YOU.
POP
LADY'S A "TREAT 'EM MEAN, KEEP 'EM KEEN" KINDA GAL.
I AIN'T SEEING NO ANNIHILATION BRIGADE, FLAG. INTEL WAS WRONG. AGAIN.
DEADSHOT'S RIGHT. THE RUSSIAN RATBAGS KNOW WE'RE BLOODY COMING, FLAG! IT'S JUST ANOTHER MINOR BASE FOR THE PEOPLE.
DAMMIT. DON'T LET THEM GET TO THE HARD DRIVES!

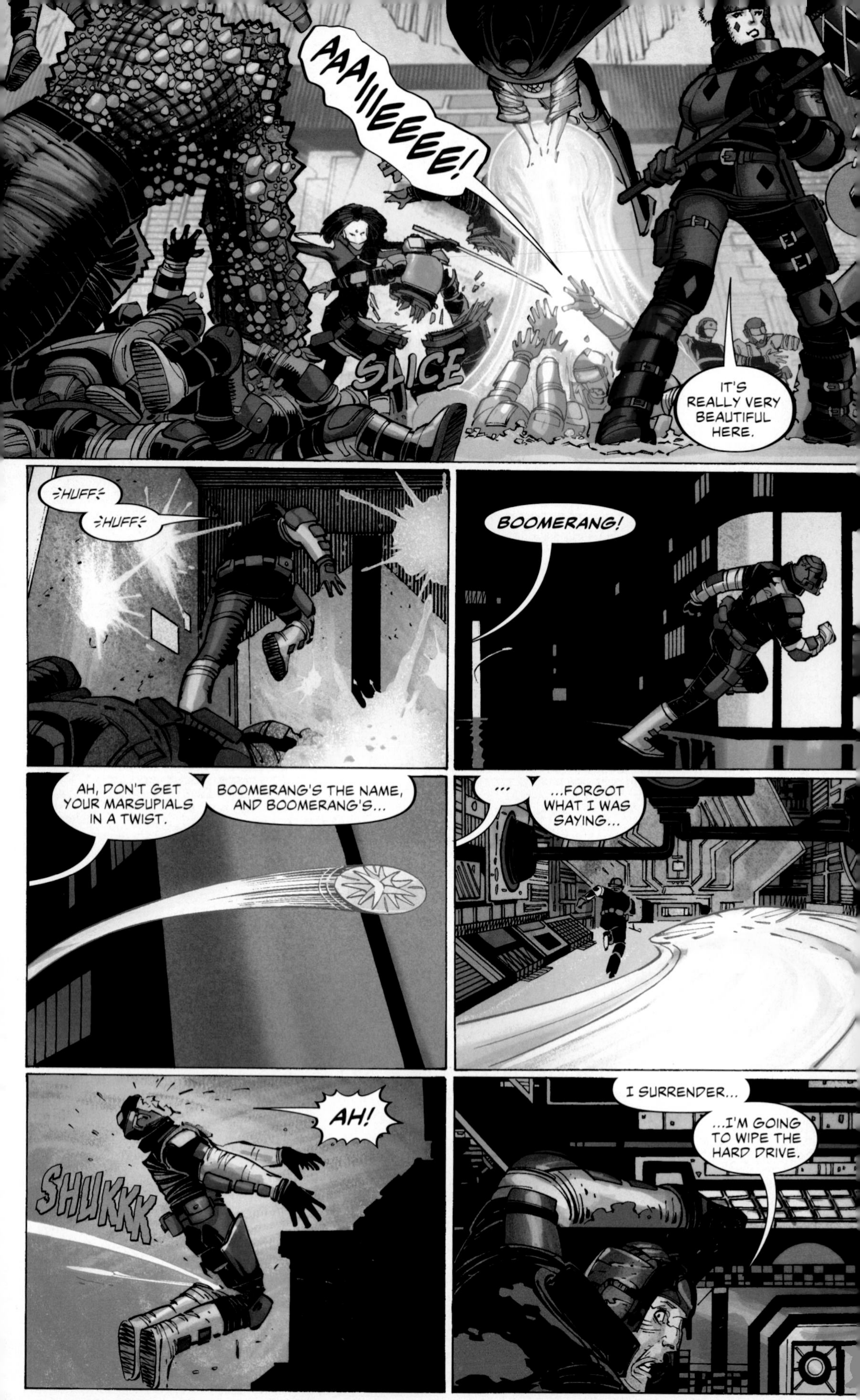
AAAIIIEEEEE!
SLICE
IT'S REALLY VERY BEAUTIFUL HERE.
HUFF
HUFF
BOOMERANG!
AH, DON'T GET YOUR MARSUPIALS IN A TWIST.
BOOMERANG'S THE NAME, AND BOOMERANG'S...
...
...FORGOT WHAT I WAS SAYING...
AH!
SHUKKK
I SURRENDER...
...I'M GOING TO WIPE THE HARD DRIVE.

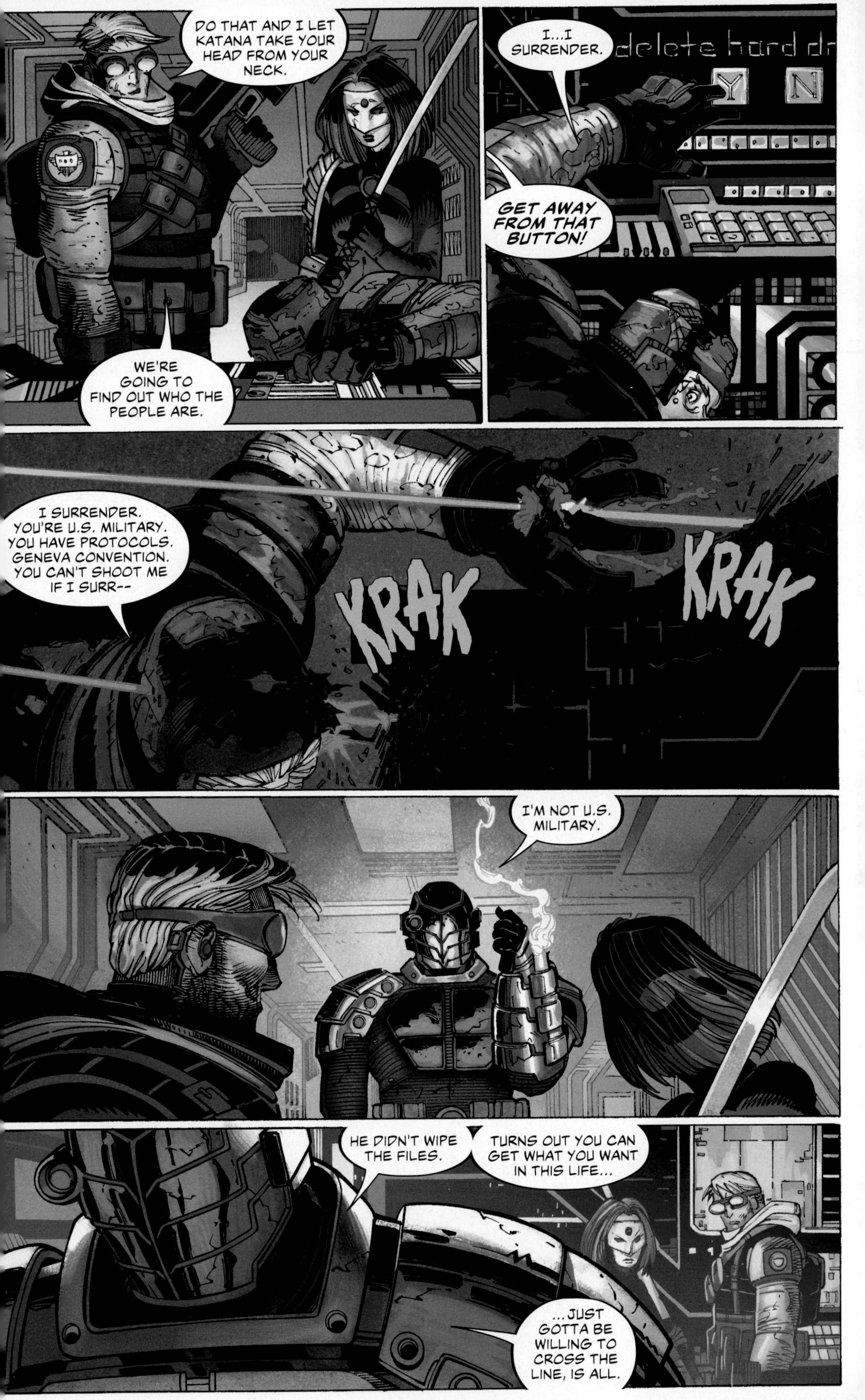
DO THAT AND I LET KATANA TAKE YOUR HEAD FROM YOUR NECK.
WE'RE GOING TO FIND OUT WHO THE PEOPLE ARE.
I...I SURRENDER.
delete hard dr
Y
N
GET AWAY FROM THAT BUTTON!
I SURRENDER. YOU'RE U.S. MILITARY. YOU HAVE PROTOCOLS. GENEVA CONVENTION. YOU CAN'T SHOOT ME IF I SURR--
KRAK
KRAK
I'M NOT U.S. MILITARY.
HE DIDN'T WIPE THE FILES.
TURNS OUT YOU CAN GET WHAT YOU WANT IN THIS LIFE...
...JUST GOTTA BE WILLING TO CROSS THE LINE, IS ALL.

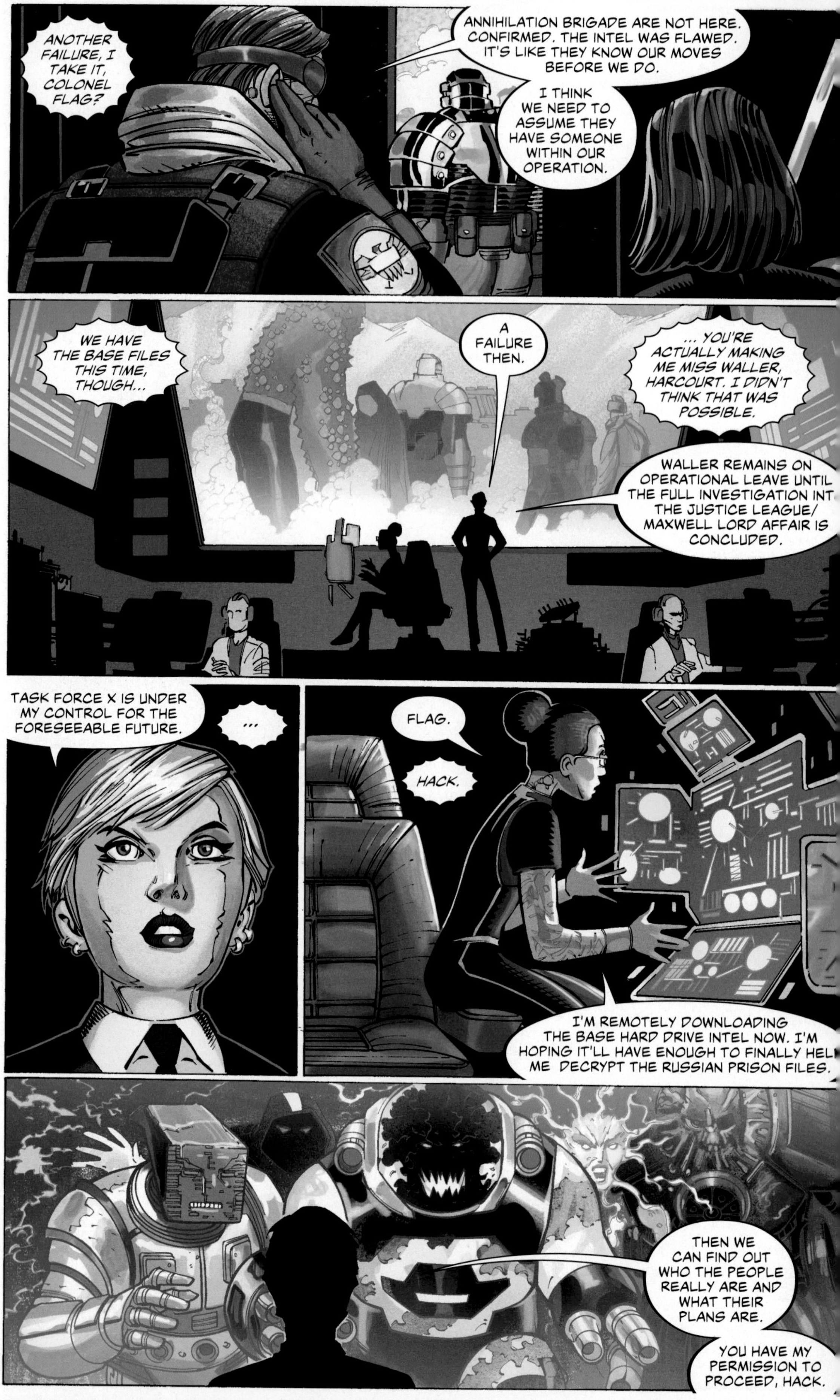
ANOTHER FAILURE, I TAKE IT, COLONEL FLAG?
ANNIHILATION BRIGADE ARE NOT HERE. CONFIRMED. THE INTEL WAS FLAWED. IT'S LIKE THEY KNOW OUR MOVES BEFORE WE DO.
I THINK WE NEED TO ASSUME THEY HAVE SOMEONE WITHIN OUR OPERATION.
WE HAVE THE BASE FILES THIS TIME, THOUGH...
A FAILURE THEN.
... YOU'RE ACTUALLY MAKING ME MISS WALLER, HARCOURT. I DIDN'T THINK THAT WAS POSSIBLE.
WALLER REMAINS ON OPERATIONAL LEAVE UNTIL THE FULL INVESTIGATION INT THE JUSTICE LEAGUE/ MAXWELL LORD AFFAIR IS CONCLUDED.
TASK FORCE X IS UNDER MY CONTROL FOR THE FORESEEABLE FUTURE.
...
FLAG.
HACK.
I'M REMOTELY DOWNLOADING THE BASE HARD DRIVE INTEL NOW. I'M HOPING IT'LL HAVE ENOUGH TO FINALLY HEL ME DECRYPT THE RUSSIAN PRISON FILES.
THEN WE CAN FIND OUT WHO THE PEOPLE REALLY ARE AND WHAT THEIR PLANS ARE.
YOU HAVE MY PERMISSION TO PROCEED, HACK.

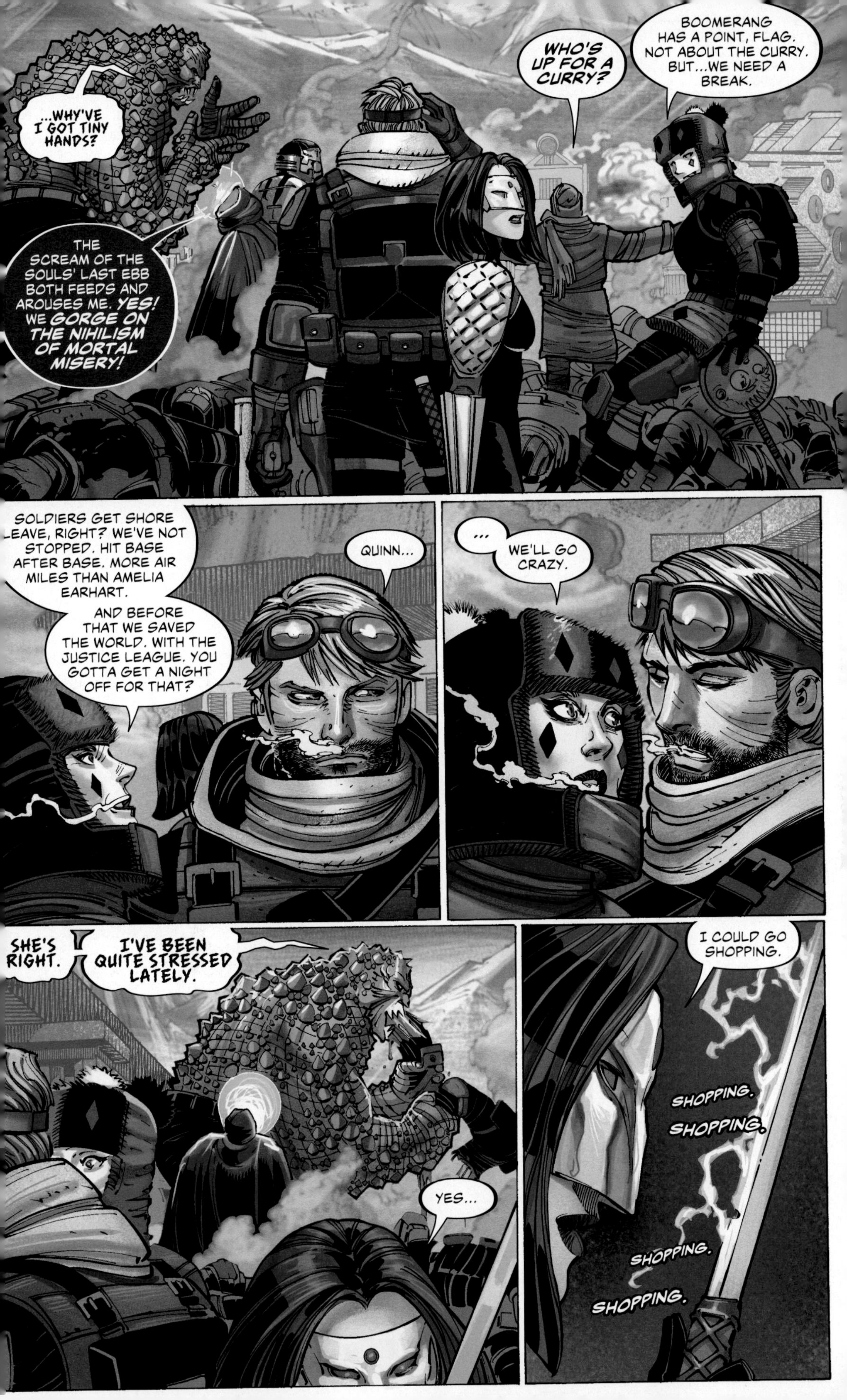
...WHY'VE I GOT TINY HANDS?
THE SCREAM OF THE SOULS' LAST EBB BOTH FEEDS AND AROUSES ME. YES! WE GORGE ON THE NIHILISM OF MORTAL MISERY!
WHO'S UP FOR A CURRY?
BOOMERANG HAS A POINT, FLAG. NOT ABOUT THE CURRY. BUT...WE NEED A BREAK.
SOLDIERS GET SHORE LEAVE, RIGHT? WE'VE NOT STOPPED. HIT BASE AFTER BASE. MORE AIR MILES THAN AMELIA EARHART.
AND BEFORE THAT WE SAVED THE WORLD. WITH THE JUSTICE LEAGUE. YOU GOTTA GET A NIGHT OFF FOR THAT?
QUINN...
...
WE'LL GO CRAZY.
SHE'S RIGHT.
I'VE BEEN QUITE STRESSED LATELY.
YES...
I COULD GO SHOPPING.
SHOPPING.
SHOPPING.
SHOPPING.
SHOPPING.

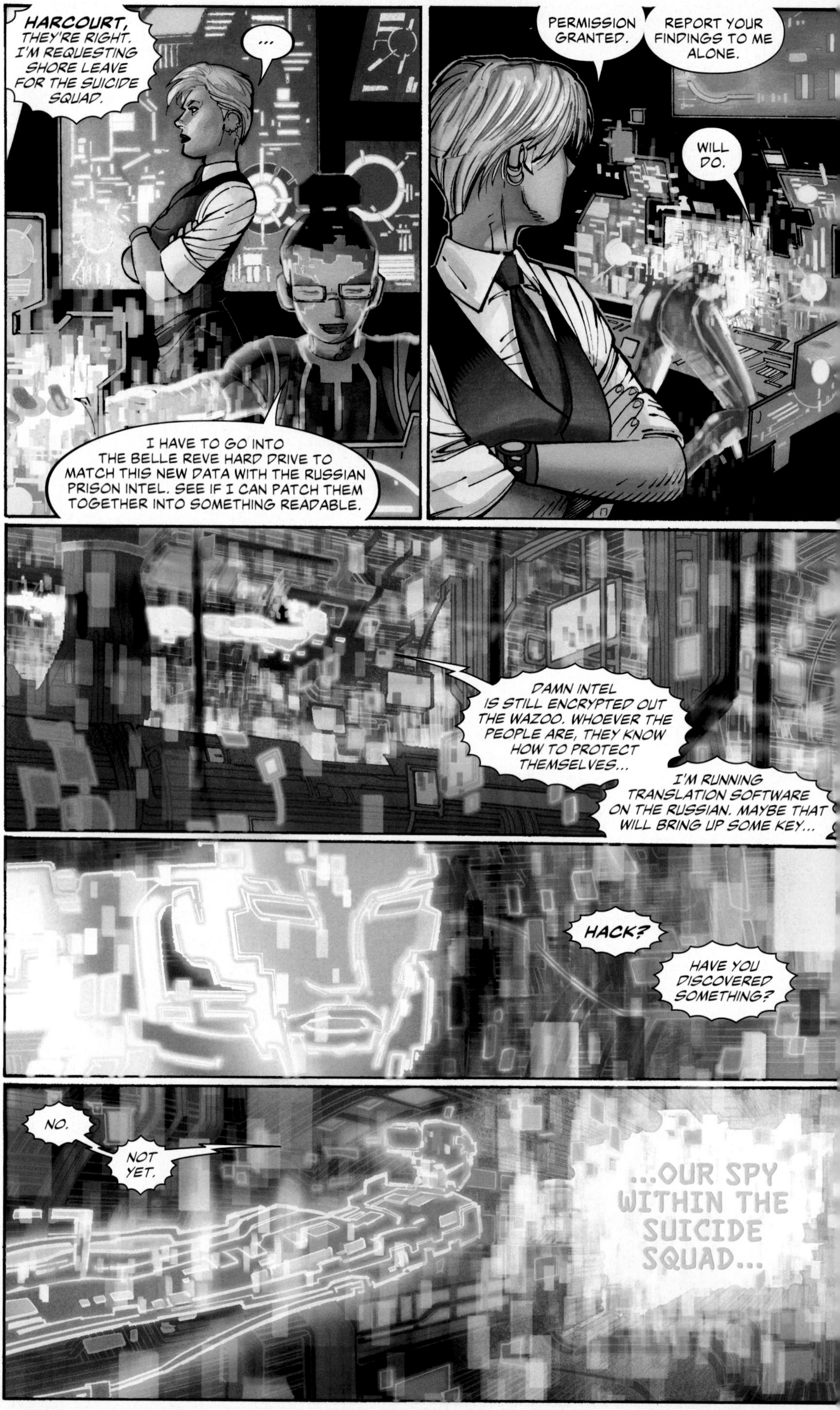
HARCOURT, THEY'RE RIGHT. I'M REQUESTING SHORE LEAVE FOR THE SUICIDE SQUAD.
...
I HAVE TO GO INTO THE BELLE REVE HARD DRIVE TO MATCH THIS NEW DATA WITH THE RUSSIAN PRISON INTEL. SEE IF I CAN PATCH THEM TOGETHER INTO SOMETHING READABLE.
PERMISSION GRANTED.
REPORT YOUR FINDINGS TO ME ALONE.
WILL DO.
DAMN INTEL IS STILL ENCRYPTED OUT THE WAZOO. WHOEVER THE PEOPLE ARE, THEY KNOW HOW TO PROTECT THEMSELVES...
I'M RUNNING TRANSLATION SOFTWARE ON THE RUSSIAN. MAYBE THAT WILL BRING UP SOME KEY...
HACK?
HAVE YOU DISCOVERED SOMETHING?
NO.
NOT YET.
...OUR SPY WITHIN THE SUICIDE SQUAD...

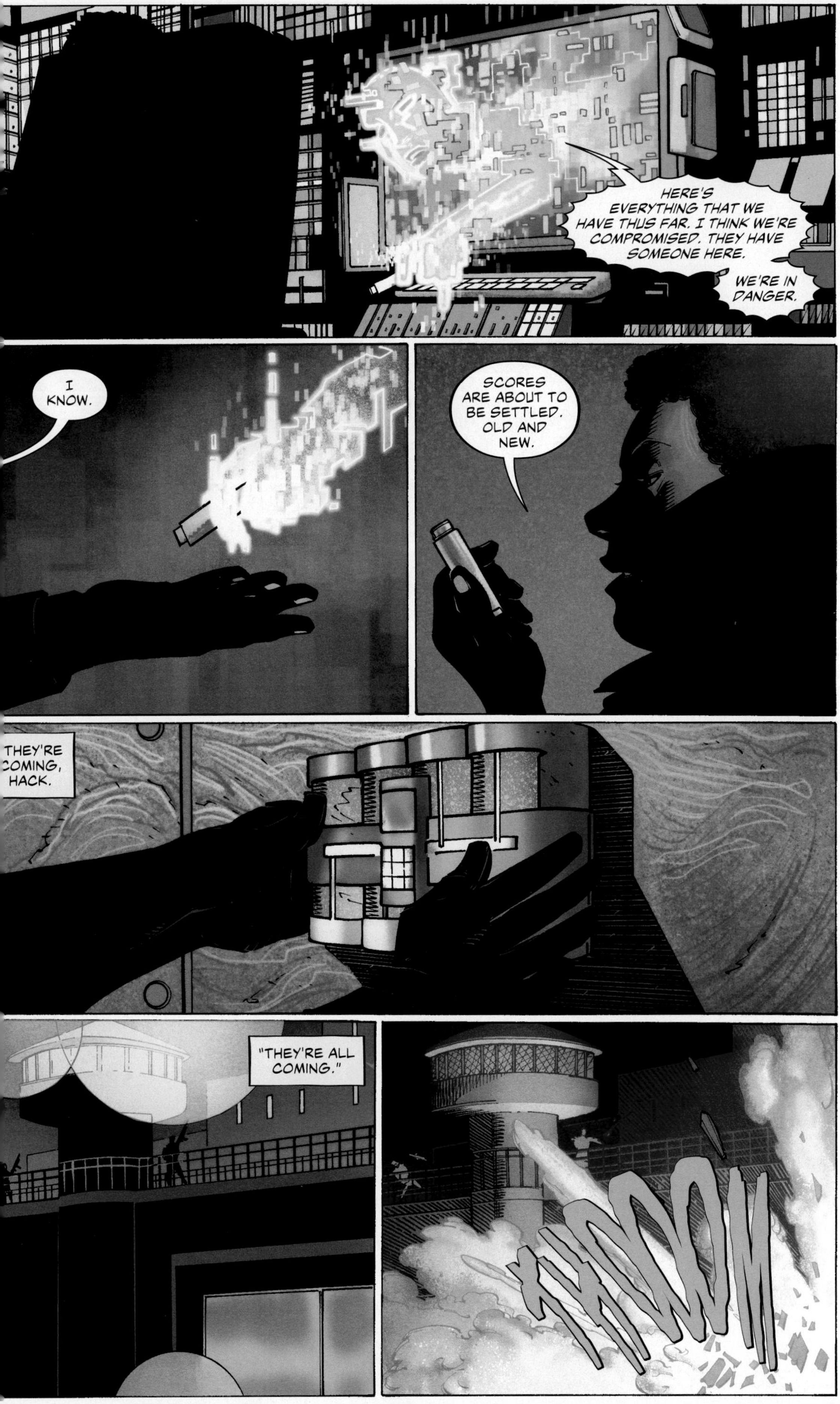
HERE'S EVERYTHING THAT WE HAVE THUS FAR. I THINK WE'RE COMPROMISED. THEY HAVE SOMEONE HERE.
WE'RE IN DANGER.
I KNOW.
SCORES ARE ABOUT TO BE SETTLED. OLD AND NEW.
THEY'RE COMING, HACK.
"THEY'RE ALL COMING."
KRADOOM

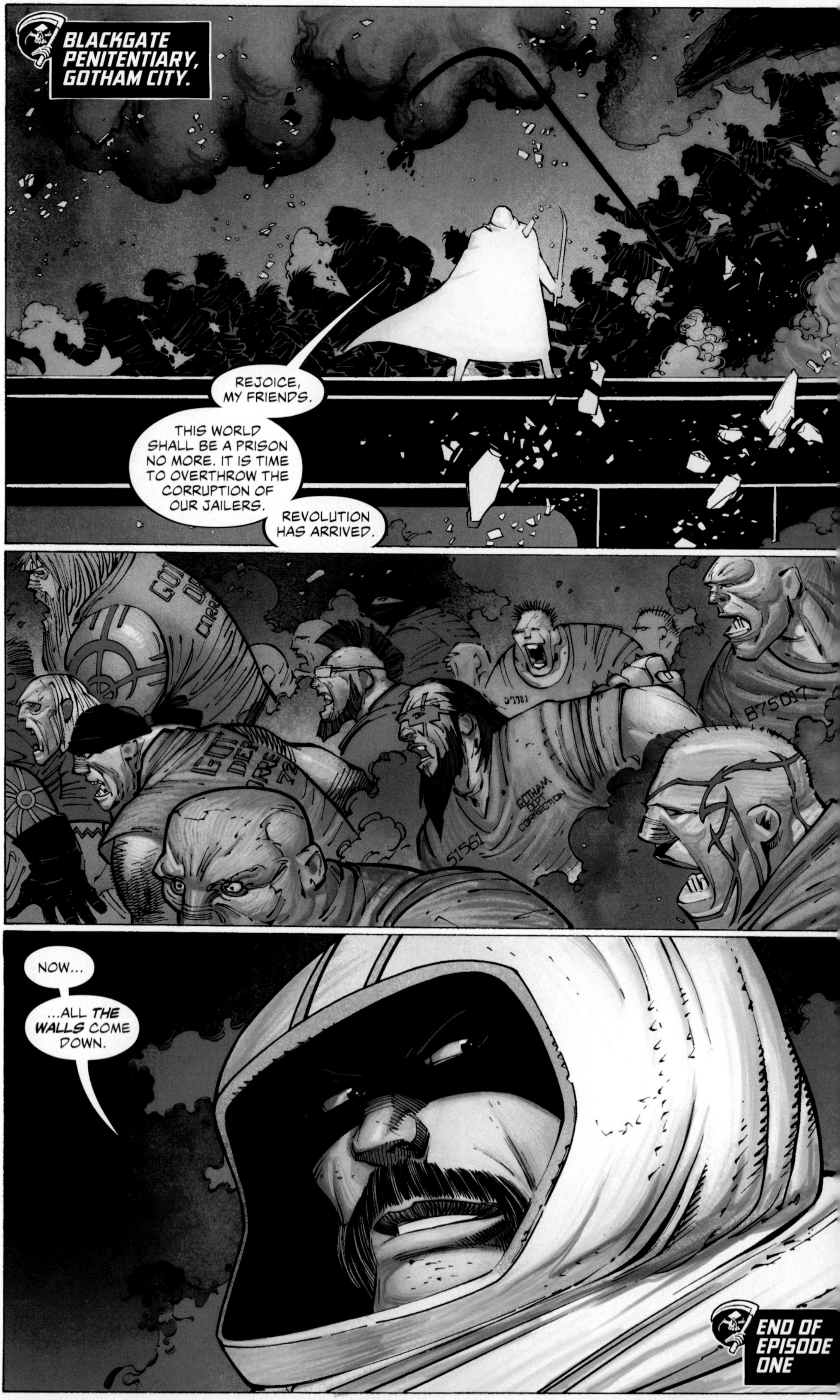
BLACKGATE PENITENTIARY, GOTHAM CITY.
REJOICE, MY FRIENDS.
THIS WORLD SHALL BE A PRISON NO MORE. IT IS TIME TO OVERTHROW THE CORRUPTION OF OUR JAILERS.
REVOLUTION HAS ARRIVED.
GOTHAM DEPT CORRECTION
51561
875017
NOW...
...ALL THE WALLS COME DOWN.
END OF EPISODE ONE

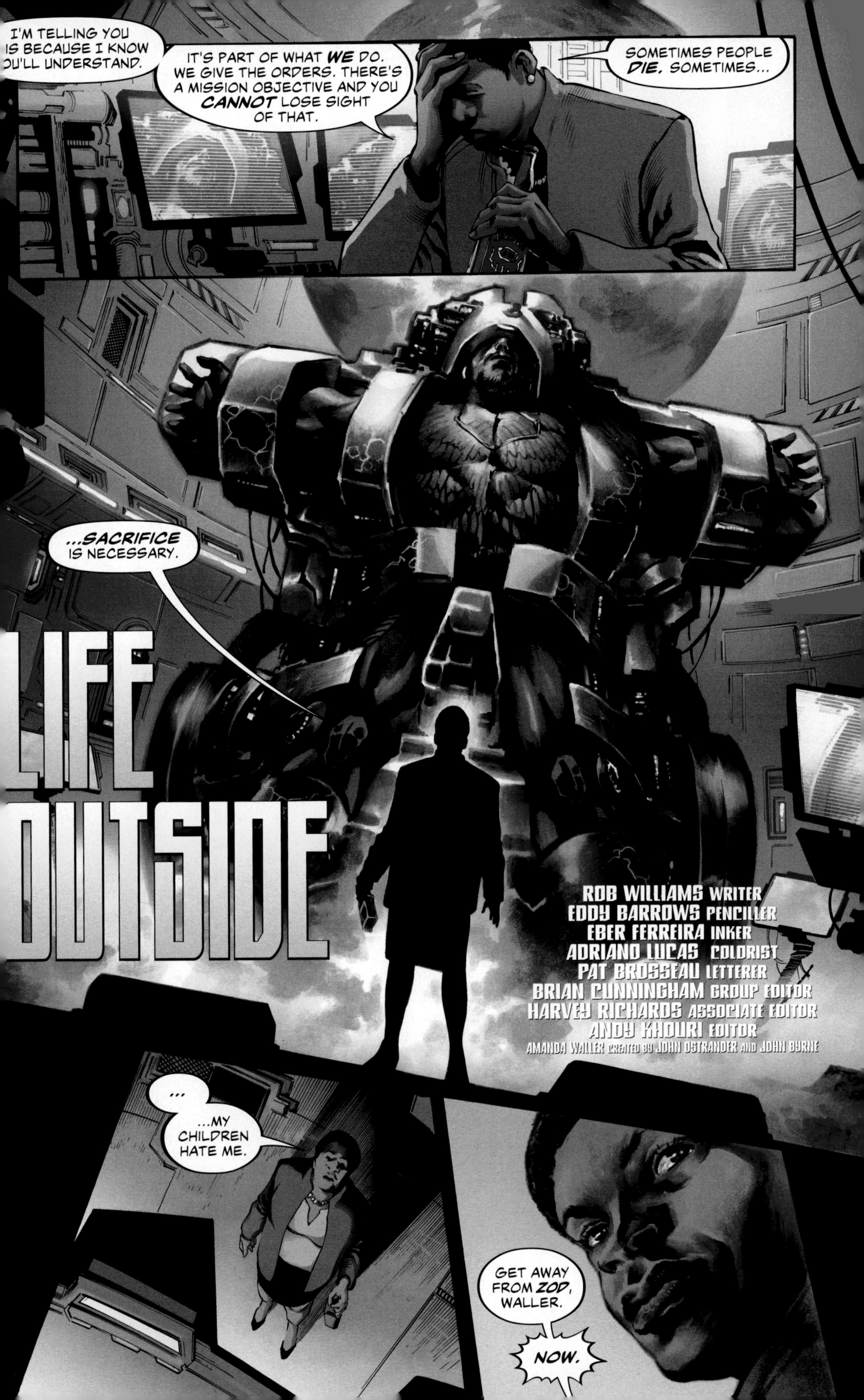
I'M TELLING YOU
IS BECAUSE I KNOW
OU'LL UNDERSTAND.
IT'S PART OF WHAT WE DO. WE GIVE THE ORDERS. THERE'S A MISSION OBJECTIVE AND YOU CANNOT LOSE SIGHT OF THAT.
SOMETIMES PEOPLE DIE. SOMETIMES...
...SACRIFICE IS NECESSARY.
LIFE OUTSIDE
ROB WILLIAMS WRITER
EDDY BARROWS PENCILLER
EBER FERREIRA INKER
ADRIANO LUCAS COLORIST
PAT BROSSEAU LETTERER
BRIAN CUNNINGHAM GROUP EDITOR
HARVEY RICHARDS ASSOCIATE EDITOR
ANDY KHOURI EDITOR
AMANDA WALLER CREATED BY JOHN OSTRANDER AND JOHN BYRNE
...
...MY CHILDREN HATE ME.
GET AWAY FROM ZOD, WALLER.
NOW.

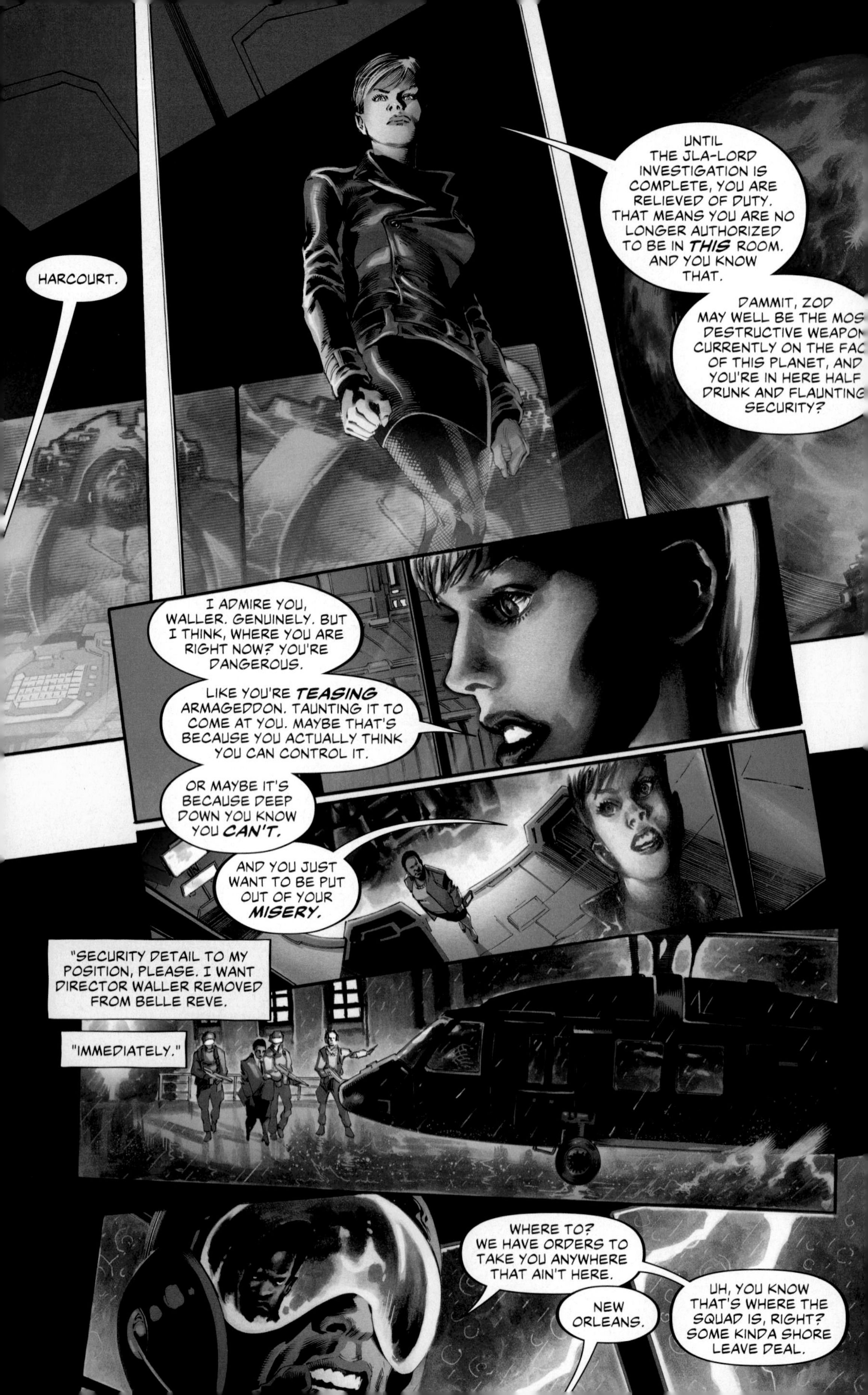
HARCOURT.
UNTIL THE JLA-LORD INVESTIGATION IS COMPLETE, YOU ARE RELIEVED OF DUTY. THAT MEANS YOU ARE NO LONGER AUTHORIZED TO BE IN THIS ROOM. AND YOU KNOW THAT.
DAMMIT, ZOD MAY WELL BE THE MOS DESTRUCTIVE WEAPON CURRENTLY ON THE FAC OF THIS PLANET, AND YOU'RE IN HERE HALF DRUNK AND FLAUNTING SECURITY?
I ADMIRE YOU, WALLER. GENUINELY. BUT I THINK, WHERE YOU ARE RIGHT NOW? YOU'RE DANGEROUS.
LIKE YOU'RE TEASING ARMAGEDDON. TAUNTING IT TO COME AT YOU. MAYBE THAT'S BECAUSE YOU ACTUALLY THINK YOU CAN CONTROL IT.
OR MAYBE IT'S BECAUSE DEEP DOWN YOU KNOW YOU CAN'T.
AND YOU JUST WANT TO BE PUT OUT OF YOUR MISERY.
"SECURITY DETAIL TO MY POSITION, PLEASE. I WANT DIRECTOR WALLER REMOVED FROM BELLE REVE.
"IMMEDIATELY."
WHERE TO? WE HAVE ORDERS TO TAKE YOU ANYWHERE THAT AIN'T HERE.
NEW ORLEANS.
UH, YOU KNOW THAT'S WHERE THE SQUAD IS, RIGHT? SOME KINDA SHORE LEAVE DEAL.

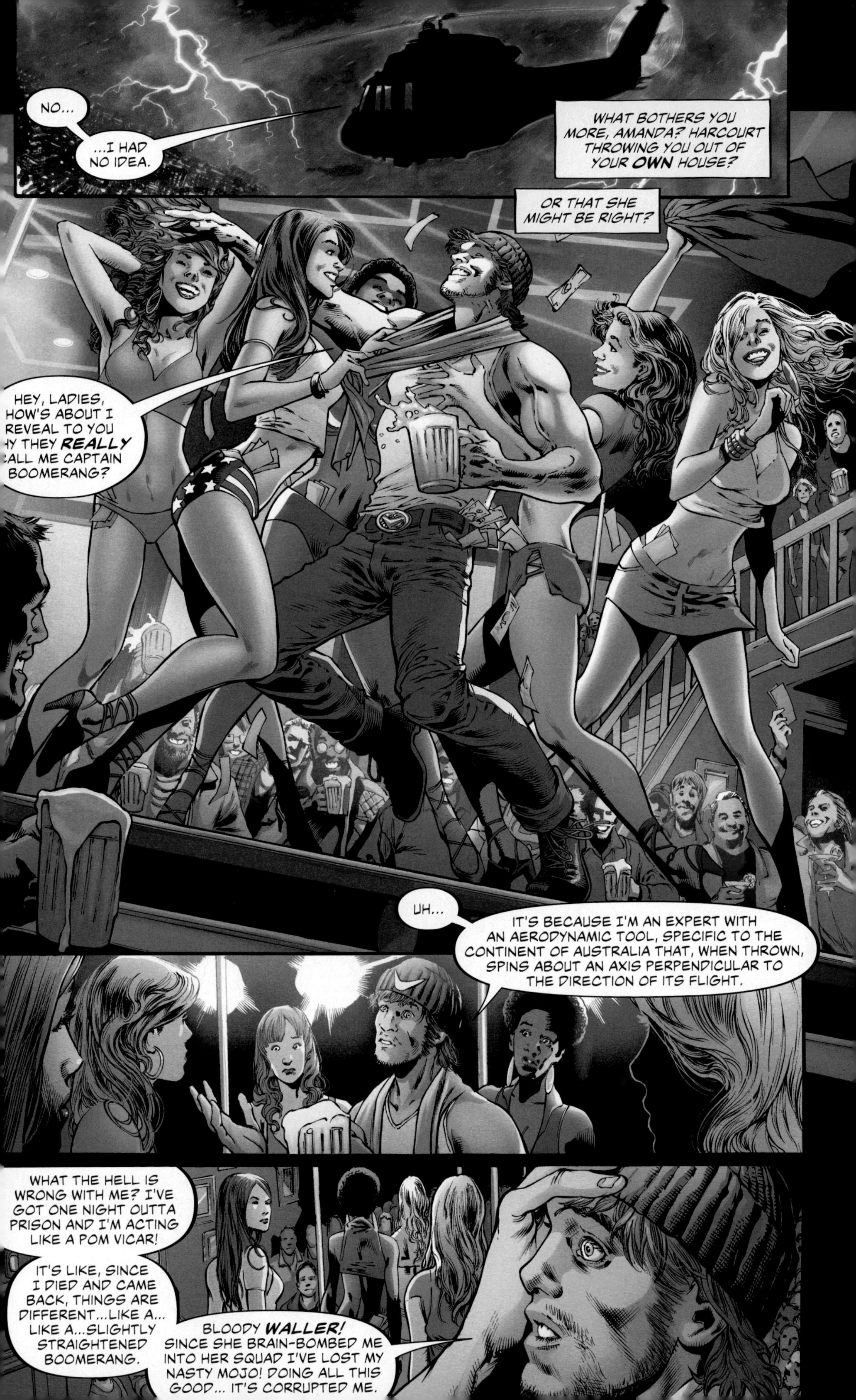
NO...
...I HAD NO IDEA.
WHAT BOTHERS YOU MORE, AMANDA? HARCOURT THROWING YOU OUT OF YOUR OWN HOUSE?
OR THAT SHE MIGHT BE RIGHT?
HEY, LADIES, HOW'S ABOUT I REVEAL TO YOU HY THEY REALLY CALL ME CAPTAIN BOOMERANG?
UH...
IT'S BECAUSE I'M AN EXPERT WITH AN AERODYNAMIC TOOL, SPECIFIC TO THE CONTINENT OF AUSTRALIA THAT, WHEN THROWN, SPINS ABOUT AN AXIS PERPENDICULAR TO THE DIRECTION OF ITS FLIGHT.
WHAT THE HELL IS WRONG WITH ME? I'VE GOT ONE NIGHT OUTTA PRISON AND I'M ACTING LIKE A POM VICAR!
IT'S LIKE, SINCE I DIED AND CAME BACK, THINGS ARE DIFFERENT...LIKE A... LIKE A...SLIGHTLY STRAIGHTENED BOOMERANG.
BLOODY WALLER! SINCE SHE BRAIN-BOMBED ME INTO HER SQUAD I'VE LOST MY NASTY MOJO! DOING ALL THIS GOOD... IT'S CORRUPTED ME.

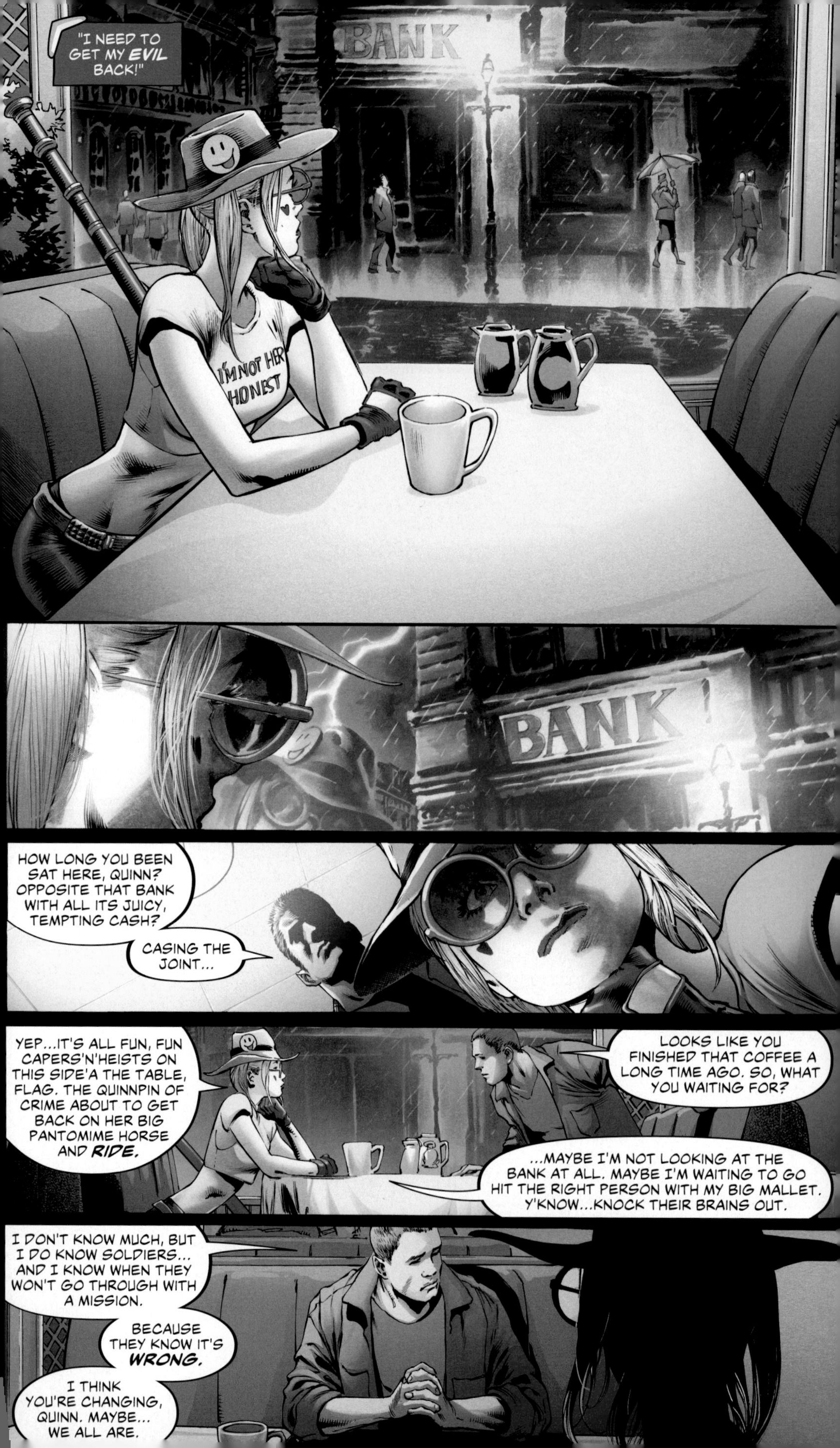
"I NEED TO GET MY EVIL BACK!"
BANK
I'M NOT HER HONEST
BANK
HOW LONG YOU BEEN SAT HERE, QUINN? OPPOSITE THAT BANK WITH ALL ITS JUICY, TEMPTING CASH?
CASING THE JOINT...
YEP...IT'S ALL FUN, FUN CAPERS'N'HEISTS ON THIS SIDE'A THE TABLE, FLAG. THE QUINNPIN OF CRIME ABOUT TO GET BACK ON HER BIG PANTOMIME HORSE AND RIDE.
LOOKS LIKE YOU FINISHED THAT COFFEE A LONG TIME AGO. SO, WHAT YOU WAITING FOR?
...MAYBE I'M NOT LOOKING AT THE BANK AT ALL. MAYBE I'M WAITING TO GO HIT THE RIGHT PERSON WITH MY BIG MALLET. Y'KNOW...KNOCK THEIR BRAINS OUT.
I DON'T KNOW MUCH, BUT I DO KNOW SOLDIERS... AND I KNOW WHEN THEY WON'T GO THROUGH WITH A MISSION.
BECAUSE THEY KNOW IT'S WRONG.
I THINK YOU'RE CHANGING, QUINN. MAYBE... WE ALL ARE.

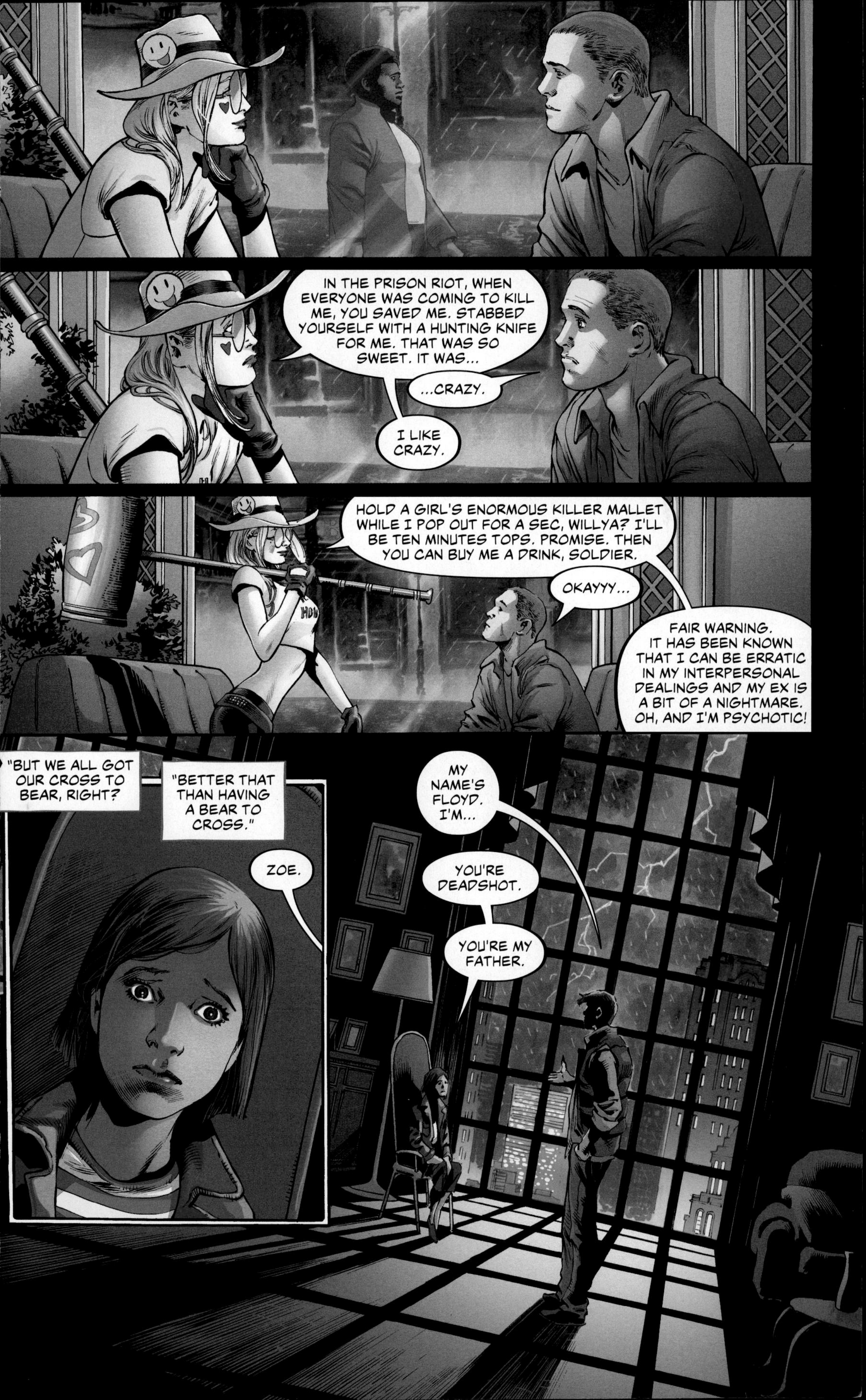
IN THE PRISON RIOT, WHEN EVERYONE WAS COMING TO KILL ME, YOU SAVED ME. STABBED YOURSELF WITH A HUNTING KNIFE FOR ME. THAT WAS SO SWEET. IT WAS...
...CRAZY.
I LIKE CRAZY.
HOLD A GIRL'S ENORMOUS KILLER MALLET WHILE I POP OUT FOR A SEC, WILLYA? I'LL BE TEN MINUTES TOPS. PROMISE. THEN YOU CAN BUY ME A DRINK, SOLDIER.
OKAYYY...
FAIR WARNING. IT HAS BEEN KNOWN THAT I CAN BE ERRATIC IN MY INTERPERSONAL DEALINGS AND MY EX IS A BIT OF A NIGHTMARE. OH, AND I'M PSYCHOTIC!
"BUT WE ALL GOT OUR CROSS TO BEAR, RIGHT?
"BETTER THAT THAN HAVING A BEAR TO CROSS."
MY NAME'S FLOYD. I'M...
ZOE.
YOU'RE DEADSHOT.
YOU'RE MY FATHER.

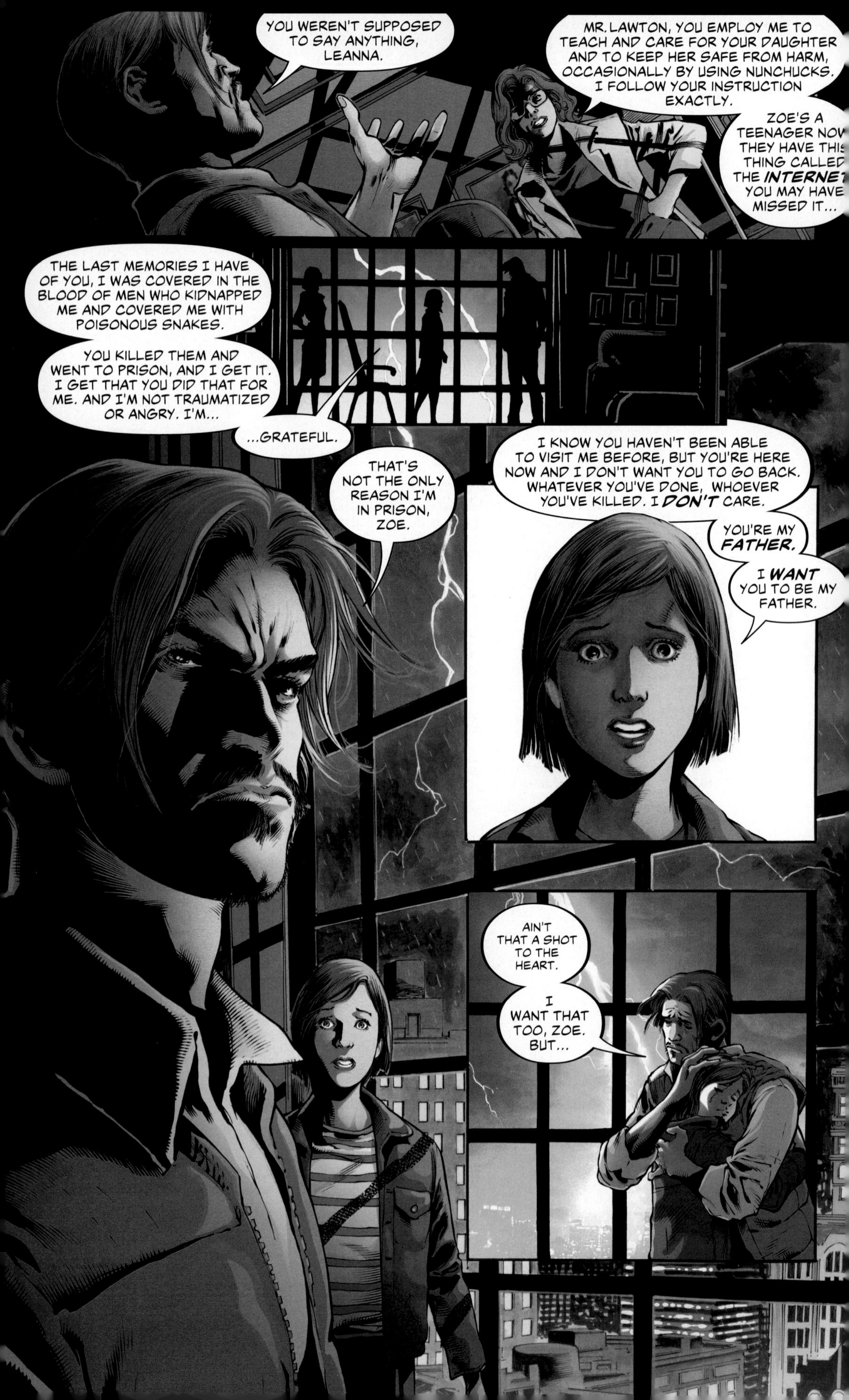
YOU WEREN'T SUPPOSED TO SAY ANYTHING, LEANNA.
MR. LAWTON, YOU EMPLOY ME TO TEACH AND CARE FOR YOUR DAUGHTER AND TO KEEP HER SAFE FROM HARM, OCCASIONALLY BY USING NUNCHUCKS. I FOLLOW YOUR INSTRUCTION EXACTLY.
ZOE'S A TEENAGER NOW. THEY HAVE THIS THING CALLED THE INTERNET. YOU MAY HAVE MISSED IT...
THE LAST MEMORIES I HAVE OF YOU, I WAS COVERED IN THE BLOOD OF MEN WHO KIDNAPPED ME AND COVERED ME WITH POISONOUS SNAKES.
YOU KILLED THEM AND WENT TO PRISON, AND I GET IT. I GET THAT YOU DID THAT FOR ME. AND I'M NOT TRAUMATIZED OR ANGRY. I'M...
...GRATEFUL.
THAT'S NOT THE ONLY REASON I'M IN PRISON, ZOE.
I KNOW YOU HAVEN'T BEEN ABLE TO VISIT ME BEFORE, BUT YOU'RE HERE NOW AND I DON'T WANT YOU TO GO BACK. WHATEVER YOU'VE DONE, WHOEVER YOU'VE KILLED. I DON'T CARE.
YOU'RE MY FATHER.
I WANT YOU TO BE MY FATHER.
AIN'T THAT A SHOT TO THE HEART.
I WANT THAT TOO, ZOE. BUT...

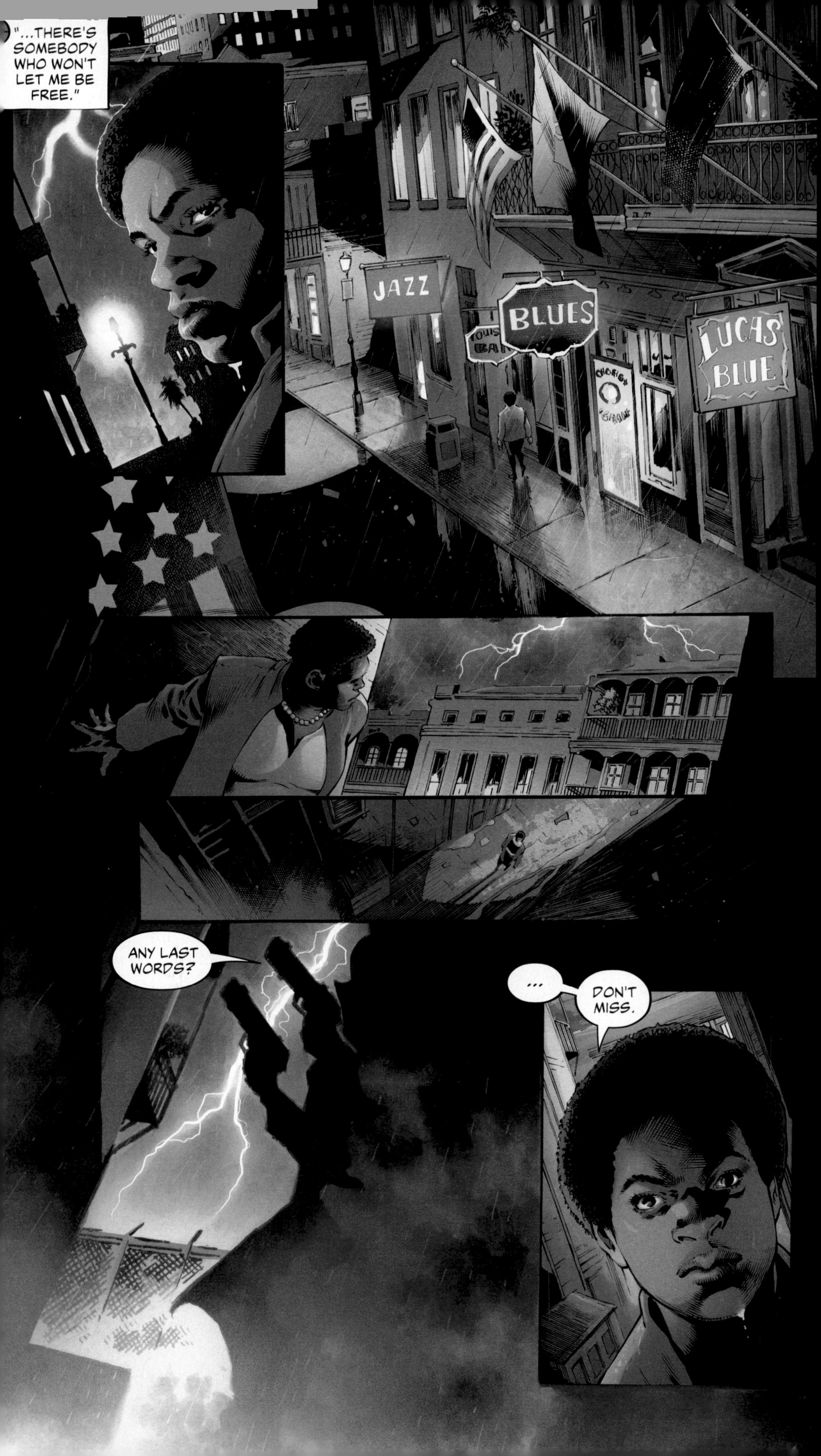
"...THERE'S SOMEBODY WHO WON'T LET ME BE FREE."
JAZZ
BLUES
LUCAS BLUE
ANY LAST WORDS?
...
DON'T MISS.

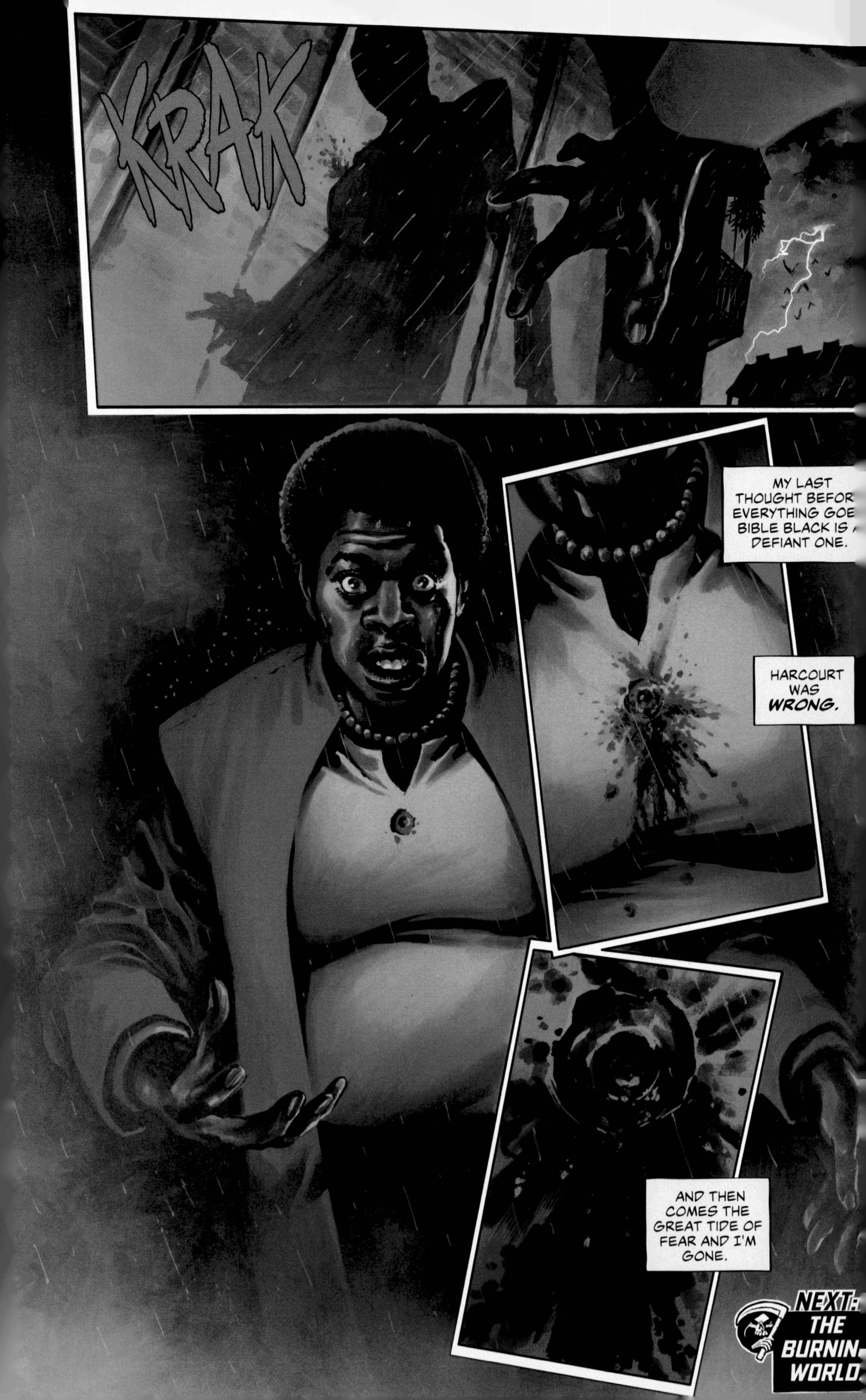
KRAK
MY LAST THOUGHT BEFOR EVERYTHING GOE BIBLE BLACK IS DEFIANT ONE.
HARCOURT WAS WRONG.
AND THEN COMES THE GREAT TIDE OF FEAR AND I'M GONE.
NEXT: THE BURNIN WORLD

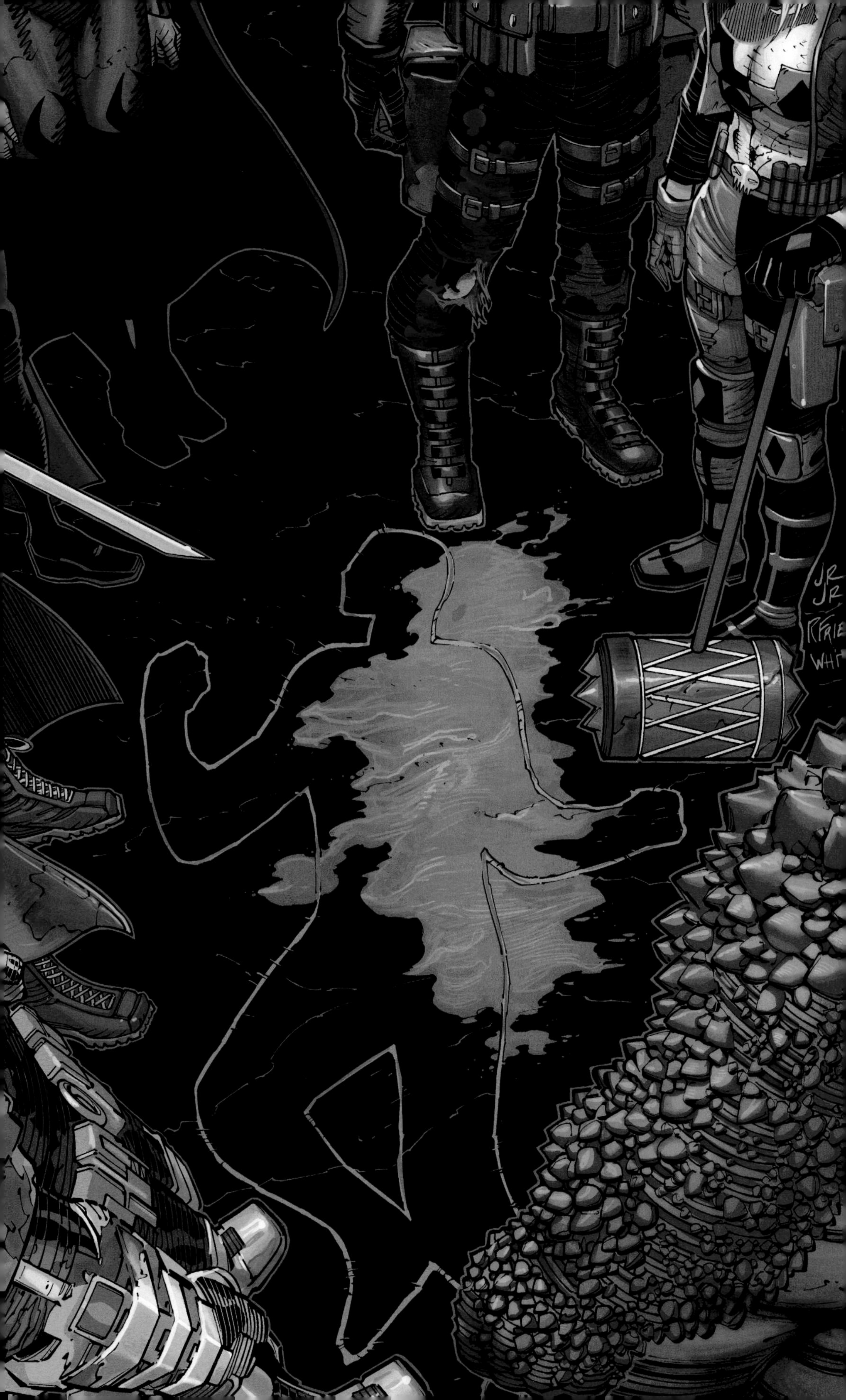
JR
JR

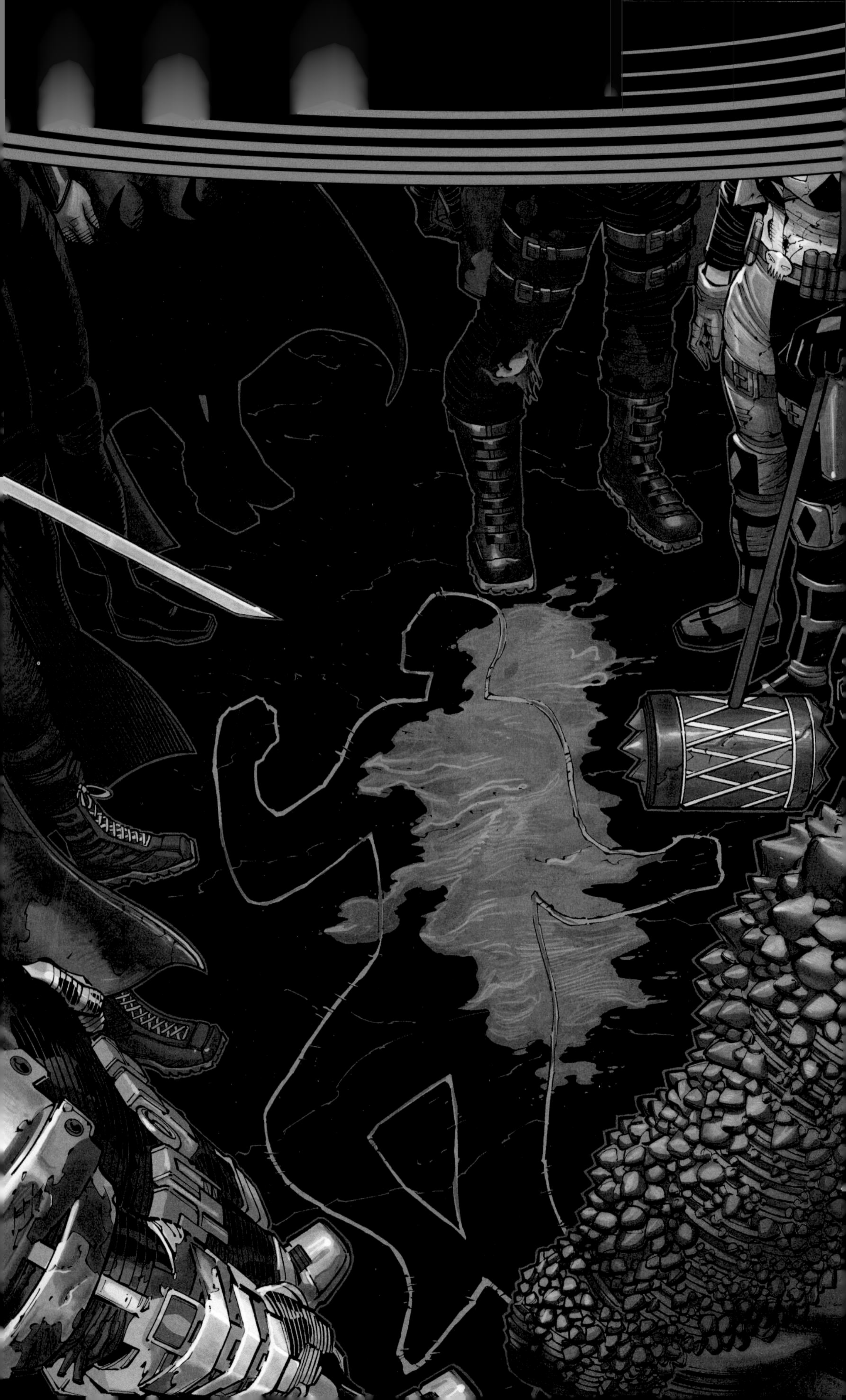

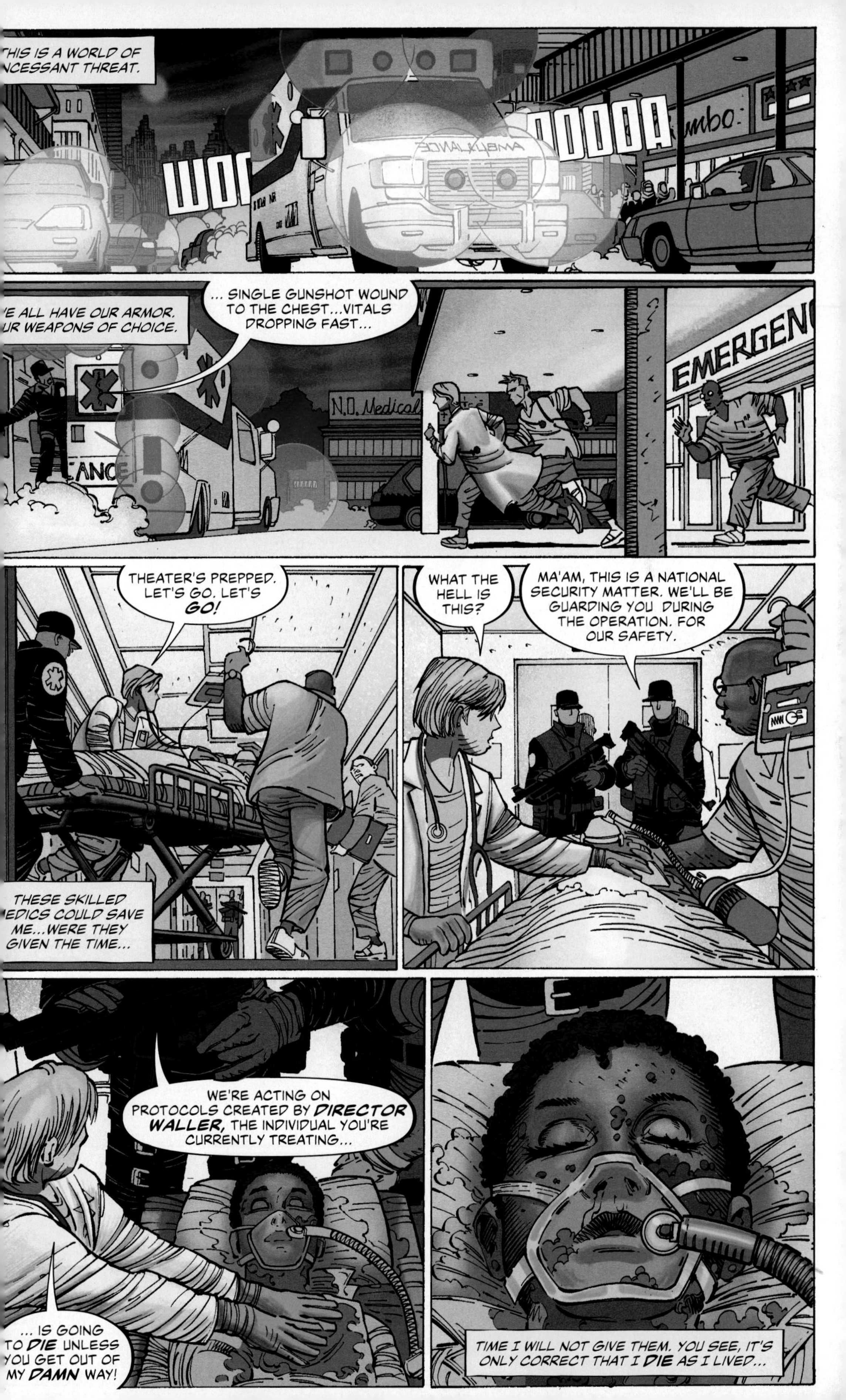
THIS IS A WORLD OF
NCESSANT THREAT.
WOOOOOOA
AMBULANCE
'E ALL HAVE OUR ARMOR.
UR WEAPONS OF CHOICE.
... SINGLE GUNSHOT WOUND TO THE CHEST...VITALS DROPPING FAST...
N.O. Medical
EMERGEN
THEATER'S PREPPED. LET'S GO. LET'S GO!
THESE SKILLED
EDICS COULD SAVE
ME...WERE THEY
GIVEN THE TIME...
WHAT THE HELL IS THIS?
MA'AM, THIS IS A NATIONAL SECURITY MATTER. WE'LL BE GUARDING YOU DURING THE OPERATION. FOR OUR SAFETY.
WE'RE ACTING ON PROTOCOLS CREATED BY DIRECTOR WALLER, THE INDIVIDUAL YOU'RE CURRENTLY TREATING...
... IS GOING TO DIE UNLESS YOU GET OUT OF MY DAMN WAY!
TIME I WILL NOT GIVE THEM. YOU SEE, IT'S ONLY CORRECT THAT I DIE AS I LIVED...

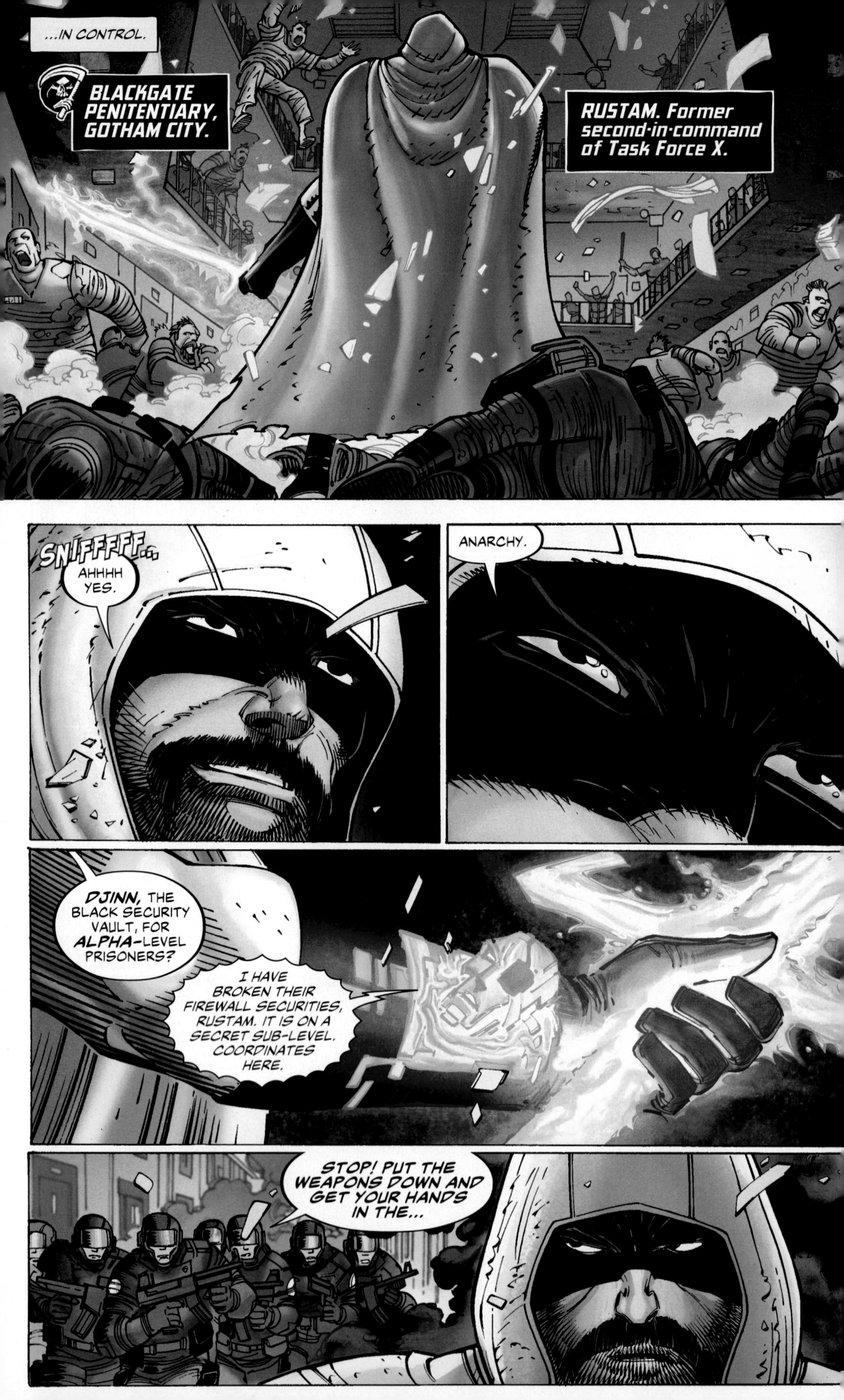
...IN CONTROL.
BLACKGATE PENITENTIARY, GOTHAM CITY.
RUSTAM. Former second-in-command of Task Force X.
SNIFFFFF...
AHHHH YES.
ANARCHY.
DJINN, THE BLACK SECURITY VAULT, FOR ALPHA-LEVEL PRISONERS?
I HAVE BROKEN THEIR FIREWALL SECURITIES, RUSTAM. IT IS ON A SECRET SUB-LEVEL. COORDINATES HERE.
STOP! PUT THE WEAPONS DOWN AND GET YOUR HANDS IN THE...

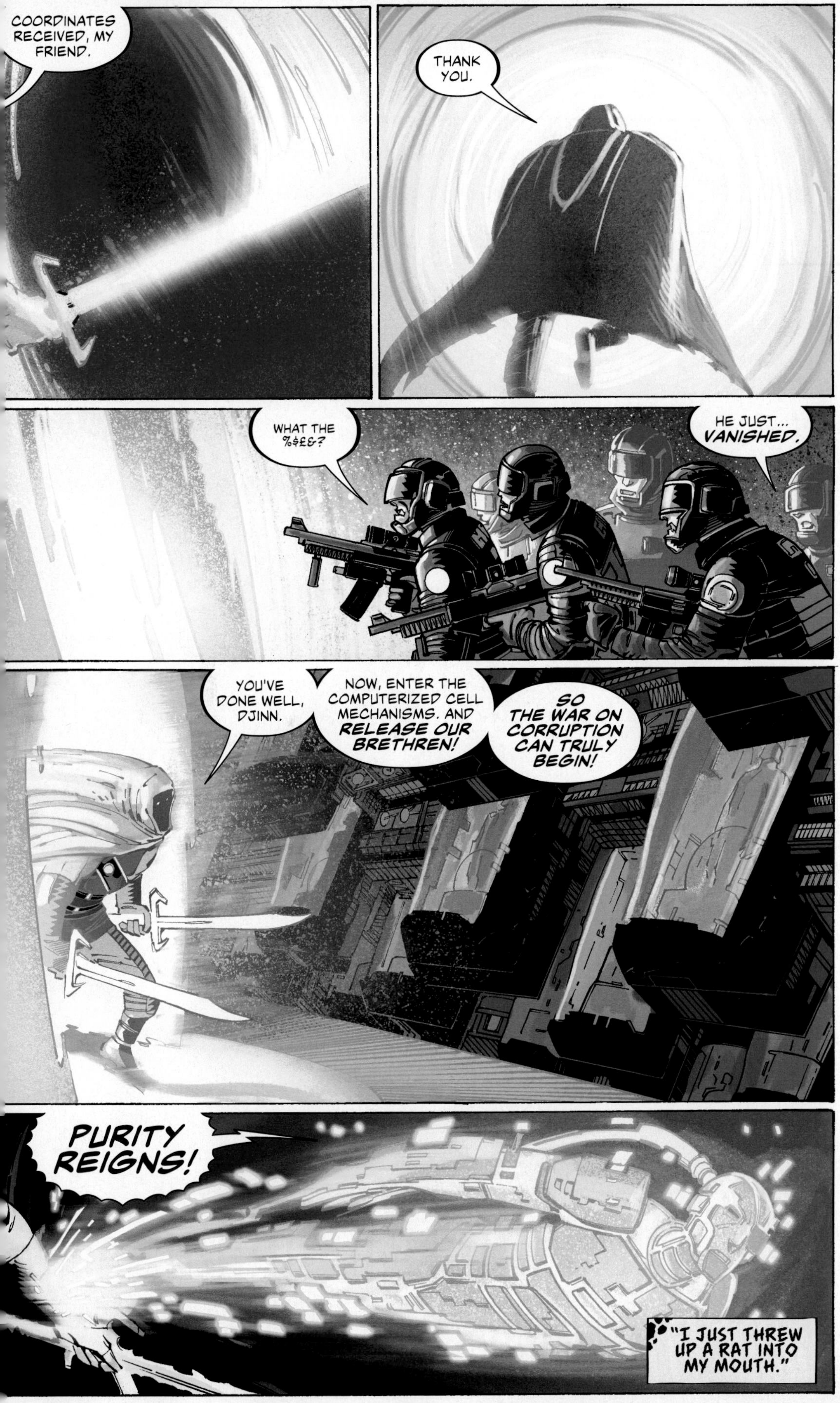

COORDINATES RECEIVED, MY FRIEND.
THANK YOU.
WHAT THE %$£&?
HE JUST... VANISHED.
YOU'VE DONE WELL, DJINN.
NOW, ENTER THE COMPUTERIZED CELL MECHANISMS. AND RELEASE OUR BRETHREN!
SO THE WAR ON CORRUPTION CAN TRULY BEGIN!
PURITY REIGNS!
"I JUST THREW UP A RAT INTO MY MOUTH."

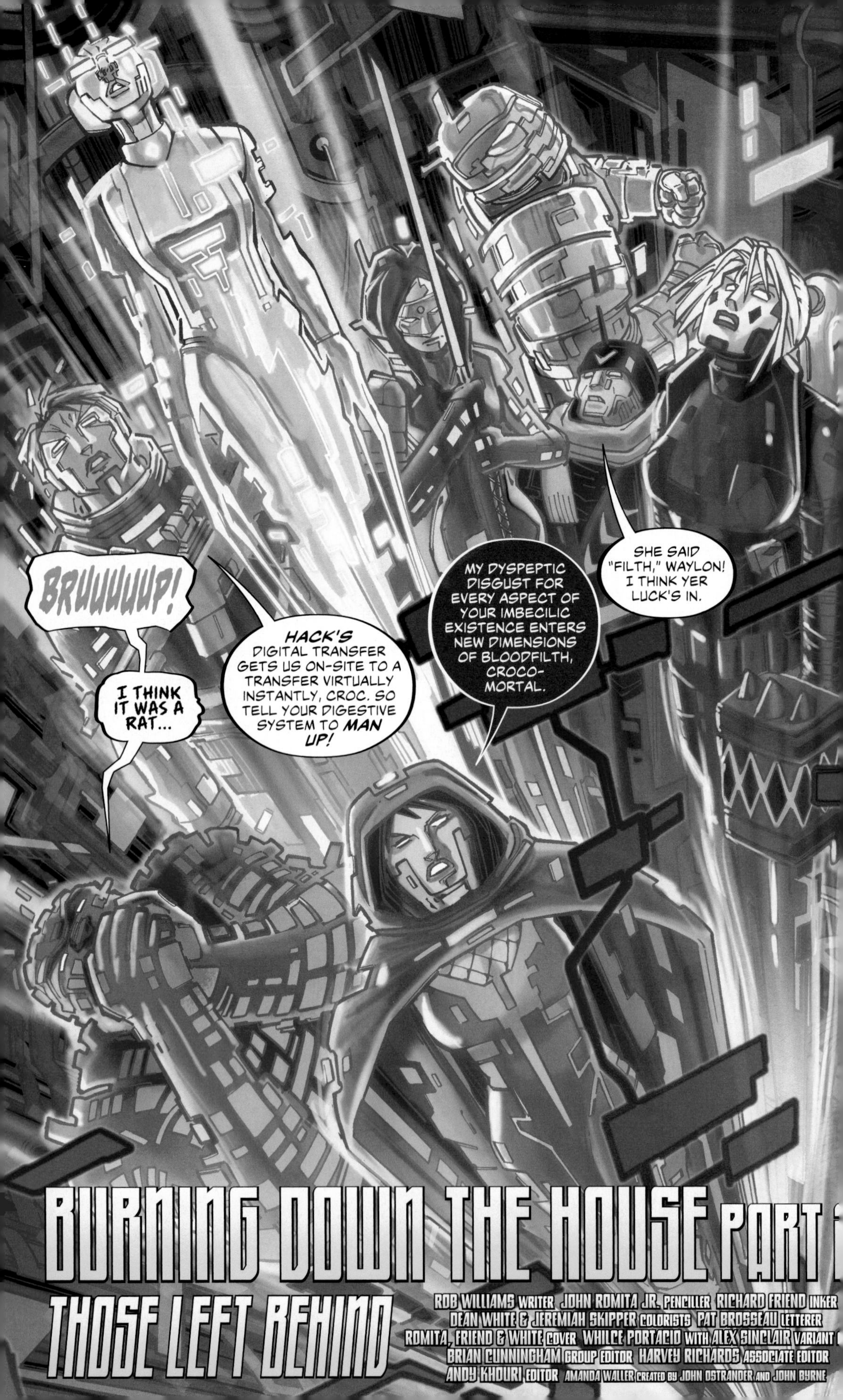
BRUUUUUP!
I THINK IT WAS A RAT...
HACK'S DIGITAL TRANSFER GETS US ON-SITE TO A TRANSFER VIRTUALLY INSTANTLY, CROC. SO TELL YOUR DIGESTIVE SYSTEM TO MAN UP!
MY DYSPEPTIC DISGUST FOR EVERY ASPECT OF YOUR IMBECILIC EXISTENCE ENTERS NEW DIMENSIONS OF BLOODFILTH, CROCO-MORTAL.
SHE SAID "FILTH," WAYLON! I THINK YER LUCK'S IN.
BURNING DOWN THE HOUSE PART
THOSE LEFT BEHIND
ROB WILLIAMS WRITER JOHN ROMITA JR. PENCILLER RICHARD FRIEND INKER
DEAN WHITE & JEREMIAH SKIPPER COLORISTS PAT BROSSEAU LETTERER
ROMITA, FRIEND & WHITE COVER WHILCE PORTACIO WITH ALEX SINCLAIR VARIANT
BRIAN CUNNINGHAM GROUP EDITOR HARVEY RICHARDS ASSOCIATE EDITOR
ANDY KHOURI EDITOR AMANDA WALLER CREATED BY JOHN OSTRANDER AND JOHN BYRNE

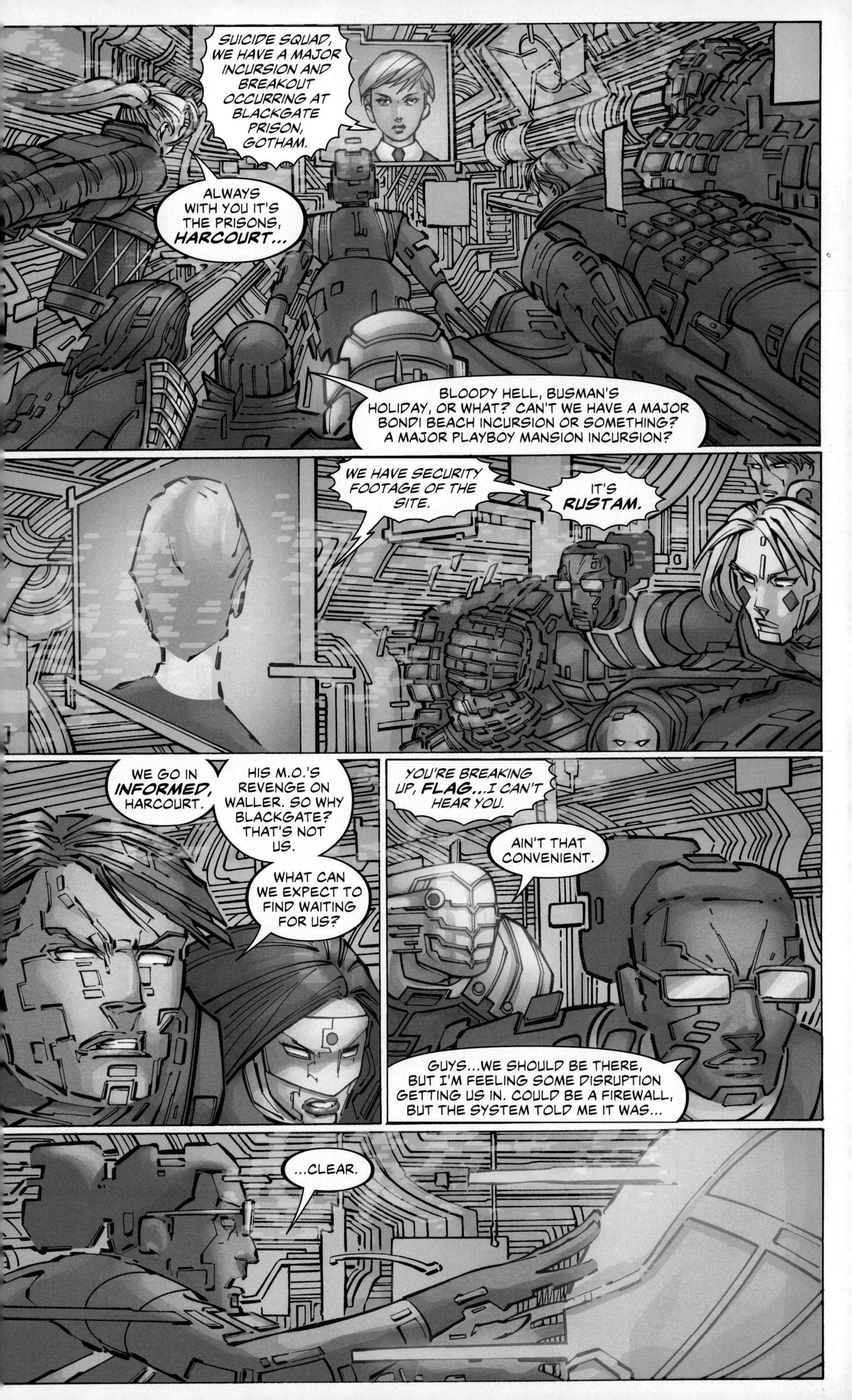
SUICIDE SQUAD, WE HAVE A MAJOR INCURSION AND BREAKOUT OCCURRING AT BLACKGATE PRISON, GOTHAM.
ALWAYS WITH YOU IT'S THE PRISONS, HARCOURT...
BLOODY HELL, BUSMAN'S HOLIDAY, OR WHAT? CAN'T WE HAVE A MAJOR BONDI BEACH INCURSION OR SOMETHING? A MAJOR PLAYBOY MANSION INCURSION?
WE HAVE SECURITY FOOTAGE OF THE SITE.
IT'S RUSTAM.
WE GO IN INFORMED, HARCOURT.
HIS M.O.'S REVENGE ON WALLER. SO WHY BLACKGATE? THAT'S NOT US.
WHAT CAN WE EXPECT TO FIND WAITING FOR US?
YOU'RE BREAKING UP, FLAG...I CAN'T HEAR YOU.
AIN'T THAT CONVENIENT.
GUYS...WE SHOULD BE THERE, BUT I'M FEELING SOME DISRUPTION GETTING US IN. COULD BE A FIREWALL, BUT THE SYSTEM TOLD ME IT WAS...
...CLEAR.

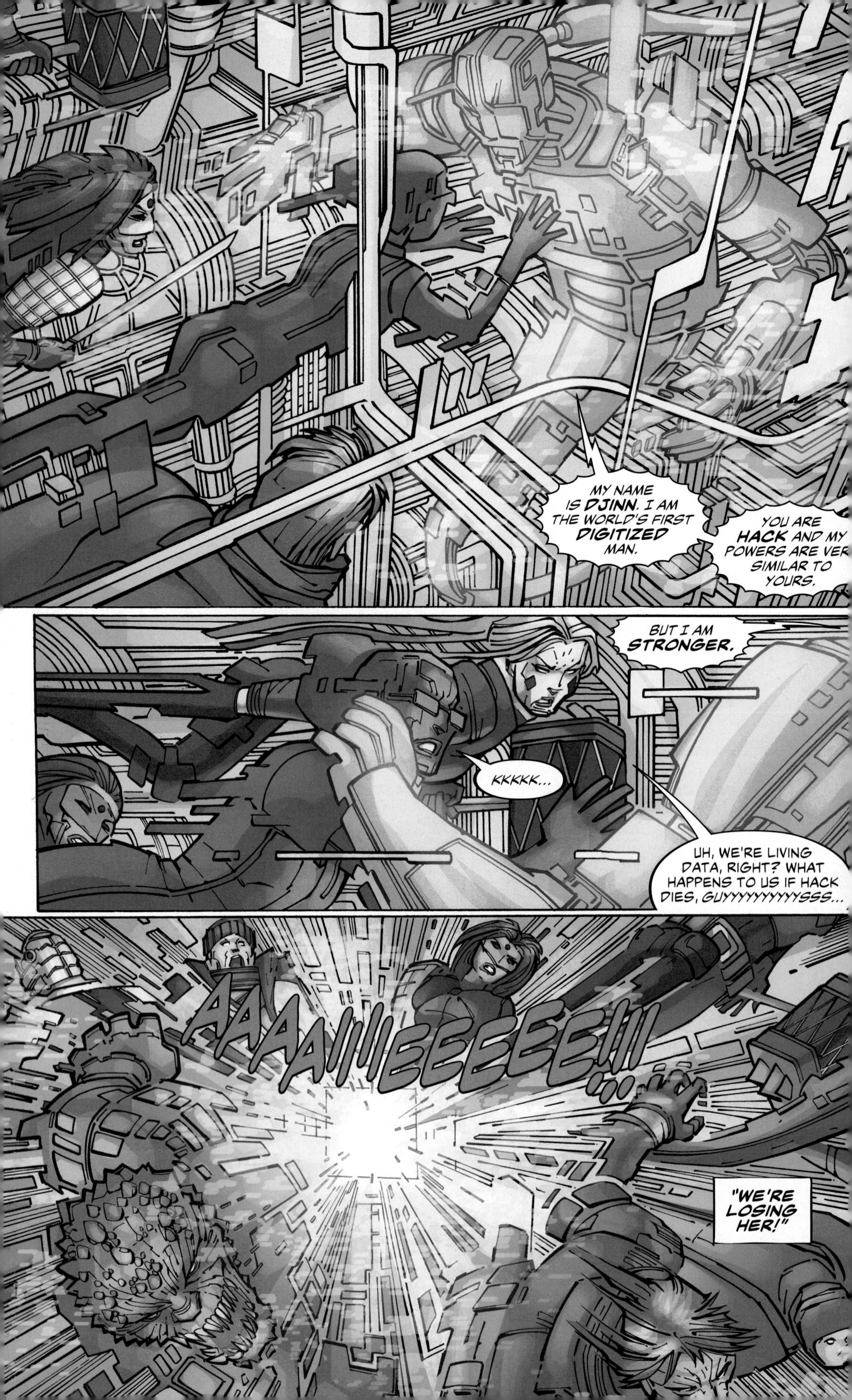
MY NAME IS DJINN. I AM THE WORLD'S FIRST DIGITIZED MAN.
YOU ARE HACK AND MY POWERS ARE VER SIMILAR TO YOURS.
BUT I AM STRONGER.
KKKKK...
UH, WE'RE LIVING DATA, RIGHT? WHAT HAPPENS TO US IF HACK DIES, GUYYYYYYYYYYSSS...
AAAAIIIIEEEEEE!!!
"WE'RE LOSING HER!"

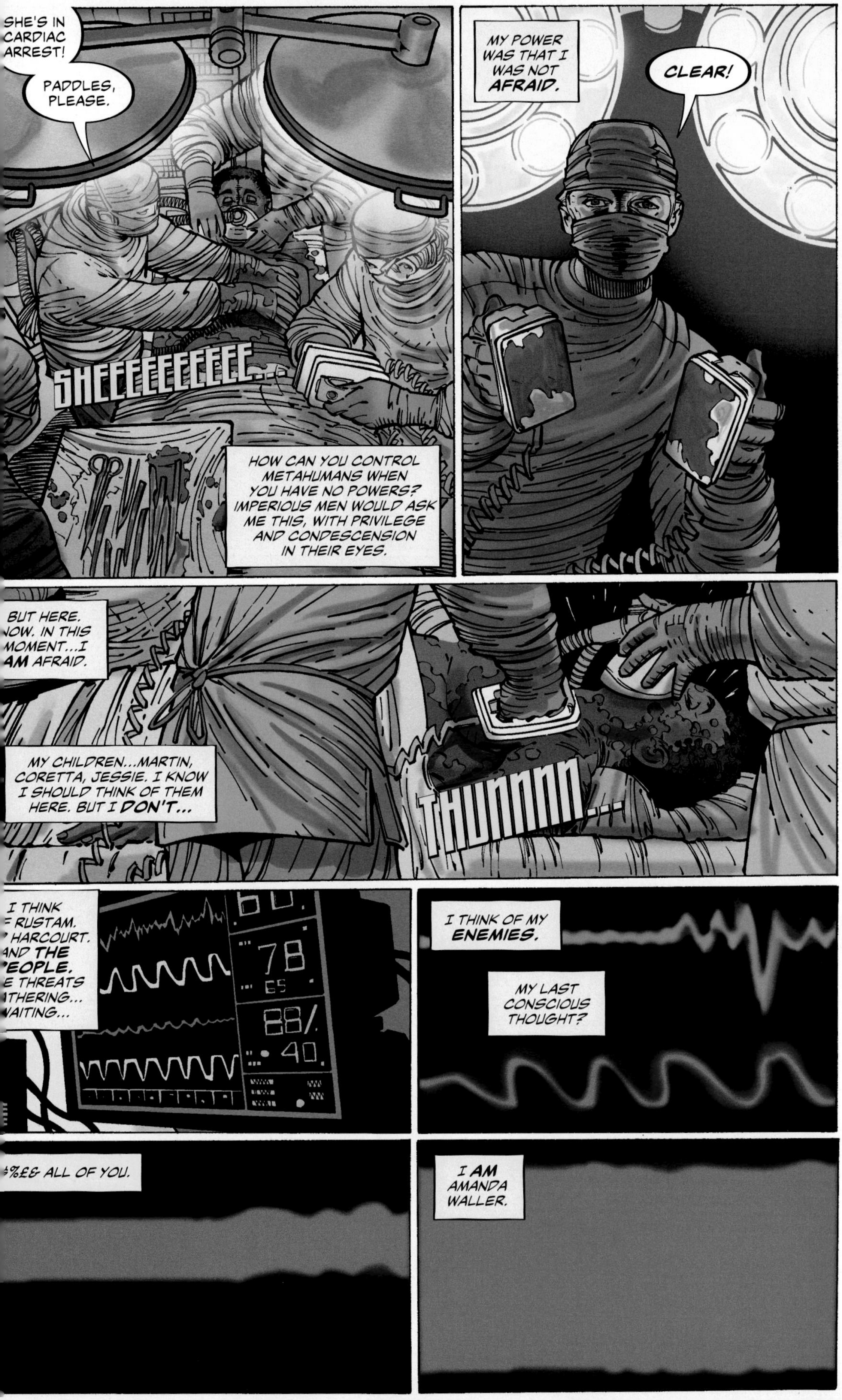
SHE'S IN CARDIAC ARREST!
PADDLES, PLEASE.
SHEEEEEEEEE...
HOW CAN YOU CONTROL METAHUMANS WHEN YOU HAVE NO POWERS? IMPERIOUS MEN WOULD ASK ME THIS, WITH PRIVILEGE AND CONDESCENSION IN THEIR EYES.
MY POWER WAS THAT I WAS NOT AFRAID.
CLEAR!
BUT HERE. NOW. IN THIS MOMENT...I AM AFRAID.
MY CHILDREN...MARTIN, CORETTA, JESSIE. I KNOW I SHOULD THINK OF THEM HERE. BUT I DON'T...
THUNNNN...
I THINK OF RUSTAM. HARCOURT. AND THE PEOPLE. THE THREATS GATHERING... WAITING...
78
88/ 40
I THINK OF MY ENEMIES.
MY LAST CONSCIOUS THOUGHT?
$%£& ALL OF YOU.
I AM AMANDA WALLER.

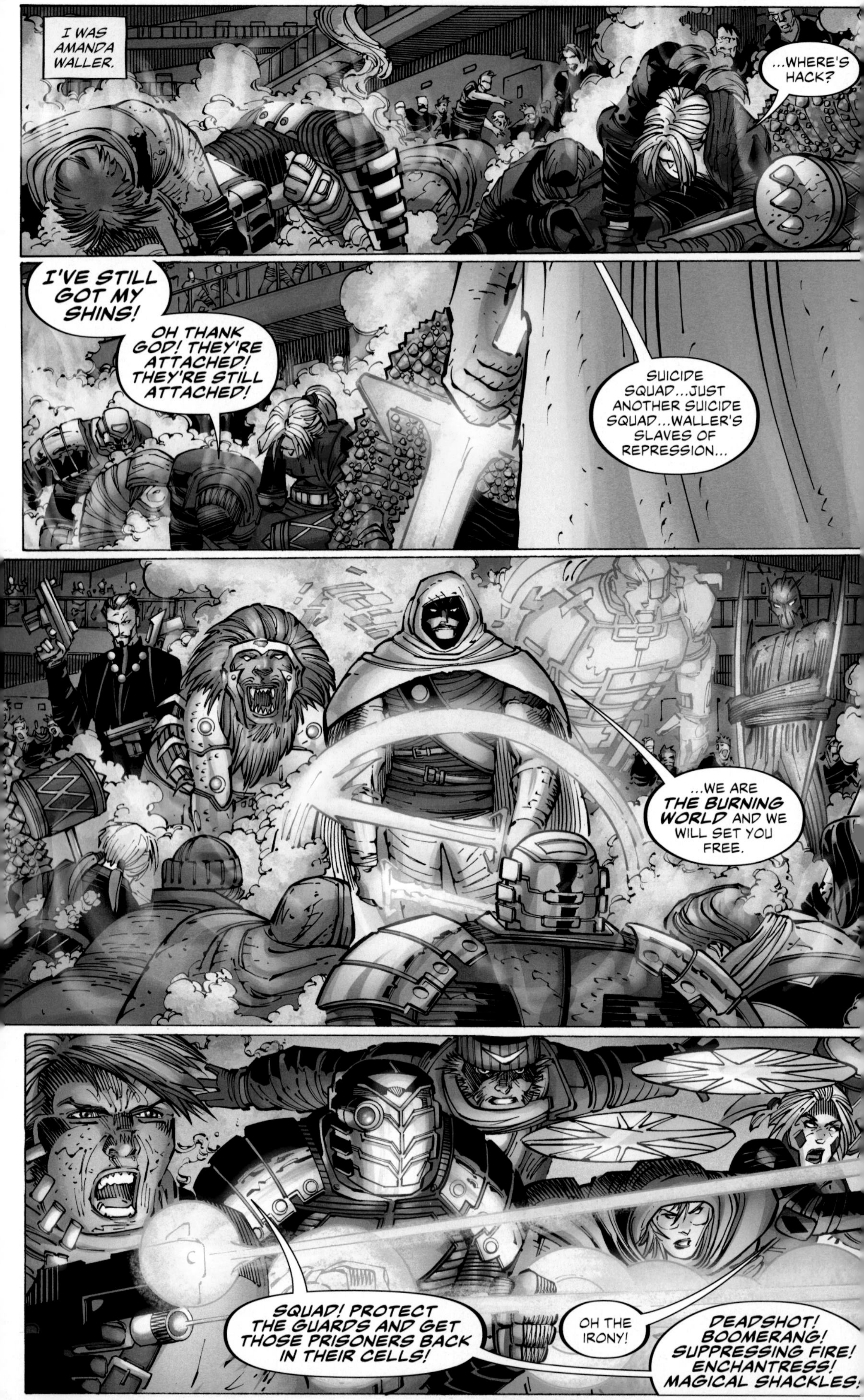
I WAS AMANDA WALLER.
...WHERE'S HACK?
I'VE STILL GOT MY SHINS!
OH THANK GOD! THEY'RE ATTACHED! THEY'RE STILL ATTACHED!
SUICIDE SQUAD...JUST ANOTHER SUICIDE SQUAD...WALLER'S SLAVES OF REPRESSION...
...WE ARE THE BURNING WORLD AND WE WILL SET YOU FREE.
SQUAD! PROTECT THE GUARDS AND GET THOSE PRISONERS BACK IN THEIR CELLS!
OH THE IRONY!
DEADSHOT! BOOMERANG! SUPPRESSING FIRE! ENCHANTRESS! MAGICAL SHACKLES.

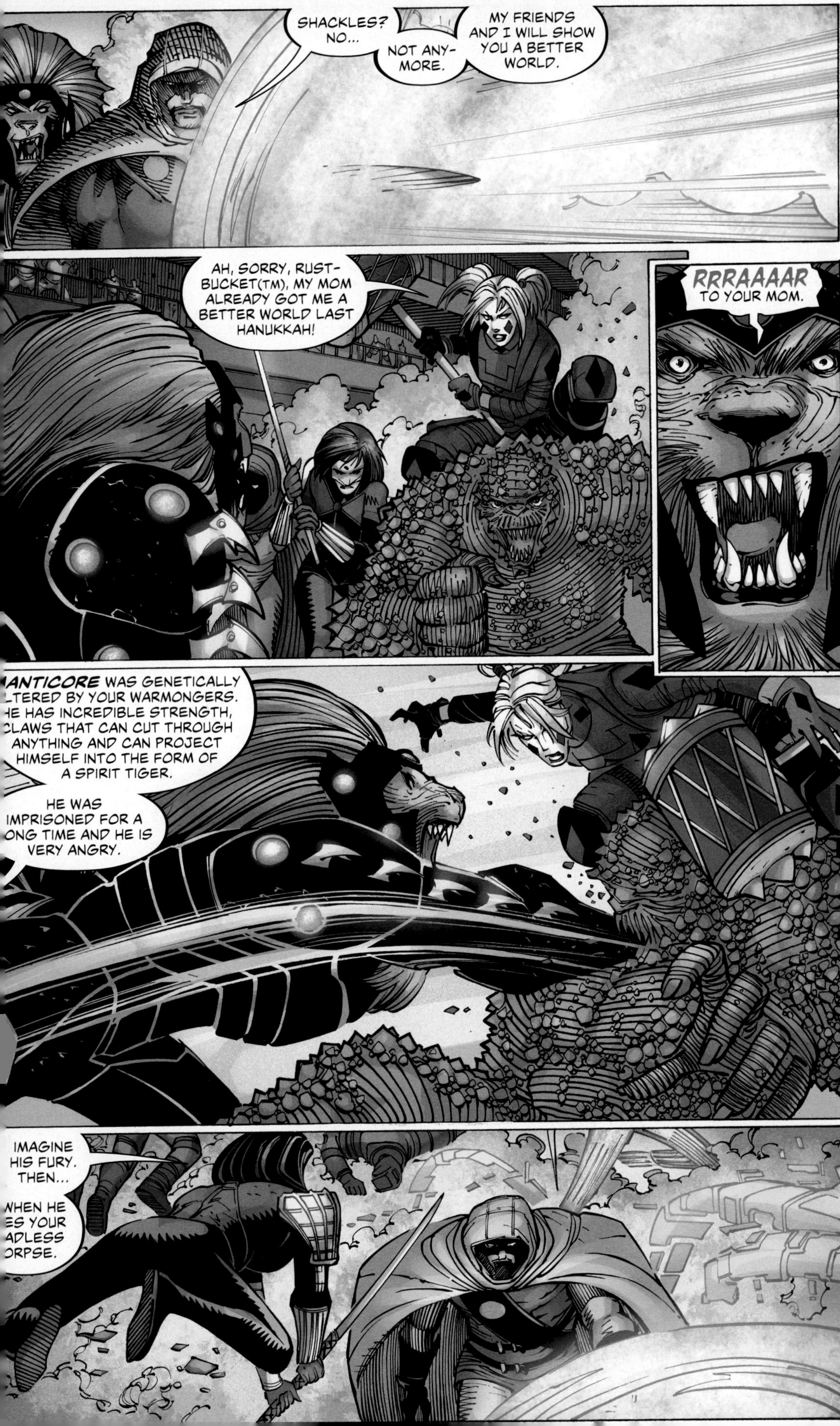
SHACKLES? NO...
NOT ANY-MORE.
MY FRIENDS AND I WILL SHOW YOU A BETTER WORLD.
AH, SORRY, RUST-BUCKET(TM), MY MOM ALREADY GOT ME A BETTER WORLD LAST HANUKKAH!
RRRAAAAR TO YOUR MOM.
ANTICORE WAS GENETICALLY LTERED BY YOUR WARMONGERS. HE HAS INCREDIBLE STRENGTH, CLAWS THAT CAN CUT THROUGH ANYTHING AND CAN PROJECT HIMSELF INTO THE FORM OF A SPIRIT TIGER.
HE WAS IMPRISONED FOR A ONG TIME AND HE IS VERY ANGRY.
IMAGINE HIS FURY. THEN...
WHEN HE ES YOUR ADLESS ORPSE.

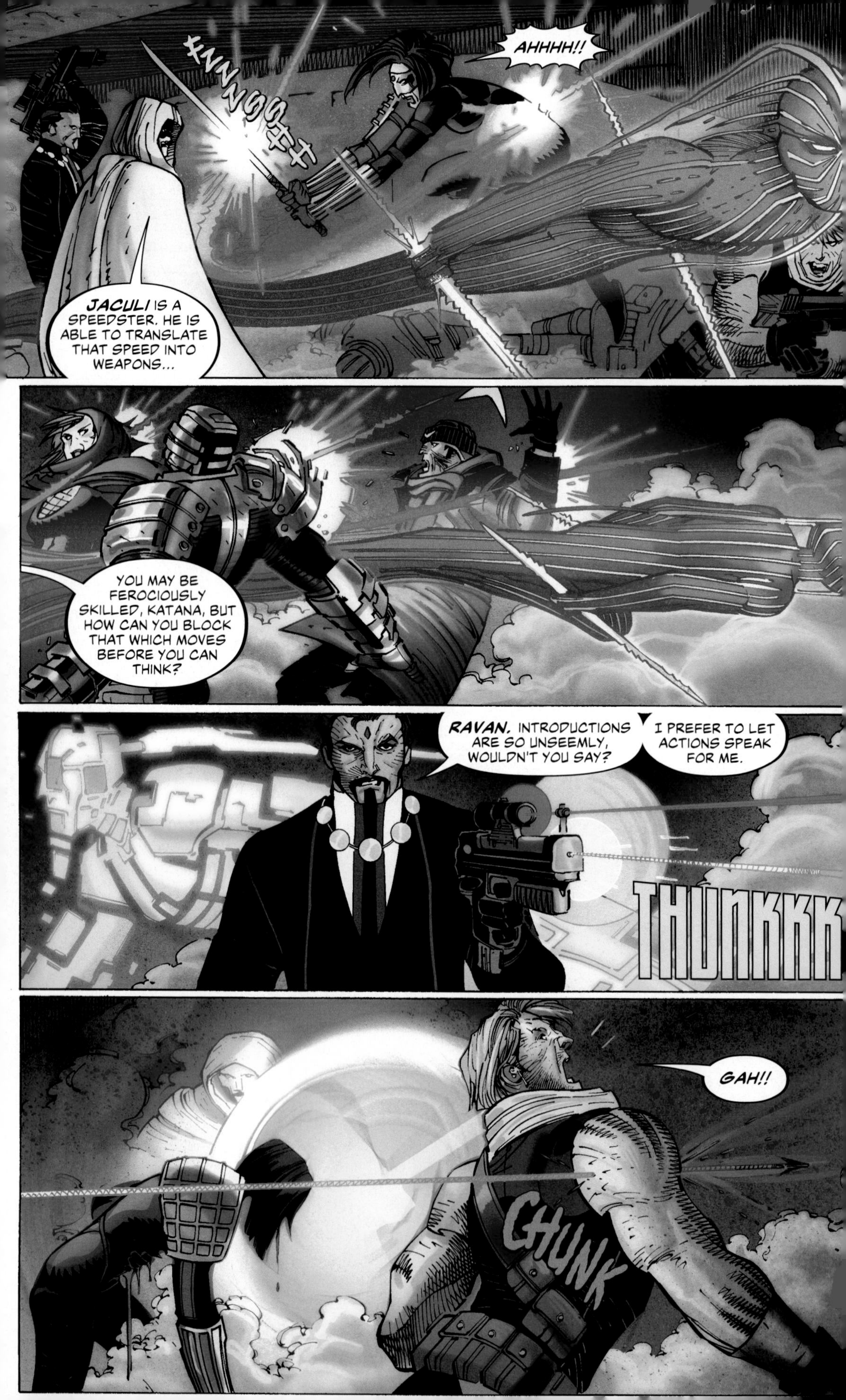

FZZZSSSTTT
AHHHH!!
JACULI IS A SPEEDSTER. HE IS ABLE TO TRANSLATE THAT SPEED INTO WEAPONS...
YOU MAY BE FEROCIOUSLY SKILLED, KATANA, BUT HOW CAN YOU BLOCK THAT WHICH MOVES BEFORE YOU CAN THINK?
RAVAN. INTRODUCTIONS ARE SO UNSEEMLY, WOULDN'T YOU SAY?
I PREFER TO LET ACTIONS SPEAK FOR ME.
THUNKKK
GAH!!
CHUNK

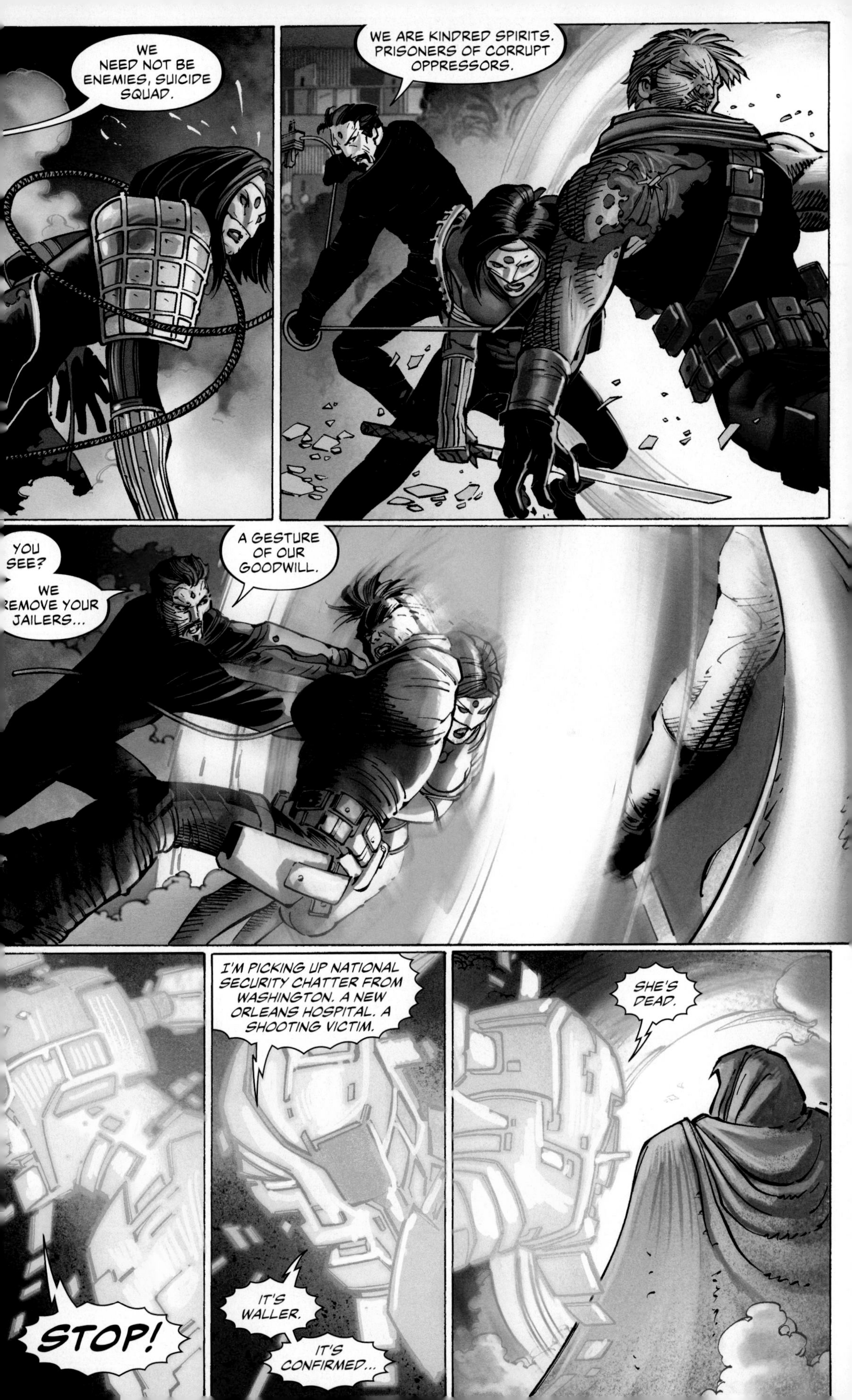
WE NEED NOT BE ENEMIES, SUICIDE SQUAD.
WE ARE KINDRED SPIRITS. PRISONERS OF CORRUPT OPPRESSORS.
YOU SEE?
WE REMOVE YOUR JAILERS...
A GESTURE OF OUR GOODWILL.
STOP!
I'M PICKING UP NATIONAL SECURITY CHATTER FROM WASHINGTON. A NEW ORLEANS HOSPITAL. A SHOOTING VICTIM.
IT'S WALLER.
IT'S CONFIRMED...
SHE'S DEAD.

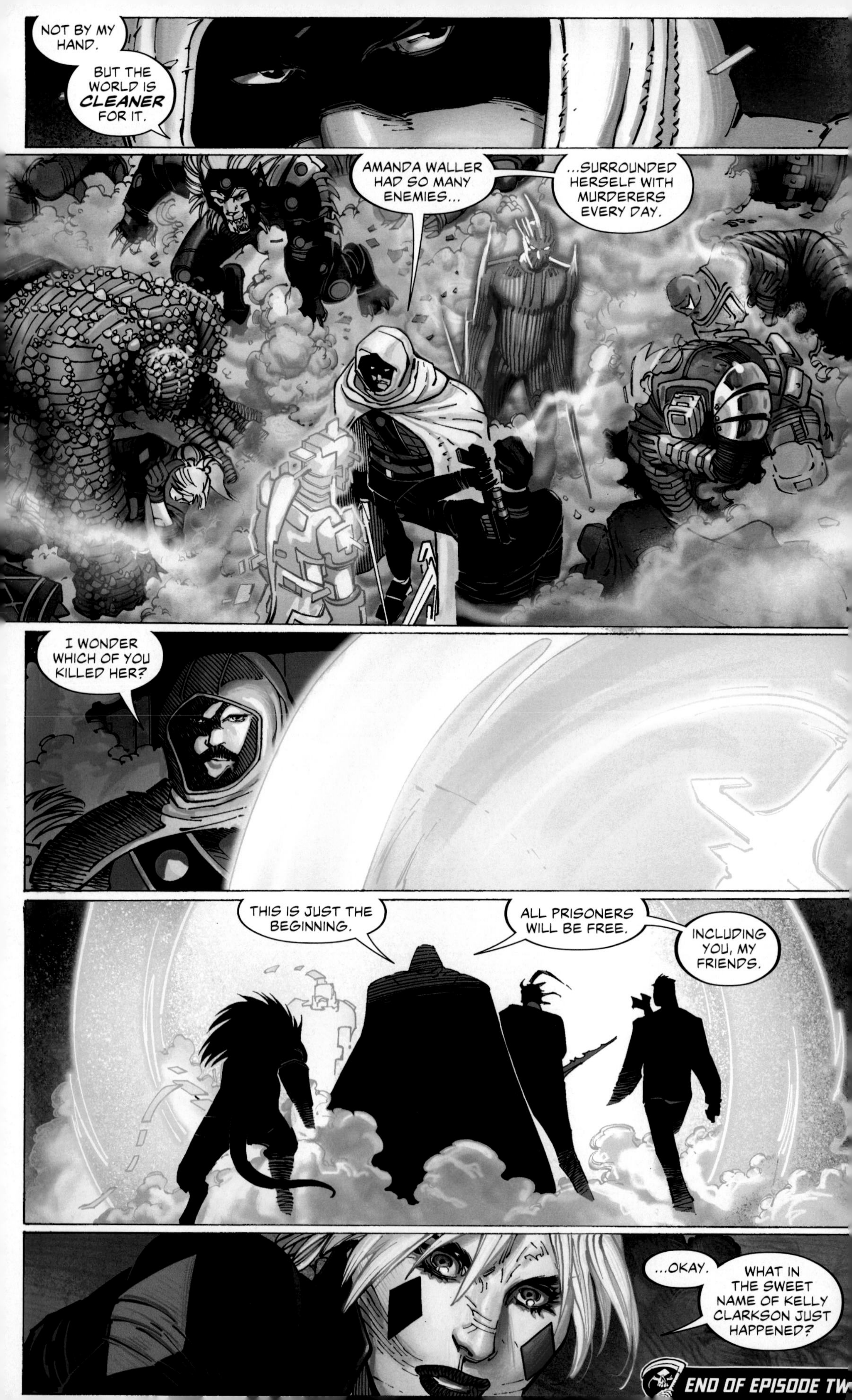
NOT BY MY HAND.
BUT THE WORLD IS CLEANER FOR IT.
AMANDA WALLER HAD SO MANY ENEMIES...
...SURROUNDED HERSELF WITH MURDERERS EVERY DAY.
I WONDER WHICH OF YOU KILLED HER?
THIS IS JUST THE BEGINNING.
ALL PRISONERS WILL BE FREE.
INCLUDING YOU, MY FRIENDS.
...OKAY.
WHAT IN THE SWEET NAME OF KELLY CLARKSON JUST HAPPENED?
END OF EPISODE TW

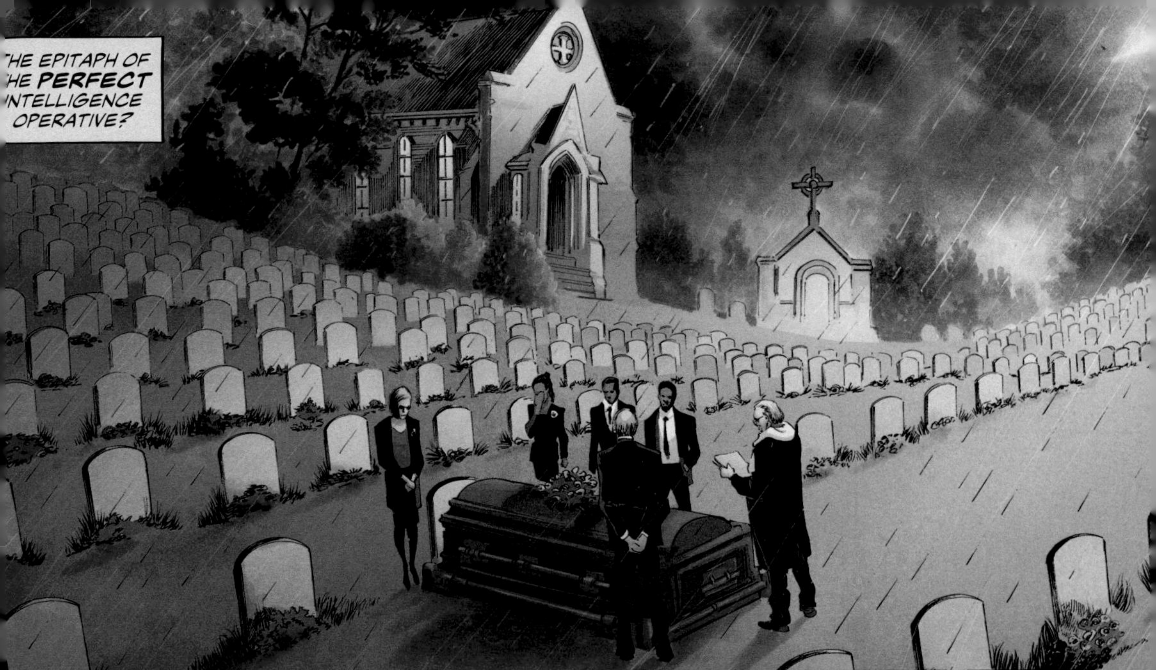
THE EPITAPH OF THE **PERFECT** INTELLIGENCE OPERATIVE?

THOSE LEFT BEHIND

ROB WILLIAMS WRITER EDDY BARROWS PENCILLER EBER FERREIRA INKER ADRIANO LUCAS COLORIST
PAT BROSSEAU LETTERER BRIAN CUNNINGHAM GROUP EDITOR HARVEY RICHARDS ASSOCIATE EDITOR
ANDY KHOURI EDITOR AMANDA WALLER CREATED BY JOHN OSTRANDER AND JOHN BYRNE

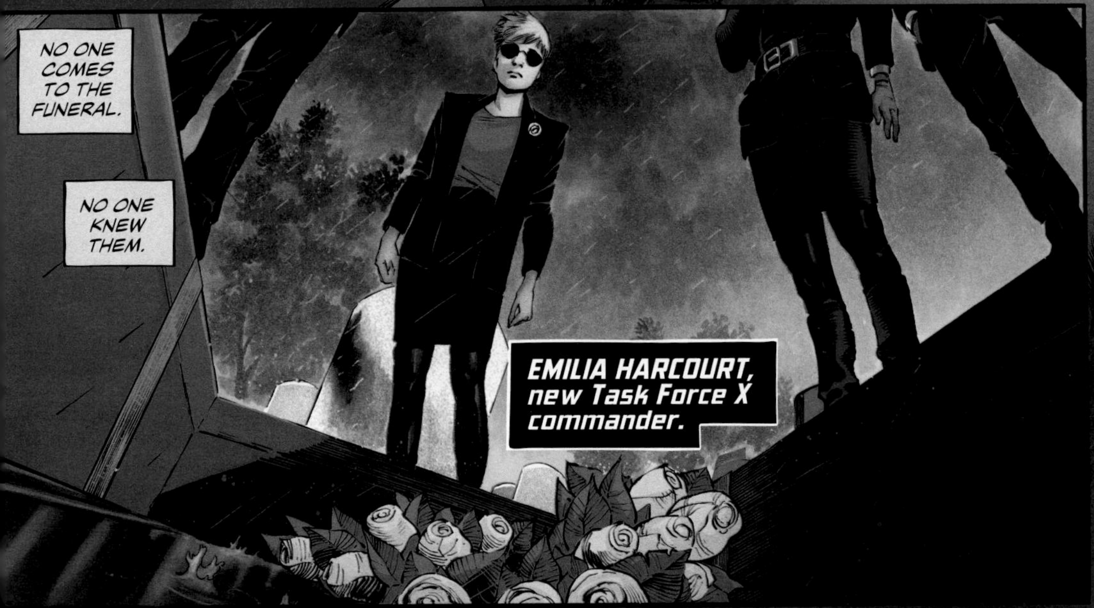
NO ONE COMES TO THE FUNERAL.
NO ONE KNEW THEM.
EMILIA HARCOURT, new Task Force X commander.

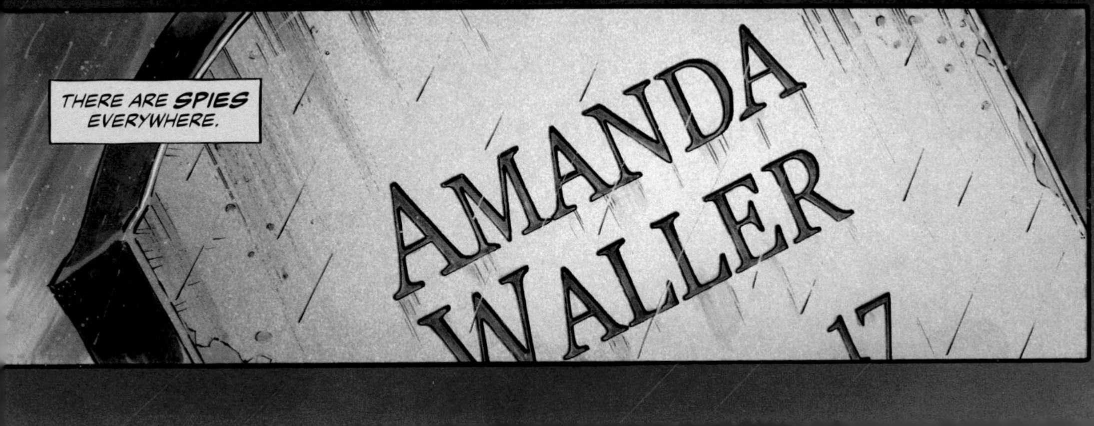
THERE ARE **SPIES** EVERYWHERE.
AMANDA WALLER

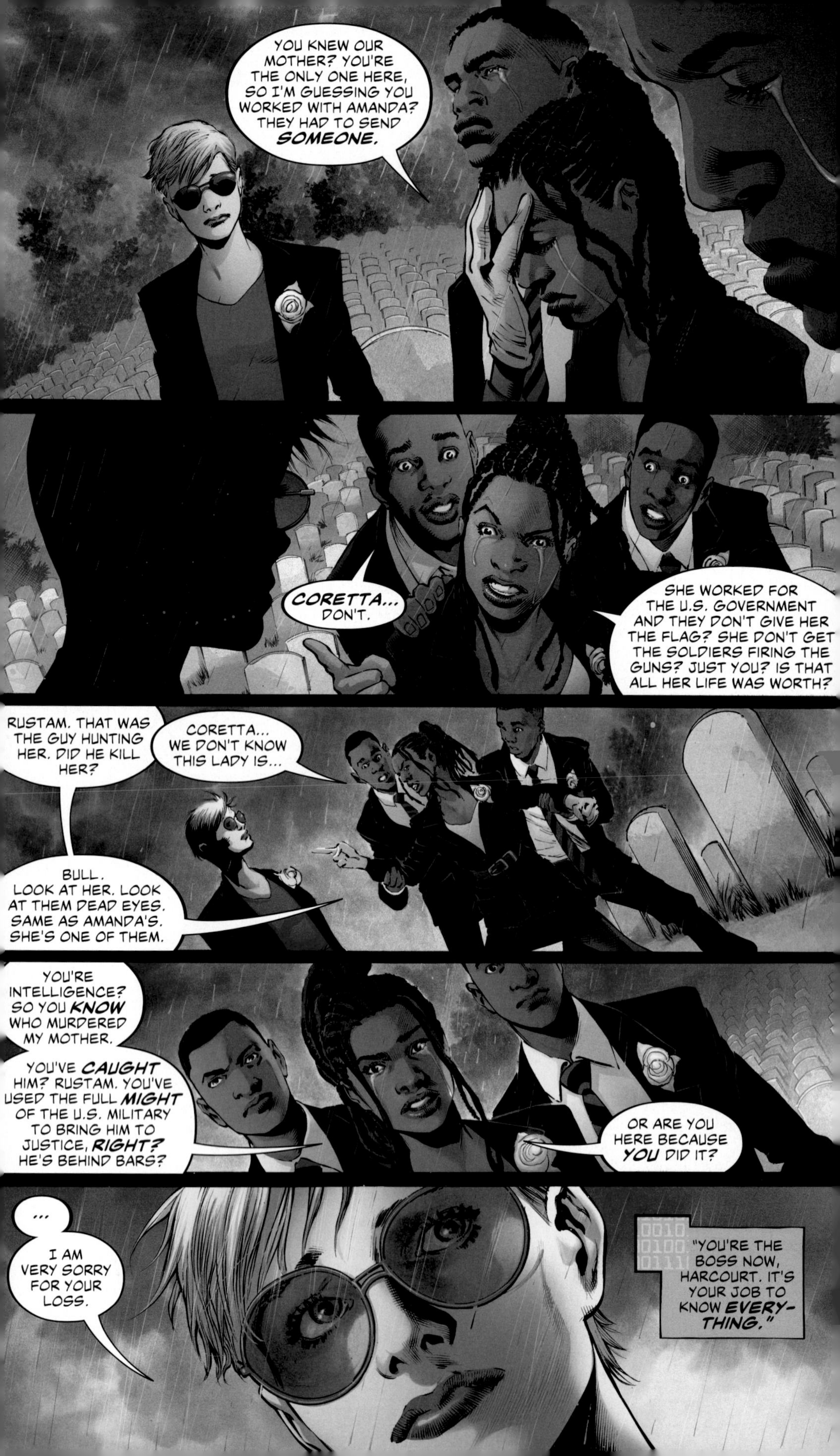

YOU KNEW OUR MOTHER? YOU'RE THE ONLY ONE HERE, SO I'M GUESSING YOU WORKED WITH AMANDA? THEY HAD TO SEND **SOMEONE.**
CORETTA... DON'T.
SHE WORKED FOR THE U.S. GOVERNMENT AND THEY DON'T GIVE HER THE FLAG? SHE DON'T GET THE SOLDIERS FIRING THE GUNS? JUST YOU? IS THAT ALL HER LIFE WAS WORTH?
RUSTAM. THAT WAS THE GUY HUNTING HER. DID HE KILL HER?
CORETTA... WE DON'T KNOW THIS LADY IS...
BULL. LOOK AT HER. LOOK AT THEM DEAD EYES. SAME AS AMANDA'S. SHE'S ONE OF THEM.
YOU'RE INTELLIGENCE? SO YOU **KNOW** WHO MURDERED MY MOTHER.
YOU'VE **CAUGHT** HIM? RUSTAM. YOU'VE USED THE FULL **MIGHT** OF THE U.S. MILITARY TO BRING HIM TO JUSTICE, **RIGHT?** HE'S BEHIND BARS?
OR ARE YOU HERE BECAUSE **YOU** DID IT?
...
I AM VERY SORRY FOR YOUR LOSS.
"YOU'RE THE BOSS NOW, HARCOURT. IT'S YOUR JOB TO KNOW **EVERY-THING.**"

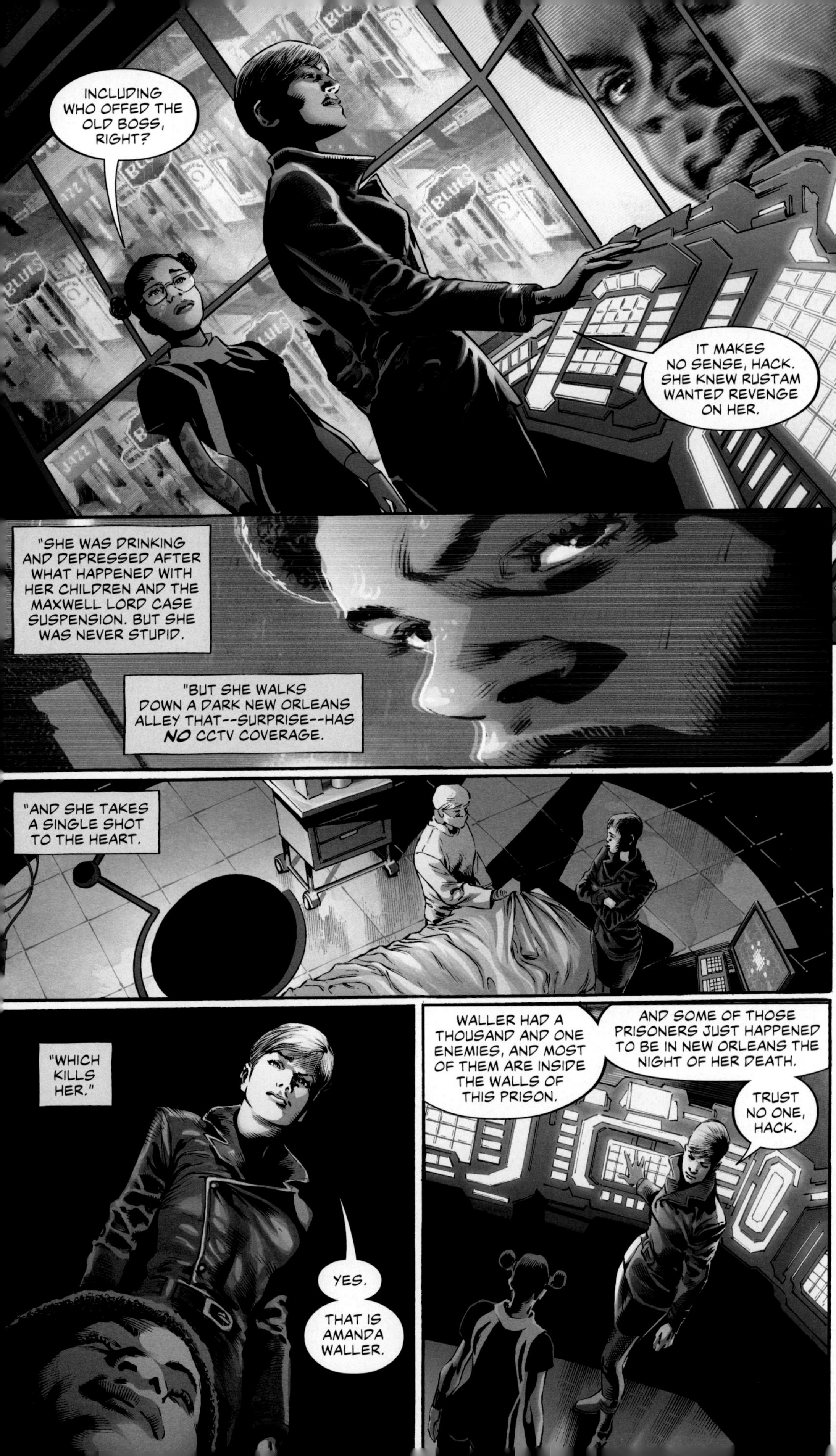
INCLUDING WHO OFFED THE OLD BOSS, RIGHT?
IT MAKES NO SENSE, HACK. SHE KNEW RUSTAM WANTED REVENGE ON HER.
"SHE WAS DRINKING AND DEPRESSED AFTER WHAT HAPPENED WITH HER CHILDREN AND THE MAXWELL LORD CASE SUSPENSION. BUT SHE WAS NEVER STUPID.
"BUT SHE WALKS DOWN A DARK NEW ORLEANS ALLEY THAT--SURPRISE--HAS *NO* CCTV COVERAGE.
"AND SHE TAKES A SINGLE SHOT TO THE HEART.
"WHICH KILLS HER."
YES.
THAT IS AMANDA WALLER.
WALLER HAD A THOUSAND AND ONE ENEMIES, AND MOST OF THEM ARE INSIDE THE WALLS OF THIS PRISON.
AND SOME OF THOSE PRISONERS JUST HAPPENED TO BE IN NEW ORLEANS THE NIGHT OF HER DEATH.
TRUST NO ONE, HACK.

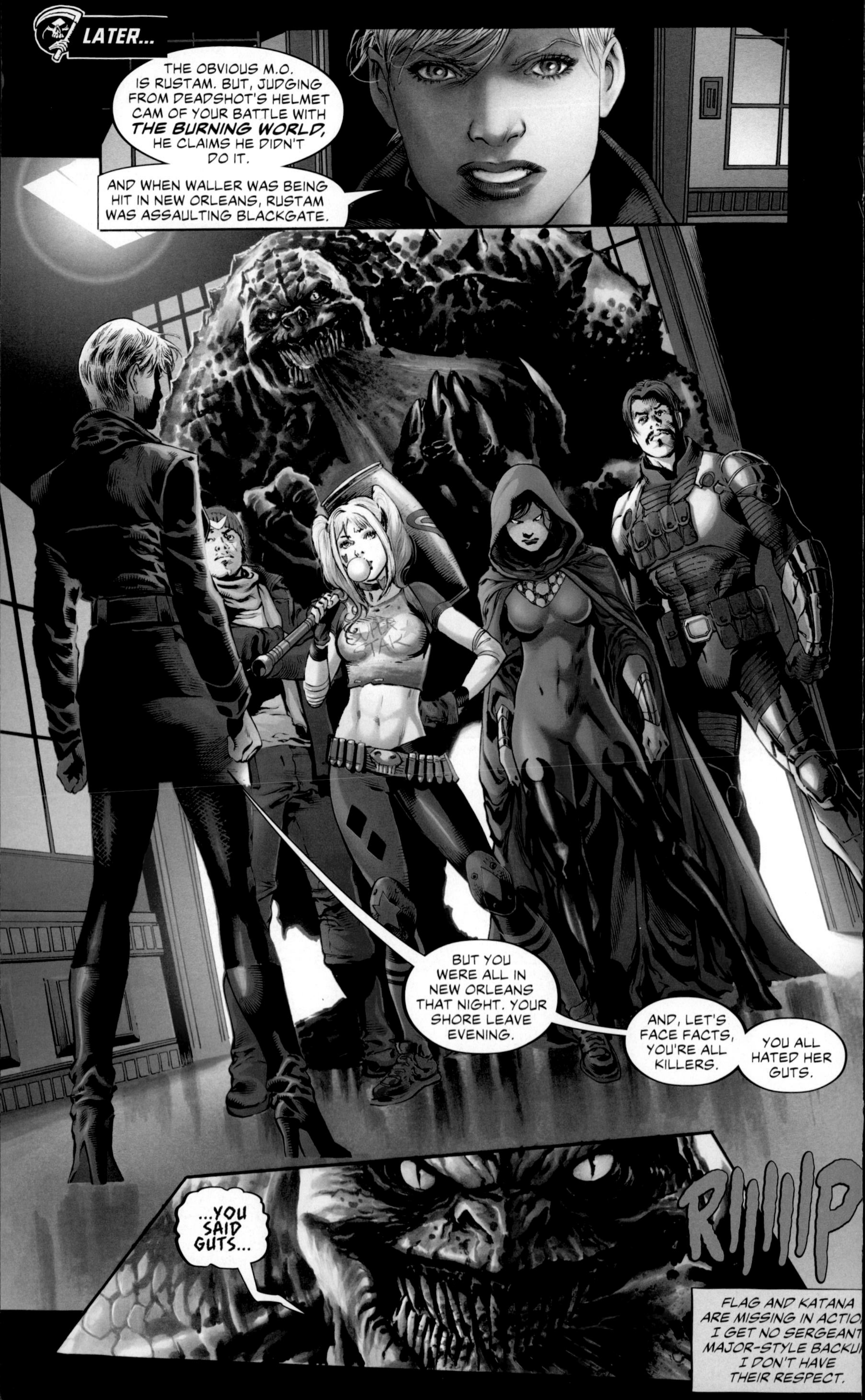
LATER...
THE OBVIOUS M.O. IS RUSTAM. BUT, JUDGING FROM DEADSHOT'S HELMET CAM OF YOUR BATTLE WITH THE BURNING WORLD, HE CLAIMS HE DIDN'T DO IT.
AND WHEN WALLER WAS BEING HIT IN NEW ORLEANS, RUSTAM WAS ASSAULTING BLACKGATE.
BUT YOU WERE ALL IN NEW ORLEANS THAT NIGHT. YOUR SHORE LEAVE EVENING.
AND, LET'S FACE FACTS, YOU'RE ALL KILLERS.
YOU ALL HATED HER GUTS.
...YOU SAID GUTS...
RIIIIP
FLAG AND KATANA ARE MISSING IN ACTIO I GET NO SERGEANT MAJOR-STYLE BACKU I DON'T HAVE THEIR RESPECT.

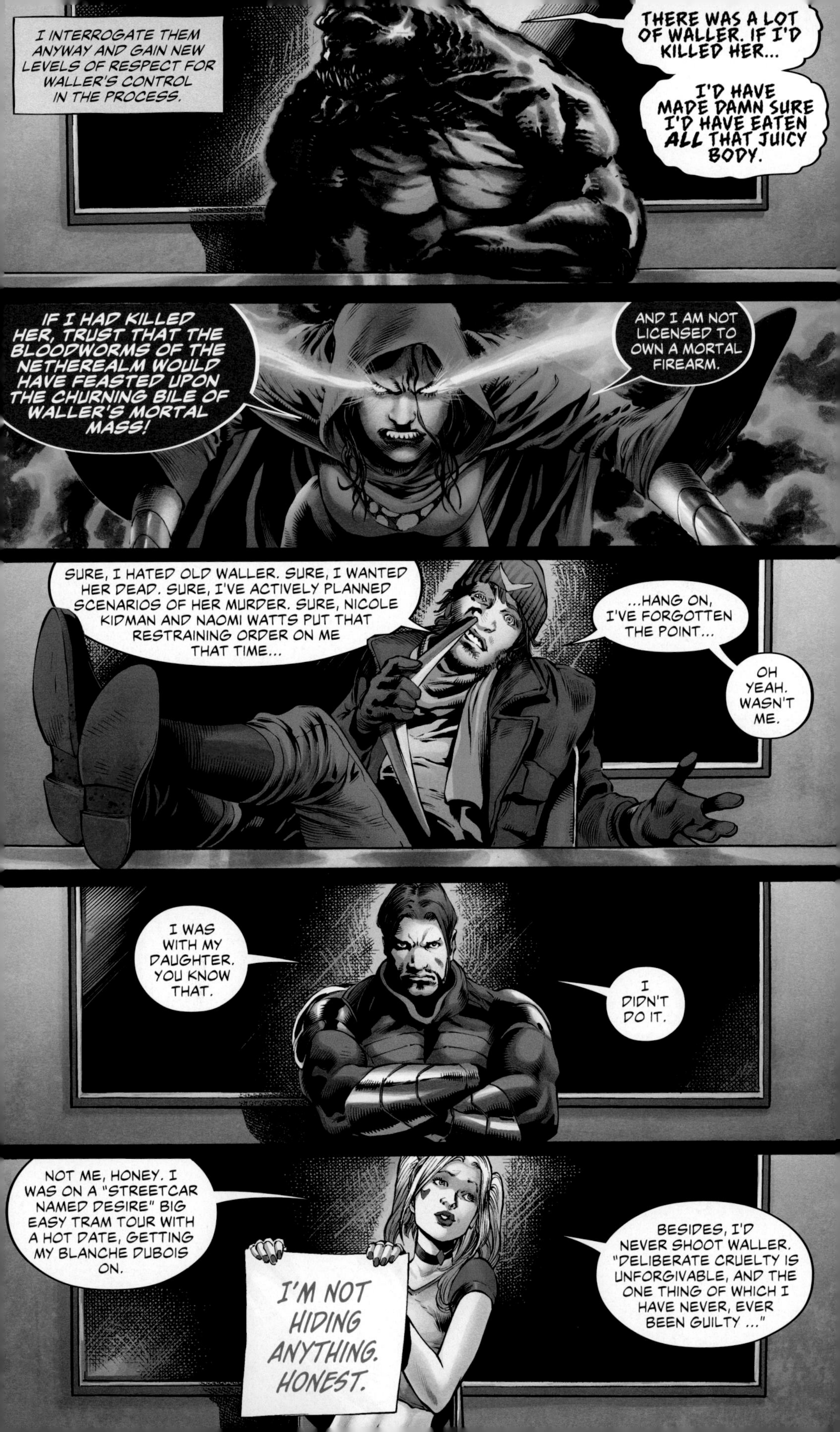
I INTERROGATE THEM ANYWAY AND GAIN NEW LEVELS OF RESPECT FOR WALLER'S CONTROL IN THE PROCESS.
THERE WAS A LOT OF WALLER. IF I'D KILLED HER...
I'D HAVE MADE DAMN SURE I'D HAVE EATEN ALL THAT JUICY BODY.
IF I HAD KILLED HER, TRUST THAT THE BLOODWORMS OF THE NETHEREALM WOULD HAVE FEASTED UPON THE CHURNING BILE OF WALLER'S MORTAL MASS!
AND I AM NOT LICENSED TO OWN A MORTAL FIREARM.
SURE, I HATED OLD WALLER. SURE, I WANTED HER DEAD. SURE, I'VE ACTIVELY PLANNED SCENARIOS OF HER MURDER. SURE, NICOLE KIDMAN AND NAOMI WATTS PUT THAT RESTRAINING ORDER ON ME THAT TIME...
...HANG ON, I'VE FORGOTTEN THE POINT...
OH YEAH. WASN'T ME.
I WAS WITH MY DAUGHTER. YOU KNOW THAT.
I DIDN'T DO IT.
NOT ME, HONEY. I WAS ON A "STREETCAR NAMED DESIRE" BIG EASY TRAM TOUR WITH A HOT DATE, GETTING MY BLANCHE DUBOIS ON.
I'M NOT HIDING ANYTHING. HONEST.
BESIDES, I'D NEVER SHOOT WALLER. "DELIBERATE CRUELTY IS UNFORGIVABLE, AND THE ONE THING OF WHICH I HAVE NEVER, EVER BEEN GUILTY ..."

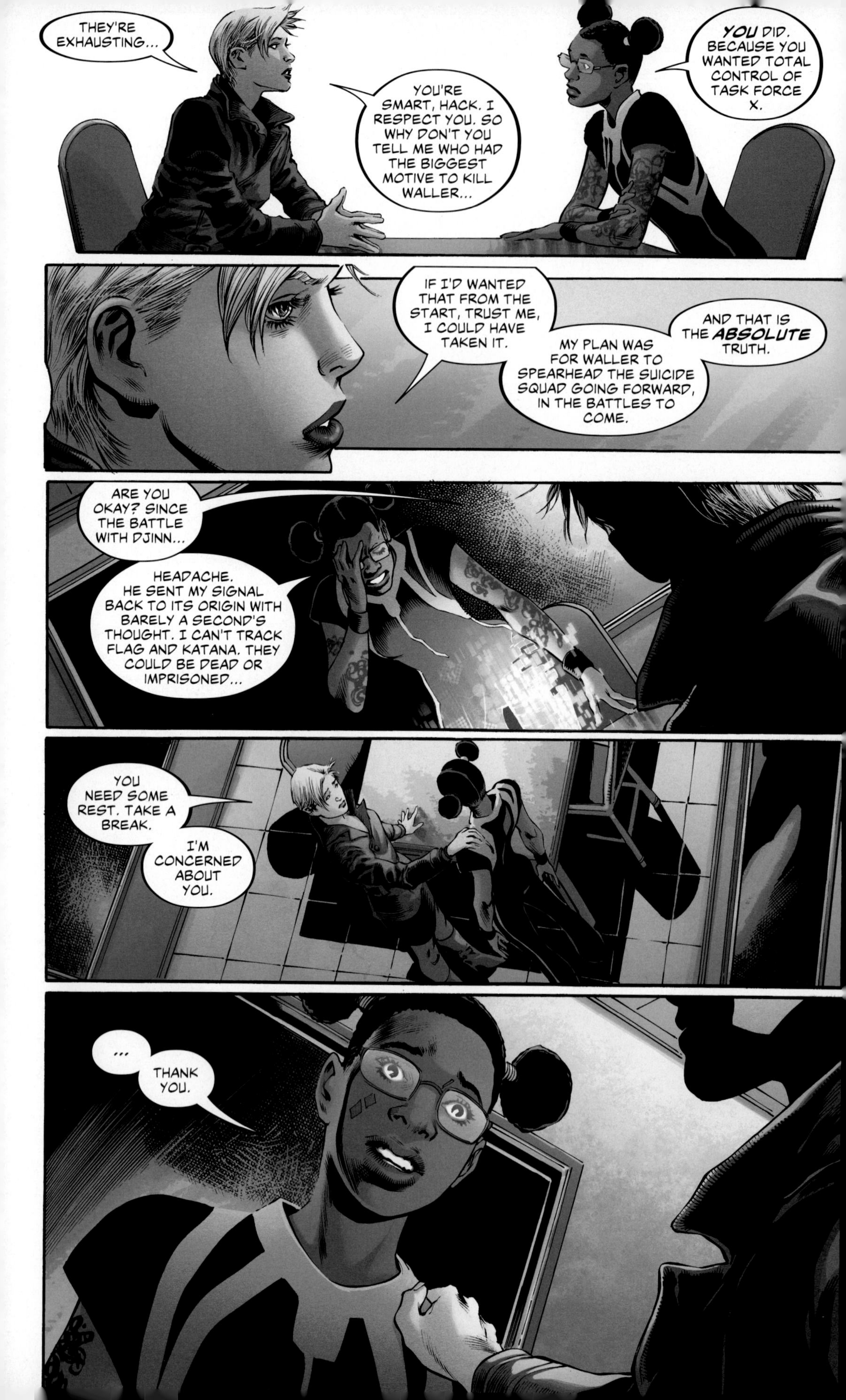
THEY'RE EXHAUSTING...
YOU'RE SMART, HACK. I RESPECT YOU. SO WHY DON'T YOU TELL ME WHO HAD THE BIGGEST MOTIVE TO KILL WALLER...
YOU DID. BECAUSE YOU WANTED TOTAL CONTROL OF TASK FORCE X.
IF I'D WANTED THAT FROM THE START, TRUST ME, I COULD HAVE TAKEN IT.
MY PLAN WAS FOR WALLER TO SPEARHEAD THE SUICIDE SQUAD GOING FORWARD, IN THE BATTLES TO COME.
AND THAT IS THE ABSOLUTE TRUTH.
ARE YOU OKAY? SINCE THE BATTLE WITH DJINN...
HEADACHE. HE SENT MY SIGNAL BACK TO ITS ORIGIN WITH BARELY A SECOND'S THOUGHT. I CAN'T TRACK FLAG AND KATANA. THEY COULD BE DEAD OR IMPRISONED...
YOU NEED SOME REST. TAKE A BREAK.
I'M CONCERNED ABOUT YOU.
...
THANK YOU.

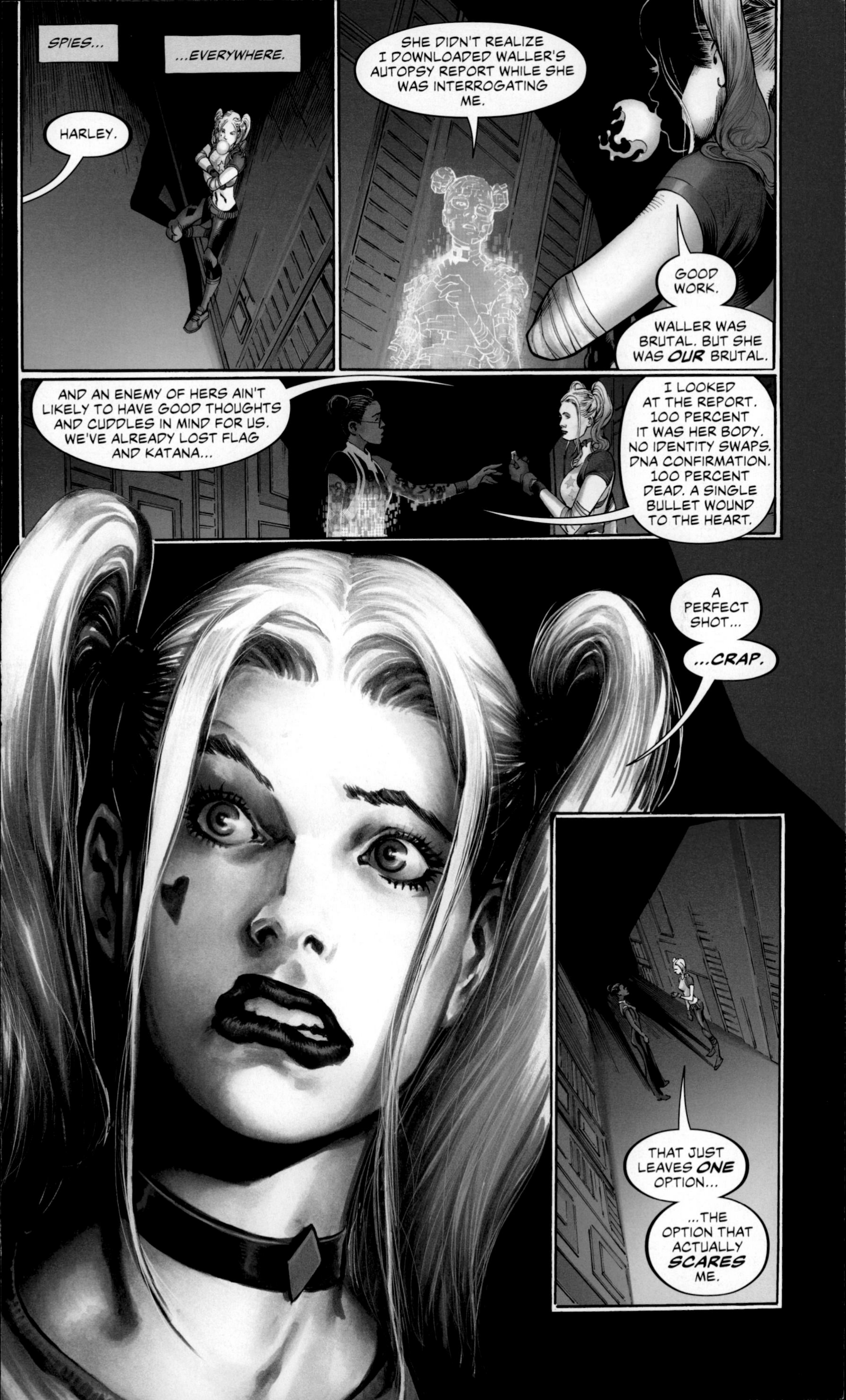
SPIES...
...EVERYWHERE.
HARLEY.
SHE DIDN'T REALIZE I DOWNLOADED WALLER'S AUTOPSY REPORT WHILE SHE WAS INTERROGATING ME.
GOOD WORK.
WALLER WAS BRUTAL. BUT SHE WAS *OUR* BRUTAL.
AND AN ENEMY OF HERS AIN'T LIKELY TO HAVE GOOD THOUGHTS AND CUDDLES IN MIND FOR US. WE'VE ALREADY LOST FLAG AND KATANA...
I LOOKED AT THE REPORT. 100 PERCENT IT WAS HER BODY. NO IDENTITY SWAPS. DNA CONFIRMATION. 100 PERCENT DEAD. A SINGLE BULLET WOUND TO THE HEART.
A PERFECT SHOT...
...CRAP.
THAT JUST LEAVES *ONE* OPTION...
...THE OPTION THAT ACTUALLY *SCARES* ME.

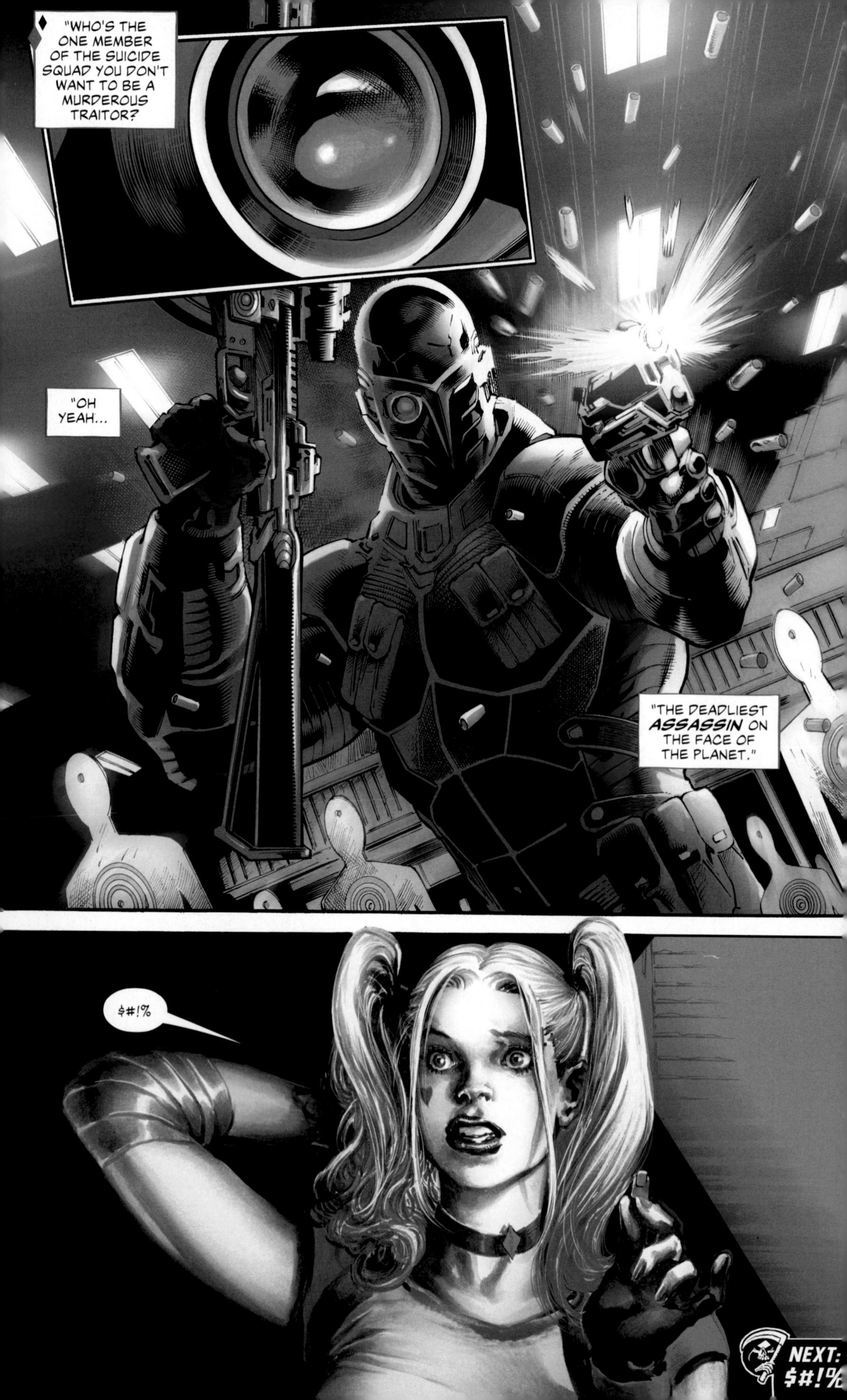
"WHO'S THE ONE MEMBER OF THE SUICIDE SQUAD YOU DON'T WANT TO BE A MURDEROUS TRAITOR?
"OH YEAH...
"THE DEADLIEST ASSASSIN ON THE FACE OF THE PLANET."
$#!%
NEXT: $#!%

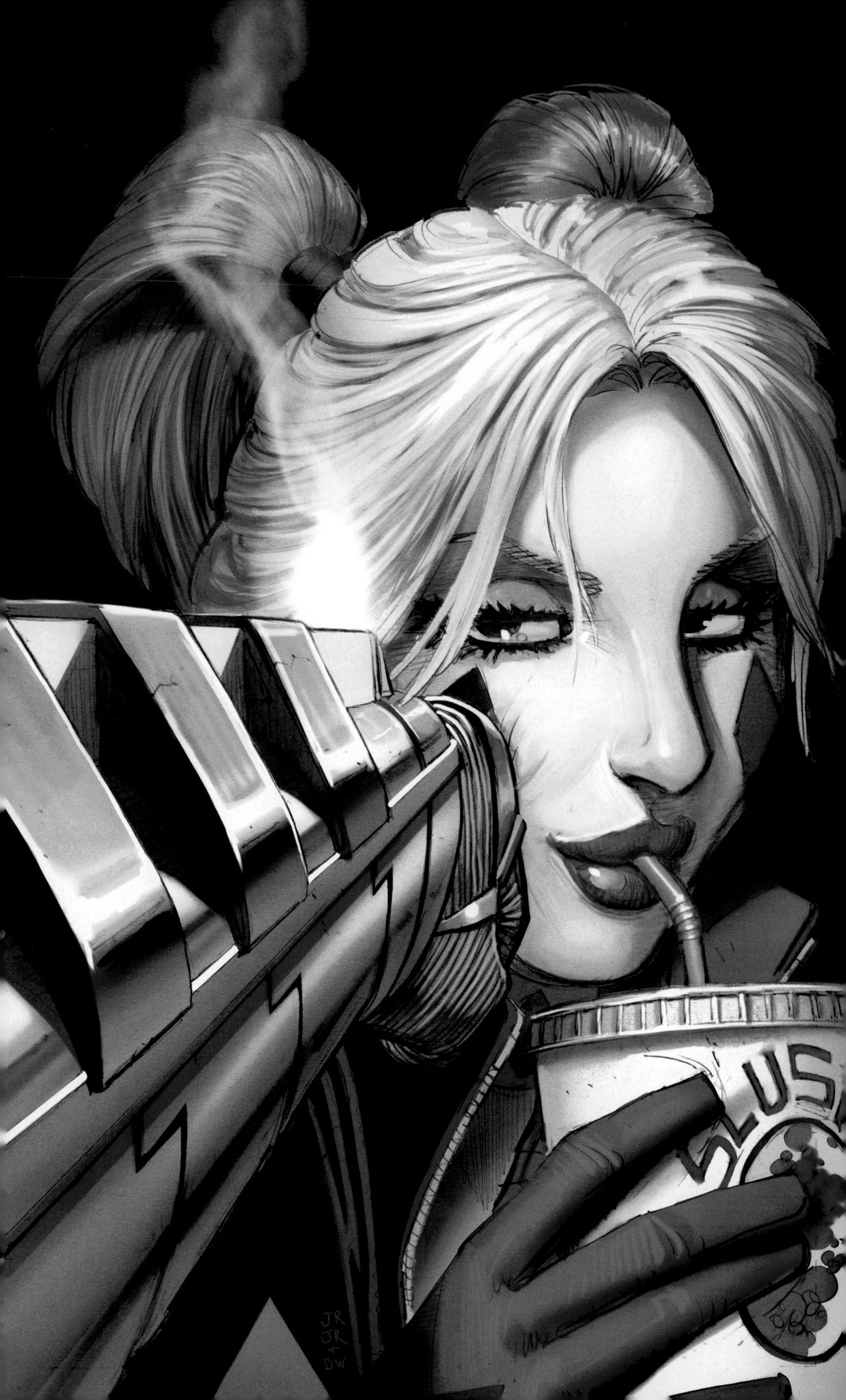

RICK FLAG, SUICIDE SQUAD FIELD COMMANDER.

UHHH

KATANA, FLAG'S SECOND-IN-COMMAND.

UNCONSCIOU.

PRISONERS OF RUSTAM AT HIS SECRET BASE.

KATANA'S... S-SWORD...

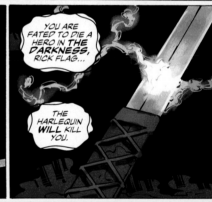

YOU ARE FATED TO DIE A HERO IN THE DARKNESS, RICK FLAG...

THE HARLEQUIN WILL KILL YOU.

WHAT?

AMANDA WALLER IS DEAD.

BUT THAT IS NOT NEARLY ENOUGH.

I WILL DESTROY ALL HER WORKS.

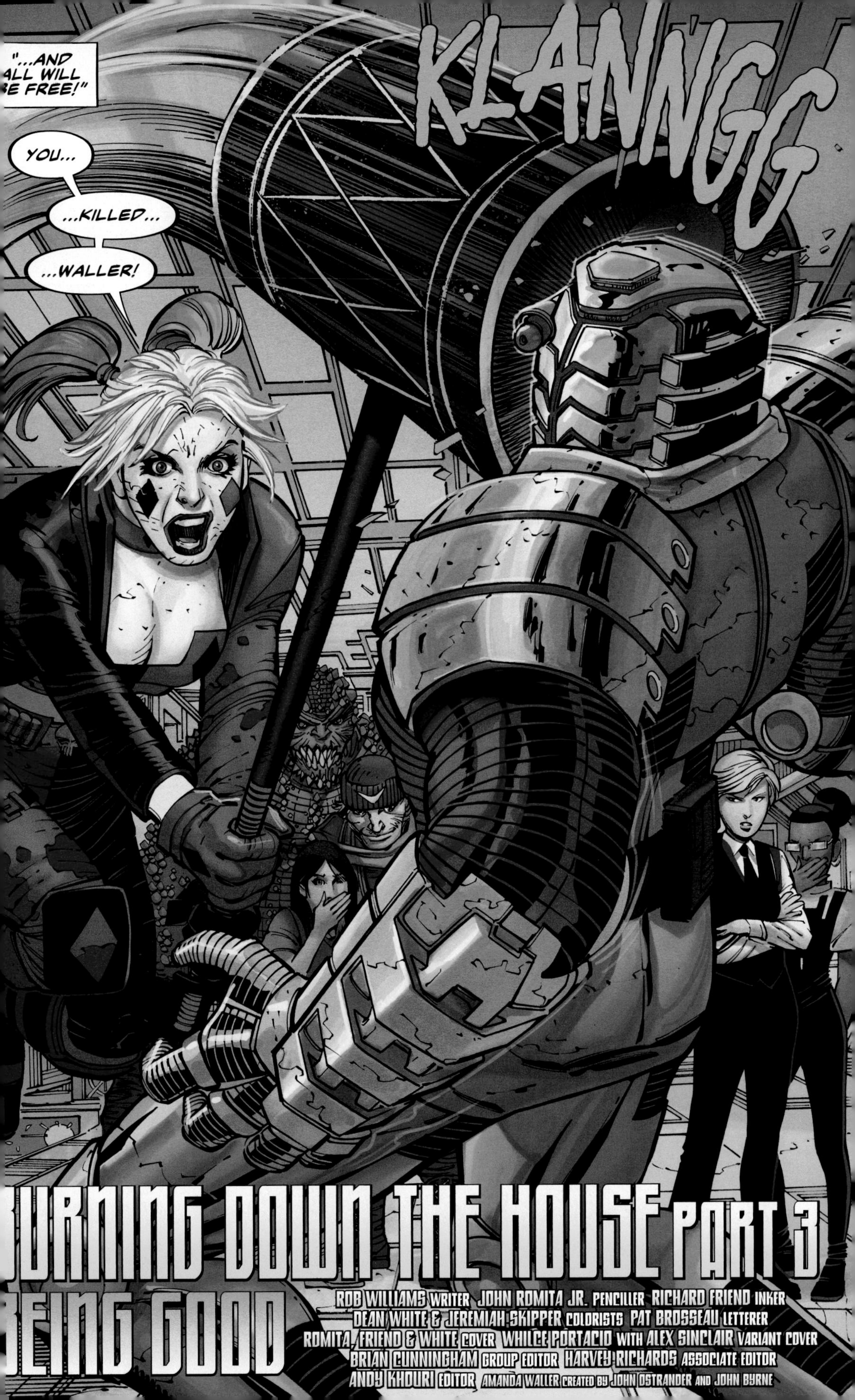
"...AND ALL WILL E FREE!"
YOU...
...KILLED...
...WALLER!
KLANNGG
URNING DOWN THE HOUSE PART 3
EING GOOD
ROB WILLIAMS WRITER JOHN ROMITA JR. PENCILLER RICHARD FRIEND INKER
DEAN WHITE & JEREMIAH SKIPPER COLORISTS PAT BROSSEAU LETTERER
ROMITA, FRIEND & WHITE COVER WHILCE PORTACIO WITH ALEX SINCLAIR VARIANT COVER
BRIAN CUNNINGHAM GROUP EDITOR HARVEY RICHARDS ASSOCIATE EDITOR
ANDY KHOURI EDITOR AMANDA WALLER CREATED BY JOHN OSTRANDER AND JOHN BYRNE

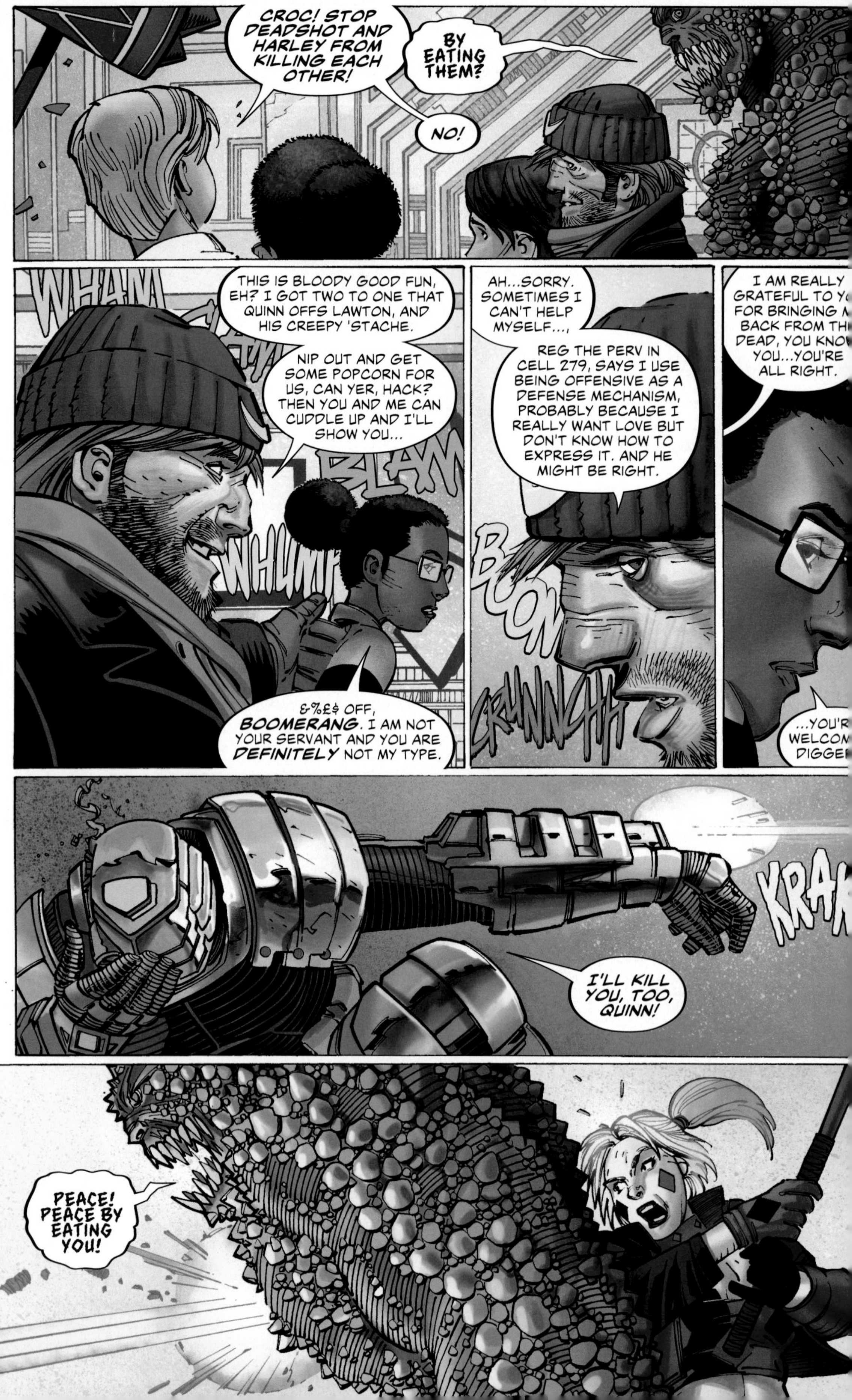
CROC! STOP DEADSHOT AND HARLEY FROM KILLING EACH OTHER!
BY EATING THEM?
NO!
WHAM
THIS IS BLOODY GOOD FUN, EH? I GOT TWO TO ONE THAT QUINN OFFS LAWTON, AND HIS CREEPY 'STACHE.
NIP OUT AND GET SOME POPCORN FOR US, CAN YER, HACK? THEN YOU AND ME CAN CUDDLE UP AND I'LL SHOW YOU...
BLAM
&%£$ OFF, BOOMERANG. I AM NOT YOUR SERVANT AND YOU ARE DEFINITELY NOT MY TYPE.
AH...SORRY. SOMETIMES I CAN'T HELP MYSELF...,
REG THE PERV IN CELL 279, SAYS I USE BEING OFFENSIVE AS A DEFENSE MECHANISM, PROBABLY BECAUSE I REALLY WANT LOVE BUT DON'T KNOW HOW TO EXPRESS IT. AND HE MIGHT BE RIGHT.
BOOM
CRUNCHH
I'LL KILL YOU, TOO, QUINN!
PEACE! PEACE BY EATING YOU!

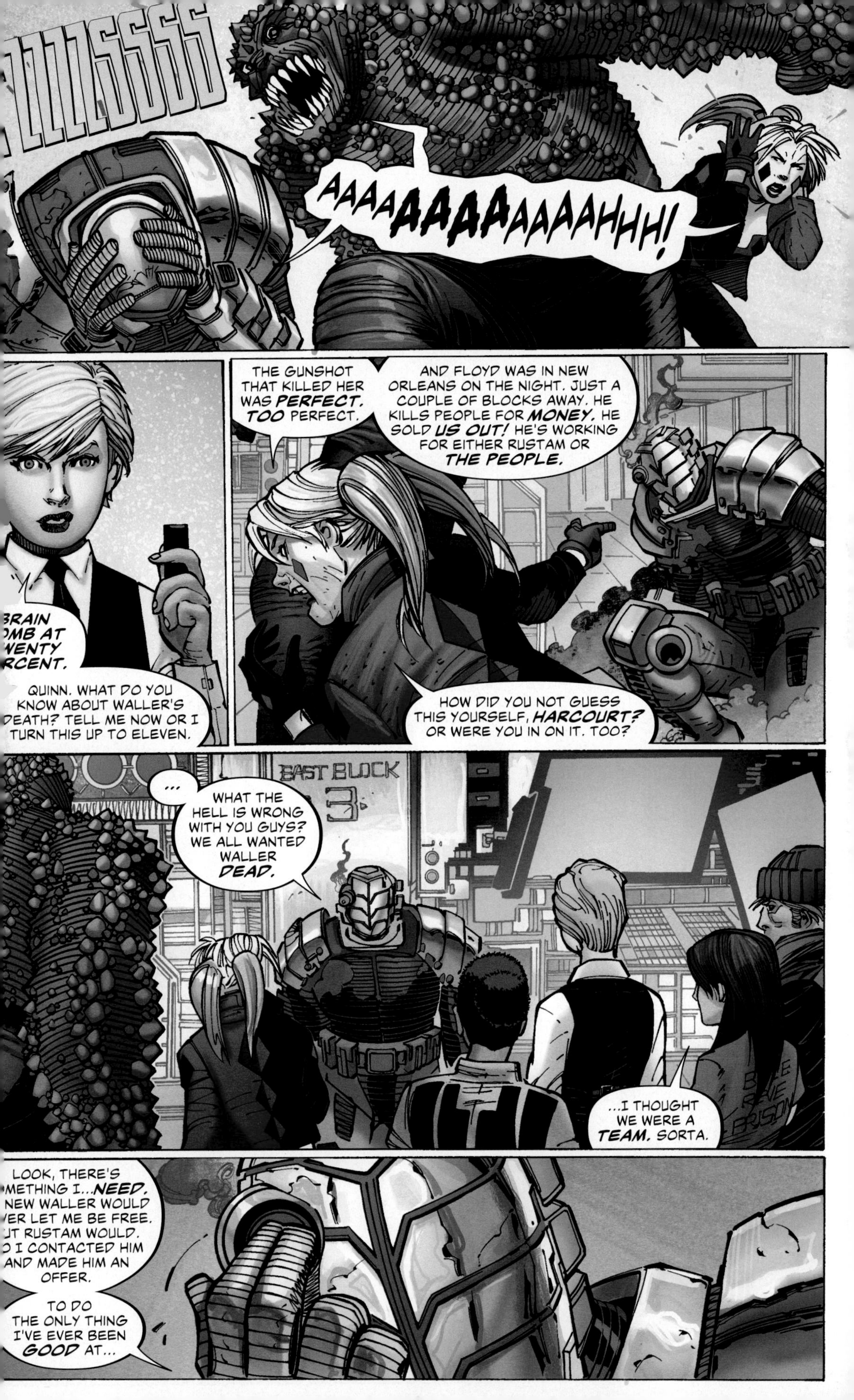
AAAAAAAAAAAAHHH!
BRAIN
OMB AT
WENTY
RCENT.
QUINN. WHAT DO YOU KNOW ABOUT WALLER'S DEATH? TELL ME NOW OR I TURN THIS UP TO ELEVEN.
THE GUNSHOT THAT KILLED HER WAS PERFECT. TOO PERFECT.
AND FLOYD WAS IN NEW ORLEANS ON THE NIGHT. JUST A COUPLE OF BLOCKS AWAY. HE KILLS PEOPLE FOR MONEY. HE SOLD US OUT! HE'S WORKING FOR EITHER RUSTAM OR THE PEOPLE.
HOW DID YOU NOT GUESS THIS YOURSELF, HARCOURT? OR WERE YOU IN ON IT, TOO?
EAST BLOCK
3
...
WHAT THE HELL IS WRONG WITH YOU GUYS? WE ALL WANTED WALLER DEAD.
...I THOUGHT WE WERE A TEAM. SORTA.
LOOK, THERE'S
METHING I...NEED.
NEW WALLER WOULD
ER LET ME BE FREE.
UT RUSTAM WOULD.
O I CONTACTED HIM
AND MADE HIM AN
OFFER.
TO DO THE ONLY THING I'VE EVER BEEN GOOD AT...

"AND HE PROMISED TO *FREE ME.*"

WALLER IS... *DEAD?*

WHY HAVEN'T YOU JUST *KILLED US,* RUSTAM?

I AM *NOT* YOUR ENEMY. WALLER WAS. YOU JUST COULD NOT *SEE* IT.

WE SHOULD BE *ALLIES.* I WOULD HAVE YOU BOTH *JOIN US* IN OUR HOLY REBELLION. OUR WAR AGAINST *CORRUPTION.*

YOU WERE *PRISONERS* OF AMANDA WALLER. OF HER LIES. OF THE FASCIST COVERT SYSTEM OF *RULES* SHE REPRESENTED.

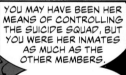

YOU MAY HAVE BEEN HER MEANS OF CONTROLLING THE SUICIDE SQUAD, BUT YOU WERE HER INMATES AS MUCH AS THE OTHER MEMBERS.

I KNOW HOW SHE *BLACKMAILED* YOU, FLAG. I KNOW HOW YOU WERE WRONGFULLY DETAINED IN PRISON.

DO YOU KNOW THAT WALLER WAS THE ONE WHO ACTUALLY ADVISED THEM TO PUT YOU BEHIND BARS FOR WHAT HAPPENED IN KAHNDAQ?

ALL BECAUSE SHE KNEW SHE COULD *USE* THAT AND OFFER YOU FREEDOM-- SO YOU WOULD *LEAD* HER SUICIDE SQUAD.

HOW DO YOU...

IT WAS ALL IN WALLER'S FILES. IN BELLE REVE. ENDLESS DETAILS. YOUR WEAKNESSES, YOUR CRIMES, YOUR *DESIRES.* ALL SO SHE COULD *RULE OVER* YOU.

THE PERNICIOUS LIBRARY OF A *DARK GOD OF BLACKMAIL.*

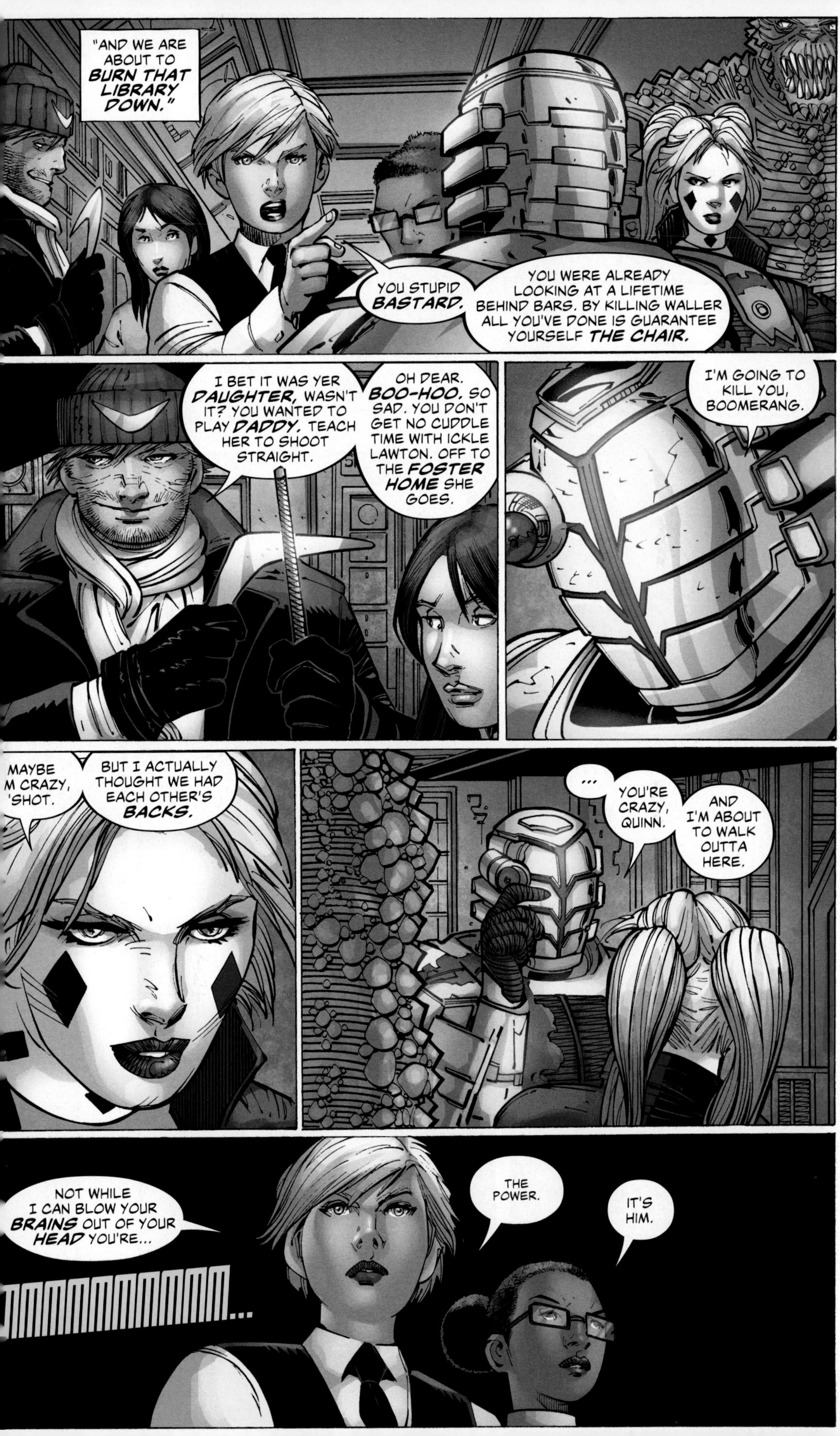
"AND WE ARE ABOUT TO BURN THAT LIBRARY DOWN."
YOU STUPID BASTARD.
YOU WERE ALREADY LOOKING AT A LIFETIME BEHIND BARS. BY KILLING WALLER ALL YOU'VE DONE IS GUARANTEE YOURSELF THE CHAIR.
I BET IT WAS YER DAUGHTER, WASN'T IT? YOU WANTED TO PLAY DADDY. TEACH HER TO SHOOT STRAIGHT.
OH DEAR. BOO-HOO. SO SAD. YOU DON'T GET NO CUDDLE TIME WITH ICKLE LAWTON. OFF TO THE FOSTER HOME SHE GOES.
I'M GOING TO KILL YOU, BOOMERANG.
MAYBE M CRAZY, 'SHOT.
BUT I ACTUALLY THOUGHT WE HAD EACH OTHER'S BACKS.
...
YOU'RE CRAZY, QUINN.
AND I'M ABOUT TO WALK OUTTA HERE.
NOT WHILE I CAN BLOW YOUR BRAINS OUT OF YOUR HEAD YOU'RE...
MMMMMMMMMM...
THE POWER.
IT'S HIM.

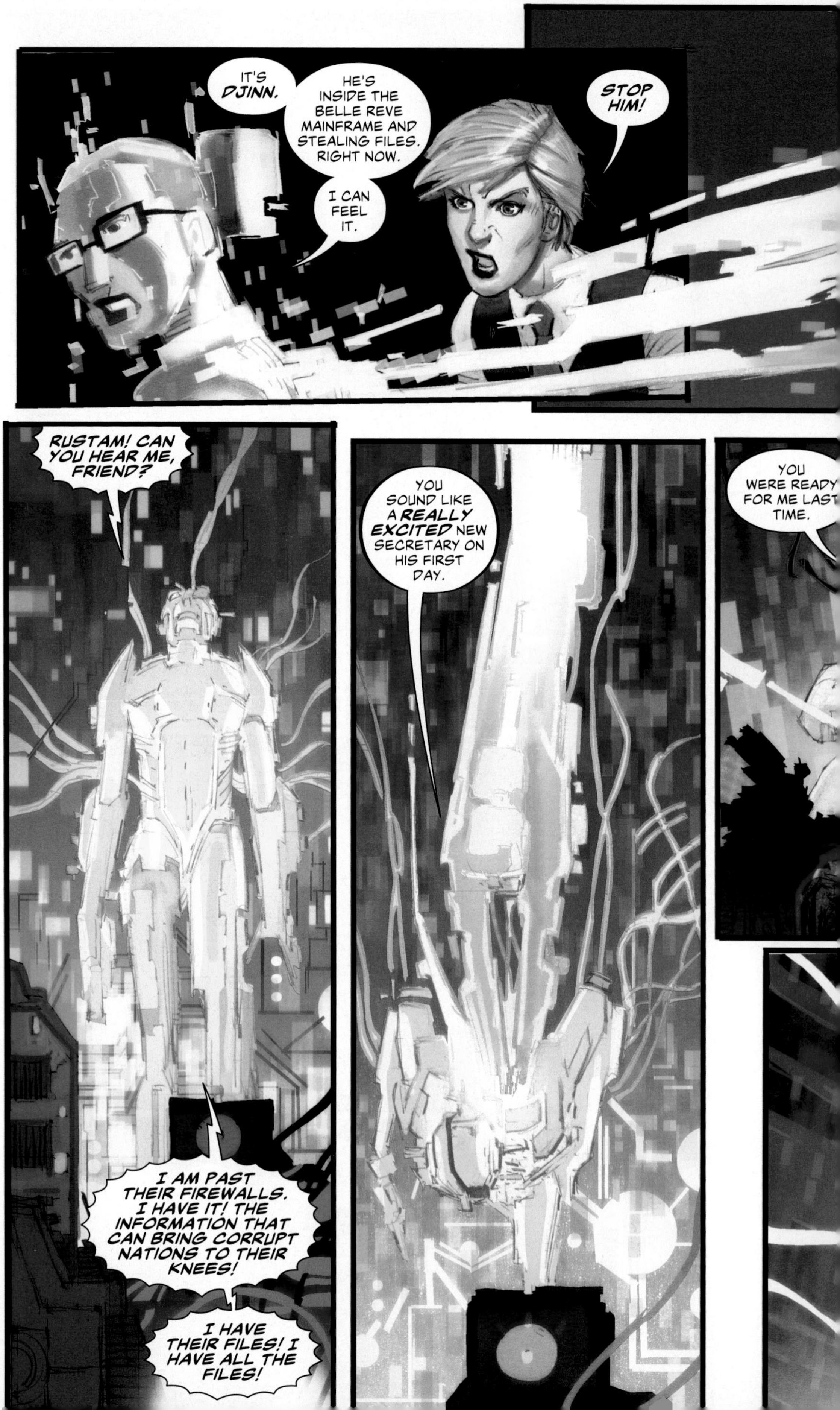
IT'S DJINN.
HE'S INSIDE THE BELLE REVE MAINFRAME AND STEALING FILES. RIGHT NOW.
I CAN FEEL IT.
STOP HIM!
RUSTAM! CAN YOU HEAR ME, FRIEND?
I AM PAST THEIR FIREWALLS. I HAVE IT! THE INFORMATION THAT CAN BRING CORRUPT NATIONS TO THEIR KNEES!
I HAVE THEIR FILES! I HAVE ALL THE FILES!
YOU SOUND LIKE A REALLY EXCITED NEW SECRETARY ON HIS FIRST DAY.
YOU WERE READY FOR ME LAST TIME.

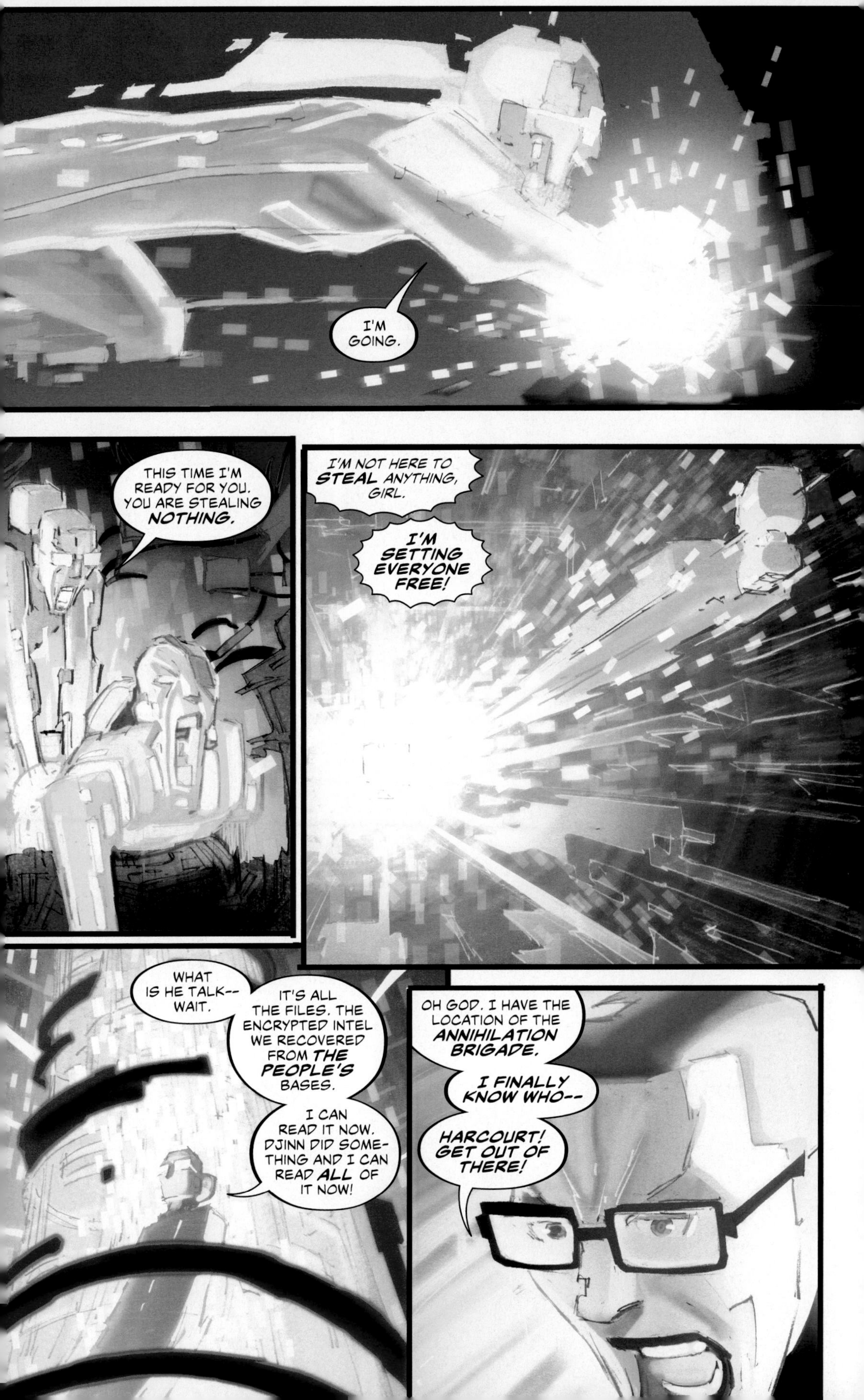
I'M GOING.
THIS TIME I'M READY FOR YOU. YOU ARE STEALING NOTHING.
I'M NOT HERE TO STEAL ANYTHING, GIRL.
I'M SETTING EVERYONE FREE!
WHAT IS HE TALK-- WAIT.
IT'S ALL THE FILES. THE ENCRYPTED INTEL WE RECOVERED FROM THE PEOPLE'S BASES.
I CAN READ IT NOW. DJINN DID SOME-THING AND I CAN READ ALL OF IT NOW!
OH GOD. I HAVE THE LOCATION OF THE ANNIHILATION BRIGADE.
I FINALLY KNOW WHO--
HARCOURT! GET OUT OF THERE!

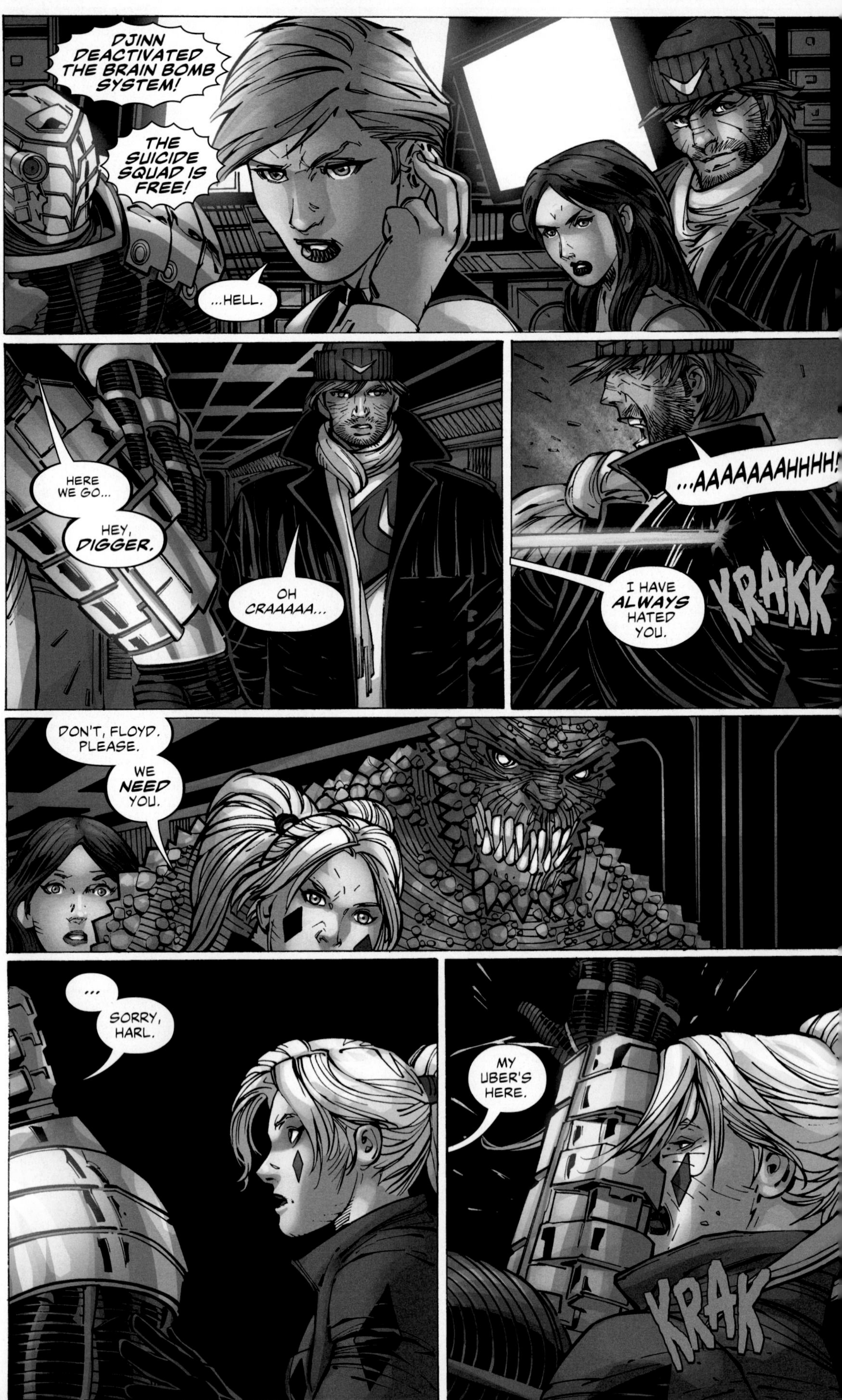
DJINN DEACTIVATED THE BRAIN BOMB SYSTEM!
THE SUICIDE SQUAD IS FREE!
...HELL.
HERE WE GO...
HEY, DIGGER.
OH CRAAAAA...
...AAAAAAAHHHH!
I HAVE ALWAYS HATED YOU.
KRAKK
DON'T, FLOYD. PLEASE.
WE NEED YOU.
...
SORRY, HARL.
MY UBER'S HERE.
KRAK

IMAGINE, FOR A SECOND, THAT YOU'VE **KILLED** AS MANY PEOPLE AS I HAVE.

REDEMPTION'S A HOUSE KEY YOU DROPPED IN THE WOODS MILES BACK.

NO ONE ER GOT IT...

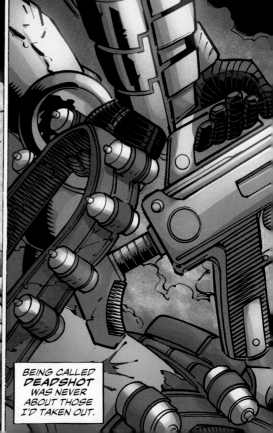

BEING CALLED **DEADSHOT** WAS NEVER ABOUT THOSE I'D TAKEN OUT.

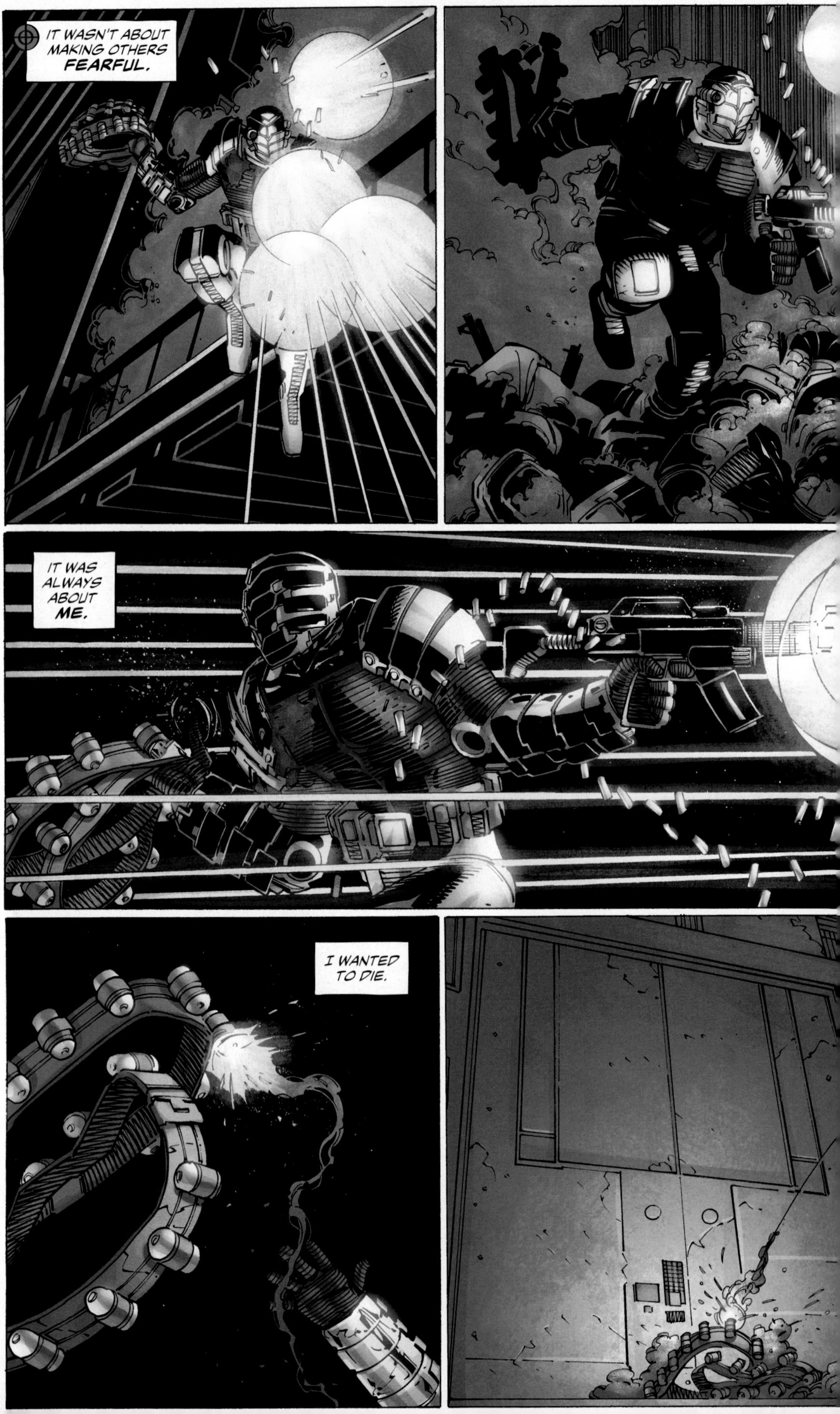
IT WASN'T ABOUT MAKING OTHERS FEARFUL.
IT WAS ALWAYS ABOUT ME.
I WANTED TO DIE.

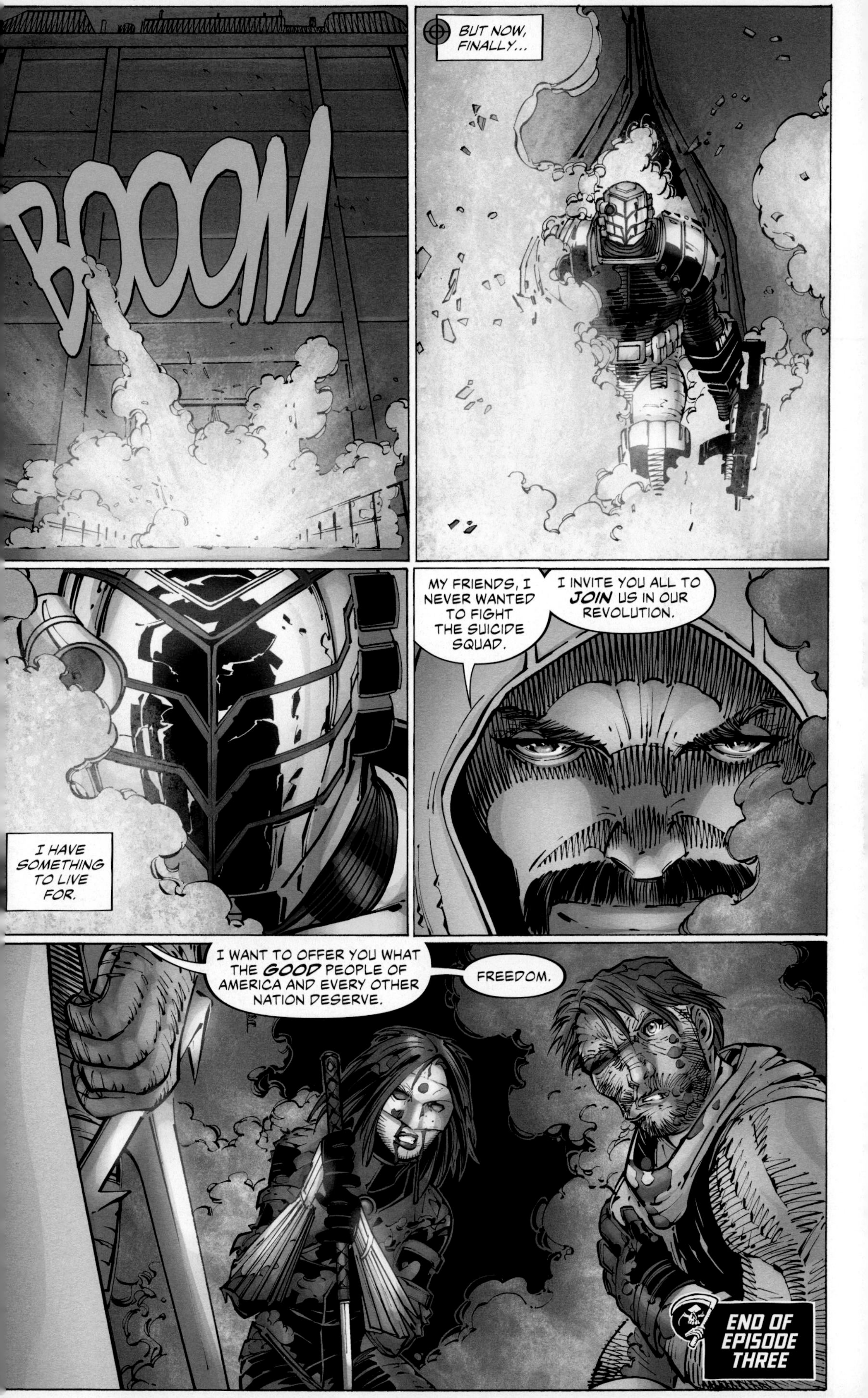
BOOOM
BUT NOW, FINALLY...
I HAVE SOMETHING TO LIVE FOR.
MY FRIENDS, I NEVER WANTED TO FIGHT THE SUICIDE SQUAD.
I INVITE YOU ALL TO JOIN US IN OUR REVOLUTION.
I WANT TO OFFER YOU WHAT THE GOOD PEOPLE OF AMERICA AND EVERY OTHER NATION DESERVE.
FREEDOM.
END OF EPISODE THREE

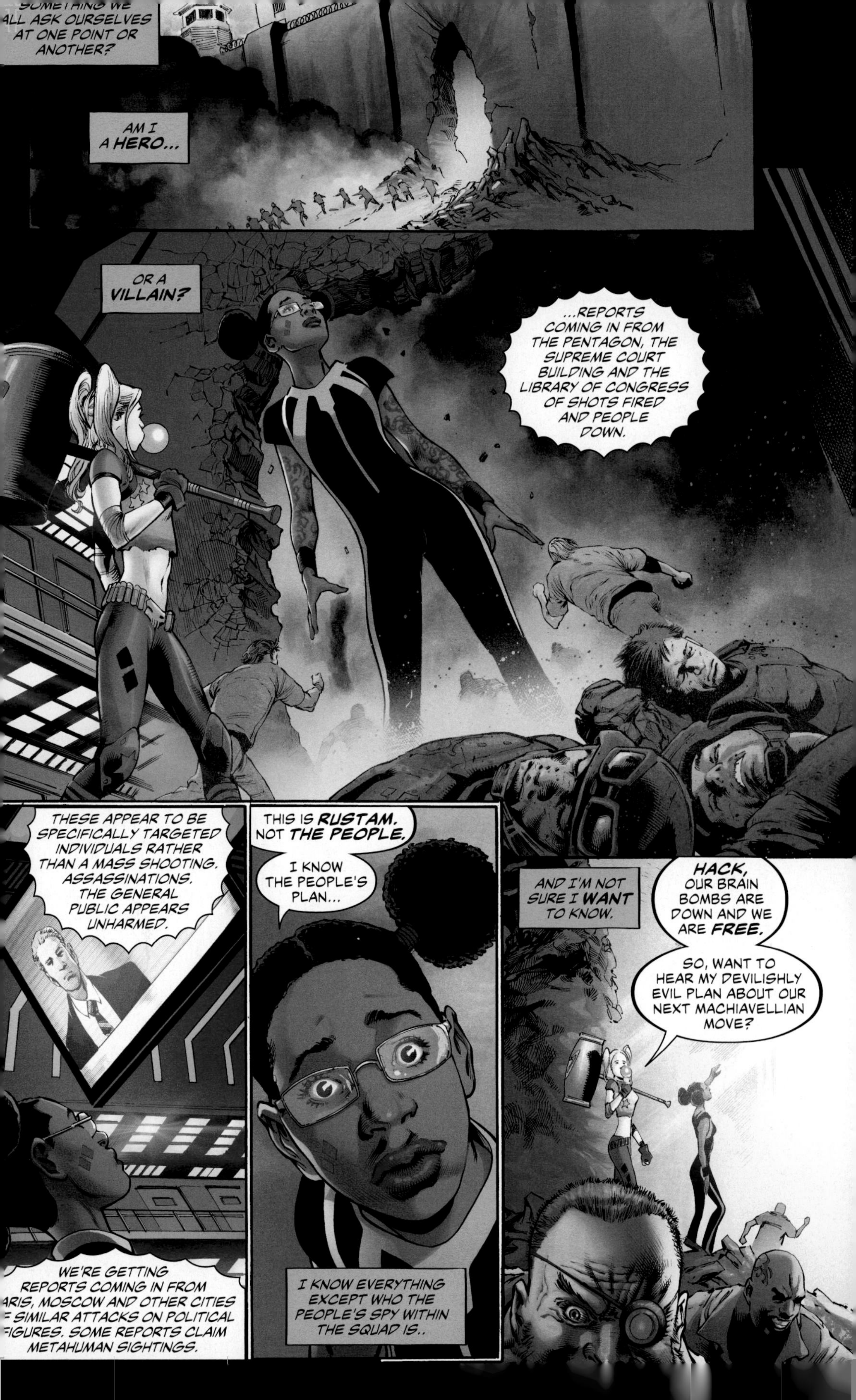
SOMETHING WE ALL ASK OURSELVES AT ONE POINT OR ANOTHER?
AM I A HERO...
OR A VILLAIN?
...REPORTS COMING IN FROM THE PENTAGON, THE SUPREME COURT BUILDING AND THE LIBRARY OF CONGRESS OF SHOTS FIRED AND PEOPLE DOWN.
THESE APPEAR TO BE SPECIFICALLY TARGETED INDIVIDUALS RATHER THAN A MASS SHOOTING. ASSASSINATIONS. THE GENERAL PUBLIC APPEARS UNHARMED.
WE'RE GETTING REPORTS COMING IN FROM ARIS, MOSCOW AND OTHER CITIES F SIMILAR ATTACKS ON POLITICAL FIGURES. SOME REPORTS CLAIM METAHUMAN SIGHTINGS.
THIS IS RUSTAM. NOT THE PEOPLE.
I KNOW THE PEOPLE'S PLAN...
I KNOW EVERYTHING EXCEPT WHO THE PEOPLE'S SPY WITHIN THE SQUAD IS..
AND I'M NOT SURE I WANT TO KNOW.
HACK, OUR BRAIN BOMBS ARE DOWN AND WE ARE FREE.
SO, WANT TO HEAR MY DEVILISHLY EVIL PLAN ABOUT OUR NEXT MACHIAVELLIAN MOVE?

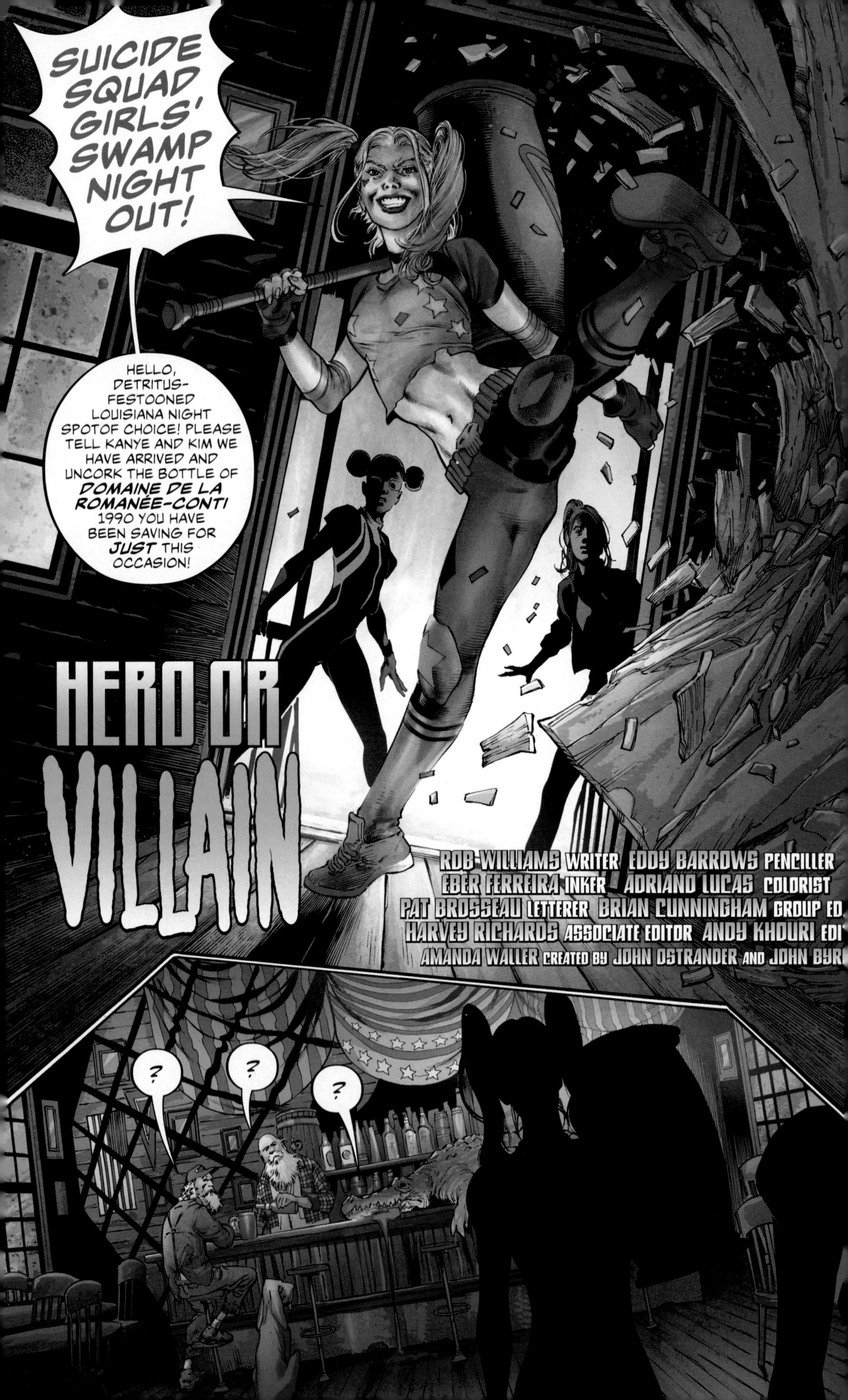

SUICIDE SQUAD GIRLS' SWAMP NIGHT OUT!
HELLO, DETRITUS-FESTOONED LOUISIANA NIGHT SPOTOF CHOICE! PLEASE TELL KANYE AND KIM WE HAVE ARRIVED AND UNCORK THE BOTTLE OF *DOMAINE DE LA ROMANÉE-CONTI* 1990 YOU HAVE BEEN SAVING FOR *JUST* THIS OCCASION!
HERO OR VILLAIN
ROB WILLIAMS WRITER EDDY BARROWS PENCILLER
EBER FERREIRA INKER ADRIANO LUCAS COLORIST
PAT BROSSEAU LETTERER BRIAN CUNNINGHAM GROUP ED
HARVEY RICHARDS ASSOCIATE EDITOR ANDY KHOURI EDI
AMANDA WALLER CREATED BY JOHN OSTRANDER AND JOHN BYR
?
?
?

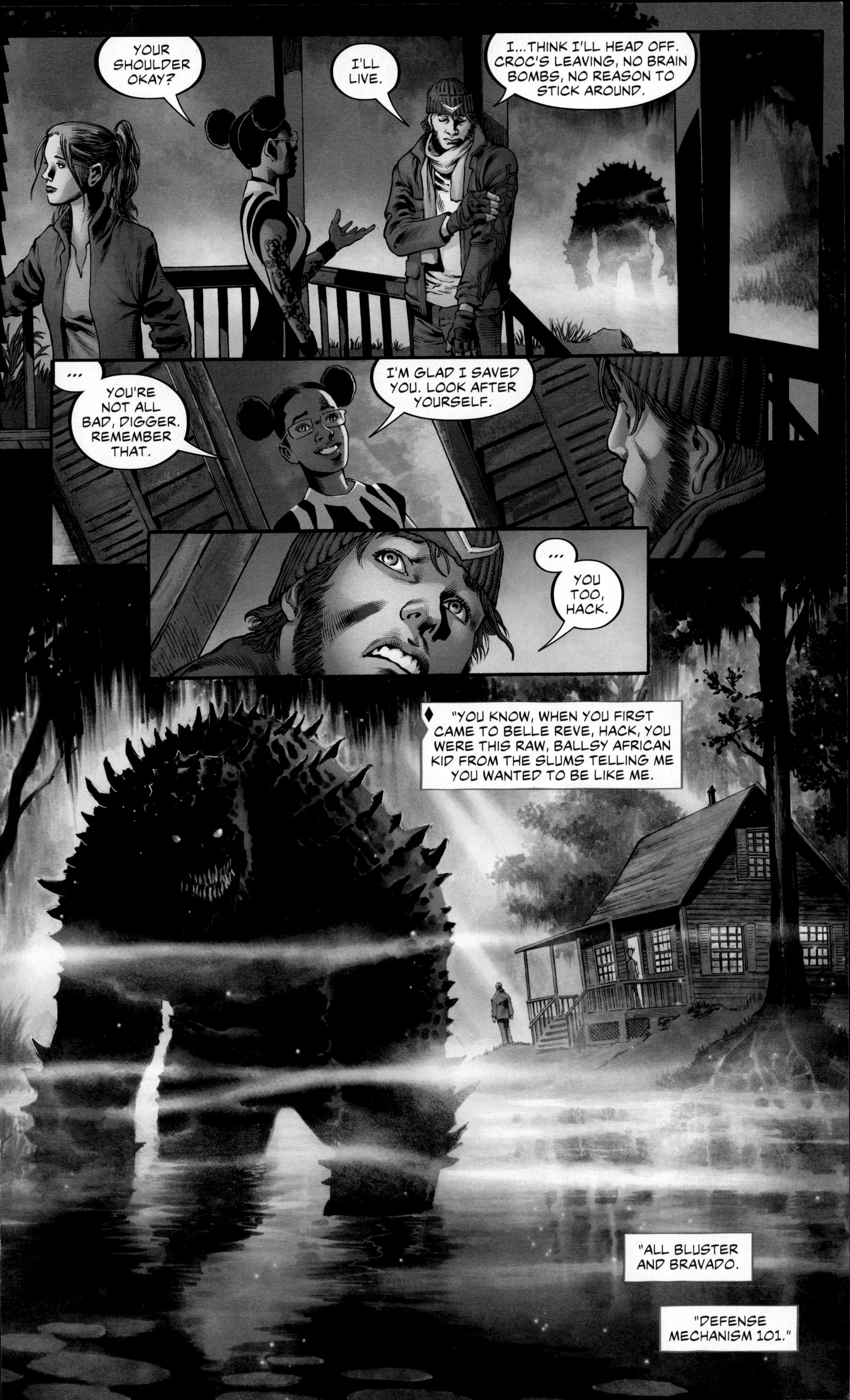
YOUR SHOULDER OKAY?
I'LL LIVE.
I...THINK I'LL HEAD OFF. CROC'S LEAVING, NO BRAIN BOMBS, NO REASON TO STICK AROUND.
... YOU'RE NOT ALL BAD, DIGGER. REMEMBER THAT.
I'M GLAD I SAVED YOU. LOOK AFTER YOURSELF.
... YOU TOO, HACK.
"YOU KNOW, WHEN YOU FIRST CAME TO BELLE REVE, HACK, YOU WERE THIS RAW, BALLSY AFRICAN KID FROM THE SLUMS TELLING ME YOU WANTED TO BE LIKE ME.
"ALL BLUSTER AND BRAVADO.
"DEFENSE MECHANISM 101."

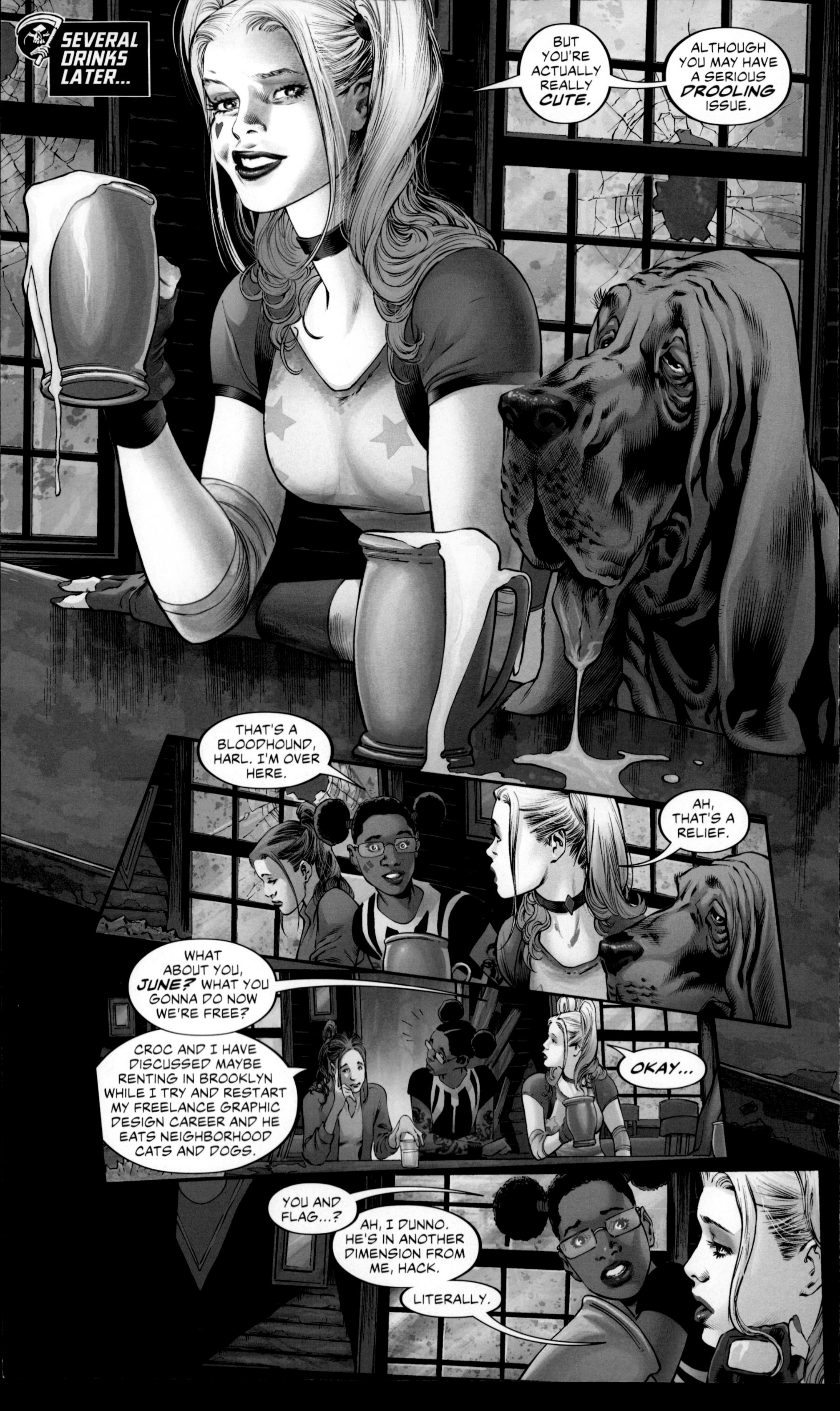
SEVERAL DRINKS LATER...
BUT YOU'RE ACTUALLY REALLY CUTE.
ALTHOUGH YOU MAY HAVE A SERIOUS DROOLING ISSUE.
THAT'S A BLOODHOUND, HARL. I'M OVER HERE.
AH, THAT'S A RELIEF.
WHAT ABOUT YOU, JUNE? WHAT YOU GONNA DO NOW WE'RE FREE?
CROC AND I HAVE DISCUSSED MAYBE RENTING IN BROOKLYN WHILE I TRY AND RESTART MY FREELANCE GRAPHIC DESIGN CAREER AND HE EATS NEIGHBORHOOD CATS AND DOGS.
OKAY...
YOU AND FLAG...?
AH, I DUNNO. HE'S IN ANOTHER DIMENSION FROM ME, HACK.
LITERALLY.

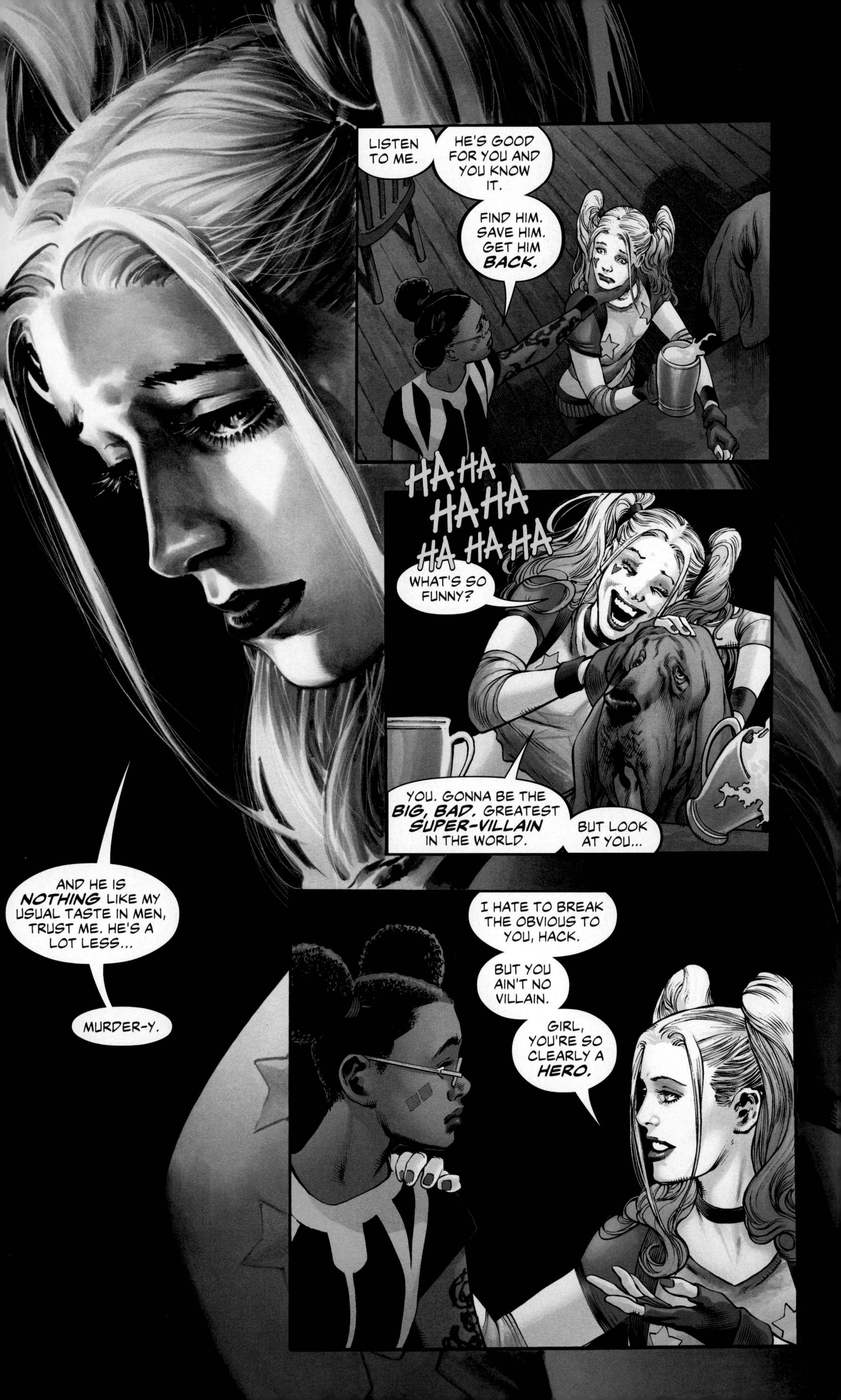
LISTEN TO ME.
HE'S GOOD FOR YOU AND YOU KNOW IT.
FIND HIM. SAVE HIM. GET HIM BACK.
HA HA HA HA HA HA HA
WHAT'S SO FUNNY?
YOU. GONNA BE THE BIG, BAD, GREATEST SUPER-VILLAIN IN THE WORLD.
BUT LOOK AT YOU...
AND HE IS NOTHING LIKE MY USUAL TASTE IN MEN, TRUST ME. HE'S A LOT LESS...
MURDER-Y.
I HATE TO BREAK THE OBVIOUS TO YOU, HACK.
BUT YOU AIN'T NO VILLAIN.
GIRL, YOU'RE SO CLEARLY A HERO.

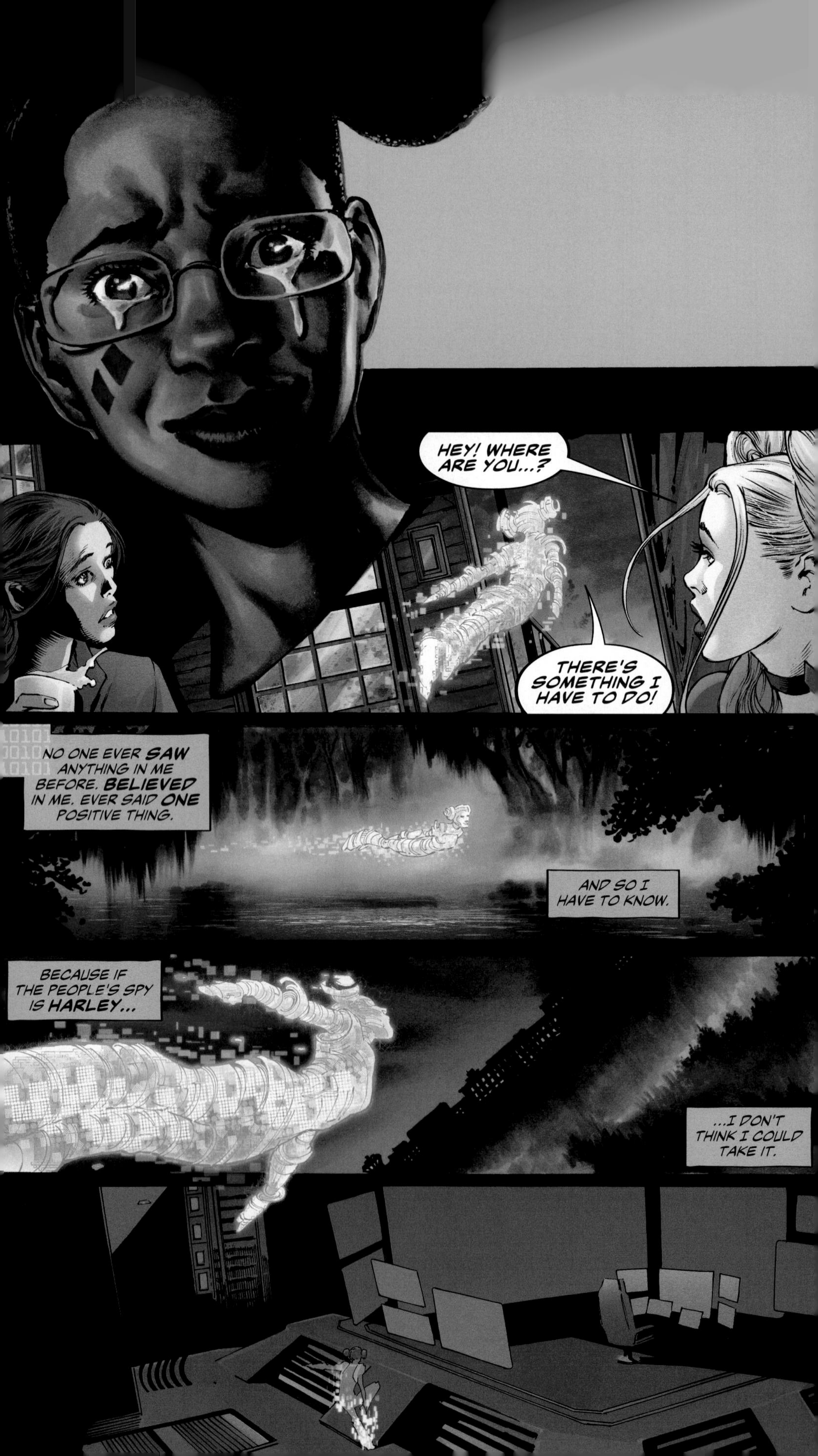
HEY! WHERE ARE YOU...?
THERE'S SOMETHING I HAVE TO DO!
NO ONE EVER SAW ANYTHING IN ME BEFORE. BELIEVED IN ME. EVER SAID ONE POSITIVE THING.
AND SO I HAVE TO KNOW.
BECAUSE IF THE PEOPLE'S SPY IS HARLEY...
...I DON'T THINK I COULD TAKE IT.

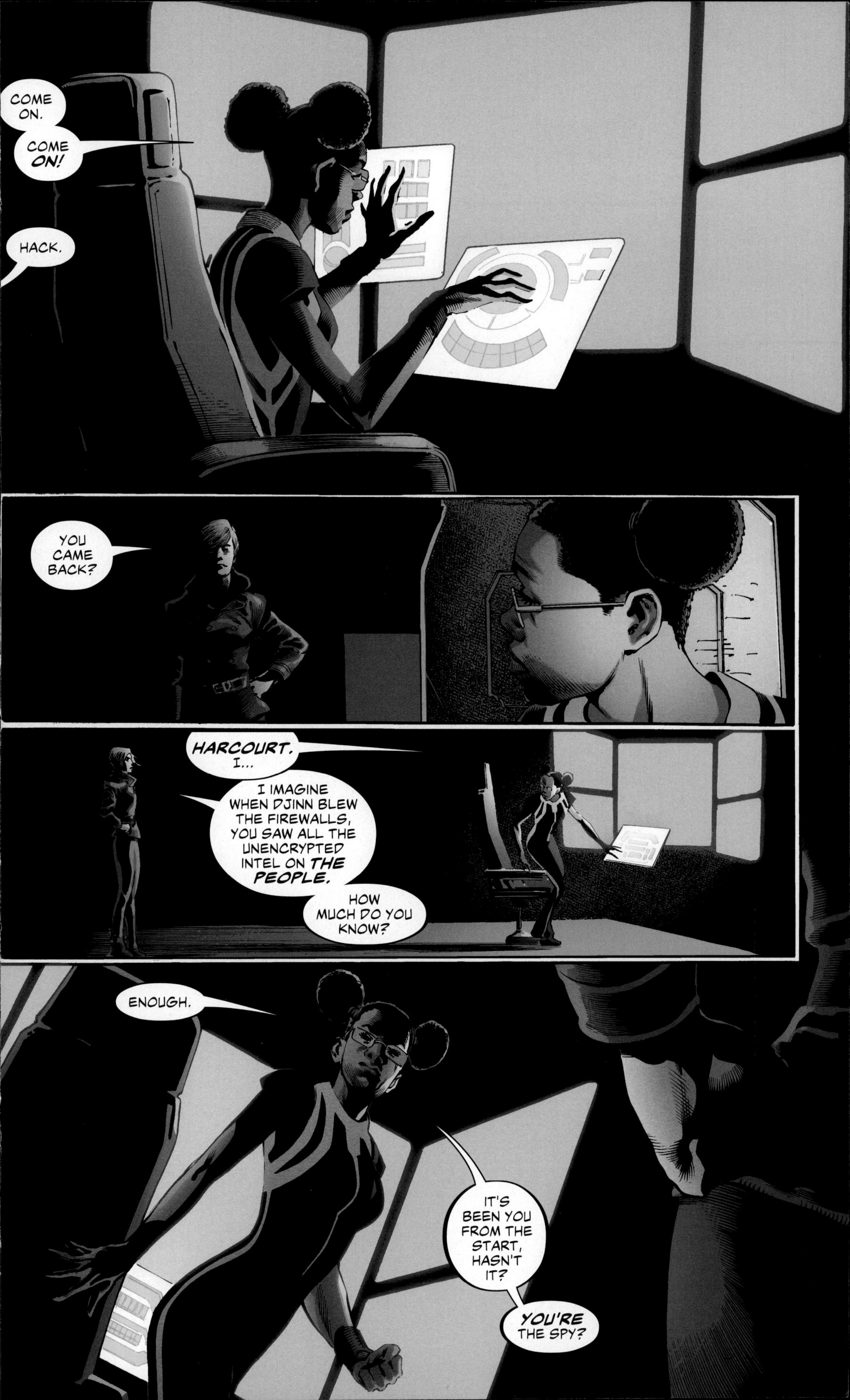
COME ON.
COME ON!
HACK.
YOU CAME BACK?
HARCOURT. I...
I IMAGINE WHEN DJINN BLEW THE FIREWALLS, YOU SAW ALL THE UNENCRYPTED INTEL ON THE PEOPLE.
HOW MUCH DO YOU KNOW?
ENOUGH.
IT'S BEEN YOU FROM THE START, HASN'T IT?
YOU'RE THE SPY?

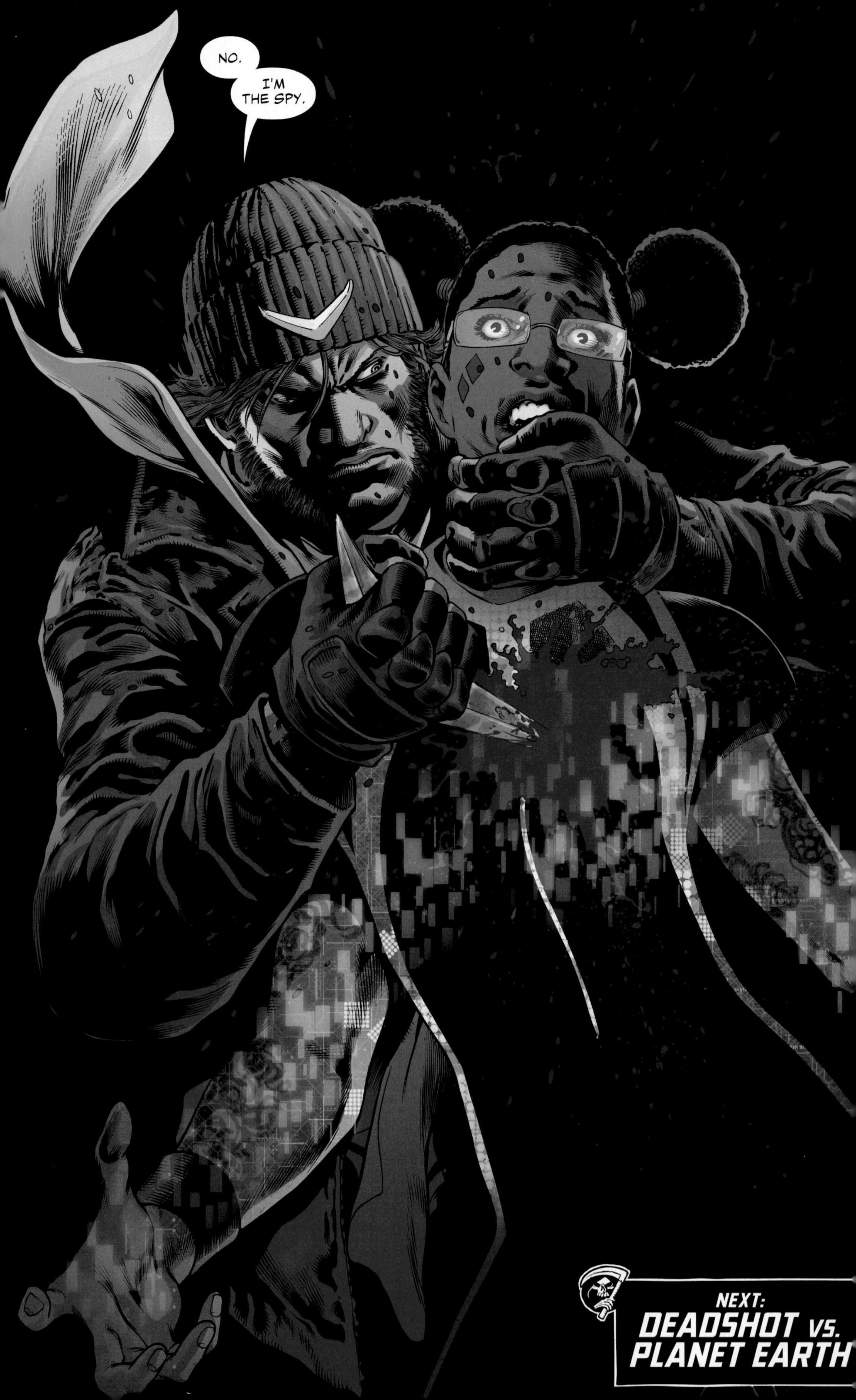
NO.
I'M THE SPY.
NEXT:
DEADSHOT VS. PLANET EARTH

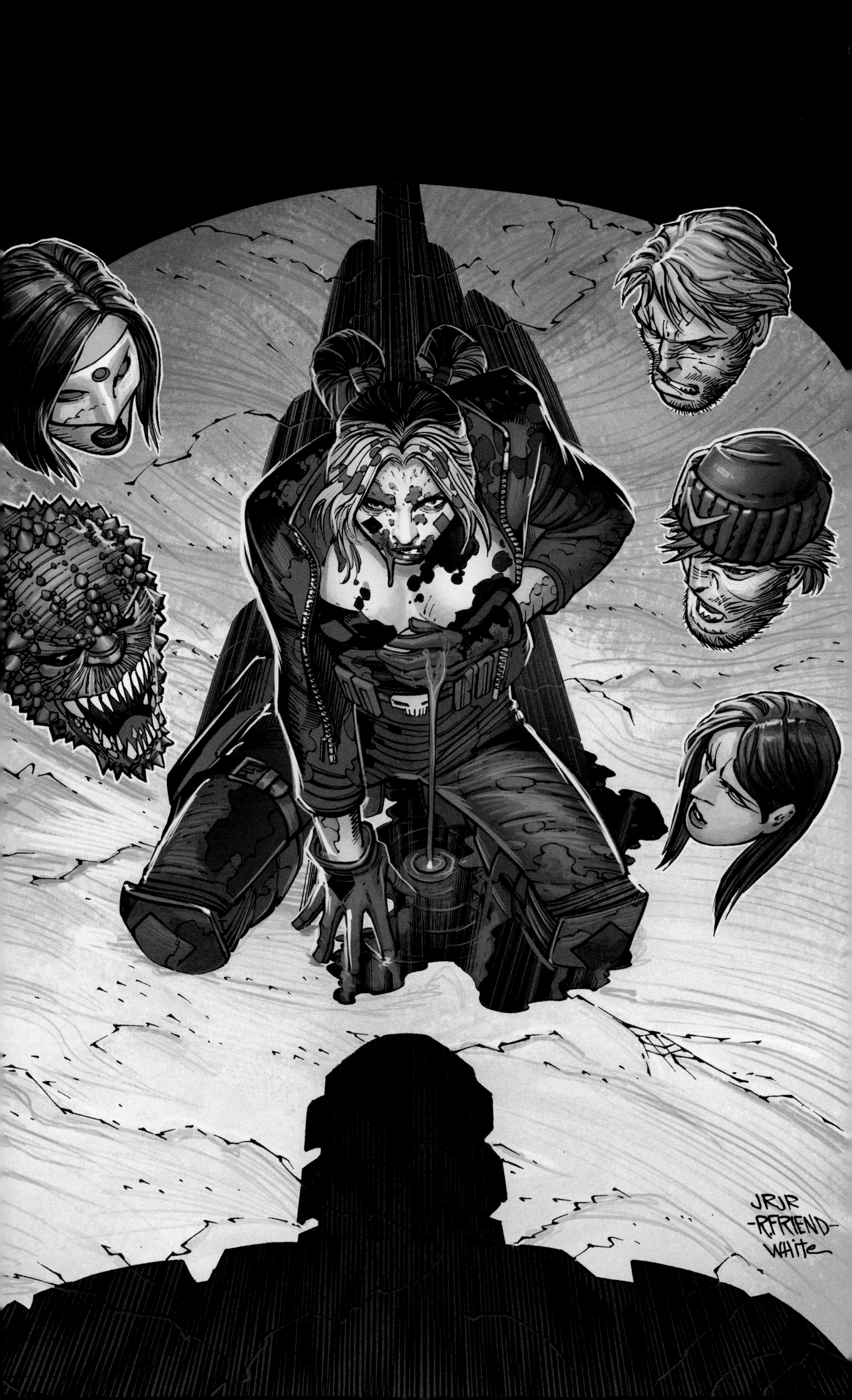
JRJR
-R.FRIEND-
White

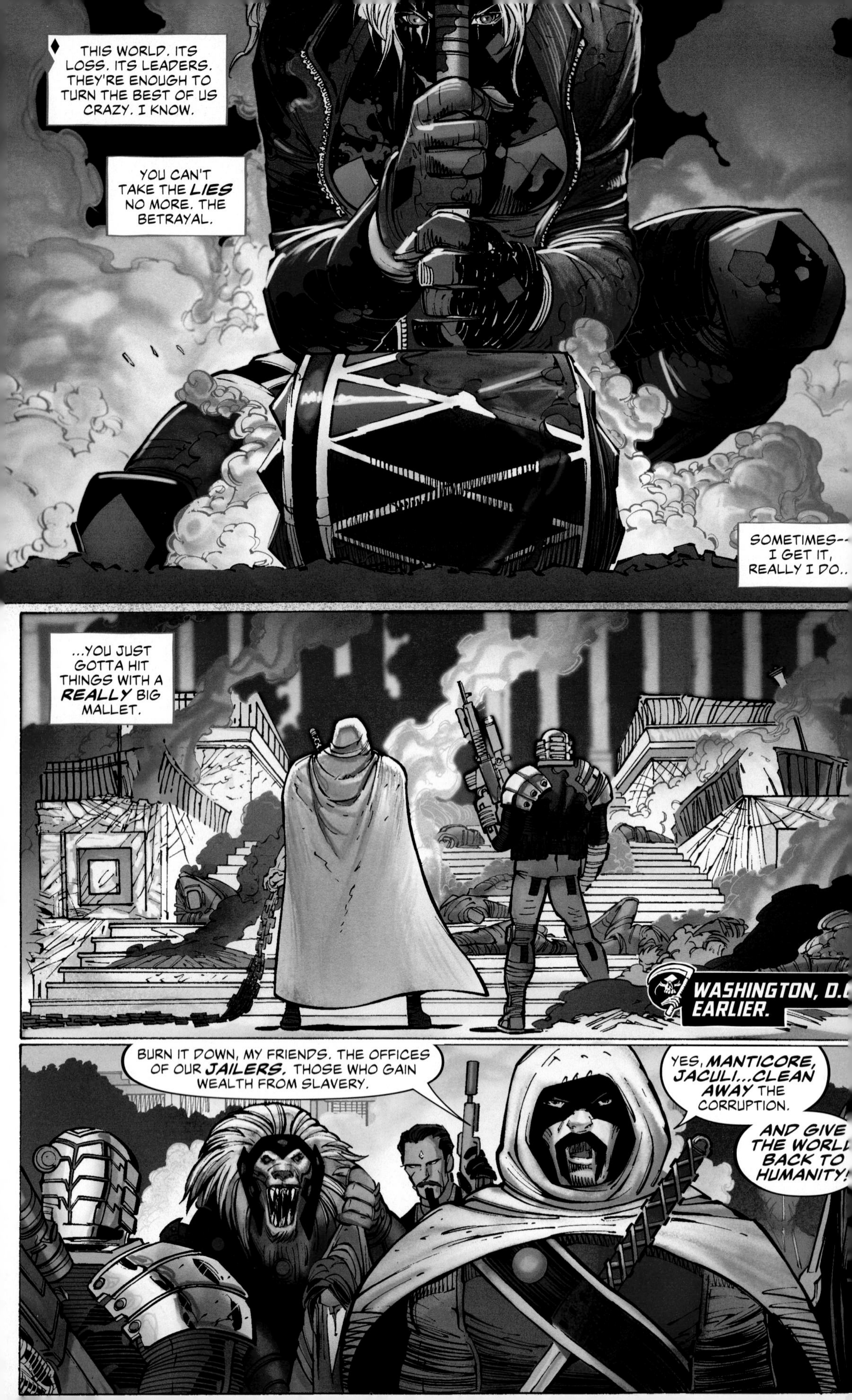
THIS WORLD. ITS LOSS. ITS LEADERS. THEY'RE ENOUGH TO TURN THE BEST OF US CRAZY. I KNOW.
YOU CAN'T TAKE THE LIES NO MORE. THE BETRAYAL.
SOMETIMES-- I GET IT, REALLY I DO...
...YOU JUST GOTTA HIT THINGS WITH A REALLY BIG MALLET.
WASHINGTON, D.C. EARLIER.
BURN IT DOWN, MY FRIENDS. THE OFFICES OF OUR JAILERS. THOSE WHO GAIN WEALTH FROM SLAVERY.
YES, MANTICORE, JACULI...CLEAN AWAY THE CORRUPTION.
AND GIVE THE WORLD BACK TO HUMANITY!

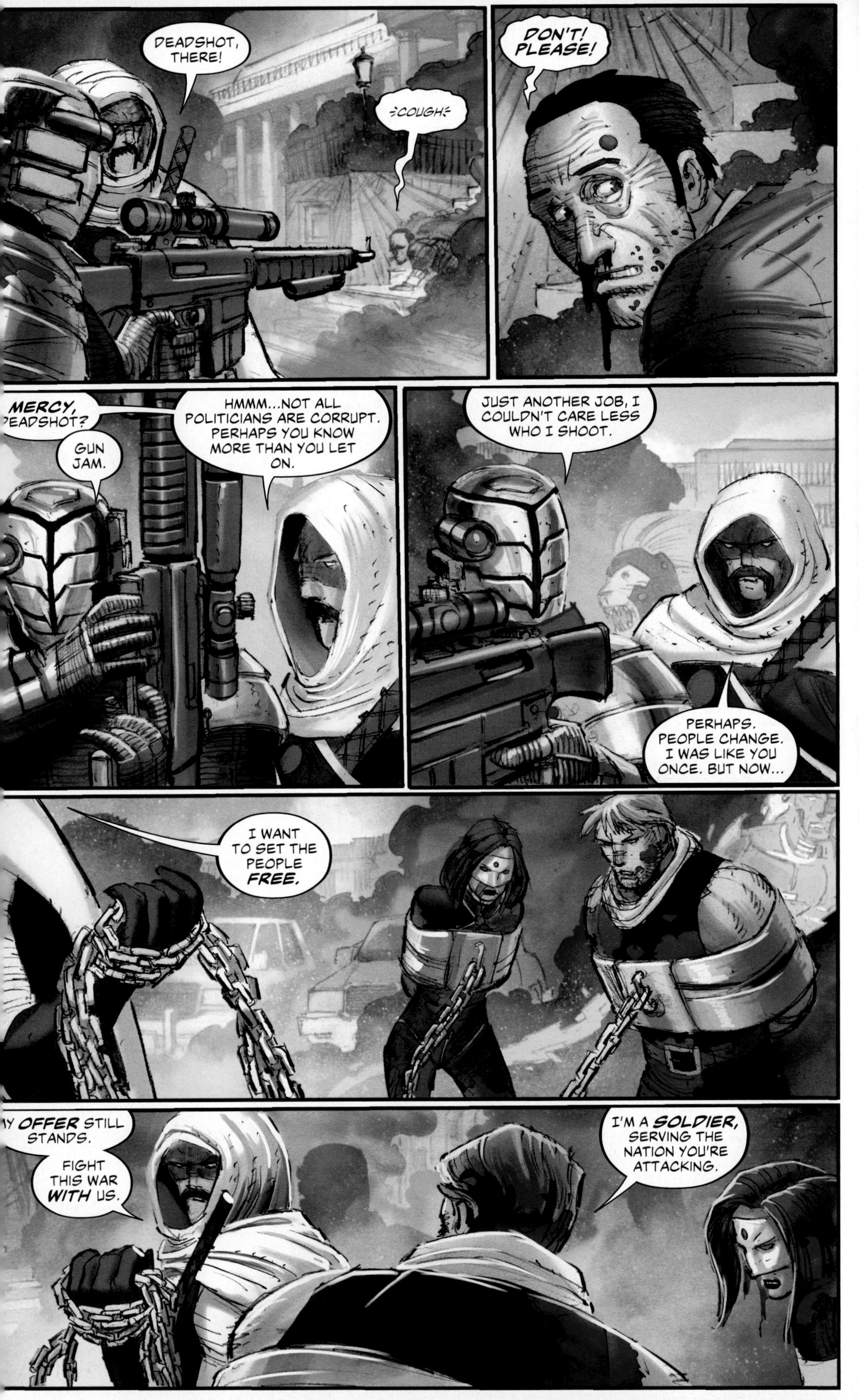
DEADSHOT, THERE!
≠COUGH≠
DON'T! PLEASE!
MERCY, DEADSHOT?
GUN JAM.
HMMM...NOT ALL POLITICIANS ARE CORRUPT. PERHAPS YOU KNOW MORE THAN YOU LET ON.
JUST ANOTHER JOB, I COULDN'T CARE LESS WHO I SHOOT.
PERHAPS. PEOPLE CHANGE. I WAS LIKE YOU ONCE. BUT NOW...
I WANT TO SET THE PEOPLE FREE.
MY OFFER STILL STANDS.
FIGHT THIS WAR WITH US.
I'M A SOLDIER, SERVING THE NATION YOU'RE ATTACKING.

FLAG, WE LIVE IN A WORLD WHERE *EIGHT* BILLIONAIRES CONTROL THE SAME WEALTH AS THE POOREST *HALF* OF THE GLOBE'S POPULATION.

SO TELL ME WHO IS ON THE SIDE OF *RIGHT* HERE?

DEADSHOT...

...MY BLADE WILL TASTE YOUR FLESH, *TRAITOR.*

I SWEAR THIS.

BRING IT, SNOWFLAKE.

RUSTAM. *TIME!* WE HAVE SUPERHUMANS INCOMING. LONDON IS NEXT. OPEN THE PORTAL.

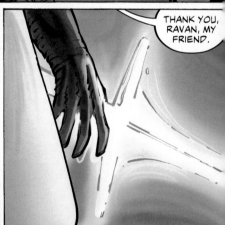

THANK YOU, RAVAN, MY FRIEND.

MY BURNING WORLD! FOLLOW ME!

IT...IT'S THE END OF THE WORLD...

NO.

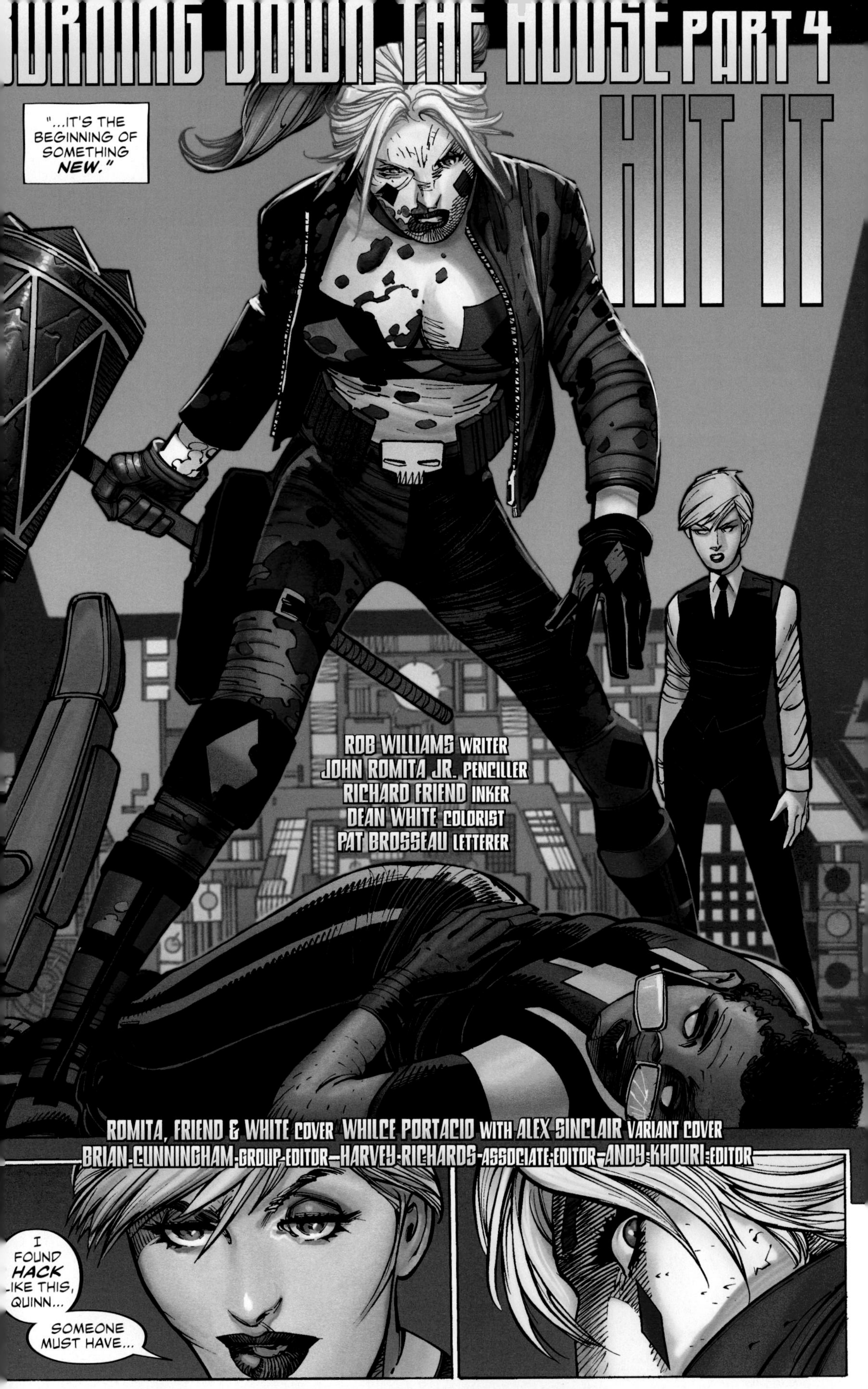
BURNING DOWN THE HOUSE PART 4
HIT IT
"...IT'S THE BEGINNING OF SOMETHING NEW."
ROB WILLIAMS WRITER
JOHN ROMITA JR. PENCILLER
RICHARD FRIEND INKER
DEAN WHITE COLORIST
PAT BROSSEAU LETTERER
ROMITA, FRIEND & WHITE COVER WHILCE PORTACIO WITH ALEX SINCLAIR VARIANT COVER
BRIAN CUNNINGHAM GROUP EDITOR HARVEY RICHARDS ASSOCIATE EDITOR ANDY KHOURI EDITOR
I FOUND HACK LIKE THIS, QUINN...
SOMEONE MUST HAVE...

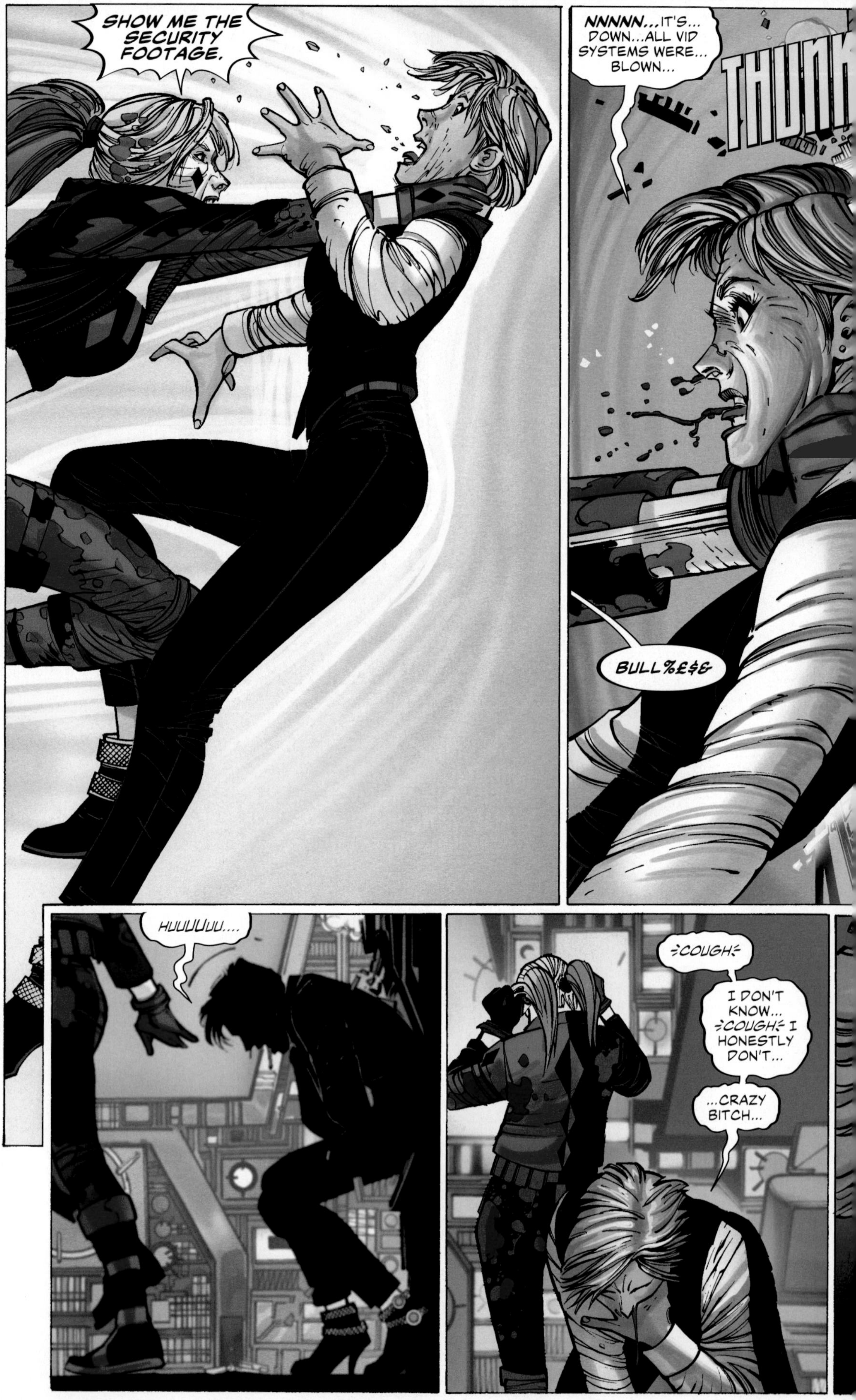
SHOW ME THE SECURITY FOOTAGE.
NNNNN...IT'S... DOWN...ALL VID SYSTEMS WERE... BLOWN...
THUNK
BULL%£$&
HUUUUUU....
=COUGH=
I DON'T KNOW... =COUGH= I HONESTLY DON'T...
...CRAZY BITCH...

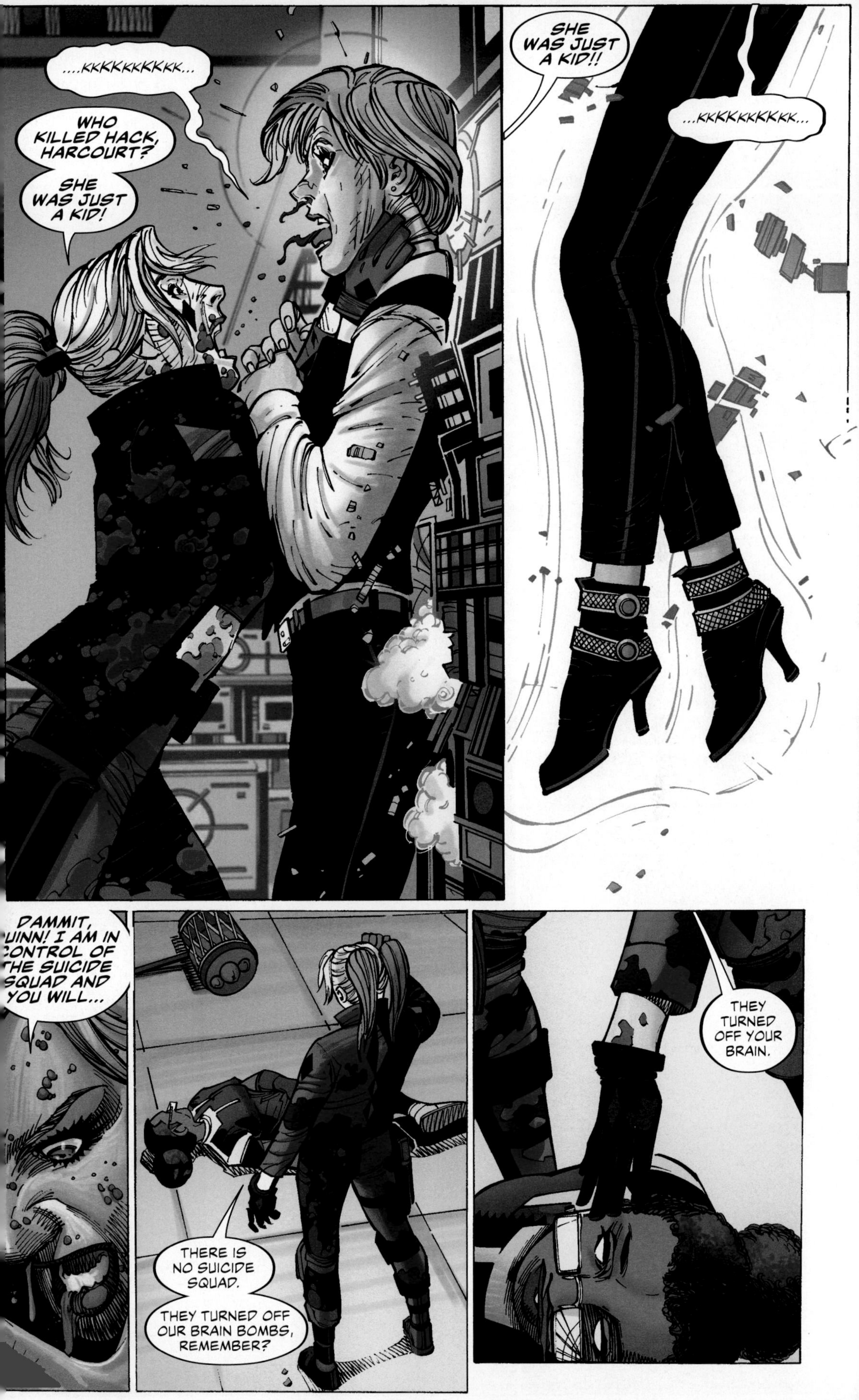
....KKKKKKKKKK...
WHO KILLED HACK, HARCOURT?
SHE WAS JUST A KID!
SHE WAS JUST A KID!!
...KKKKKKKKKK...
DAMMIT, UINN! I AM IN CONTROL OF THE SUICIDE SQUAD AND YOU WILL...
THERE IS NO SUICIDE SQUAD.
THEY TURNED OFF OUR BRAIN BOMBS, REMEMBER?
THEY TURNED OFF YOUR BRAIN.

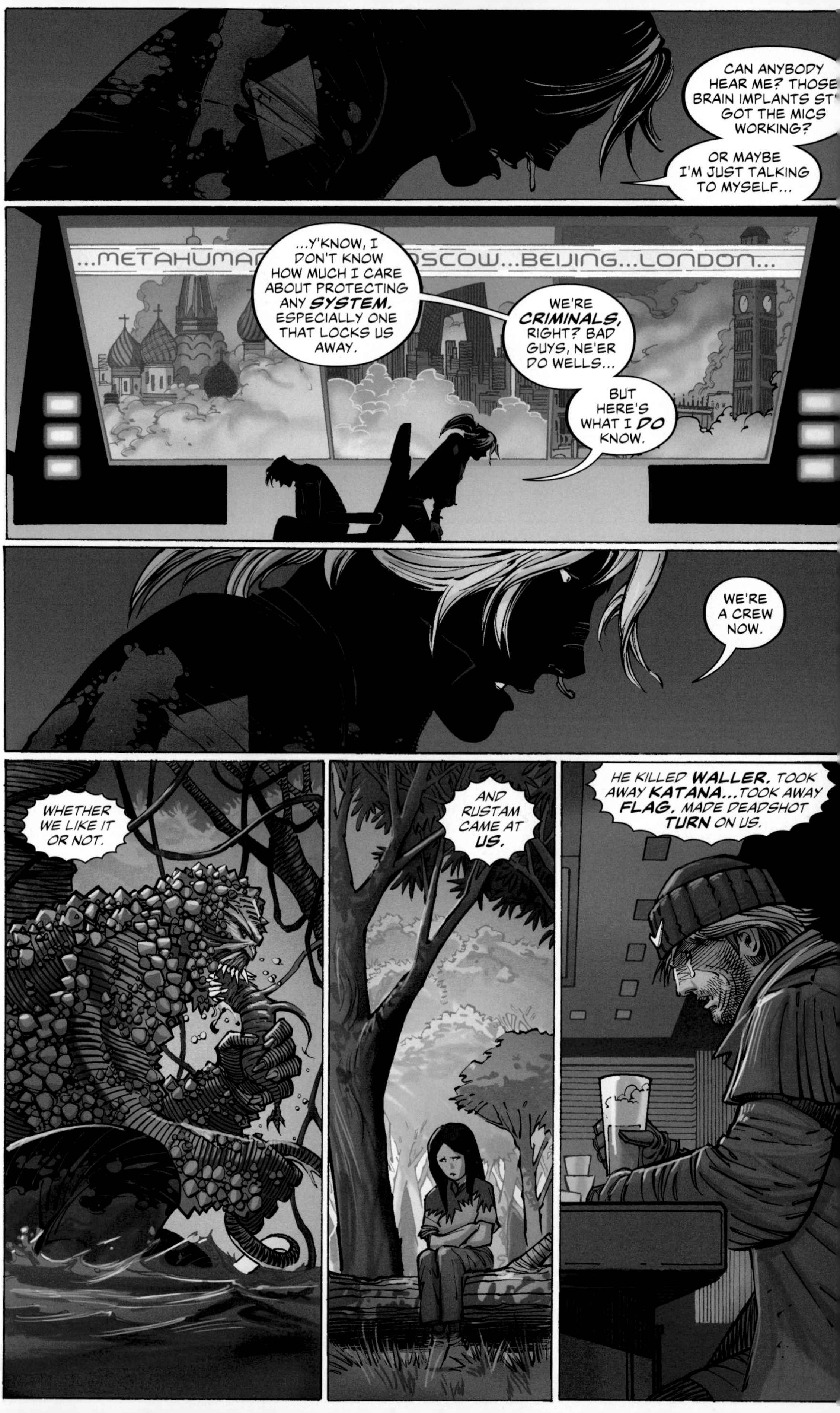
CAN ANYBODY HEAR ME? THOSE BRAIN IMPLANTS ST' GOT THE MICS WORKING?
OR MAYBE I'M JUST TALKING TO MYSELF...
...METAHUMAN
OSCOW...BEIJING...LONDON...
...Y'KNOW, I DON'T KNOW HOW MUCH I CARE ABOUT PROTECTING ANY SYSTEM. ESPECIALLY ONE THAT LOCKS US AWAY.
WE'RE CRIMINALS, RIGHT? BAD GUYS, NE'ER DO WELLS...
BUT HERE'S WHAT I DO KNOW.
WE'RE A CREW NOW.
WHETHER WE LIKE IT OR NOT.
AND RUSTAM CAME AT US.
HE KILLED WALLER. TOOK AWAY KATANA...TOOK AWAY FLAG. MADE DEADSHOT TURN ON US.

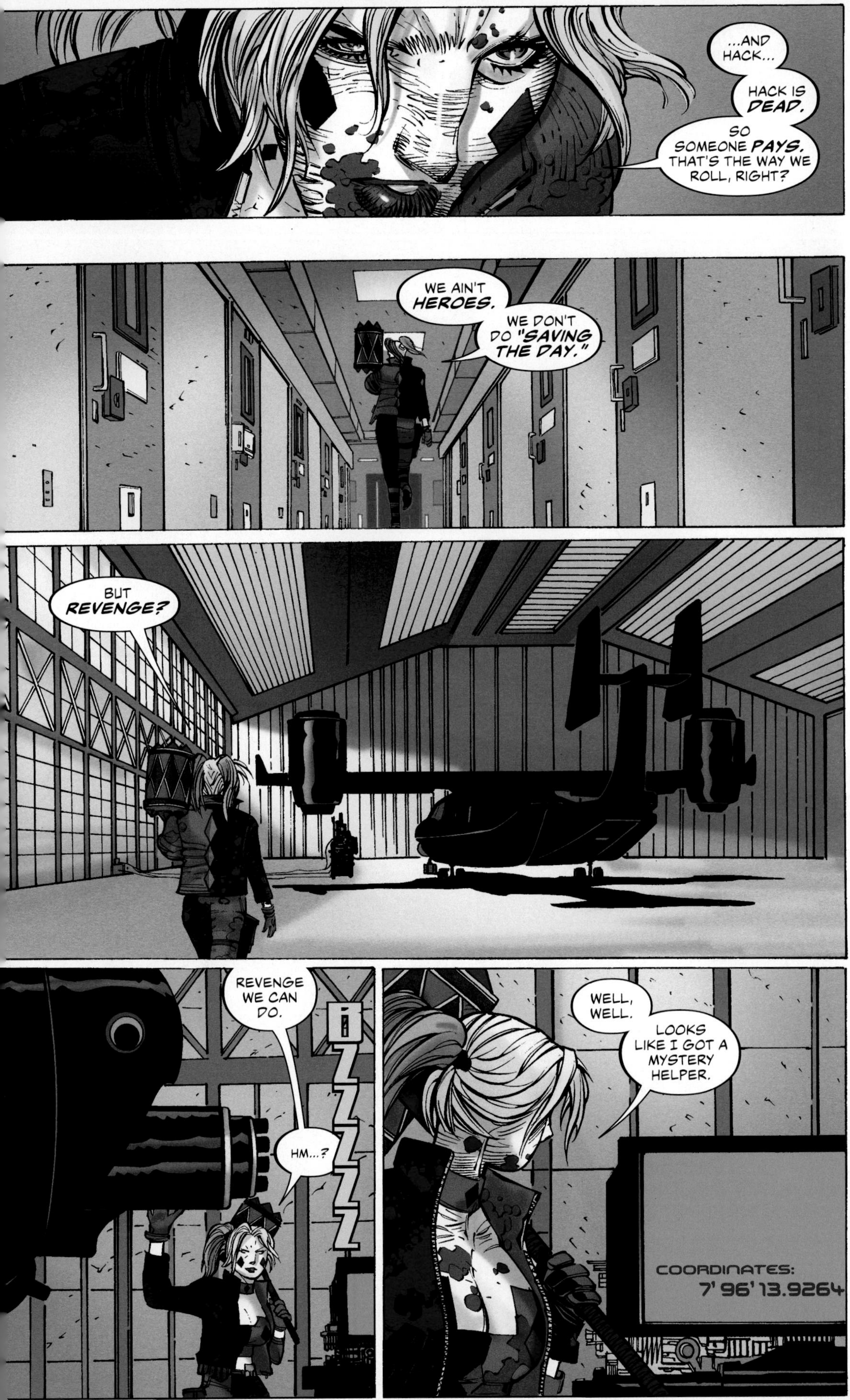
...AND HACK...
HACK IS DEAD.
SO SOMEONE PAYS. THAT'S THE WAY WE ROLL, RIGHT?
WE AIN'T HEROES.
WE DON'T DO "SAVING THE DAY."
BUT REVENGE?
REVENGE WE CAN DO.
BZZZZZ
HM...?
WELL, WELL.
LOOKS LIKE I GOT A MYSTERY HELPER.
COORDINATES:
7' 96' 13.9264

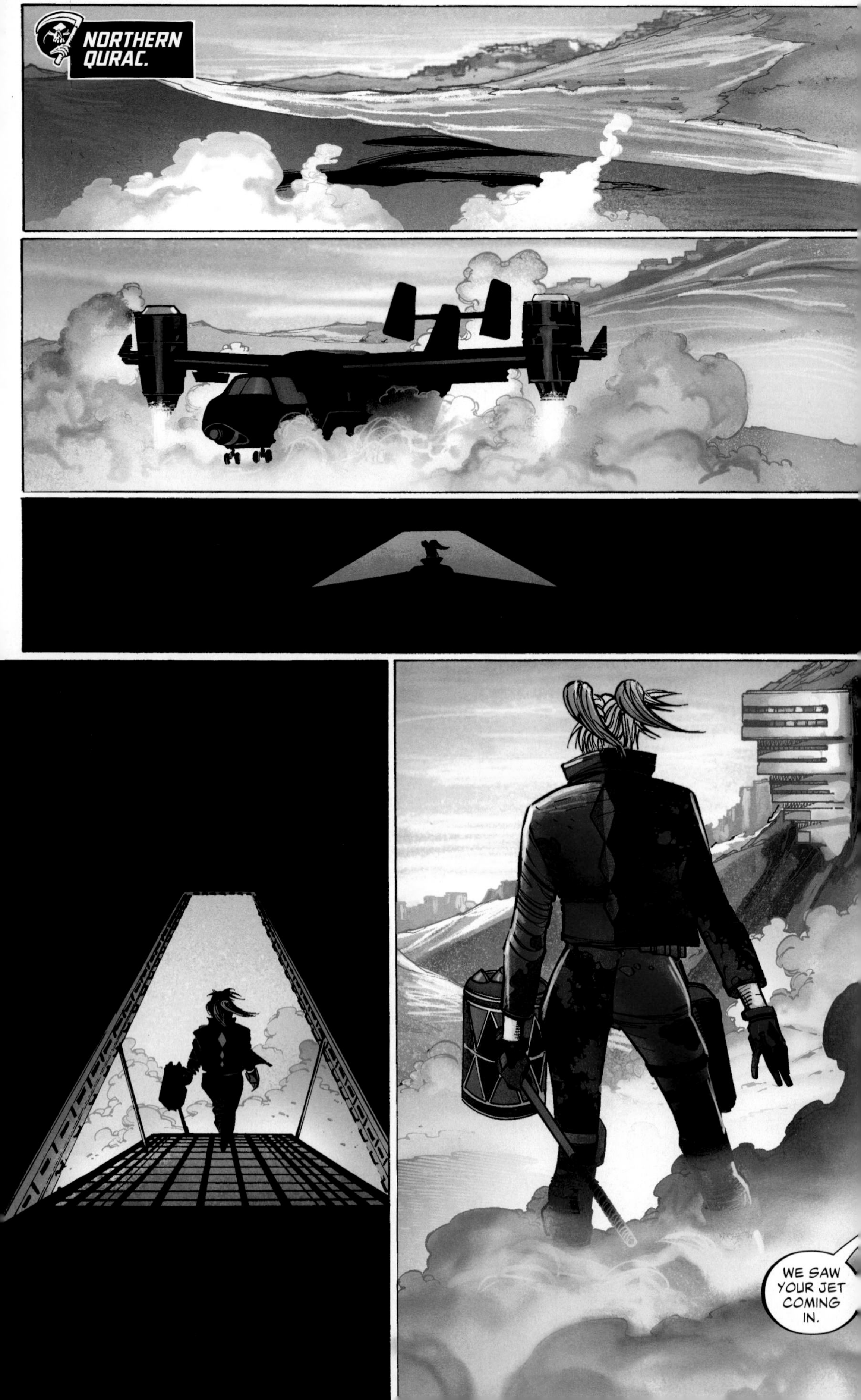
NORTHERN QURAC.
WE SAW YOUR JET COMING IN.

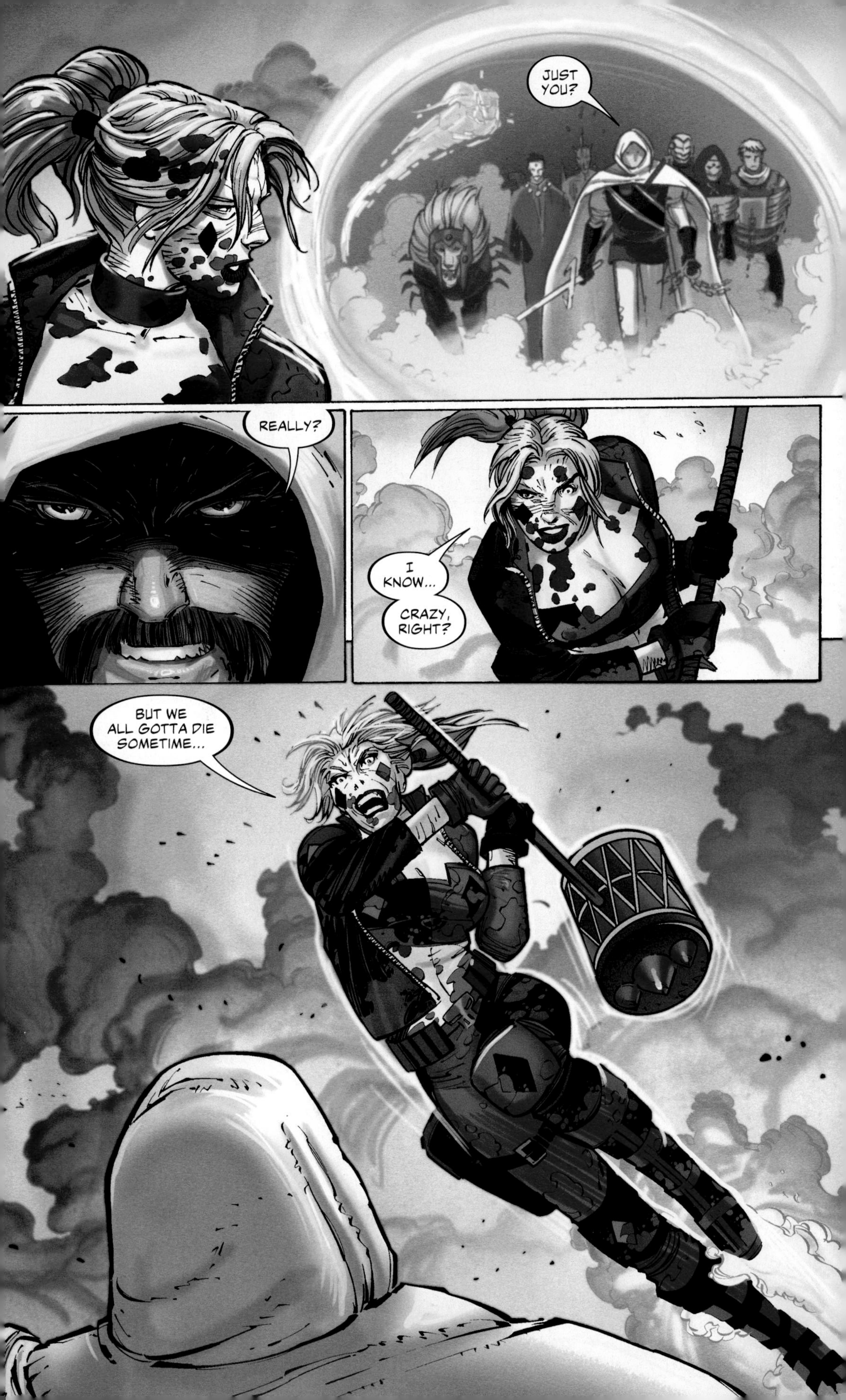
JUST YOU?
REALLY?
I KNOW...
CRAZY, RIGHT?
BUT WE ALL GOTTA DIE SOMETIME...

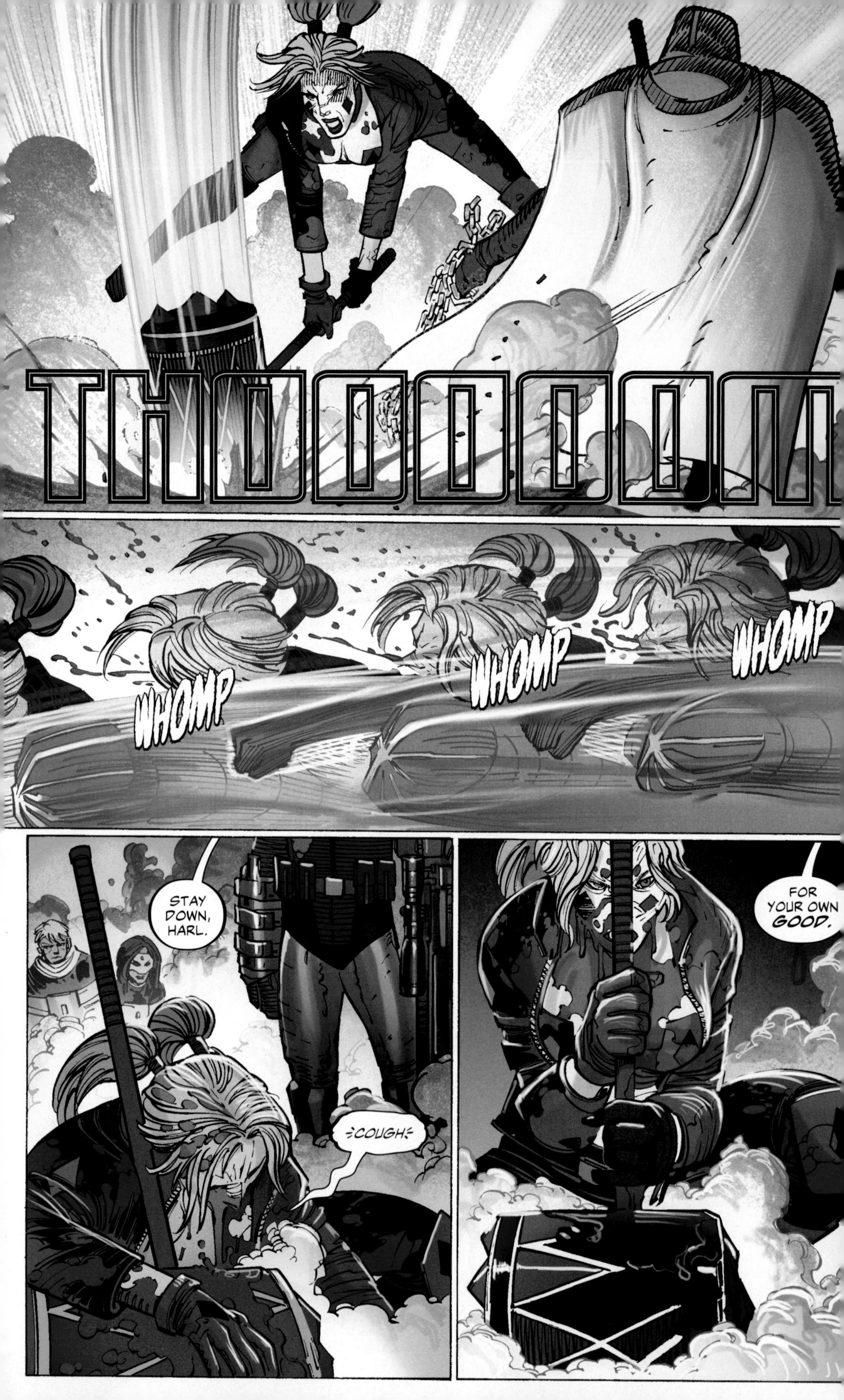
THOOOOOM
WHOMP
WHOMP
WHOMP
STAY DOWN, HARL.
COUGH
FOR YOUR OWN GOOD.

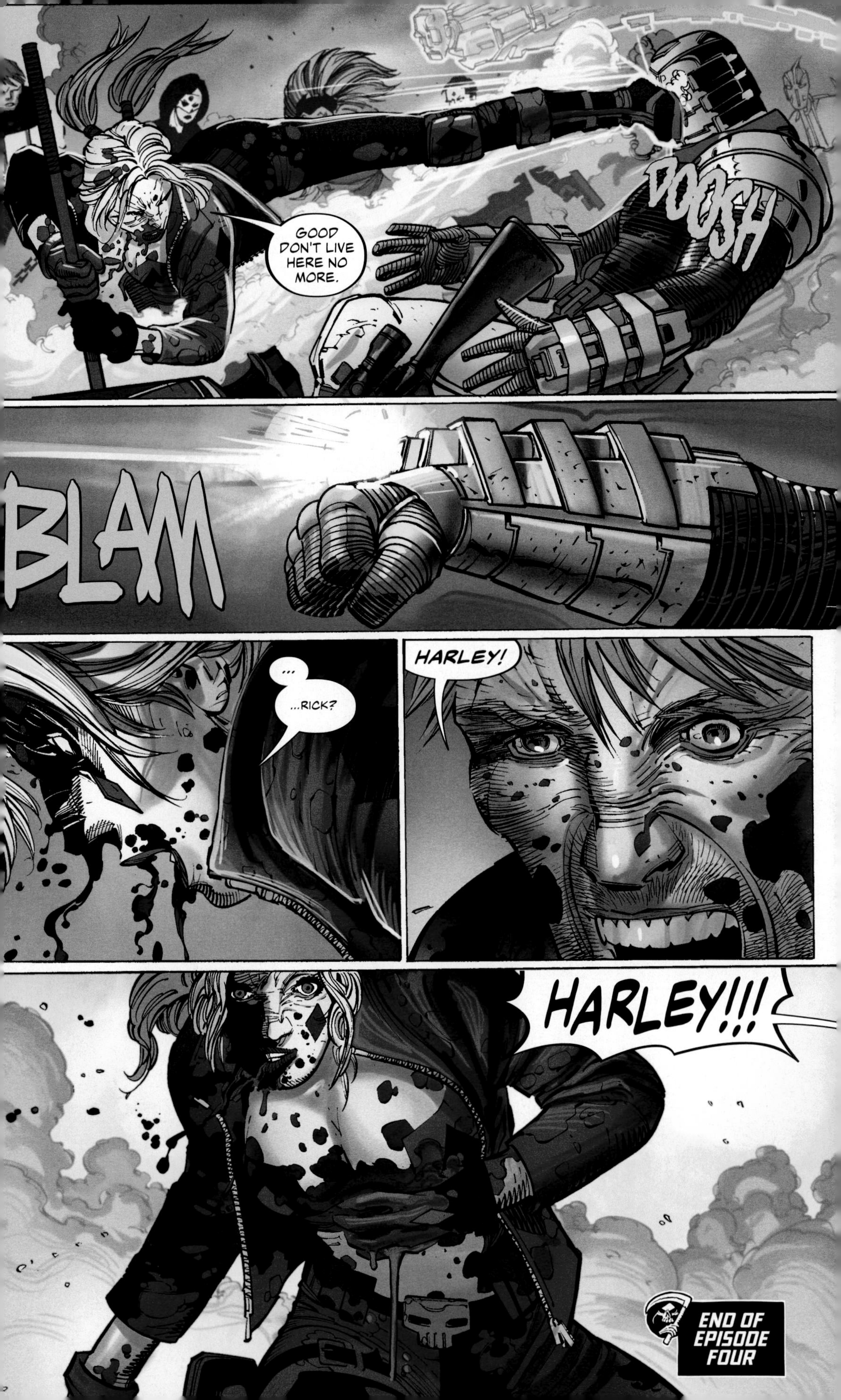

GOOD DON'T LIVE HERE NO MORE.
DOOSH
BLAM
...
...RICK?
HARLEY!
HARLEY!!!
END OF EPISODE FOUR

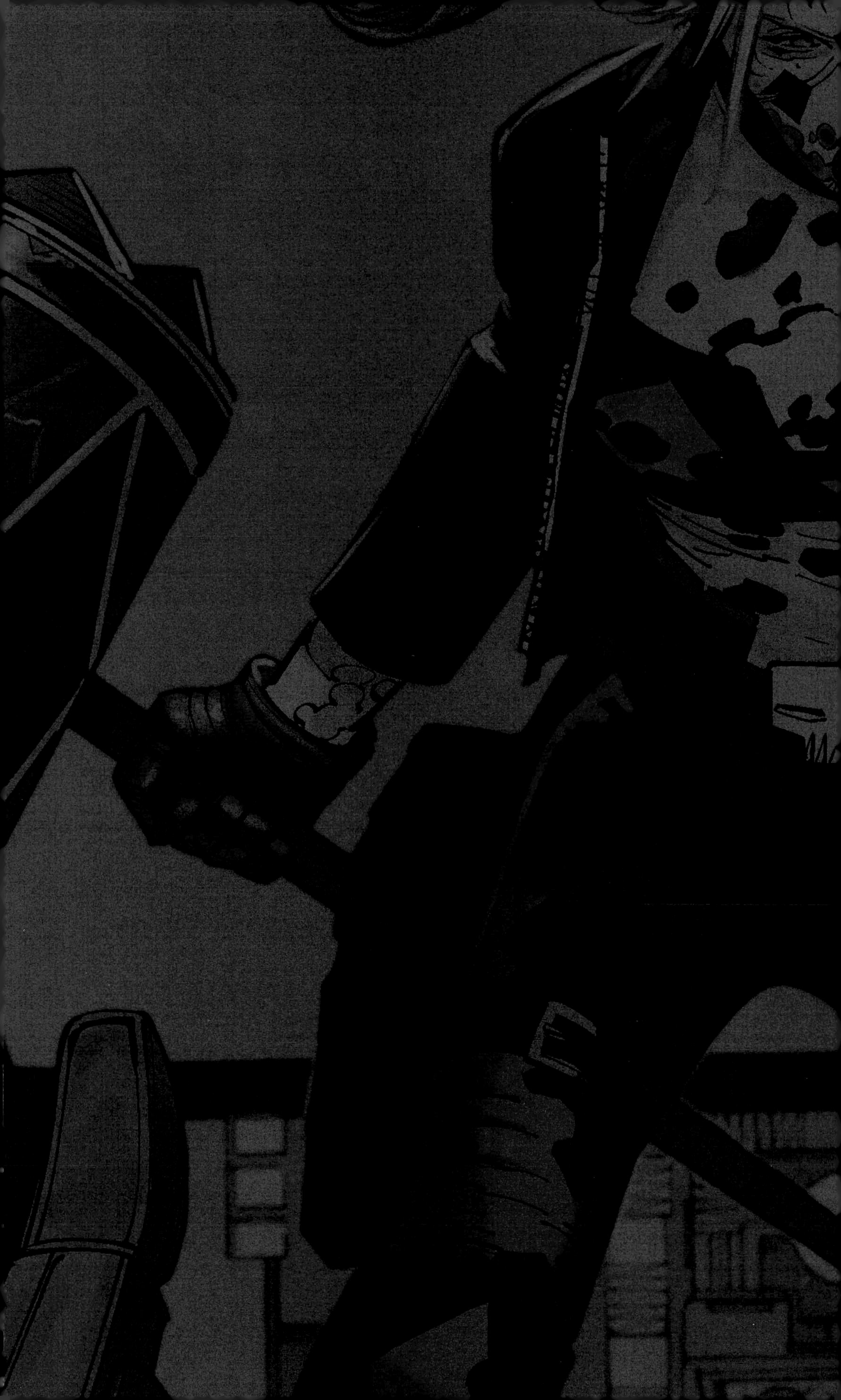

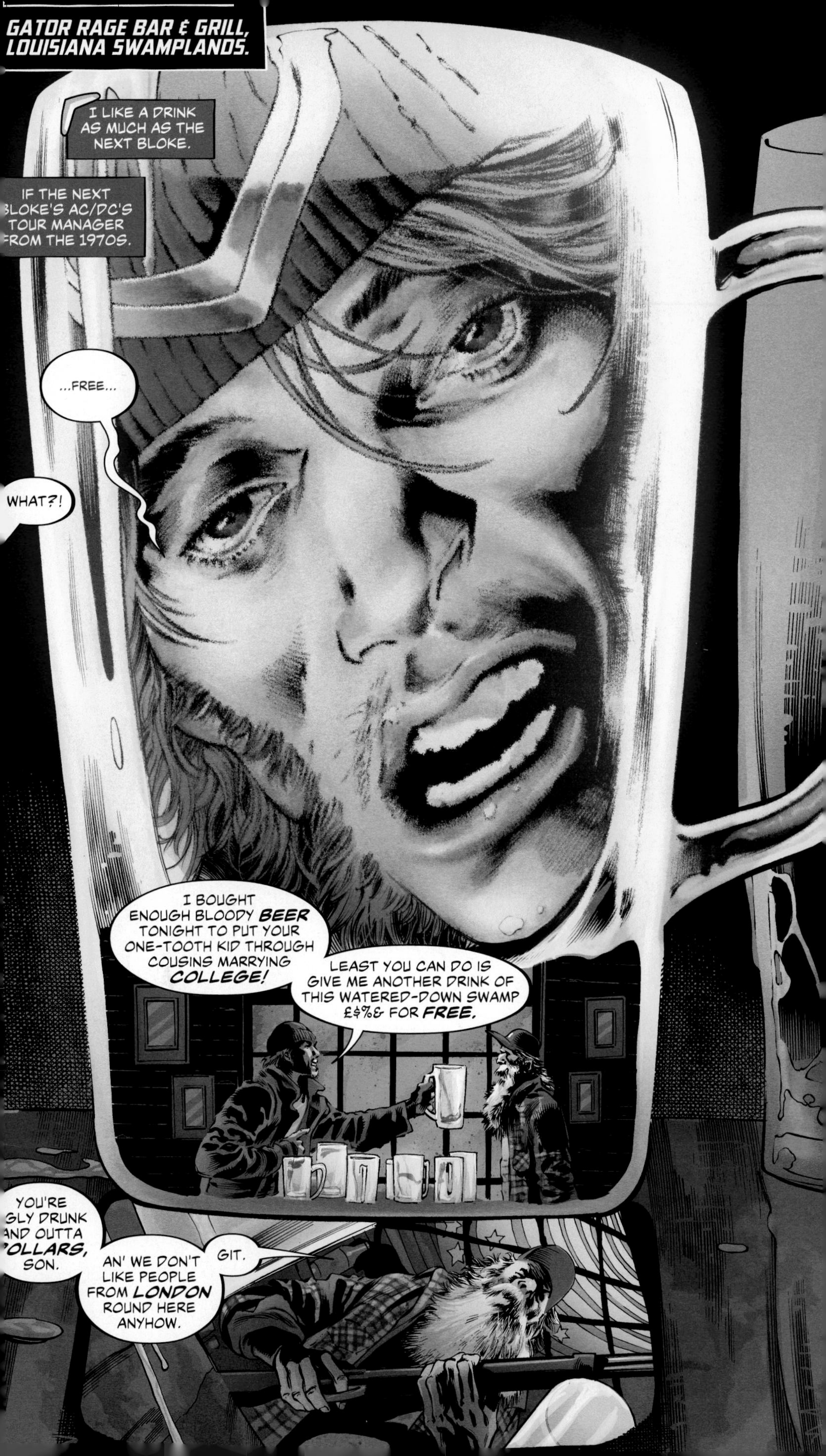
GATOR RAGE BAR & GRILL, LOUISIANA SWAMPLANDS.
I LIKE A DRINK AS MUCH AS THE NEXT BLOKE.
IF THE NEXT BLOKE'S AC/DC'S TOUR MANAGER FROM THE 1970S.
...FREE...
WHAT?!
I BOUGHT ENOUGH BLOODY BEER TONIGHT TO PUT YOUR ONE-TOOTH KID THROUGH COUSINS MARRYING COLLEGE!
LEAST YOU CAN DO IS GIVE ME ANOTHER DRINK OF THIS WATERED-DOWN SWAMP £$%& FOR FREE.
YOU'RE UGLY DRUNK AND OUTTA DOLLARS, SON.
GIT.
AN' WE DON'T LIKE PEOPLE FROM LONDON ROUND HERE ANYHOW.

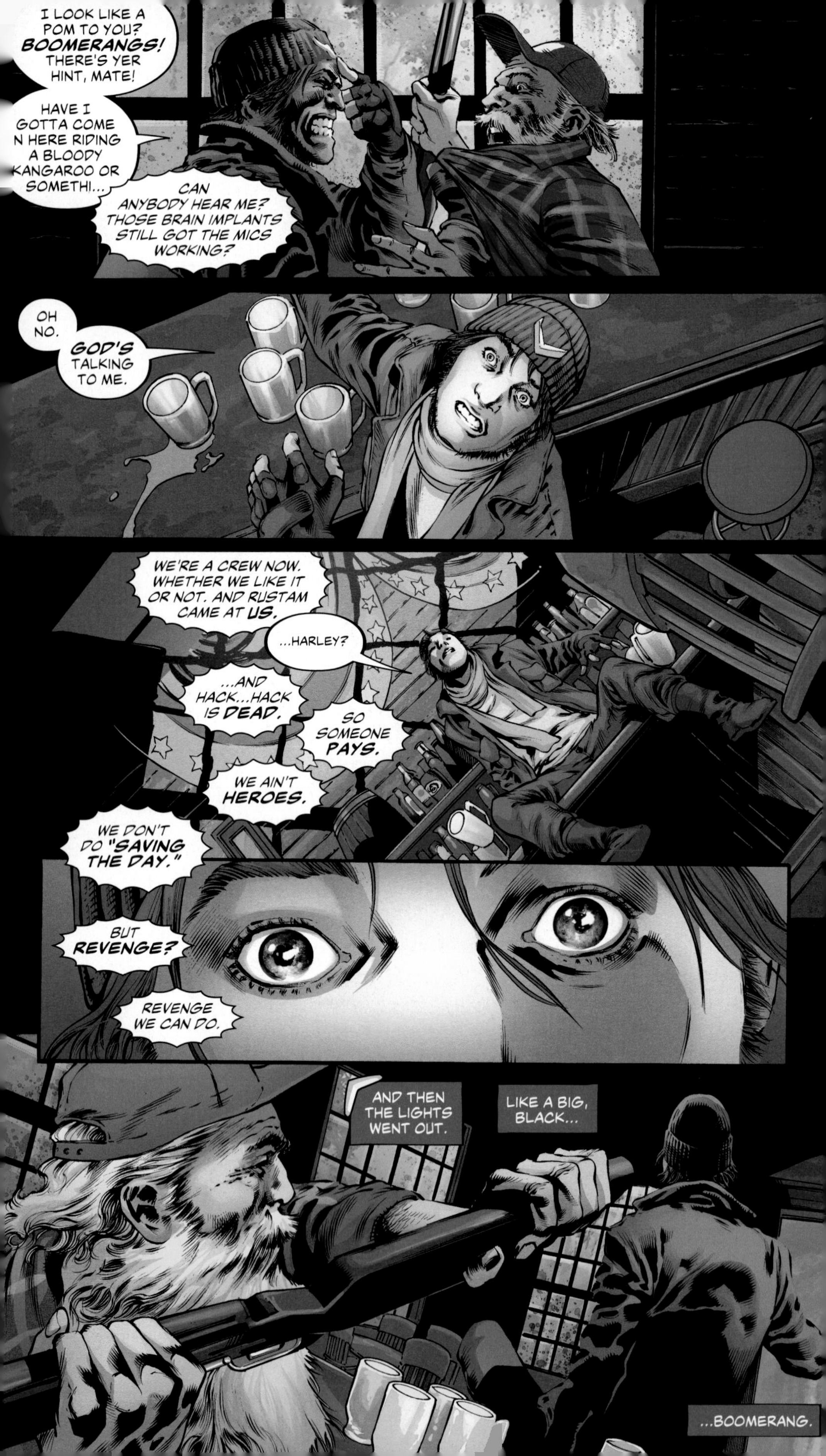
I LOOK LIKE A POM TO YOU? BOOMERANGS! THERE'S YER HINT, MATE!
HAVE I GOTTA COME N HERE RIDING A BLOODY KANGAROO OR SOMETHI...
CAN ANYBODY HEAR ME? THOSE BRAIN IMPLANTS STILL GOT THE MICS WORKING?
OH NO.
GOD'S TALKING TO ME.
WE'RE A CREW NOW. WHETHER WE LIKE IT OR NOT. AND RUSTAM CAME AT US.
...HARLEY?
...AND HACK...HACK IS DEAD.
SO SOMEONE PAYS.
WE AIN'T HEROES.
WE DON'T DO "SAVING THE DAY."
BUT REVENGE?
REVENGE WE CAN DO.
AND THEN THE LIGHTS WENT OUT.
LIKE A BIG, BLACK...
...BOOMERANG.

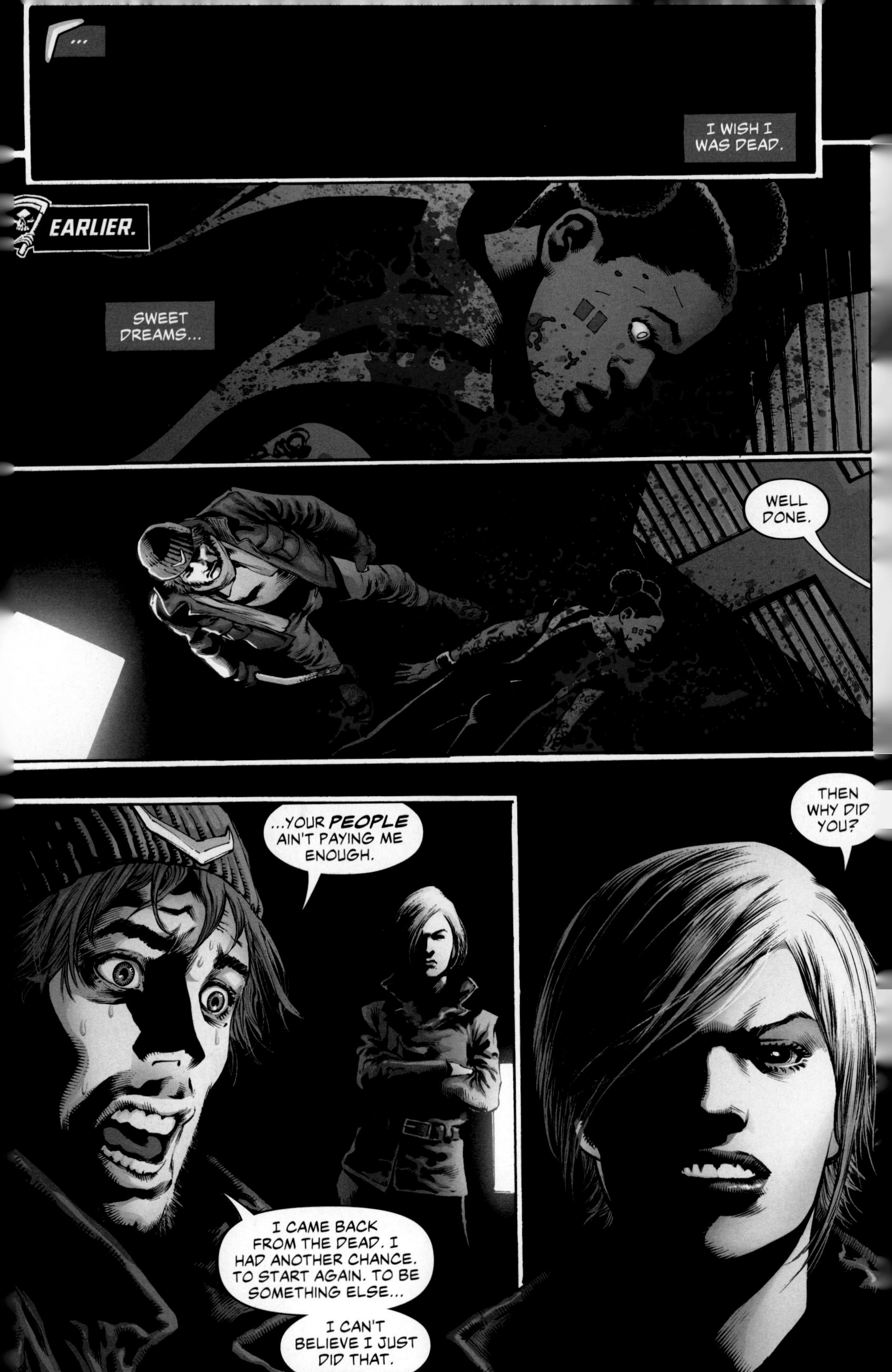
...
I WISH I WAS DEAD.
EARLIER.
SWEET DREAMS...
WELL DONE.
...YOUR PEOPLE AIN'T PAYING ME ENOUGH.
THEN WHY DID YOU?
I CAME BACK FROM THE DEAD. I HAD ANOTHER CHANCE. TO START AGAIN. TO BE SOMETHING ELSE...
I CAN'T BELIEVE I JUST DID THAT.

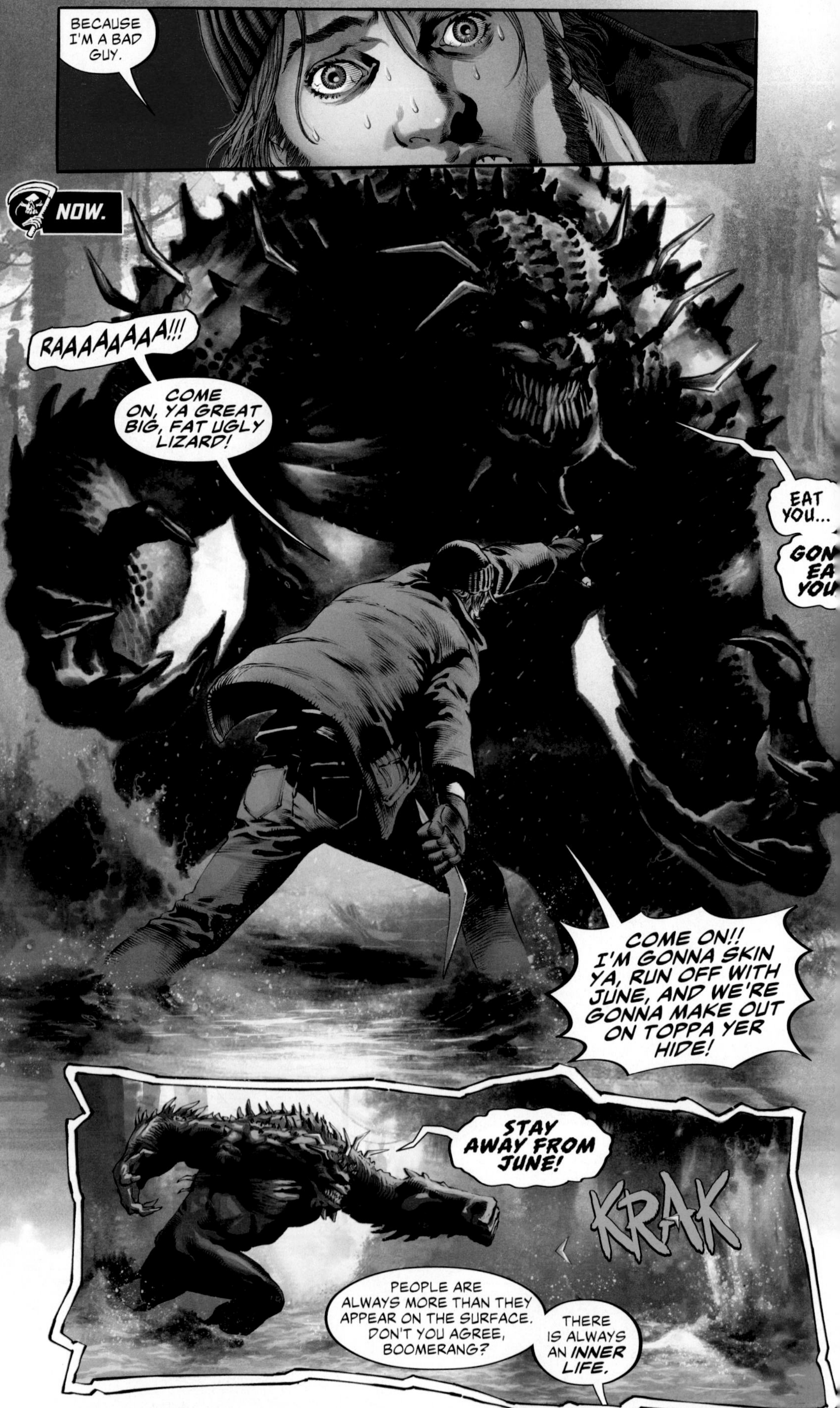
BECAUSE I'M A BAD GUY.
NOW.
RAAAAAAAA!!!
COME ON, YA GREAT BIG, FAT UGLY LIZARD!
EAT YOU...
COME ON!! I'M GONNA SKIN YA, RUN OFF WITH JUNE, AND WE'RE GONNA MAKE OUT ON TOPPA YER HIDE!
STAY AWAY FROM JUNE!
KRAK
PEOPLE ARE ALWAYS MORE THAN THEY APPEAR ON THE SURFACE. DON'T YOU AGREE, BOOMERANG?
THERE IS ALWAYS AN INNER LIFE.

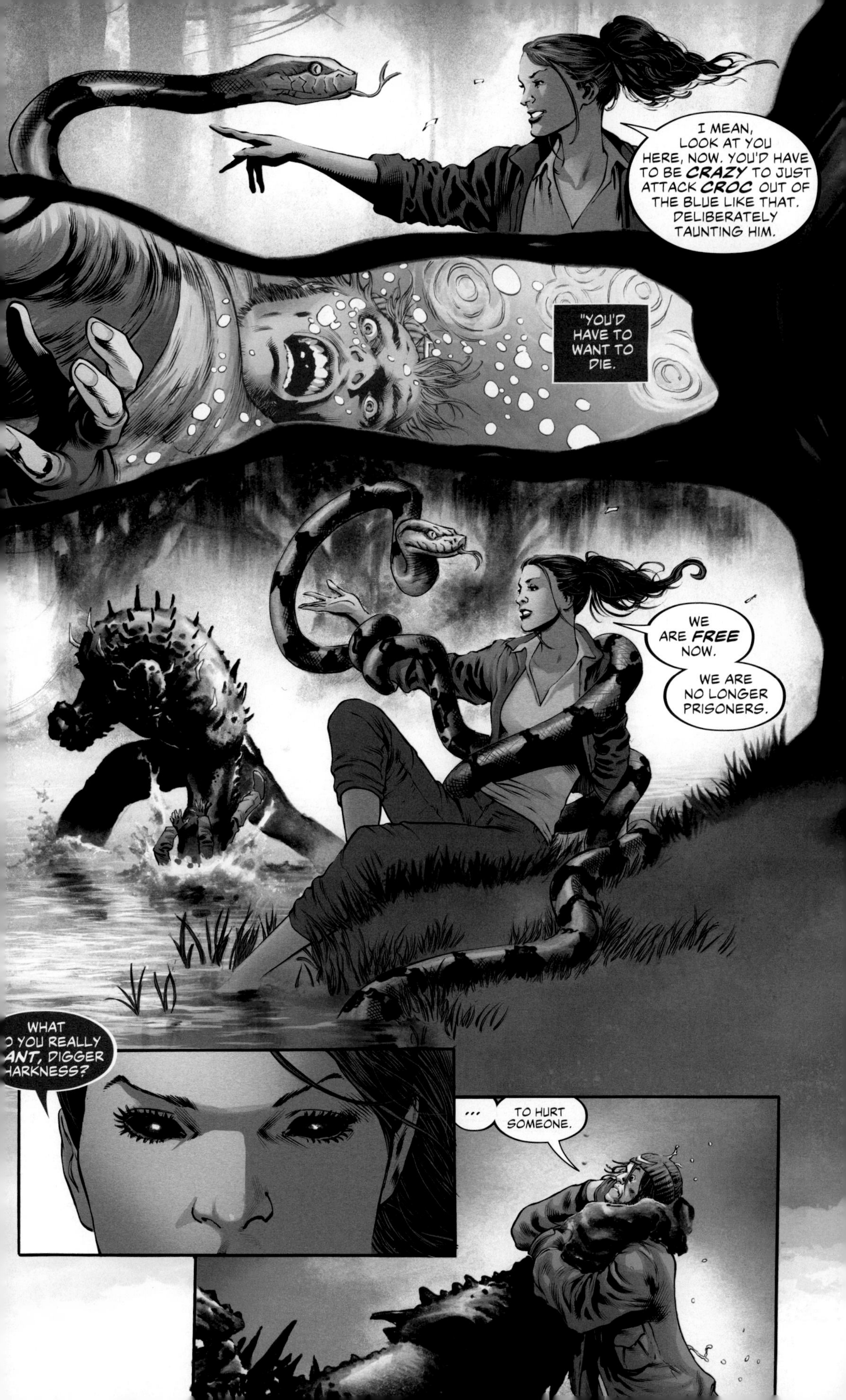
I MEAN, LOOK AT YOU HERE, NOW. YOU'D HAVE TO BE CRAZY TO JUST ATTACK CROC OUT OF THE BLUE LIKE THAT. DELIBERATELY TAUNTING HIM.
"YOU'D HAVE TO WANT TO DIE.
WE ARE FREE NOW.
WE ARE NO LONGER PRISONERS.
WHAT
YOU REALLY
ANT, DIGGER
HARKNESS?
...
TO HURT SOMEONE.

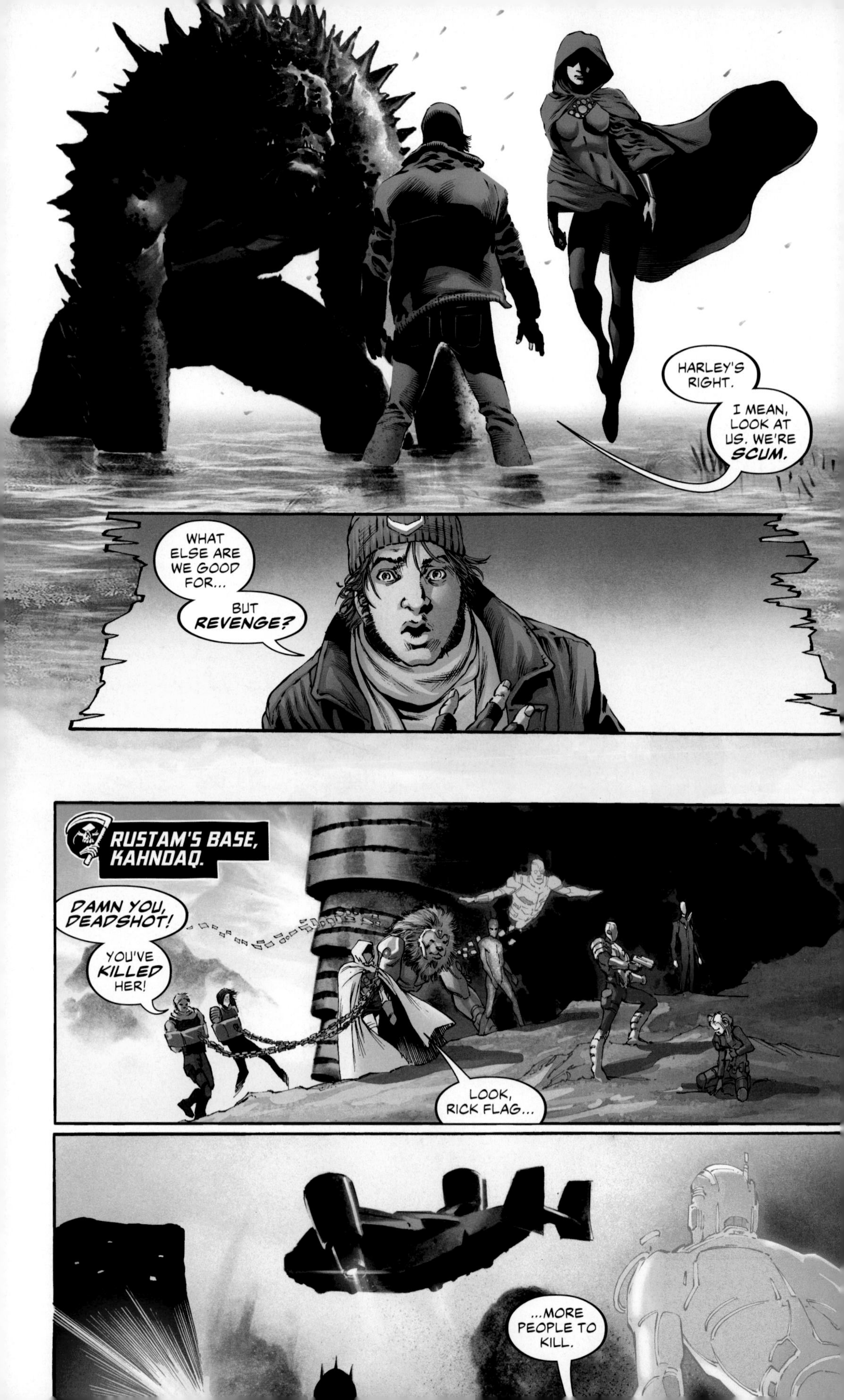
HARLEY'S RIGHT.
I MEAN, LOOK AT US. WE'RE SCUM.
WHAT ELSE ARE WE GOOD FOR...
BUT REVENGE?
RUSTAM'S BASE, KAHNDAQ.
DAMN YOU, DEADSHOT!
YOU'VE KILLED HER!
LOOK, RICK FLAG...
...MORE PEOPLE TO KILL.

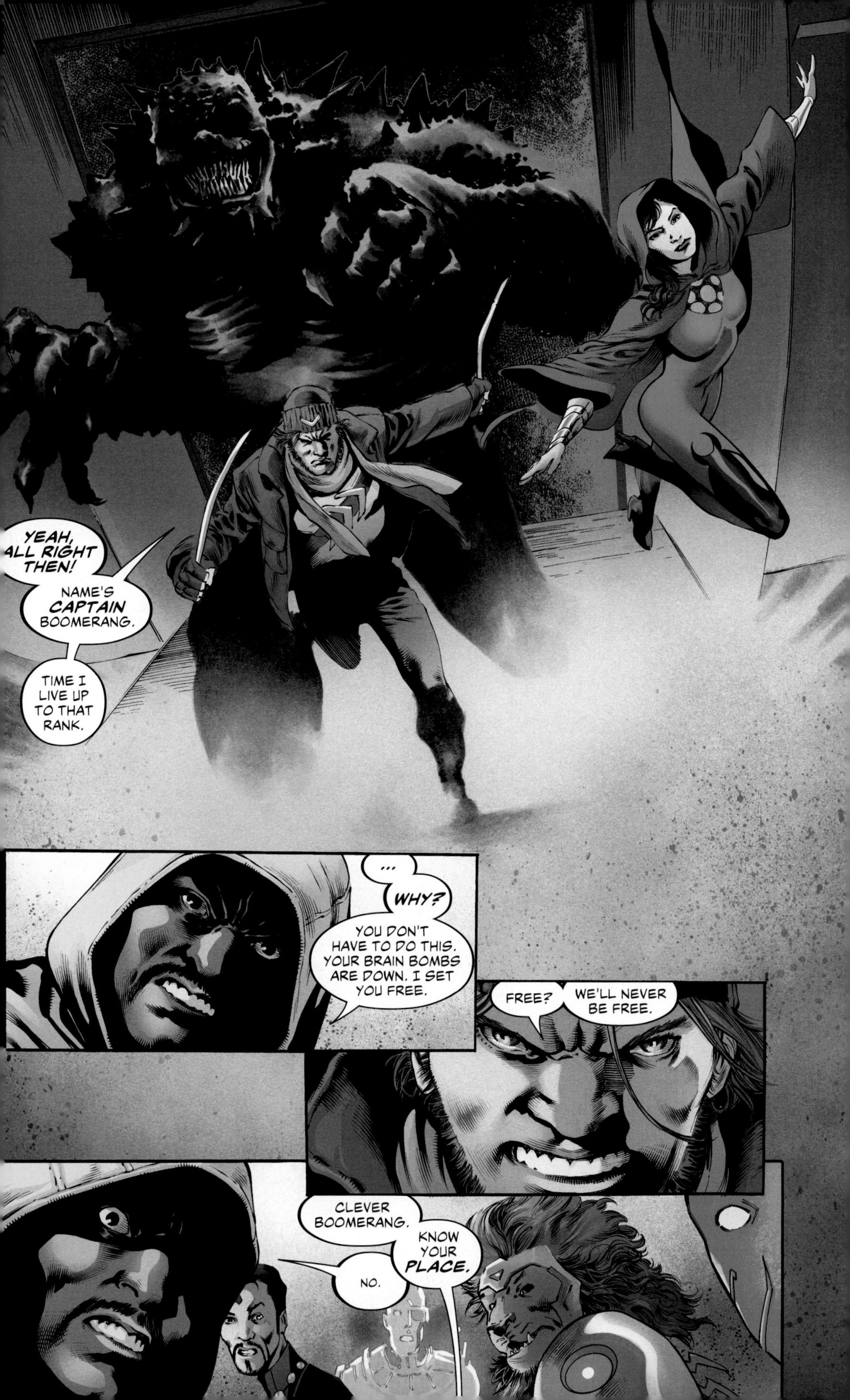
YEAH, ALL RIGHT THEN!
NAME'S CAPTAIN BOOMERANG.
TIME I LIVE UP TO THAT RANK.
...
WHY?
YOU DON'T HAVE TO DO THIS. YOUR BRAIN BOMBS ARE DOWN. I SET YOU FREE.
FREE?
WE'LL NEVER BE FREE.
CLEVER BOOMERANG.
KNOW YOUR PLACE.
NO.

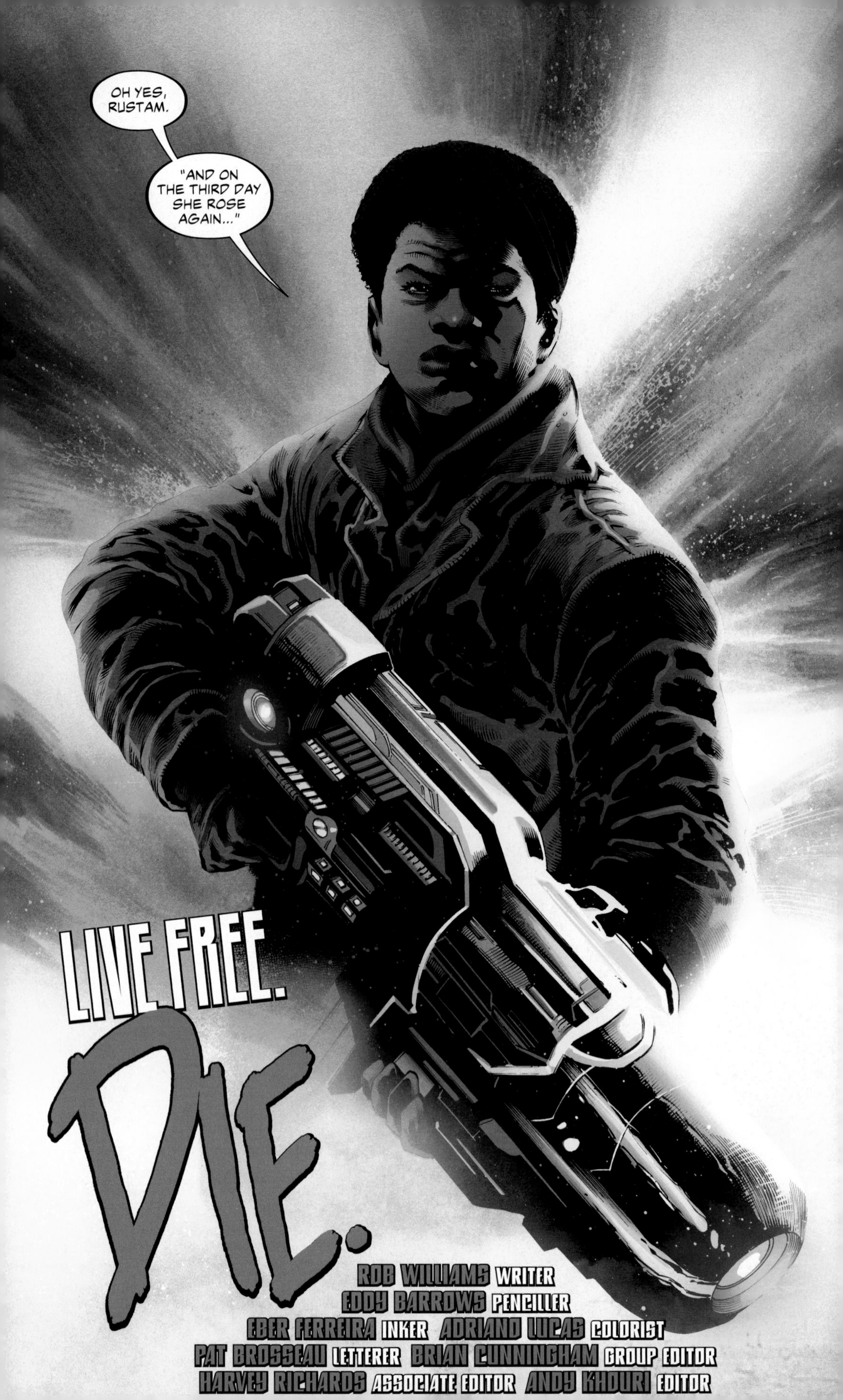

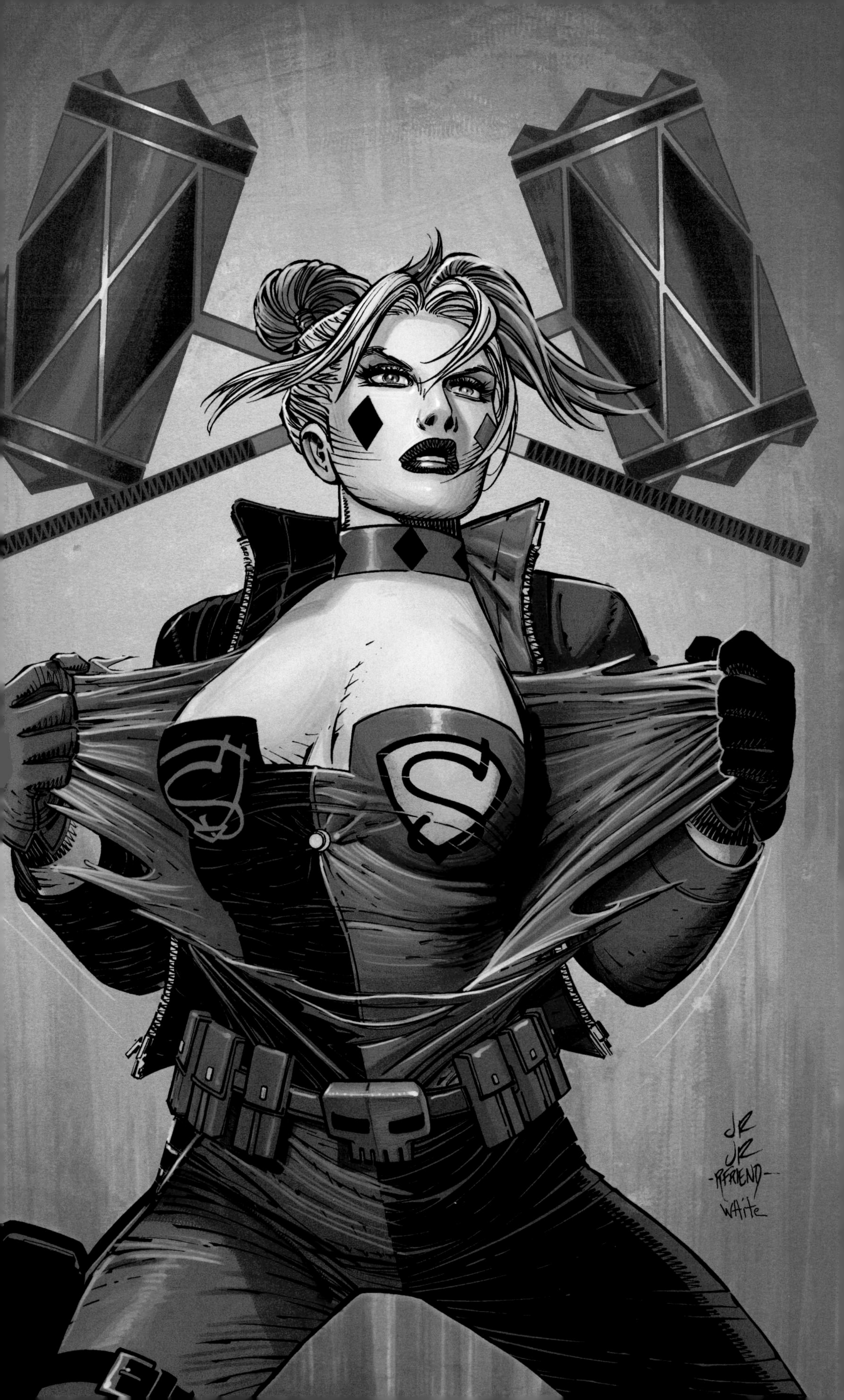
JR
JR
-RFRIEND-
White

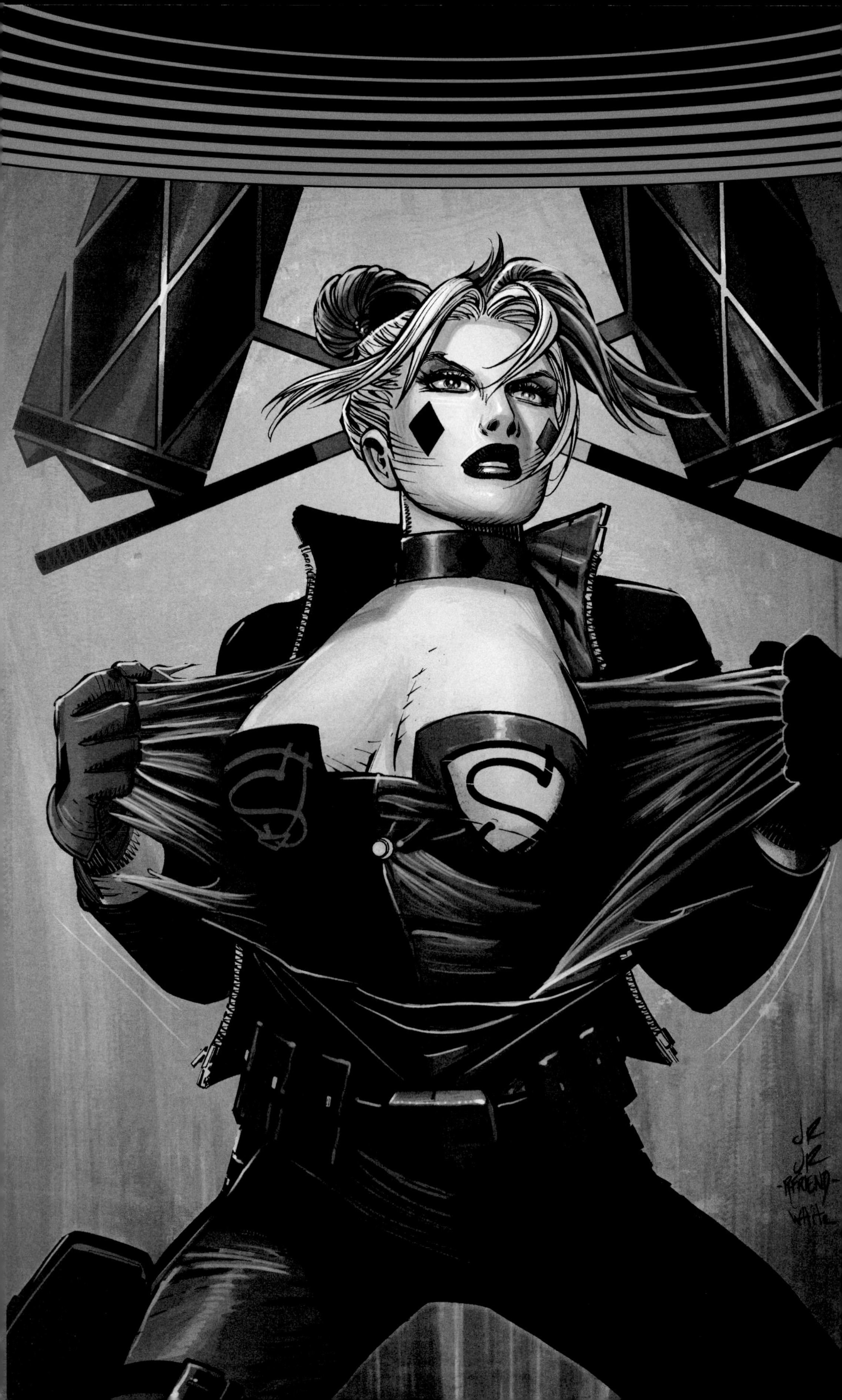

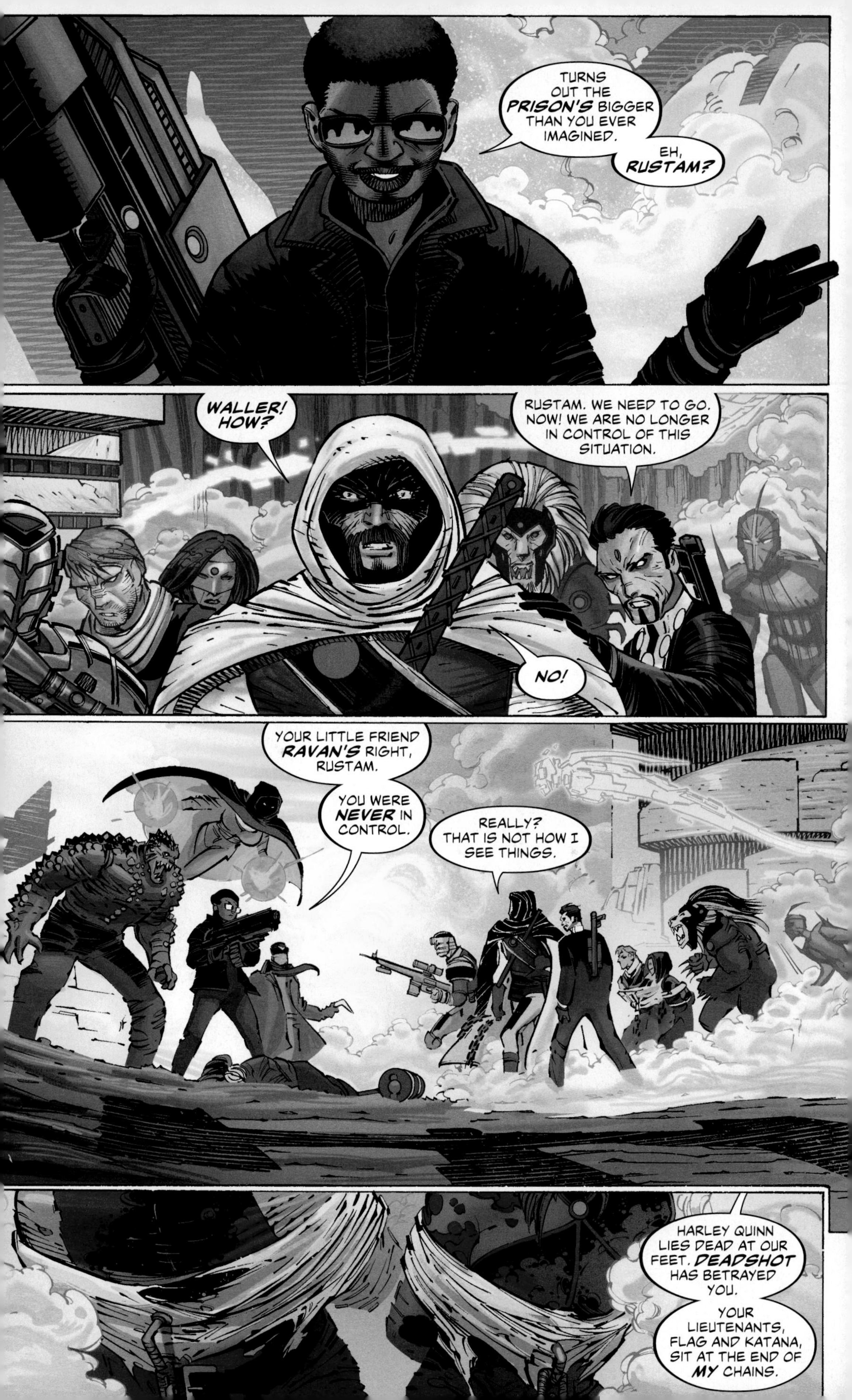
TURNS OUT THE PRISON'S BIGGER THAN YOU EVER IMAGINED.
EH, RUSTAM?
WALLER! HOW?
RUSTAM. WE NEED TO GO. NOW! WE ARE NO LONGER IN CONTROL OF THIS SITUATION.
NO!
YOUR LITTLE FRIEND RAVAN'S RIGHT, RUSTAM.
YOU WERE NEVER IN CONTROL.
REALLY? THAT IS NOT HOW I SEE THINGS.
HARLEY QUINN LIES DEAD AT OUR FEET. DEADSHOT HAS BETRAYED YOU.
YOUR LIEUTENANTS, FLAG AND KATANA, SIT AT THE END OF MY CHAINS.

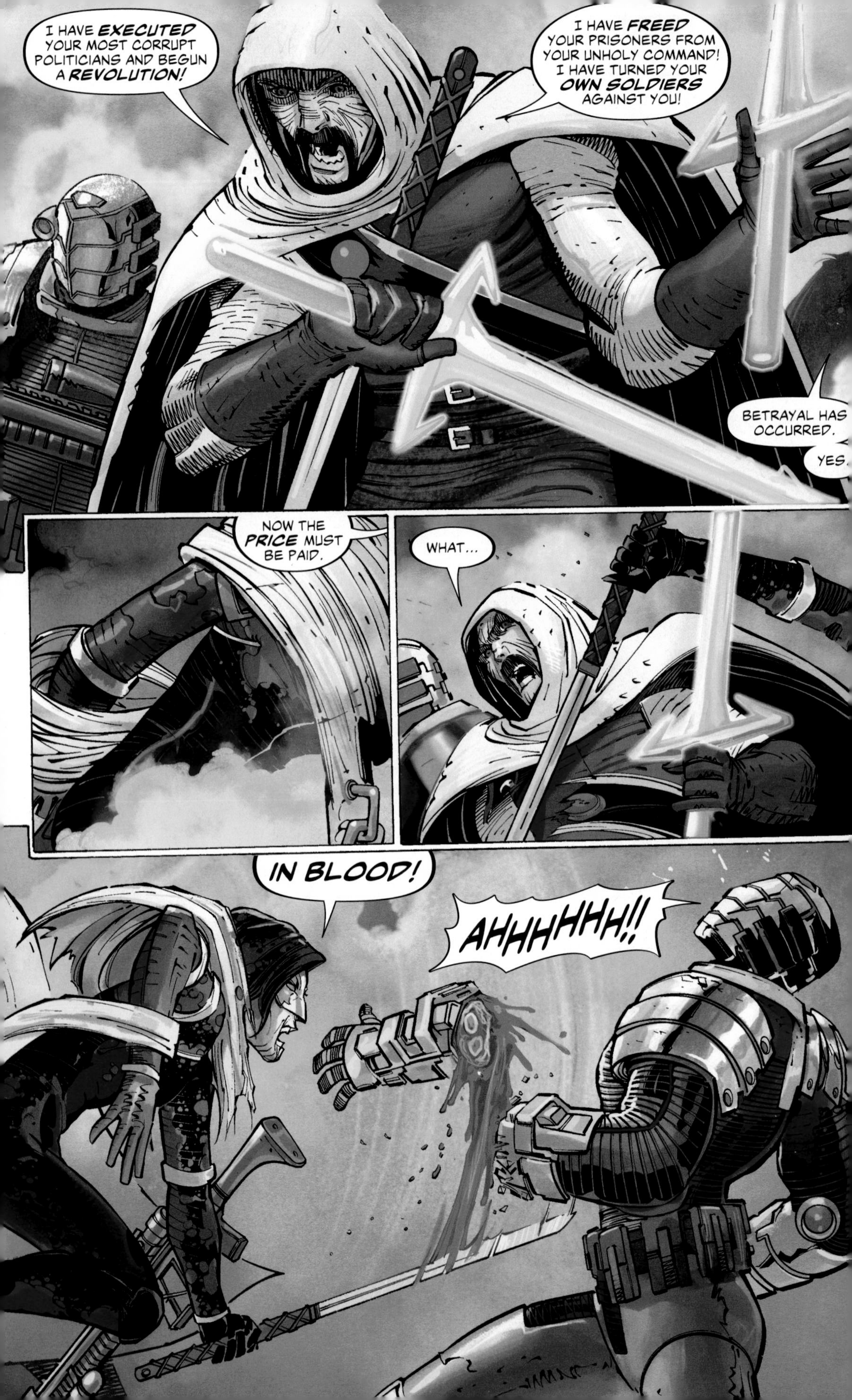
I HAVE EXECUTED YOUR MOST CORRUPT POLITICIANS AND BEGUN A REVOLUTION!
I HAVE FREED YOUR PRISONERS FROM YOUR UNHOLY COMMAND! I HAVE TURNED YOUR OWN SOLDIERS AGAINST YOU!
BETRAYAL HAS OCCURRED.
YES.
NOW THE PRICE MUST BE PAID.
WHAT...
IN BLOOD!
AHHHHHH!!

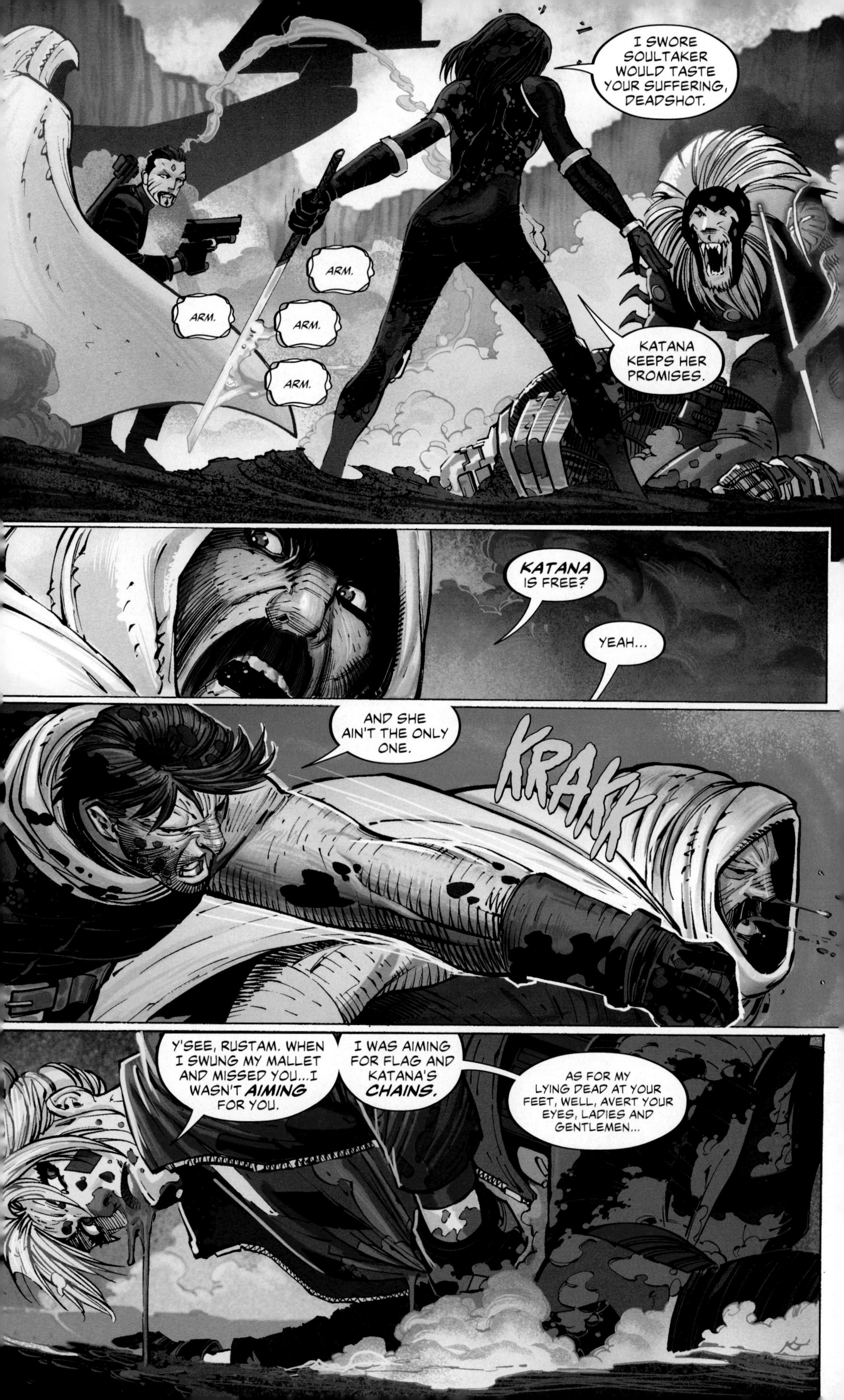
I SWORE SOULTAKER WOULD TASTE YOUR SUFFERING, DEADSHOT.
ARM.
ARM.
ARM.
ARM.
KATANA KEEPS HER PROMISES.
KATANA IS FREE?
YEAH...
AND SHE AIN'T THE ONLY ONE.
KRAKK
Y'SEE, RUSTAM. WHEN I SWUNG MY MALLET AND MISSED YOU...I WASN'T AIMING FOR YOU.
I WAS AIMING FOR FLAG AND KATANA'S CHAINS.
AS FOR MY LYING DEAD AT YOUR FEET, WELL, AVERT YOUR EYES, LADIES AND GENTLEMEN...

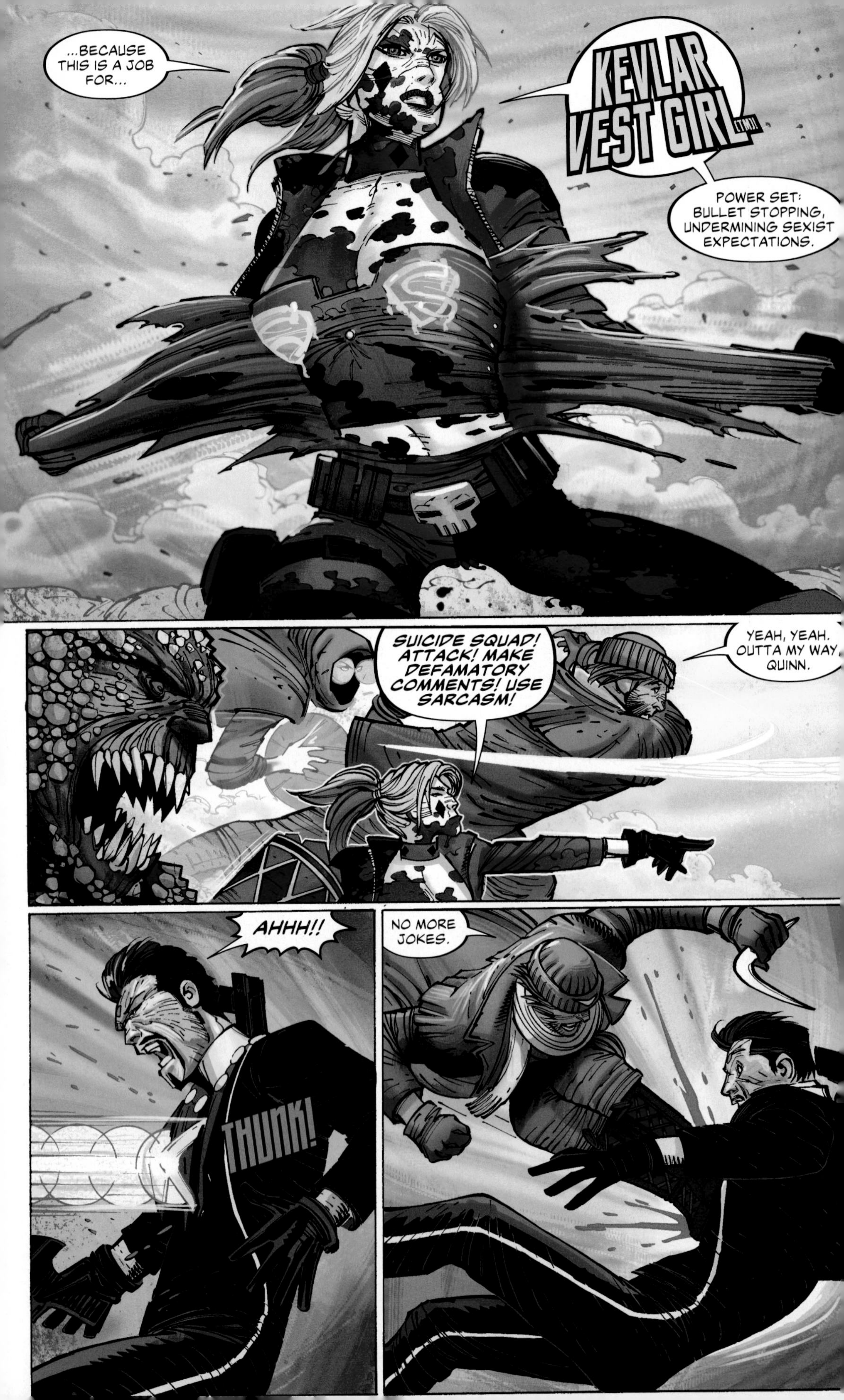
...BECAUSE THIS IS A JOB FOR...
KEVLAR VEST GIRL(TM)!
POWER SET: BULLET STOPPING, UNDERMINING SEXIST EXPECTATIONS.
SUICIDE SQUAD! ATTACK! MAKE DEFAMATORY COMMENTS! USE SARCASM!
YEAH, YEAH. OUTTA MY WAY, QUINN.
AHHH!!
THUNK!
NO MORE JOKES.

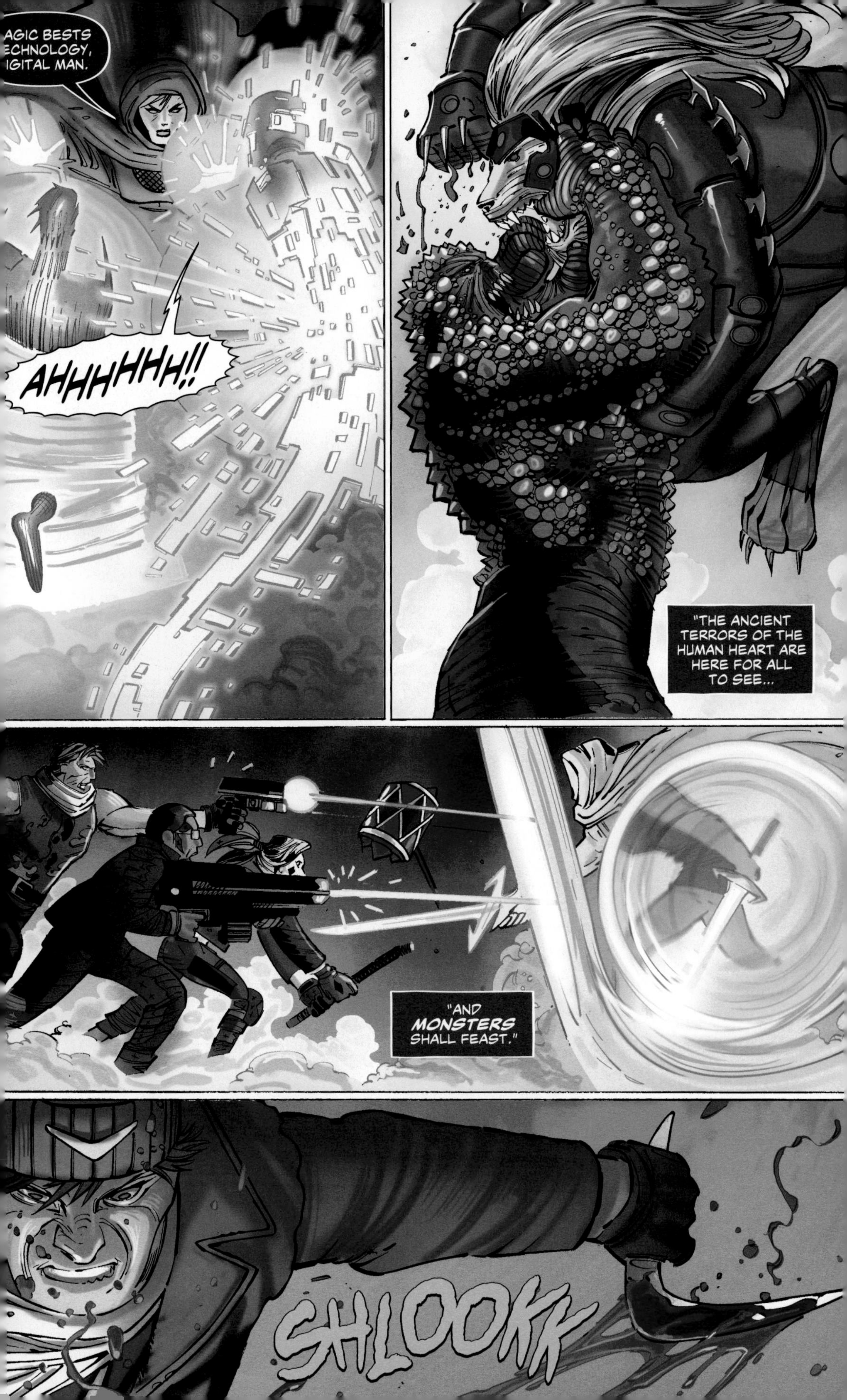
AGIC BESTS
ECHNOLOGY,
IGITAL MAN.
AHHHHHH!!
"THE ANCIENT TERRORS OF THE HUMAN HEART ARE HERE FOR ALL TO SEE...
"AND MONSTERS SHALL FEAST."
SHLOOKK

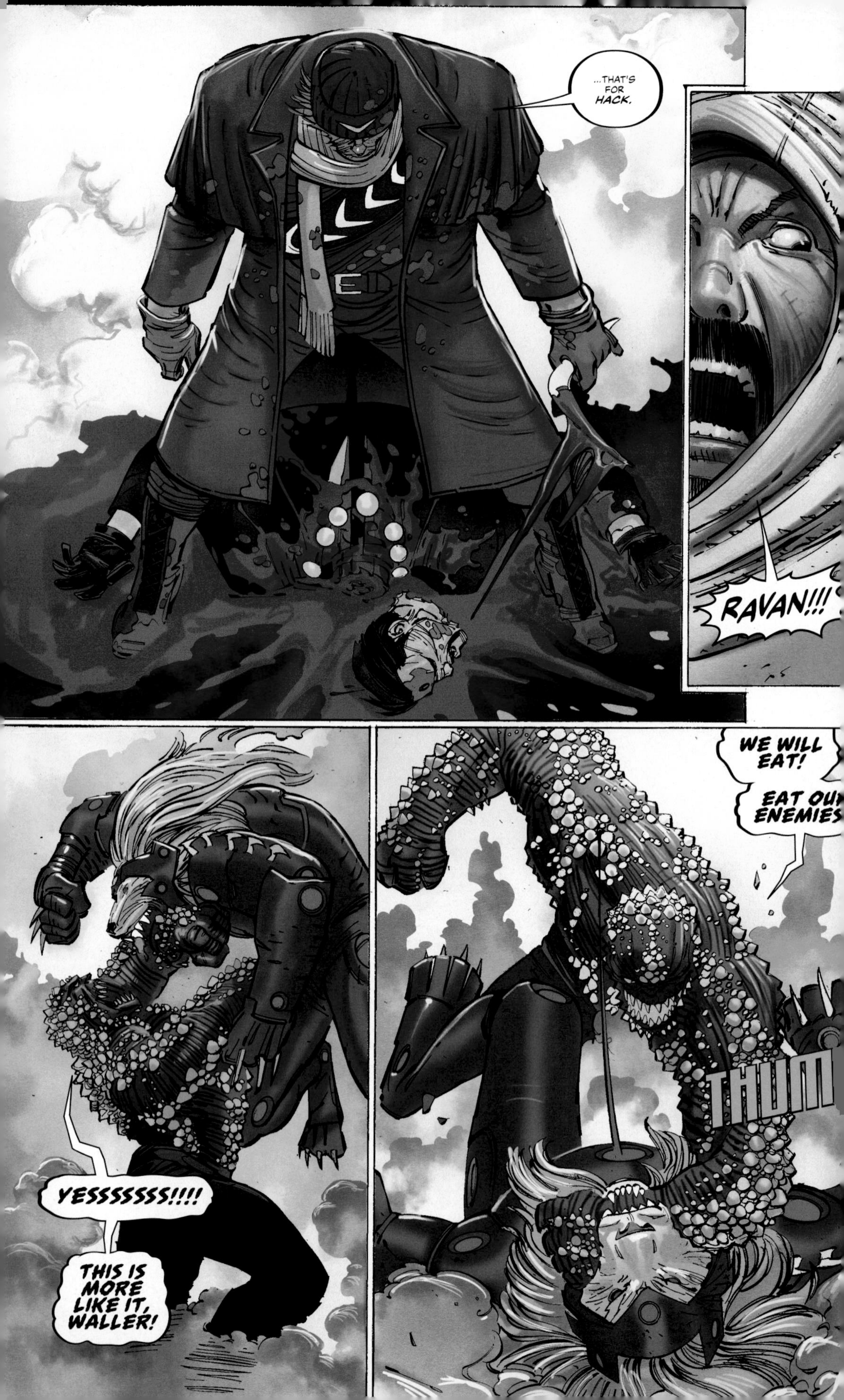
...THAT'S FOR HACK.
RAVAN!!!
YESSSSSSS!!!!
THIS IS MORE LIKE IT, WALLER!
WE WILL EAT!
EAT OU ENEMIES
THUM

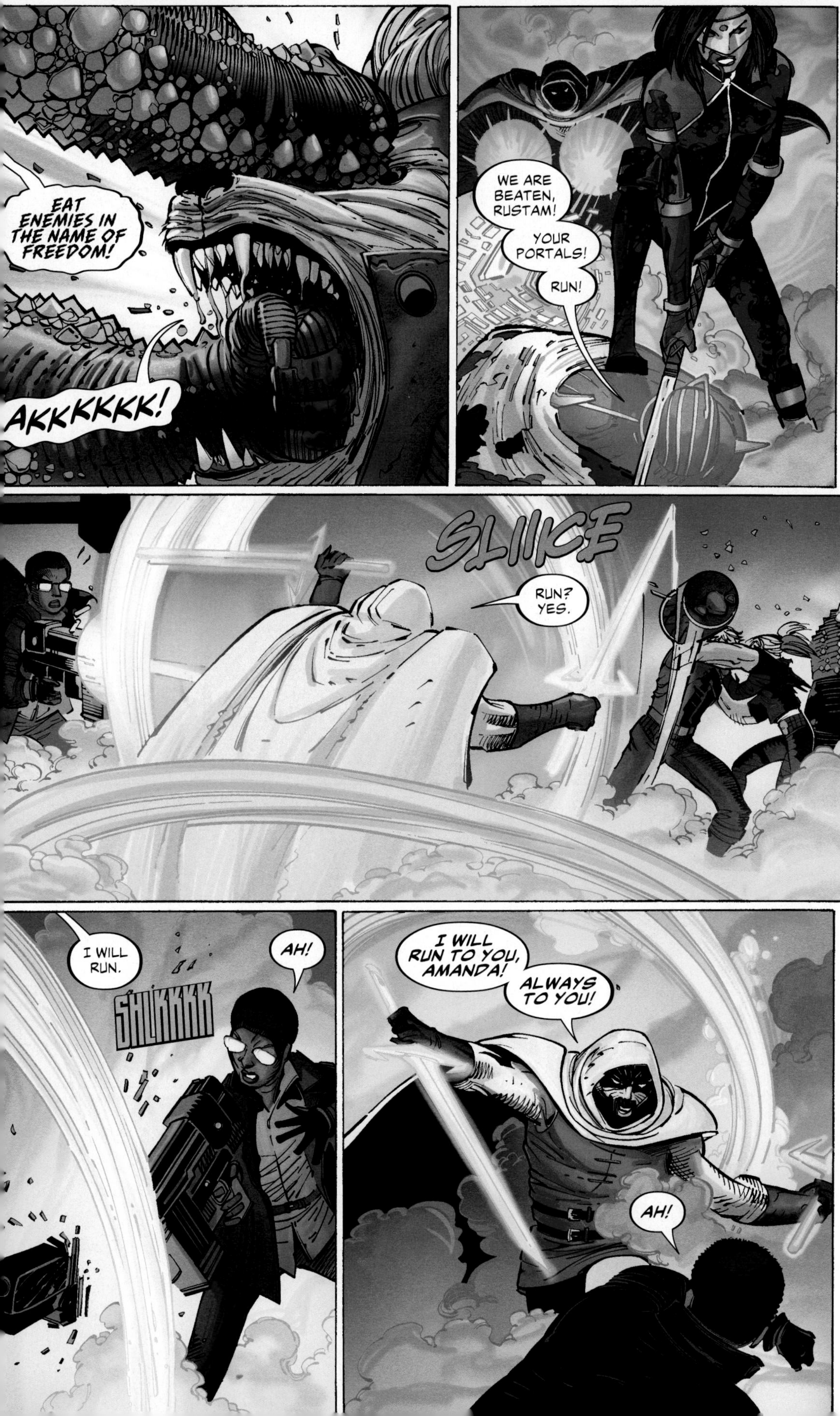
EAT ENEMIES IN THE NAME OF FREEDOM!
AKKKKKK!
WE ARE BEATEN, RUSTAM!
YOUR PORTALS!
RUN!
SLIICE
RUN? YES.
I WILL RUN.
AH!
SHLKKKK
I WILL RUN TO YOU, AMANDA!
ALWAYS TO YOU!
AH!

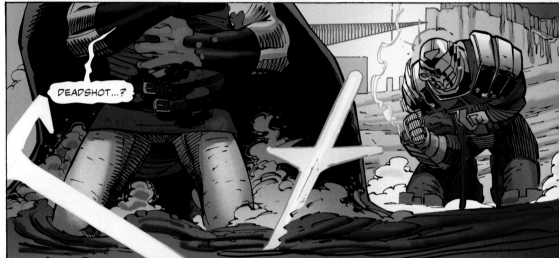

DEADSHOT...?

BUT...YOU FOLLOWED ME.

YOU KILLED FOR ME.

I SAID I'D GIVE YOU YOUR DAUGHTER.

...SO DID WALLER...

AND I FIGURED...

...SHE ALWAYS WINS.

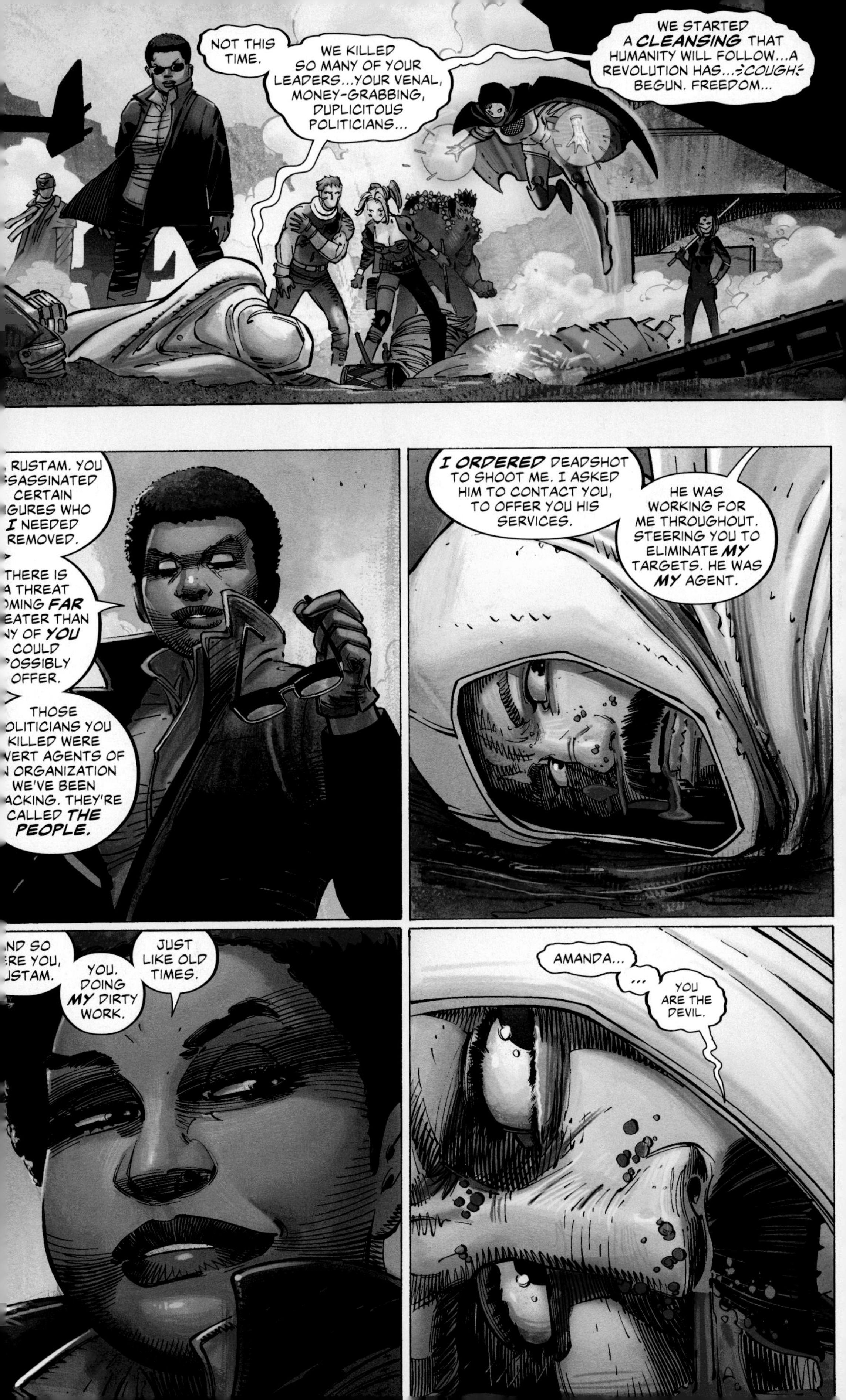

NOT THIS TIME.
WE KILLED SO MANY OF YOUR LEADERS...YOUR VENAL, MONEY-GRABBING, DUPLICITOUS POLITICIANS...
WE STARTED A **CLEANSING** THAT HUMANITY WILL FOLLOW...A REVOLUTION HAS...*COUGH* BEGUN. FREEDOM...
RUSTAM. YOU SSASSINATED CERTAIN IGURES WHO **I** NEEDED REMOVED.
THERE IS A THREAT OMING **FAR** EATER THAN NY OF **YOU** COULD POSSIBLY OFFER.
THOSE OLITICIANS YOU KILLED WERE VERT AGENTS OF N ORGANIZATION WE'VE BEEN ACKING. THEY'RE CALLED **THE PEOPLE.**
I ORDERED DEADSHOT TO SHOOT ME. I ASKED HIM TO CONTACT YOU, TO OFFER YOU HIS SERVICES.
HE WAS WORKING FOR ME THROUGHOUT. STEERING YOU TO ELIMINATE **MY** TARGETS. HE WAS **MY** AGENT.
ND SO ERE YOU, USTAM.
YOU. DOING **MY** DIRTY WORK.
JUST LIKE OLD TIMES.
AMANDA...
...
YOU ARE THE DEVIL.

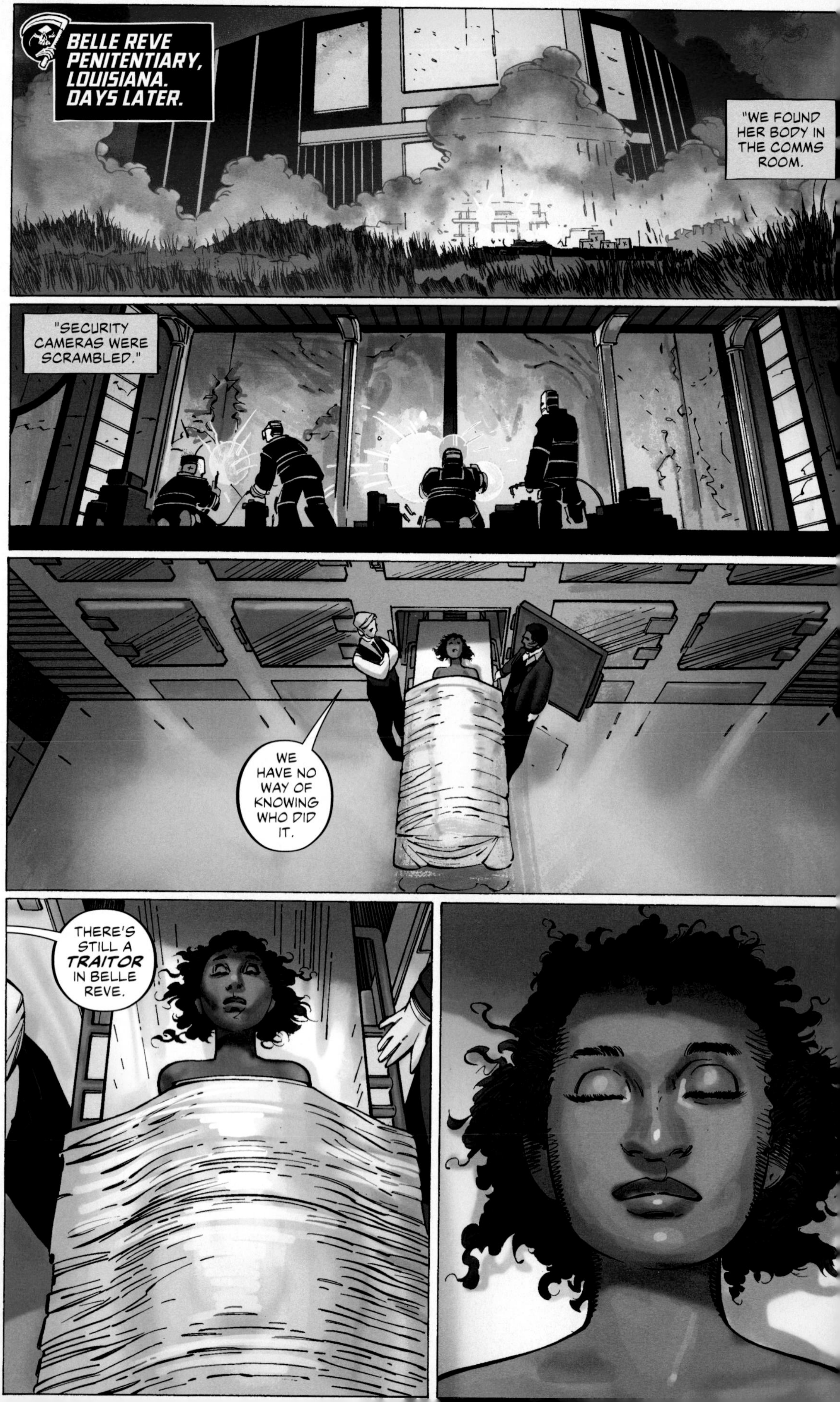
BELLE REVE PENITENTIARY, LOUISIANA. DAYS LATER.
"WE FOUND HER BODY IN THE COMMS ROOM.
"SECURITY CAMERAS WERE SCRAMBLED."
WE HAVE NO WAY OF KNOWING WHO DID IT.
THERE'S STILL A TRAITOR IN BELLE REVE.

SOME STAY DEAD...

I'M SORRY, HACK.

I WILL FIND OUT WHO KILLED THIS GIRL, HARCOURT. AND I WILL MAKE THEM *PAY.*

THE OUTSIDE.

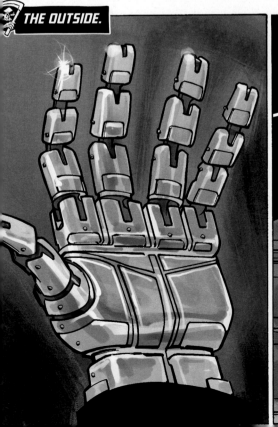

WELL, WELL.

IF IT ISN'T FLOYD LAWTON.

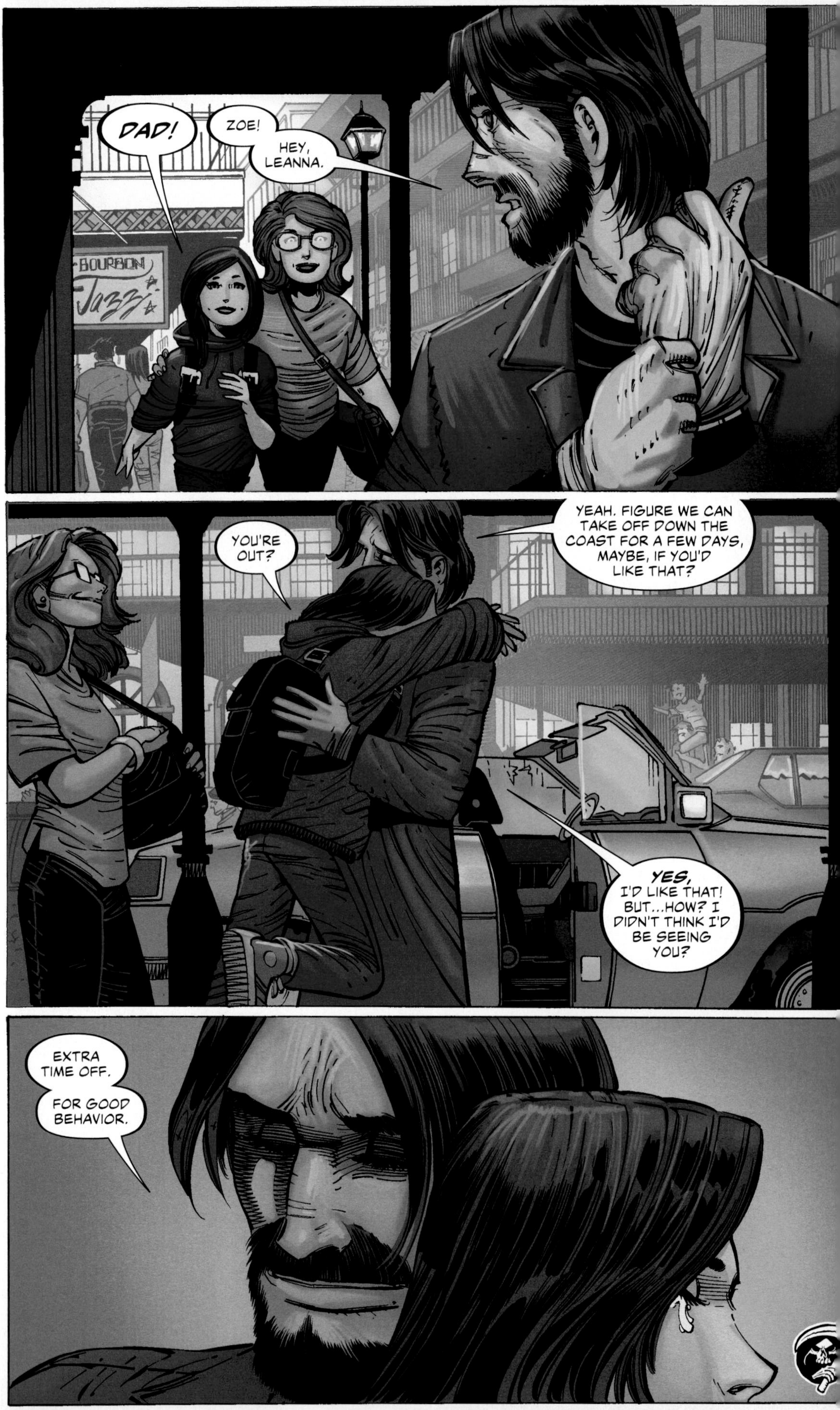
DAD!
ZOE!
HEY, LEANNA.
BOURBON Jazz
YOU'RE OUT?
YEAH. FIGURE WE CAN TAKE OFF DOWN THE COAST FOR A FEW DAYS, MAYBE, IF YOU'D LIKE THAT?
YES, I'D LIKE THAT! BUT...HOW? I DIDN'T THINK I'D BE SEEING YOU?
EXTRA TIME OFF.
FOR GOOD BEHAVIOR.

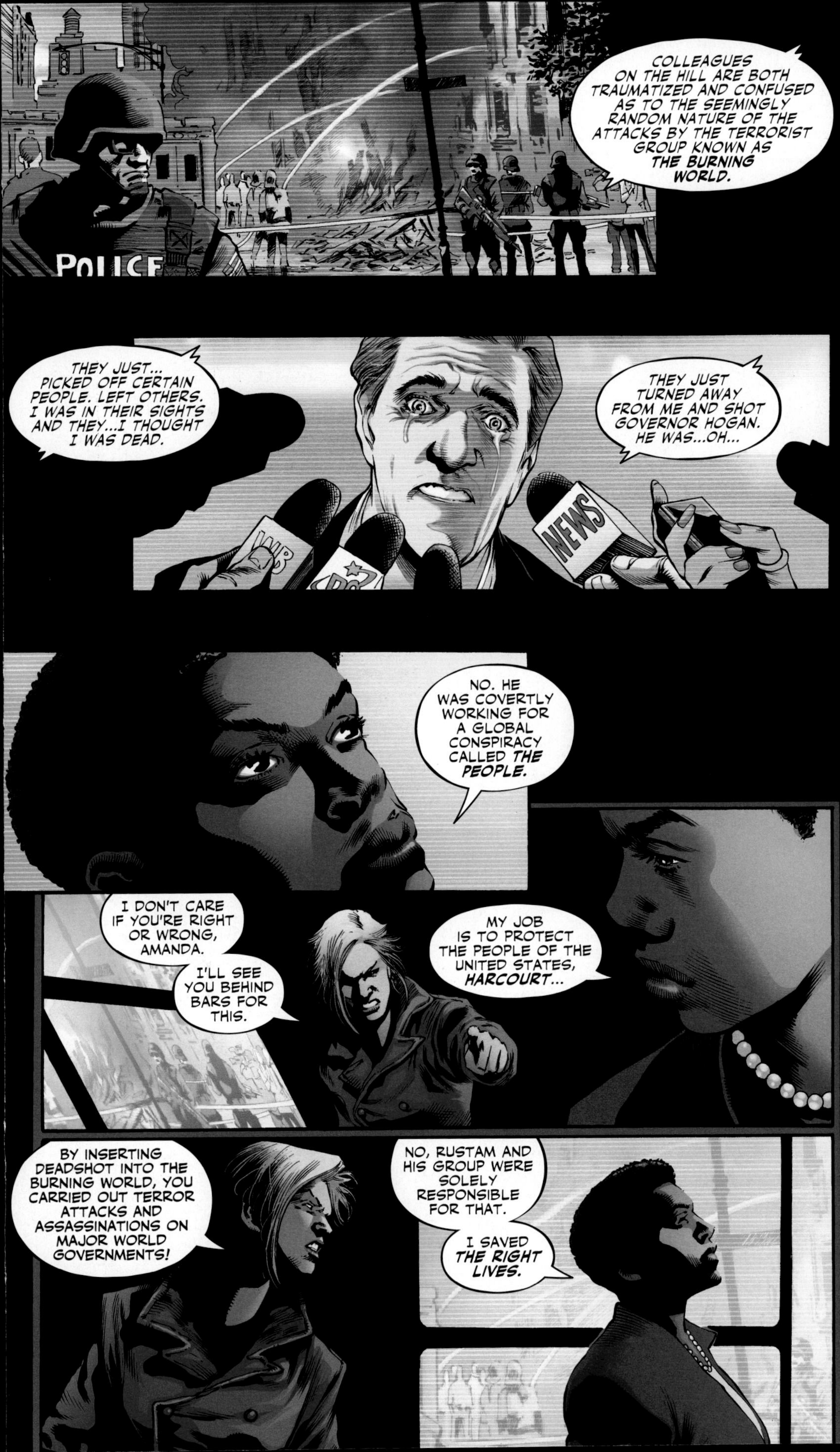
COLLEAGUES ON THE HILL ARE BOTH TRAUMATIZED AND CONFUSED AS TO THE SEEMINGLY RANDOM NATURE OF THE ATTACKS BY THE TERRORIST GROUP KNOWN AS THE BURNING WORLD.
POLICE
THEY JUST... PICKED OFF CERTAIN PEOPLE. LEFT OTHERS. I WAS IN THEIR SIGHTS AND THEY...I THOUGHT I WAS DEAD.
THEY JUST TURNED AWAY FROM ME AND SHOT GOVERNOR HOGAN. HE WAS...OH...
NEWS
NO. HE WAS COVERTLY WORKING FOR A GLOBAL CONSPIRACY CALLED THE PEOPLE.
I DON'T CARE IF YOU'RE RIGHT OR WRONG, AMANDA.
I'LL SEE YOU BEHIND BARS FOR THIS.
MY JOB IS TO PROTECT THE PEOPLE OF THE UNITED STATES, HARCOURT...
BY INSERTING DEADSHOT INTO THE BURNING WORLD, YOU CARRIED OUT TERROR ATTACKS AND ASSASSINATIONS ON MAJOR WORLD GOVERNMENTS!
NO, RUSTAM AND HIS GROUP WERE SOLELY RESPONSIBLE FOR THAT.
I SAVED THE RIGHT LIVES.

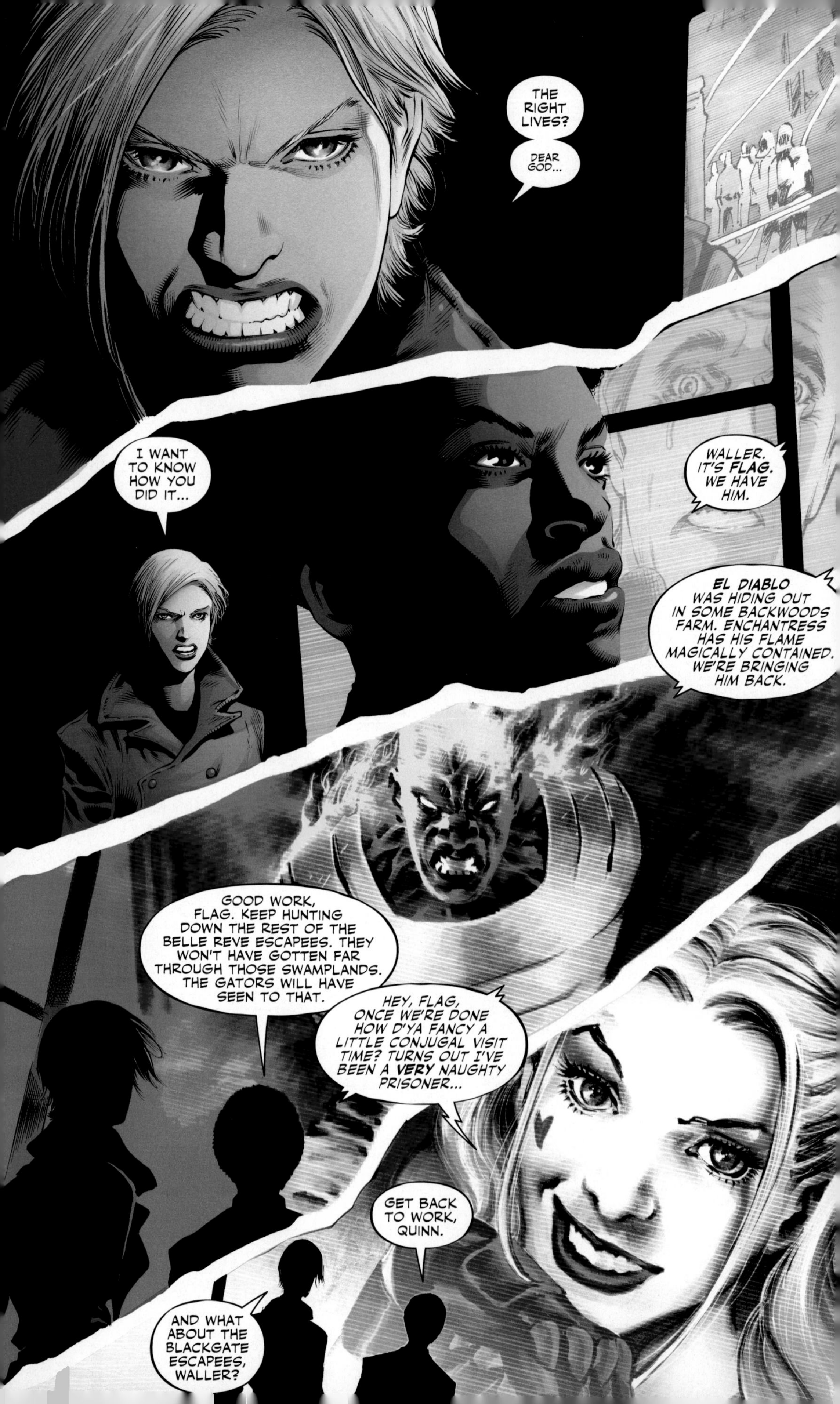
THE RIGHT LIVES?
DEAR GOD...
I WANT TO KNOW HOW YOU DID IT...
WALLER. IT'S FLAG. WE HAVE HIM.
EL DIABLO WAS HIDING OUT IN SOME BACKWOODS FARM. ENCHANTRESS HAS HIS FLAME MAGICALLY CONTAINED. WE'RE BRINGING HIM BACK.
GOOD WORK, FLAG. KEEP HUNTING DOWN THE REST OF THE BELLE REVE ESCAPEES. THEY WON'T HAVE GOTTEN FAR THROUGH THOSE SWAMPLANDS. THE GATORS WILL HAVE SEEN TO THAT.
HEY, FLAG, ONCE WE'RE DONE HOW D'YA FANCY A LITTLE CONJUGAL VISIT TIME? TURNS OUT I'VE BEEN A VERY NAUGHTY PRISONER...
GET BACK TO WORK, QUINN.
AND WHAT ABOUT THE BLACKGATE ESCAPEES, WALLER?

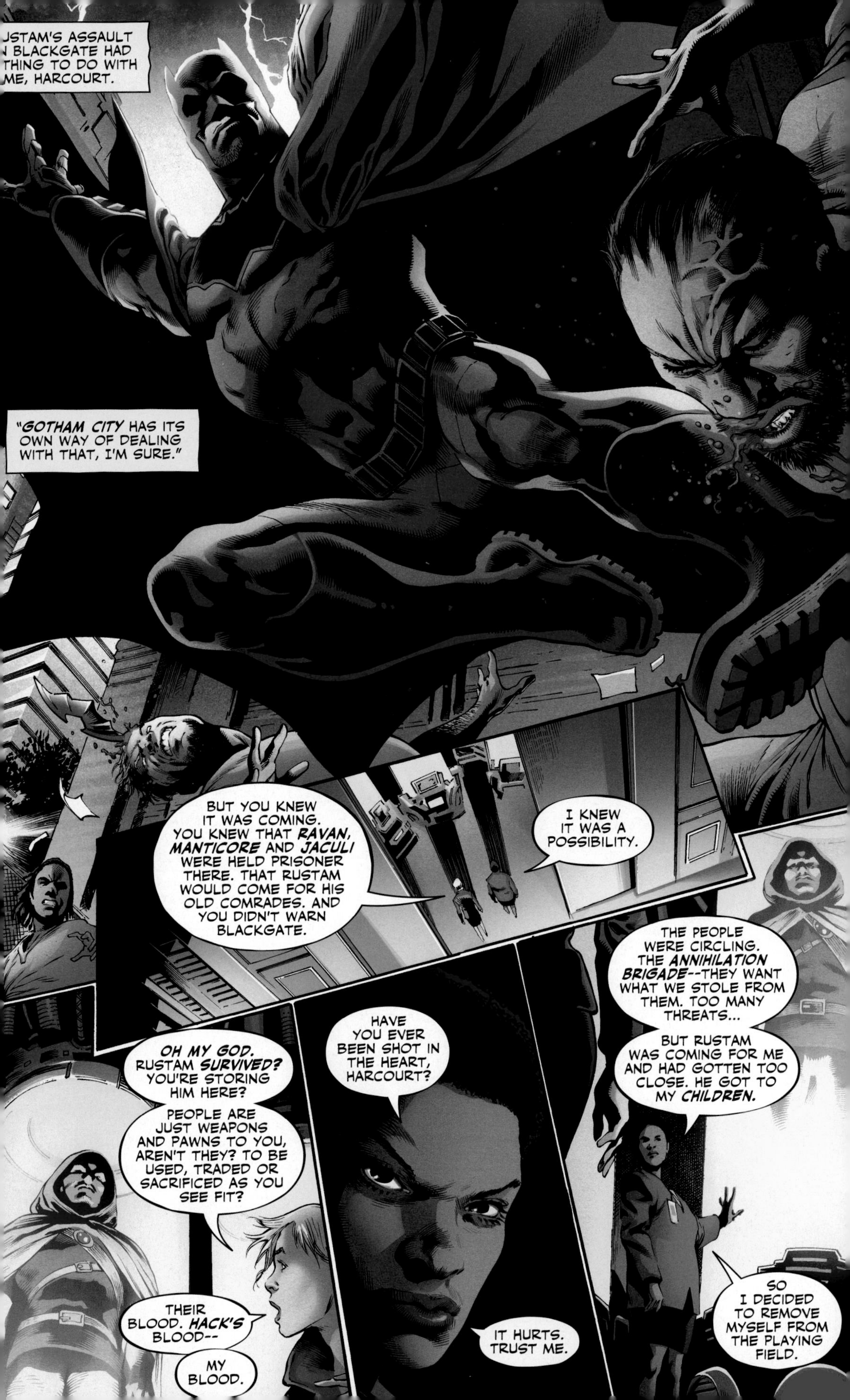

JSTAM'S ASSAULT
N BLACKGATE HAD
THING TO DO WITH
ME, HARCOURT.
"GOTHAM CITY HAS ITS
OWN WAY OF DEALING
WITH THAT, I'M SURE."
BUT YOU KNEW IT WAS COMING. YOU KNEW THAT RAVAN, MANTICORE AND JACULI WERE HELD PRISONER THERE. THAT RUSTAM WOULD COME FOR HIS OLD COMRADES. AND YOU DIDN'T WARN BLACKGATE.
I KNEW IT WAS A POSSIBILITY.
THE PEOPLE WERE CIRCLING. THE ANNIHILATION BRIGADE--THEY WANT WHAT WE STOLE FROM THEM. TOO MANY THREATS...
BUT RUSTAM WAS COMING FOR ME AND HAD GOTTEN TOO CLOSE. HE GOT TO MY CHILDREN.
OH MY GOD. RUSTAM SURVIVED? YOU'RE STORING HIM HERE?
PEOPLE ARE JUST WEAPONS AND PAWNS TO YOU, AREN'T THEY? TO BE USED, TRADED OR SACRIFICED AS YOU SEE FIT?
HAVE YOU EVER BEEN SHOT IN THE HEART, HARCOURT?
THEIR BLOOD. HACK'S BLOOD--
MY BLOOD.
IT HURTS. TRUST ME.
SO I DECIDED TO REMOVE MYSELF FROM THE PLAYING FIELD.

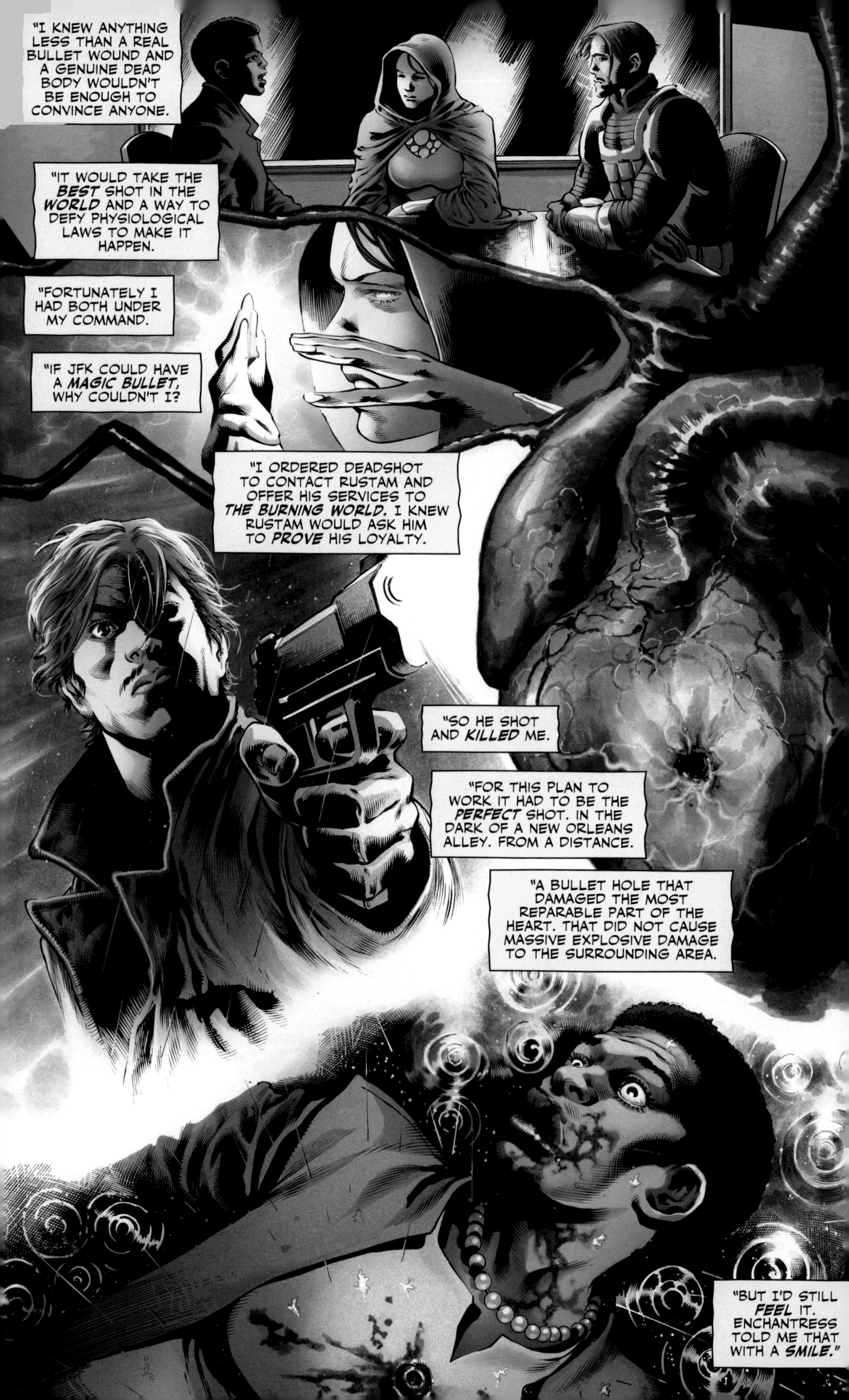
"I KNEW ANYTHING LESS THAN A REAL BULLET WOUND AND A GENUINE DEAD BODY WOULDN'T BE ENOUGH TO CONVINCE ANYONE.
"IT WOULD TAKE THE BEST SHOT IN THE WORLD AND A WAY TO DEFY PHYSIOLOGICAL LAWS TO MAKE IT HAPPEN.
"FORTUNATELY I HAD BOTH UNDER MY COMMAND.
"IF JFK COULD HAVE A MAGIC BULLET, WHY COULDN'T I?
"I ORDERED DEADSHOT TO CONTACT RUSTAM AND OFFER HIS SERVICES TO THE BURNING WORLD. I KNEW RUSTAM WOULD ASK HIM TO PROVE HIS LOYALTY.
"SO HE SHOT AND KILLED ME.
"FOR THIS PLAN TO WORK IT HAD TO BE THE PERFECT SHOT. IN THE DARK OF A NEW ORLEANS ALLEY. FROM A DISTANCE.
"A BULLET HOLE THAT DAMAGED THE MOST REPARABLE PART OF THE HEART. THAT DID NOT CAUSE MASSIVE EXPLOSIVE DAMAGE TO THE SURROUNDING AREA.
"BUT I'D STILL FEEL IT. ENCHANTRESS TOLD ME THAT WITH A SMILE."

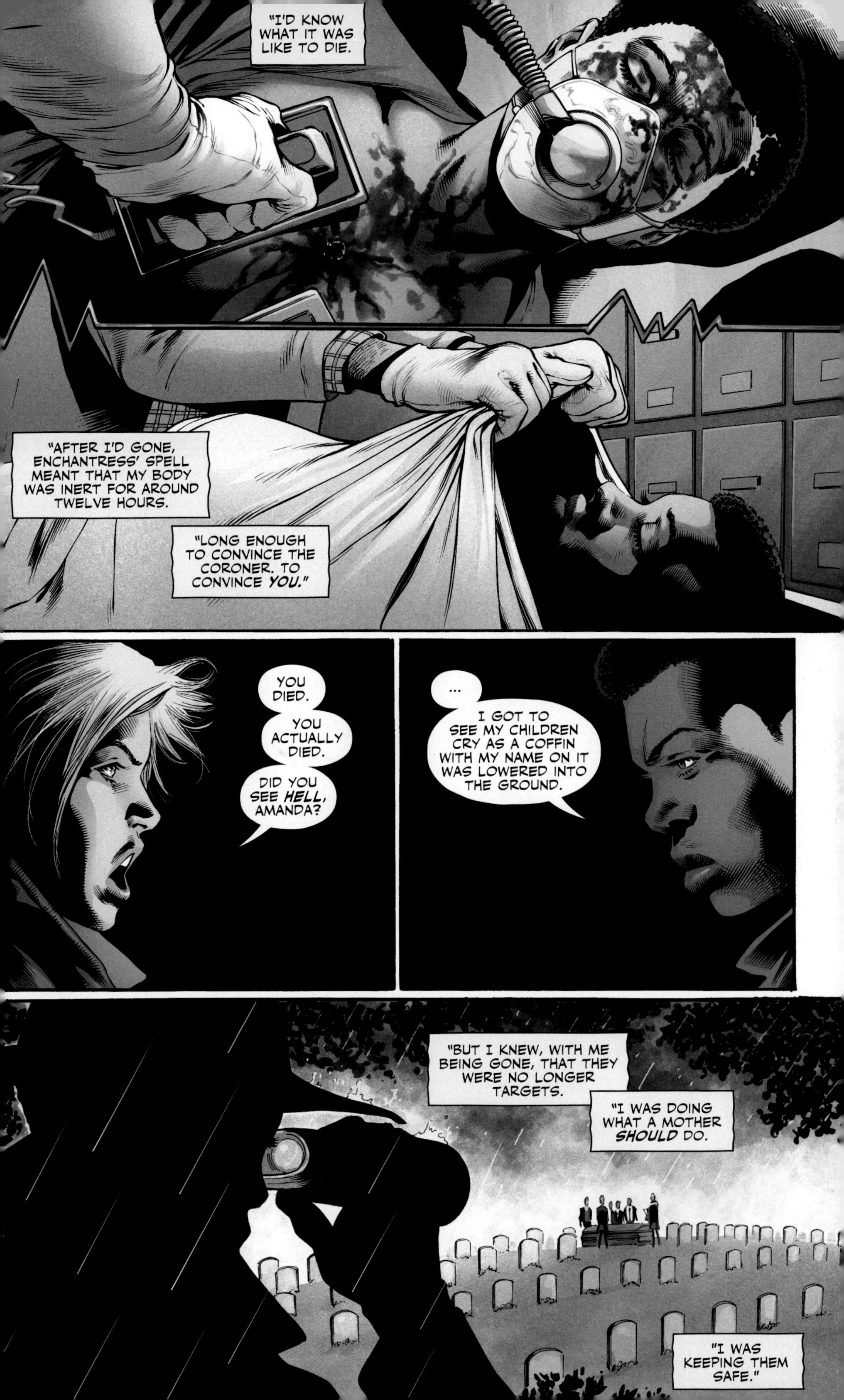

"I'D KNOW WHAT IT WAS LIKE TO DIE.
"AFTER I'D GONE, ENCHANTRESS' SPELL MEANT THAT MY BODY WAS INERT FOR AROUND TWELVE HOURS.
"LONG ENOUGH TO CONVINCE THE CORONER. TO CONVINCE *YOU.*"
YOU DIED.
YOU ACTUALLY DIED.
DID YOU SEE *HELL,* AMANDA?
...
I GOT TO SEE MY CHILDREN CRY AS A COFFIN WITH MY NAME ON IT WAS LOWERED INTO THE GROUND.
"BUT I KNEW, WITH ME BEING GONE, THAT THEY WERE NO LONGER TARGETS.
"I WAS DOING WHAT A MOTHER *SHOULD* DO.
"I WAS KEEPING THEM SAFE."

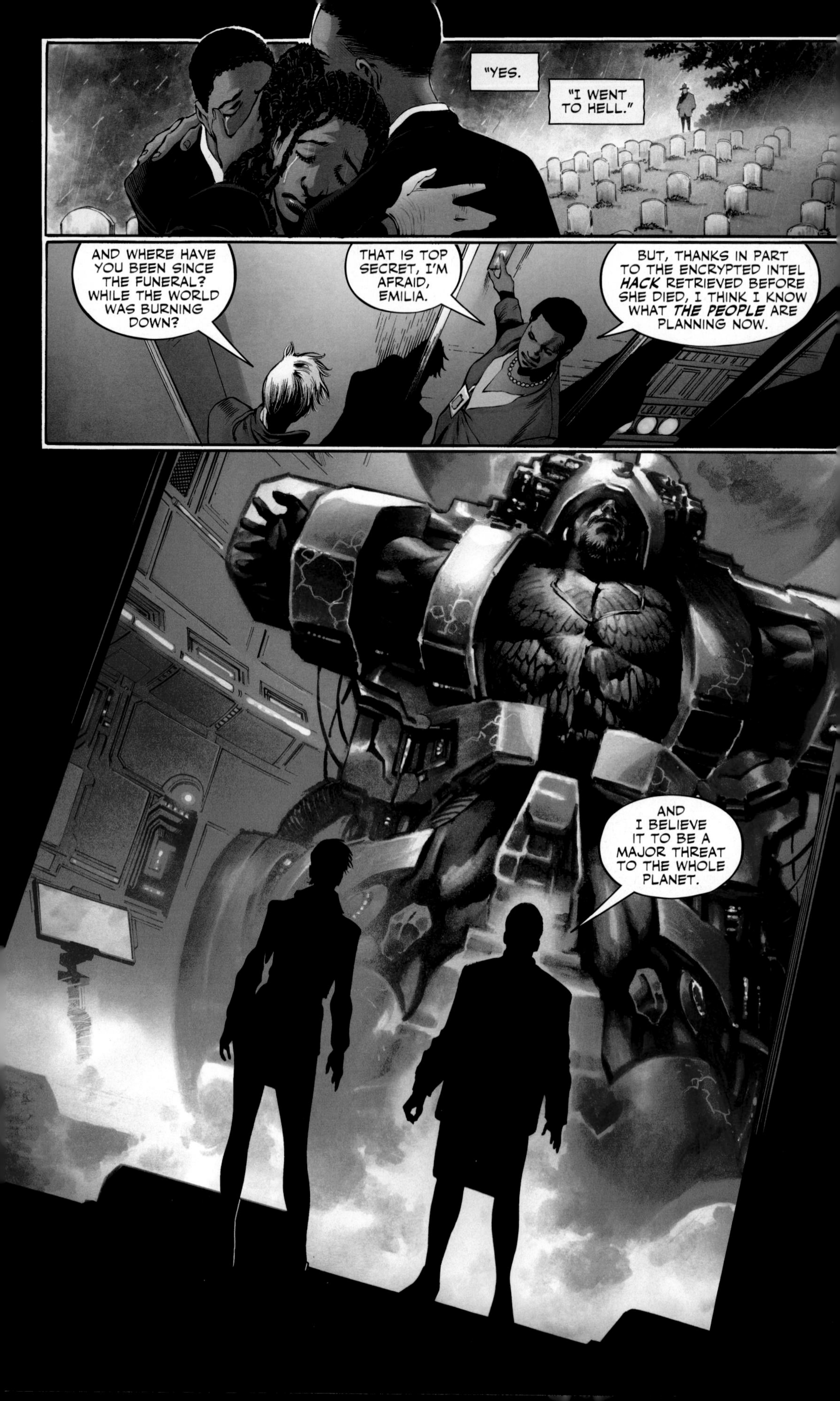
"YES.
"I WENT TO HELL."
AND WHERE HAVE YOU BEEN SINCE THE FUNERAL? WHILE THE WORLD WAS BURNING DOWN?
THAT IS TOP SECRET, I'M AFRAID, EMILIA.
BUT, THANKS IN PART TO THE ENCRYPTED INTEL HACK RETRIEVED BEFORE SHE DIED, I THINK I KNOW WHAT THE PEOPLE ARE PLANNING NOW.
AND I BELIEVE IT TO BE A MAJOR THREAT TO THE WHOLE PLANET.

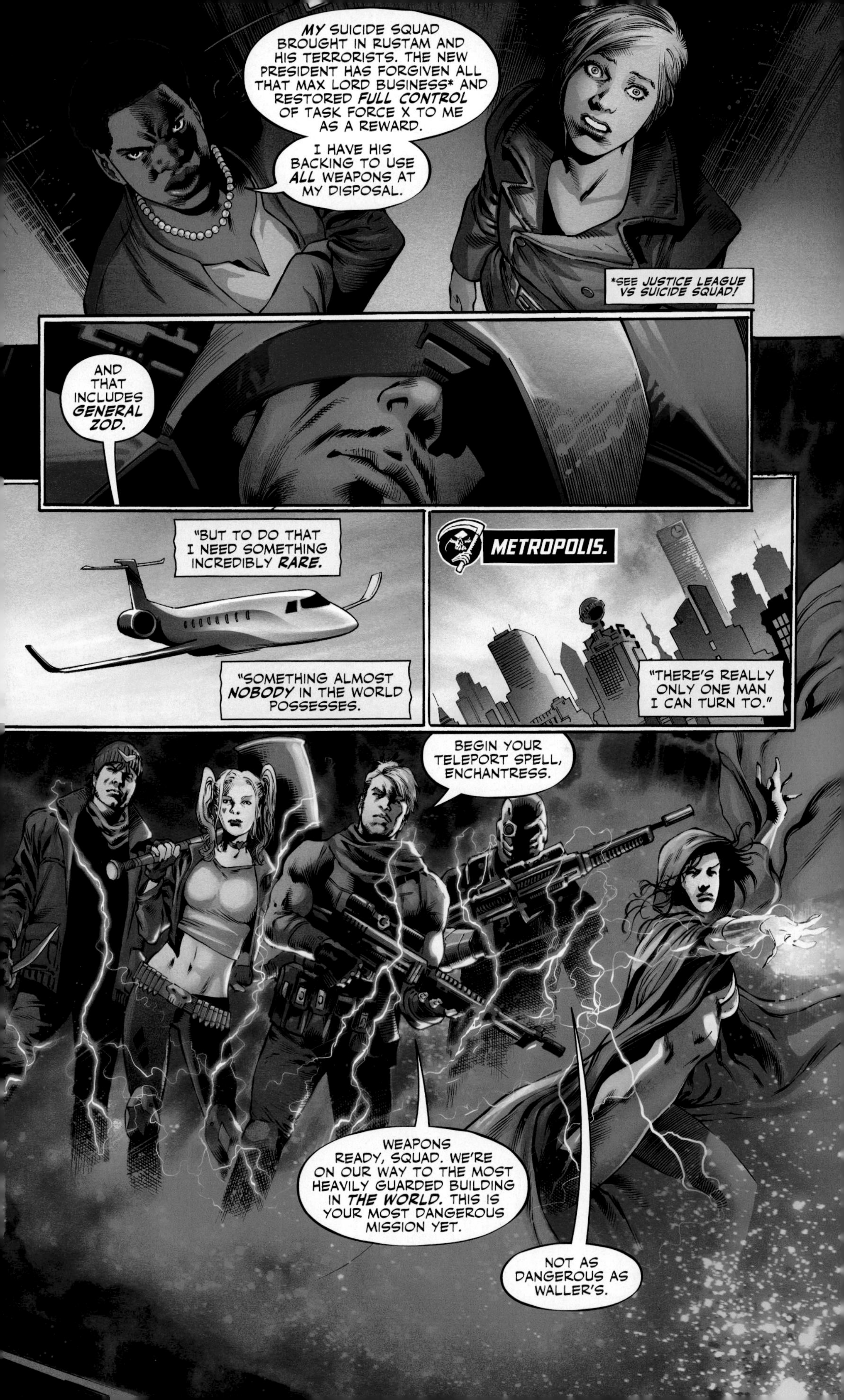
MY SUICIDE SQUAD BROUGHT IN RUSTAM AND HIS TERRORISTS. THE NEW PRESIDENT HAS FORGIVEN ALL THAT MAX LORD BUSINESS* AND RESTORED *FULL CONTROL* OF TASK FORCE X TO ME AS A REWARD.
I HAVE HIS BACKING TO USE *ALL* WEAPONS AT MY DISPOSAL.
*SEE *JUSTICE LEAGUE VS SUICIDE SQUAD!*
AND THAT INCLUDES *GENERAL ZOD.*
"BUT TO DO THAT I NEED SOMETHING INCREDIBLY *RARE.*
"SOMETHING ALMOST *NOBODY* IN THE WORLD POSSESSES.
METROPOLIS.
"THERE'S REALLY ONLY ONE MAN I CAN TURN TO."
BEGIN YOUR TELEPORT SPELL, ENCHANTRESS.
WEAPONS READY, SQUAD. WE'RE ON OUR WAY TO THE MOST HEAVILY GUARDED BUILDING IN *THE WORLD.* THIS IS YOUR MOST DANGEROUS MISSION YET.
NOT AS DANGEROUS AS WALLER'S.

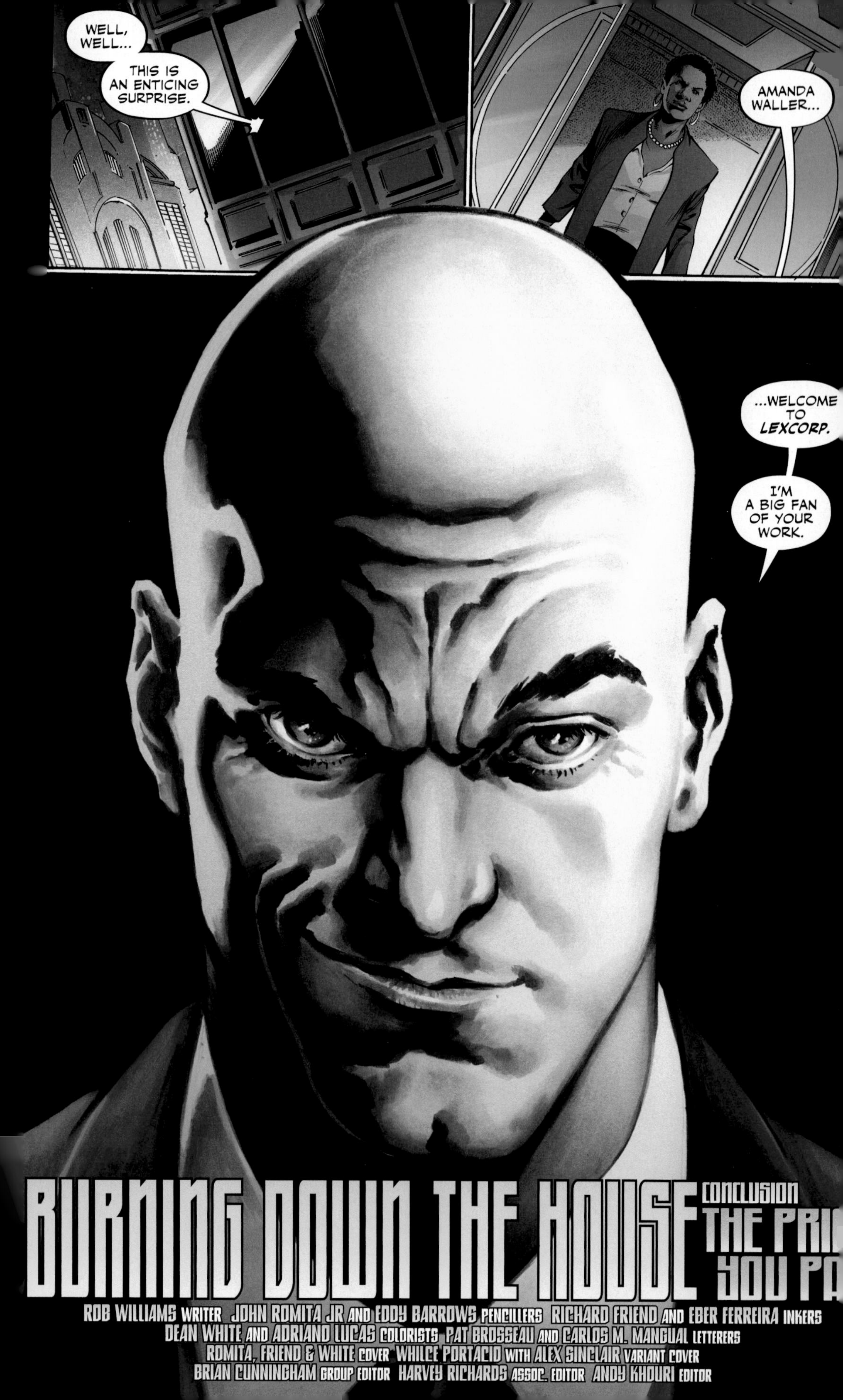

WELL, WELL...
THIS IS AN ENTICING SURPRISE.
AMANDA WALLER...
...WELCOME TO LEXCORP.
I'M A BIG FAN OF YOUR WORK.
BURNING DOWN THE HOUSE CONCLUSION THE PRI YOU PA
ROB WILLIAMS WRITER JOHN ROMITA JR AND EDDY BARROWS PENCILLERS RICHARD FRIEND AND EBER FERREIRA INKERS
DEAN WHITE AND ADRIANO LUCAS COLORISTS PAT BROSSEAU AND CARLOS M. MANGUAL LETTERERS
ROMITA, FRIEND & WHITE COVER WHILCE PORTACIO WITH ALEX SINCLAIR VARIANT COVER
BRIAN CUNNINGHAM GROUP EDITOR HARVEY RICHARDS ASSOC. EDITOR ANDY KHOURI EDITOR

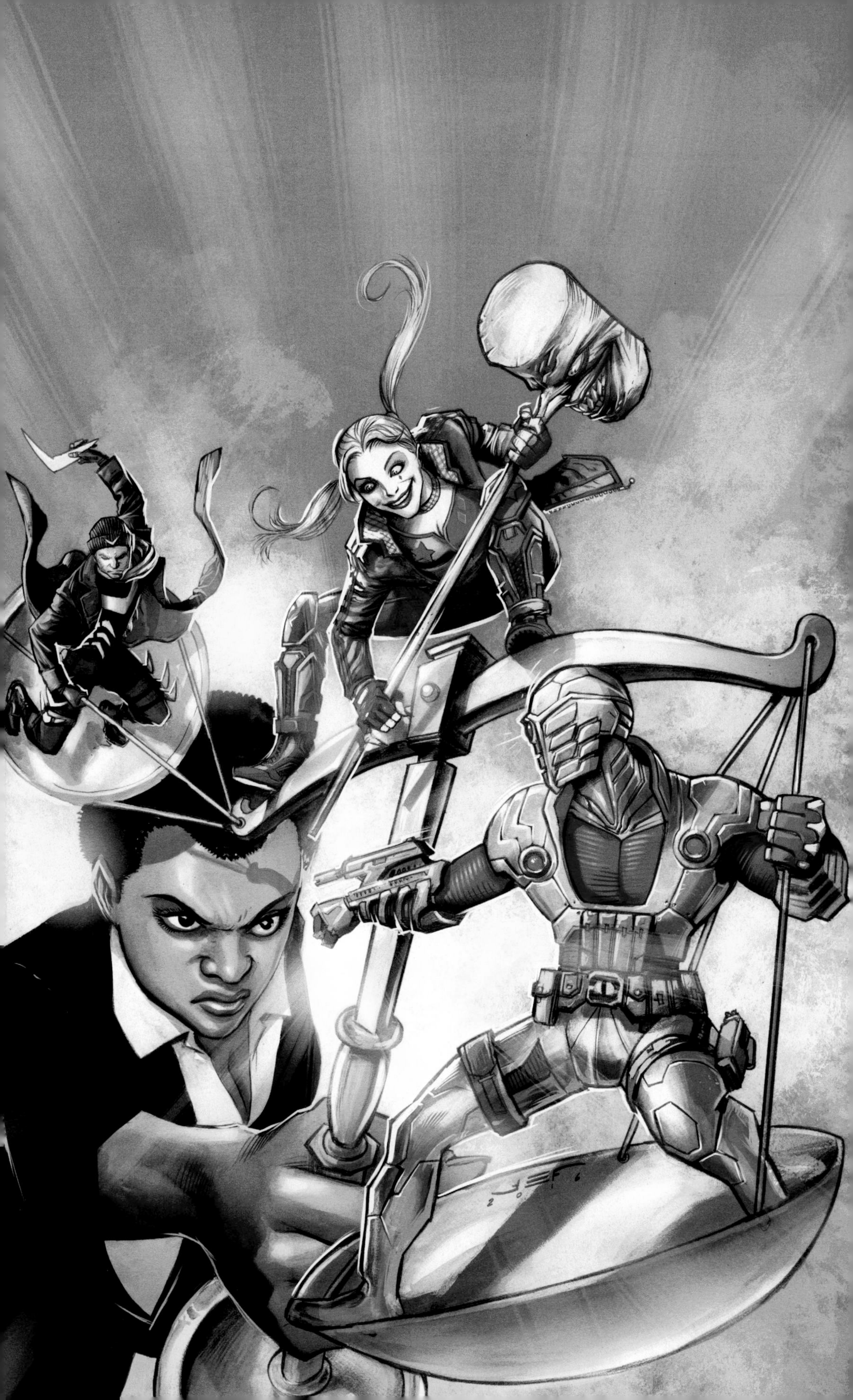

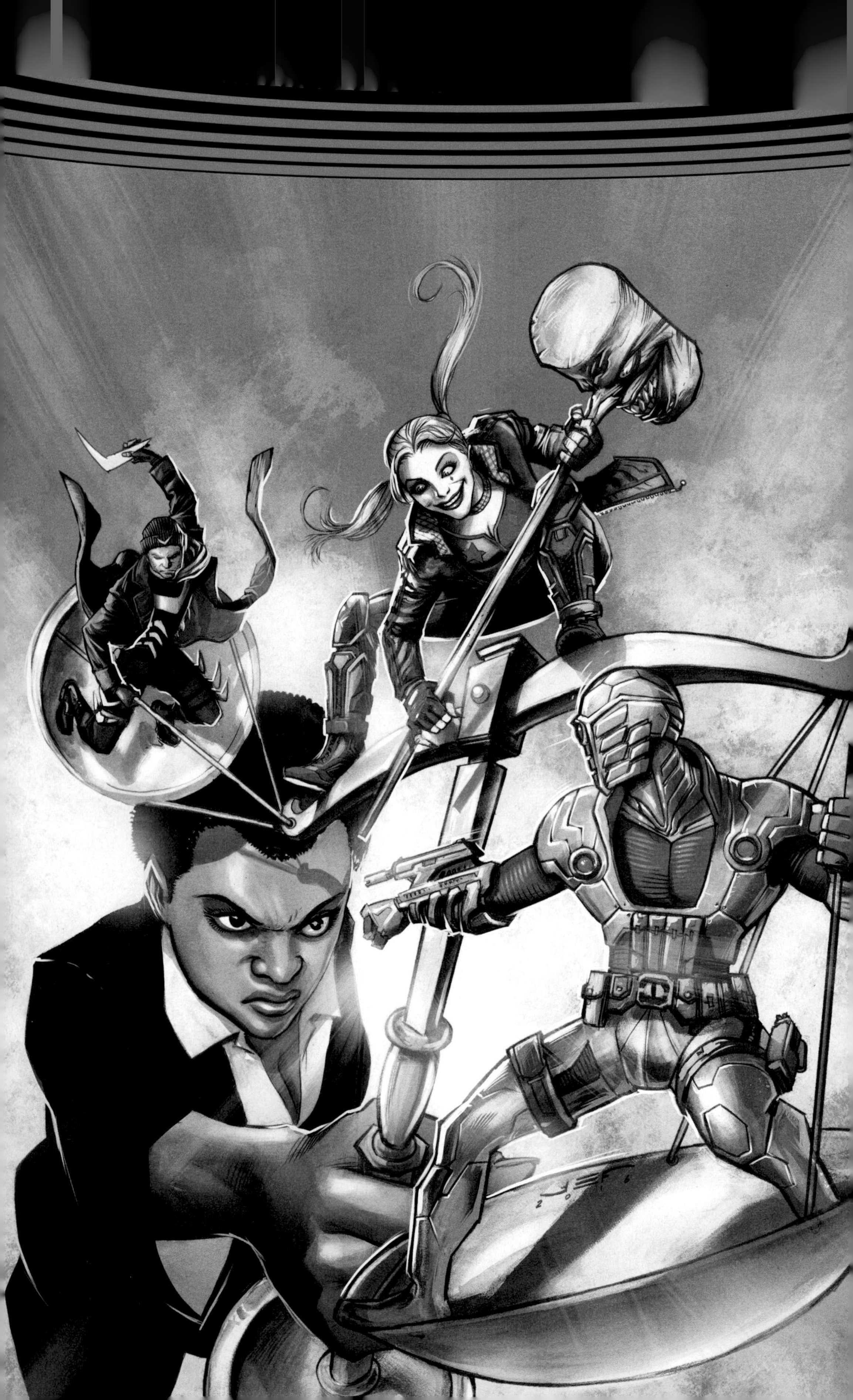

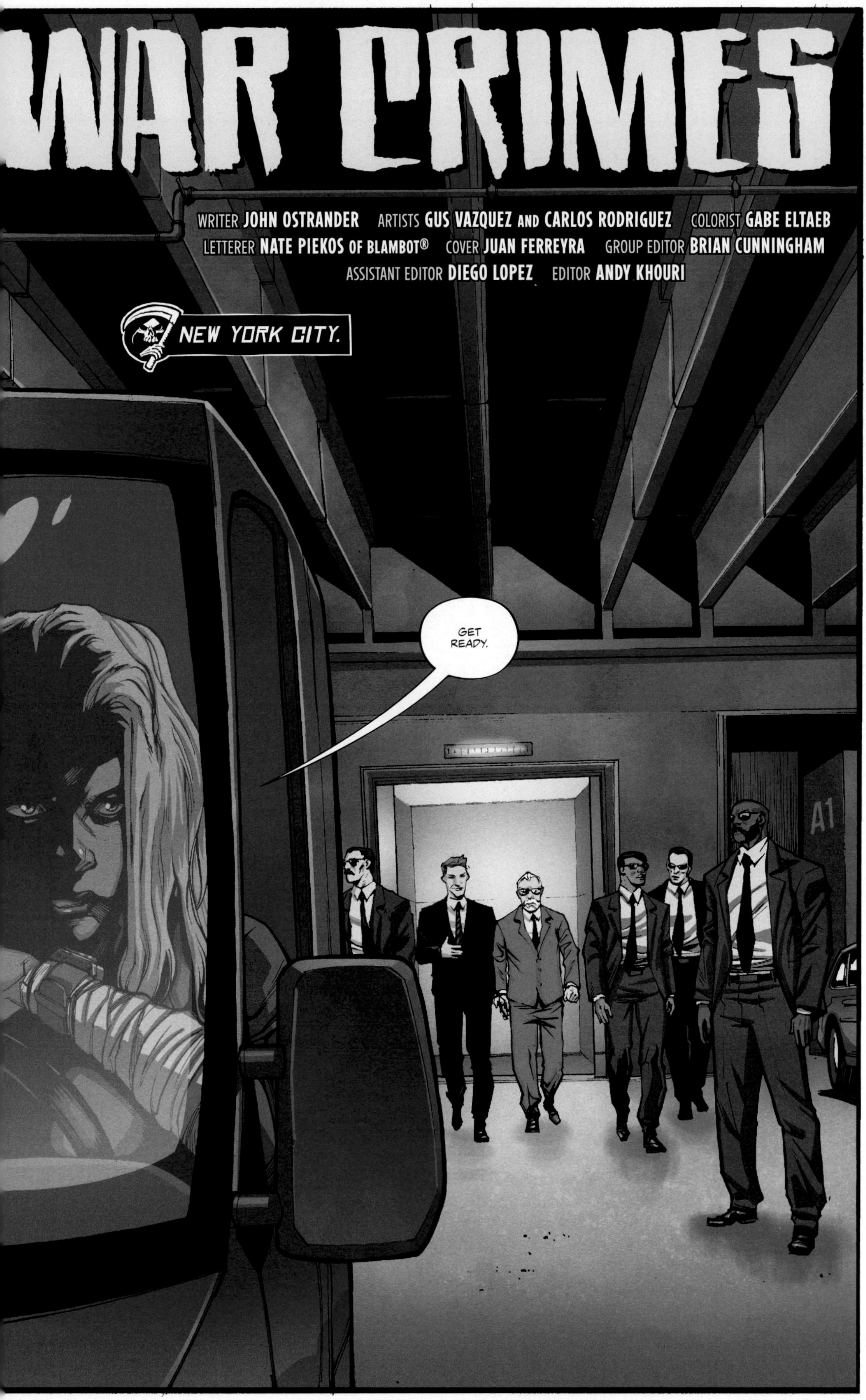
WAR CRIMES
WRITER JOHN OSTRANDER ARTISTS GUS VAZQUEZ AND CARLOS RODRIGUEZ COLORIST GABE ELTAEB
LETTERER NATE PIEKOS OF BLAMBOT® COVER JUAN FERREYRA GROUP EDITOR BRIAN CUNNINGHAM
ASSISTANT EDITOR DIEGO LOPEZ EDITOR ANDY KHOURI
NEW YORK CITY.
GET READY.
A1

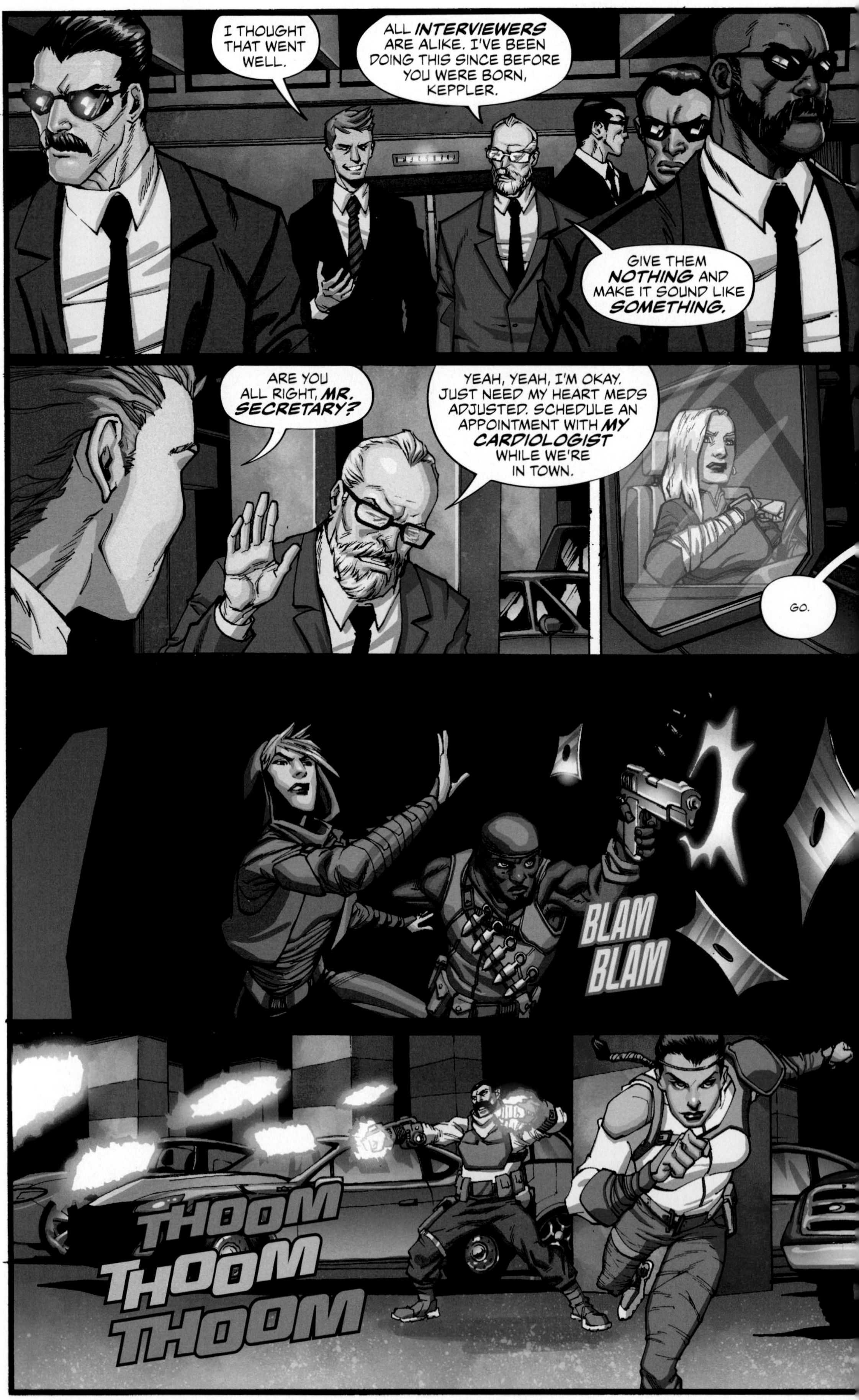

I THOUGHT THAT WENT WELL.
ALL INTERVIEWERS ARE ALIKE. I'VE BEEN DOING THIS SINCE BEFORE YOU WERE BORN, KEPPLER.
GIVE THEM NOTHING AND MAKE IT SOUND LIKE SOMETHING.
ARE YOU ALL RIGHT, MR. SECRETARY?
YEAH, YEAH, I'M OKAY. JUST NEED MY HEART MEDS ADJUSTED. SCHEDULE AN APPOINTMENT WITH MY CARDIOLOGIST WHILE WE'RE IN TOWN.
GO.
BLAM BLAM
THOOM THOOM THOOM

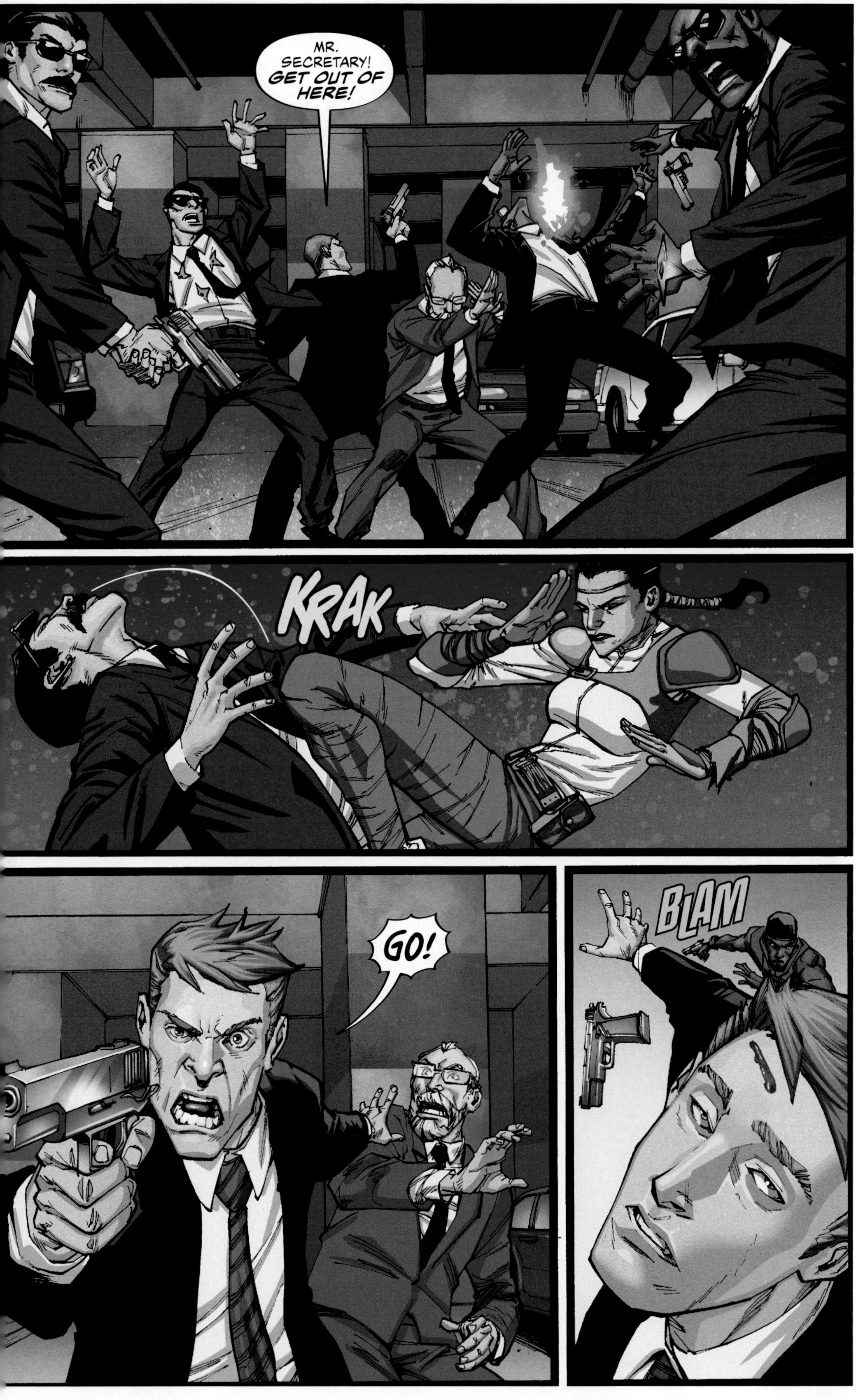
MR. SECRETARY! GET OUT OF HERE!
KRAK
GO!
BLAM

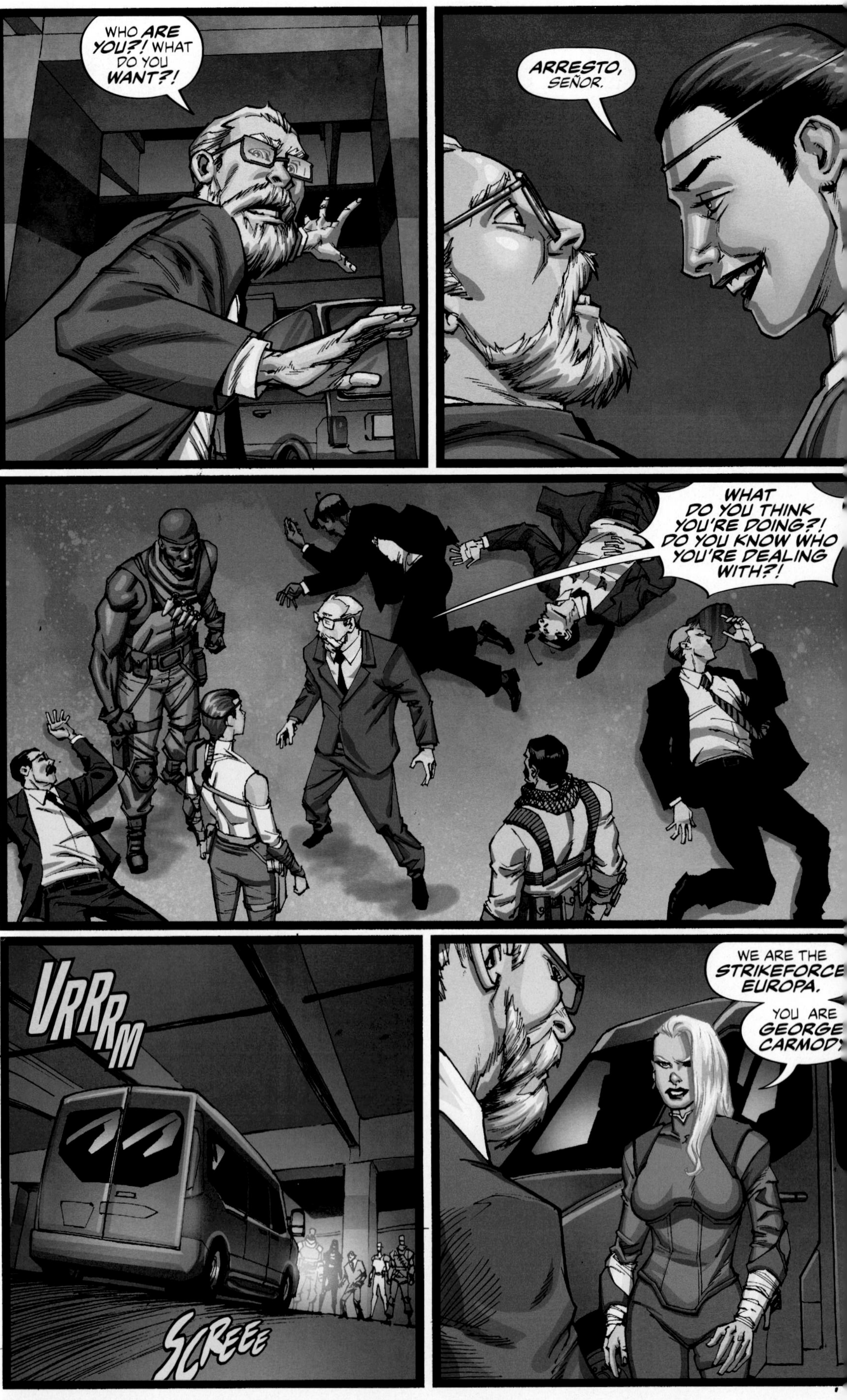
WHO ARE YOU?! WHAT DO YOU WANT?!
ARRESTO, SEÑOR.
WHAT DO YOU THINK YOU'RE DOING?! DO YOU KNOW WHO YOU'RE DEALING WITH?!
URRRM
SCREEE
WE ARE THE STRIKEFORCE EUROPA.
YOU ARE GEORGE CARMOD

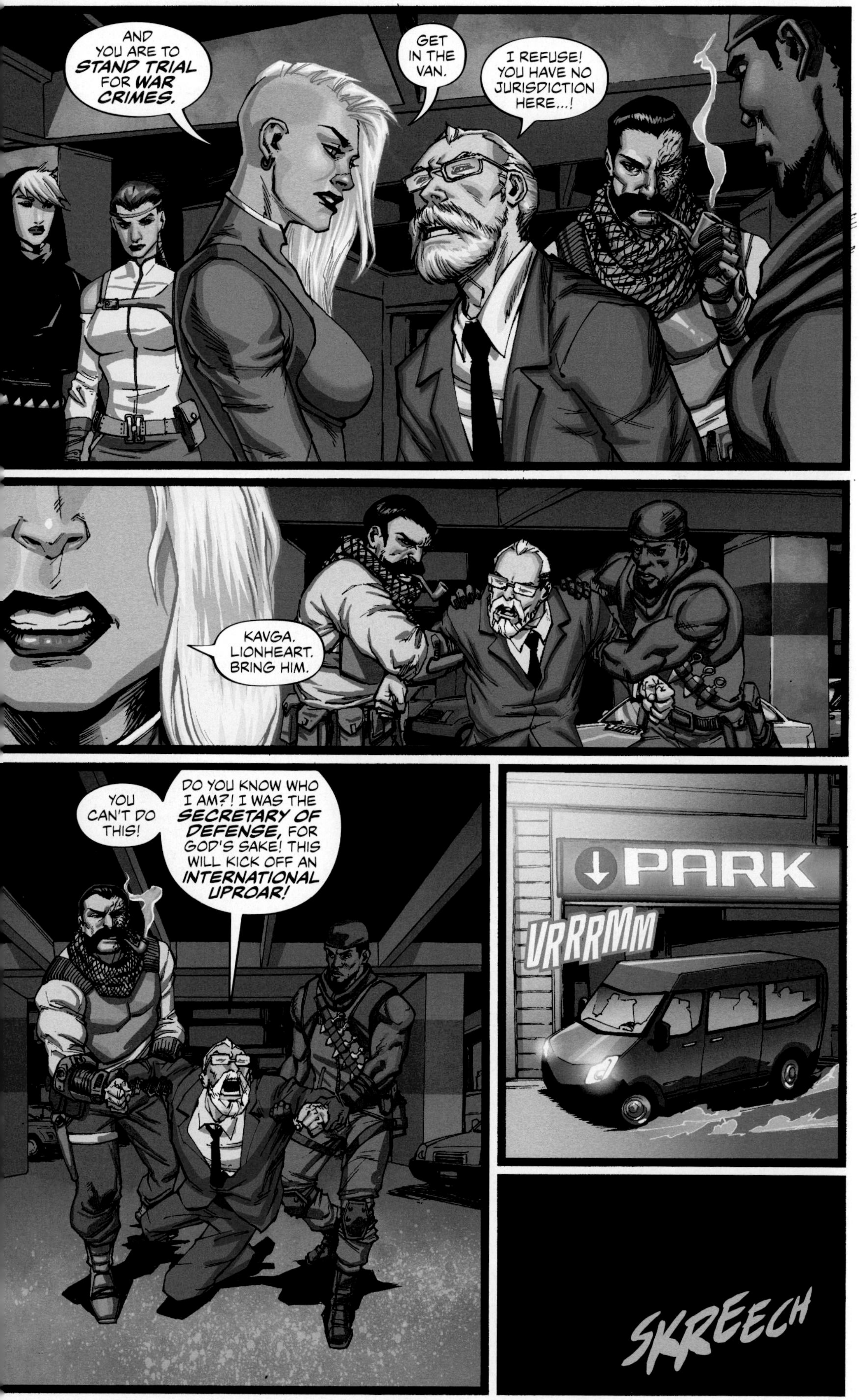
AND YOU ARE TO STAND TRIAL FOR WAR CRIMES.
GET IN THE VAN.
I REFUSE! YOU HAVE NO JURISDICTION HERE...!
KAVGA. LIONHEART. BRING HIM.
YOU CAN'T DO THIS!
DO YOU KNOW WHO I AM?! I WAS THE SECRETARY OF DEFENSE, FOR GOD'S SAKE! THIS WILL KICK OFF AN INTERNATIONAL UPROAR!
PARK
VRRRMM
SKREECH

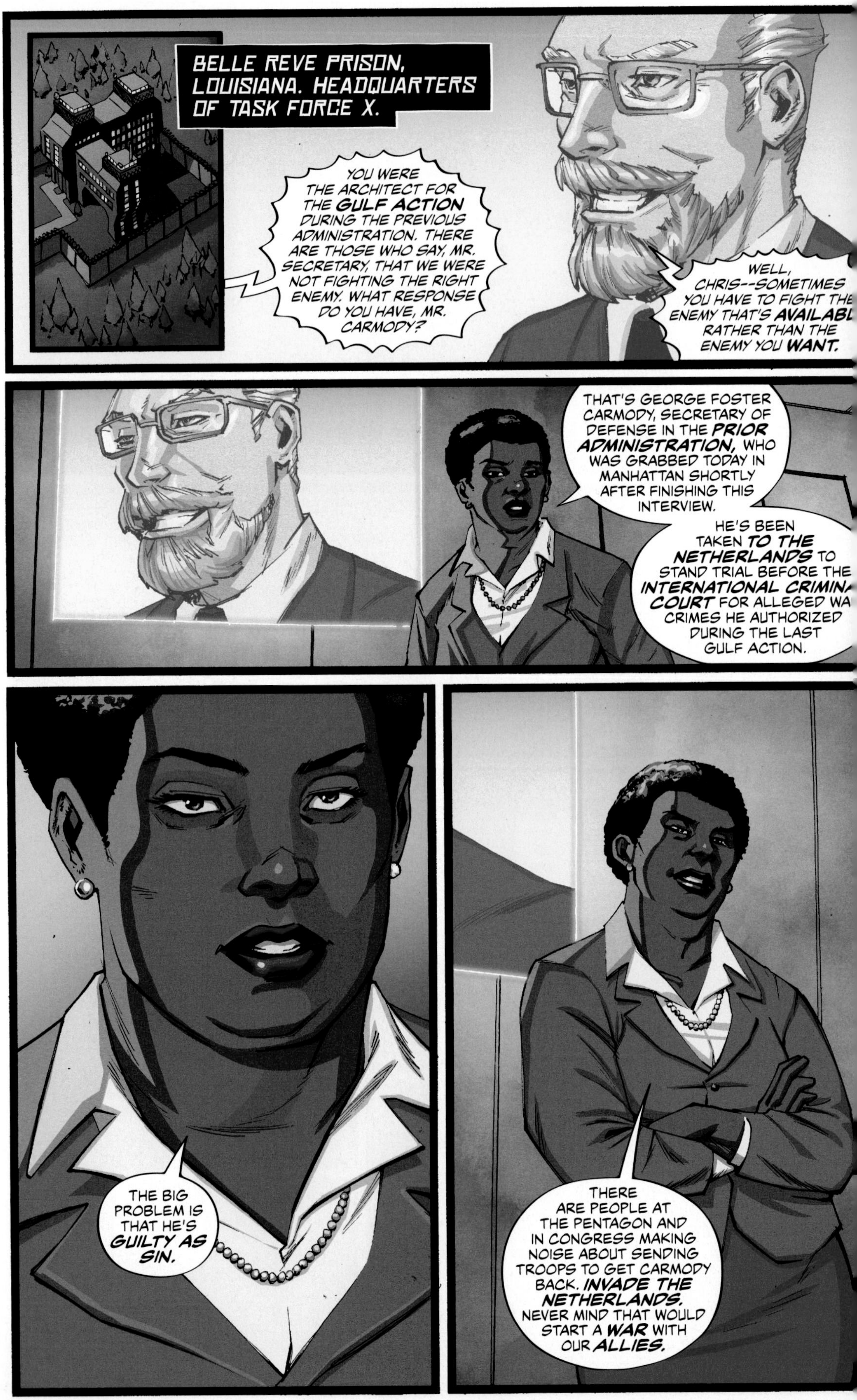
BELLE REVE PRISON, LOUISIANA. HEADQUARTERS OF TASK FORCE X.
YOU WERE THE ARCHITECT FOR THE GULF ACTION DURING THE PREVIOUS ADMINISTRATION. THERE ARE THOSE WHO SAY, MR. SECRETARY, THAT WE WERE NOT FIGHTING THE RIGHT ENEMY. WHAT RESPONSE DO YOU HAVE, MR. CARMODY?
WELL, CHRIS--SOMETIMES YOU HAVE TO FIGHT THE ENEMY THAT'S AVAILABL RATHER THAN THE ENEMY YOU WANT.
THAT'S GEORGE FOSTER CARMODY, SECRETARY OF DEFENSE IN THE PRIOR ADMINISTRATION, WHO WAS GRABBED TODAY IN MANHATTAN SHORTLY AFTER FINISHING THIS INTERVIEW.
HE'S BEEN TAKEN TO THE NETHERLANDS TO STAND TRIAL BEFORE THE INTERNATIONAL CRIMINA COURT FOR ALLEGED WA CRIMES HE AUTHORIZED DURING THE LAST GULF ACTION.
THE BIG PROBLEM IS THAT HE'S GUILTY AS SIN.
THERE ARE PEOPLE AT THE PENTAGON AND IN CONGRESS MAKING NOISE ABOUT SENDING TROOPS TO GET CARMODY BACK. INVADE THE NETHERLANDS. NEVER MIND THAT WOULD START A WAR WITH OUR ALLIES.

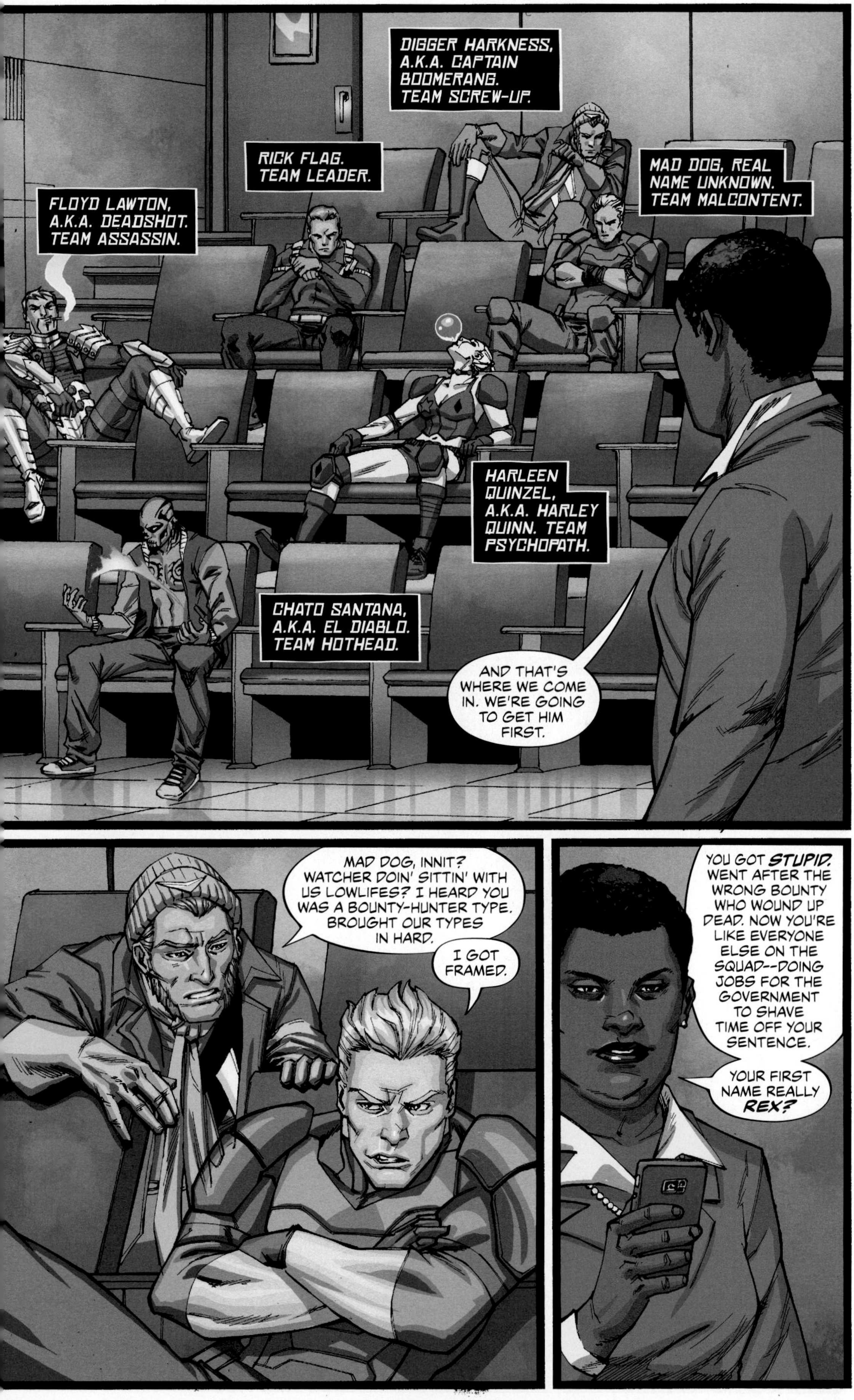
FLOYD LAWTON, A.K.A. DEADSHOT. TEAM ASSASSIN.
RICK FLAG. TEAM LEADER.
DIGGER HARKNESS, A.K.A. CAPTAIN BOOMERANG. TEAM SCREW-UP.
MAD DOG, REAL NAME UNKNOWN. TEAM MALCONTENT.
HARLEEN QUINZEL, A.K.A. HARLEY QUINN. TEAM PSYCHOPATH.
CHATO SANTANA, A.K.A. EL DIABLO. TEAM HOTHEAD.
AND THAT'S WHERE WE COME IN. WE'RE GOING TO GET HIM FIRST.
MAD DOG, INNIT? WATCHER DOIN' SITTIN' WITH US LOWLIFES? I HEARD YOU WAS A BOUNTY-HUNTER TYPE. BROUGHT OUR TYPES IN HARD.
I GOT FRAMED.
YOU GOT STUPID. WENT AFTER THE WRONG BOUNTY WHO WOUND UP DEAD. NOW YOU'RE LIKE EVERYONE ELSE ON THE SQUAD--DOING JOBS FOR THE GOVERNMENT TO SHAVE TIME OFF YOUR SENTENCE.
YOUR FIRST NAME REALLY REX?

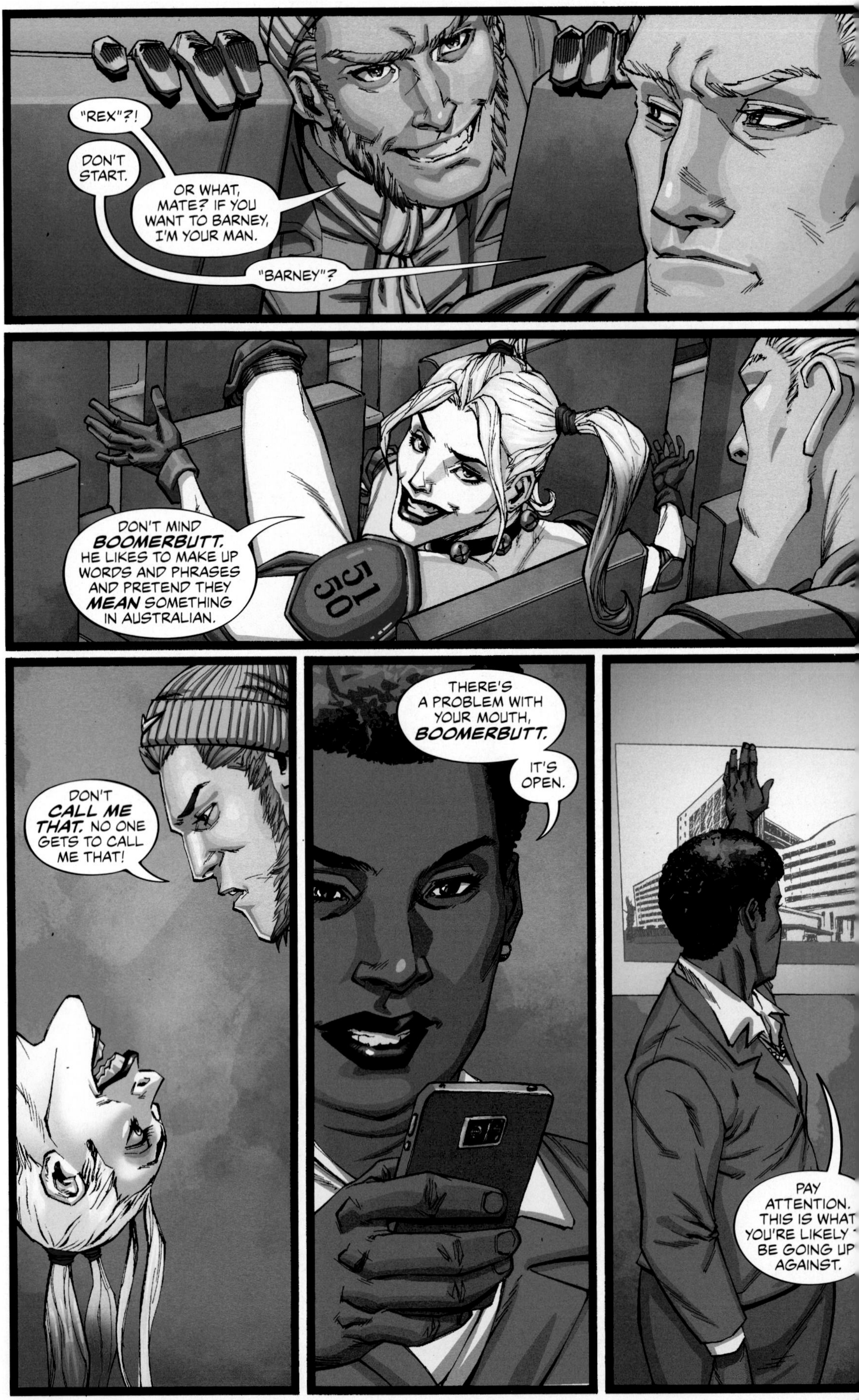
"REX"?!
DON'T START.
OR WHAT, MATE? IF YOU WANT TO BARNEY, I'M YOUR MAN.
"BARNEY"?
DON'T MIND BOOMERBUTT. HE LIKES TO MAKE UP WORDS AND PHRASES AND PRETEND THEY MEAN SOMETHING IN AUSTRALIAN.
51 50
DON'T CALL ME THAT. NO ONE GETS TO CALL ME THAT!
THERE'S A PROBLEM WITH YOUR MOUTH, BOOMERBUTT.
IT'S OPEN.
PAY ATTENTION. THIS IS WHAT YOU'RE LIKELY BE GOING UP AGAINST.

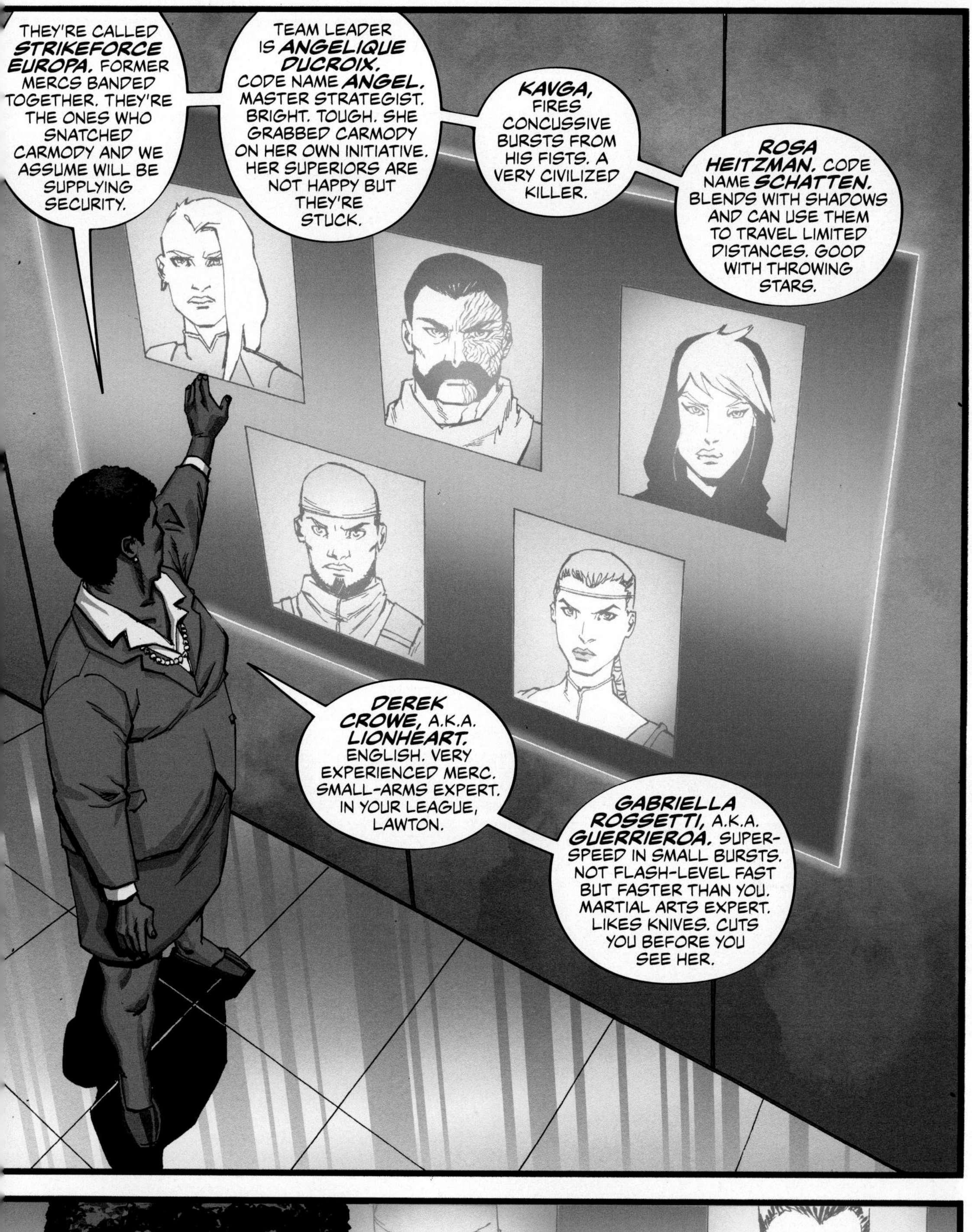
THEY'RE CALLED STRIKEFORCE EUROPA. FORMER MERCS BANDED TOGETHER. THEY'RE THE ONES WHO SNATCHED CARMODY AND WE ASSUME WILL BE SUPPLYING SECURITY.
TEAM LEADER IS ANGELIQUE DUCROIX. CODE NAME ANGEL. MASTER STRATEGIST. BRIGHT. TOUGH. SHE GRABBED CARMODY ON HER OWN INITIATIVE. HER SUPERIORS ARE NOT HAPPY BUT THEY'RE STUCK.
KAVGA, FIRES CONCUSSIVE BURSTS FROM HIS FISTS. A VERY CIVILIZED KILLER.
ROSA HEITZMAN. CODE NAME SCHATTEN. BLENDS WITH SHADOWS AND CAN USE THEM TO TRAVEL LIMITED DISTANCES. GOOD WITH THROWING STARS.
DEREK CROWE, A.K.A. LIONHEART. ENGLISH. VERY EXPERIENCED MERC. SMALL-ARMS EXPERT. IN YOUR LEAGUE, LAWTON.
GABRIELLA ROSSETTI, A.K.A. GUERRIEROA. SUPER-SPEED IN SMALL BURSTS. NOT FLASH-LEVEL FAST BUT FASTER THAN YOU. MARTIAL ARTS EXPERT. LIKES KNIVES. CUTS YOU BEFORE YOU SEE HER.

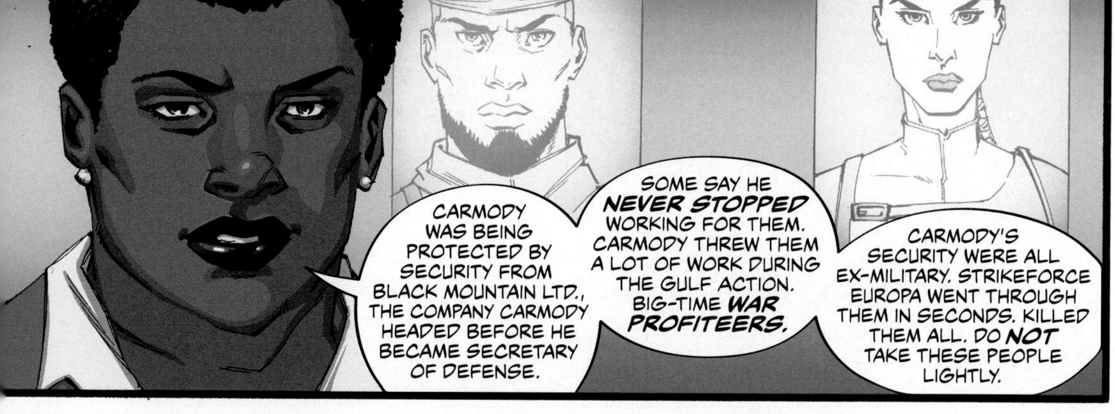
CARMODY WAS BEING PROTECTED BY SECURITY FROM BLACK MOUNTAIN LTD., THE COMPANY CARMODY HEADED BEFORE HE BECAME SECRETARY OF DEFENSE.
SOME SAY HE NEVER STOPPED WORKING FOR THEM. CARMODY THREW THEM A LOT OF WORK DURING THE GULF ACTION. BIG-TIME WAR PROFITEERS.
CARMODY'S SECURITY WERE ALL EX-MILITARY. STRIKEFORCE EUROPA WENT THROUGH THEM IN SECONDS. KILLED THEM ALL. DO NOT TAKE THESE PEOPLE LIGHTLY.

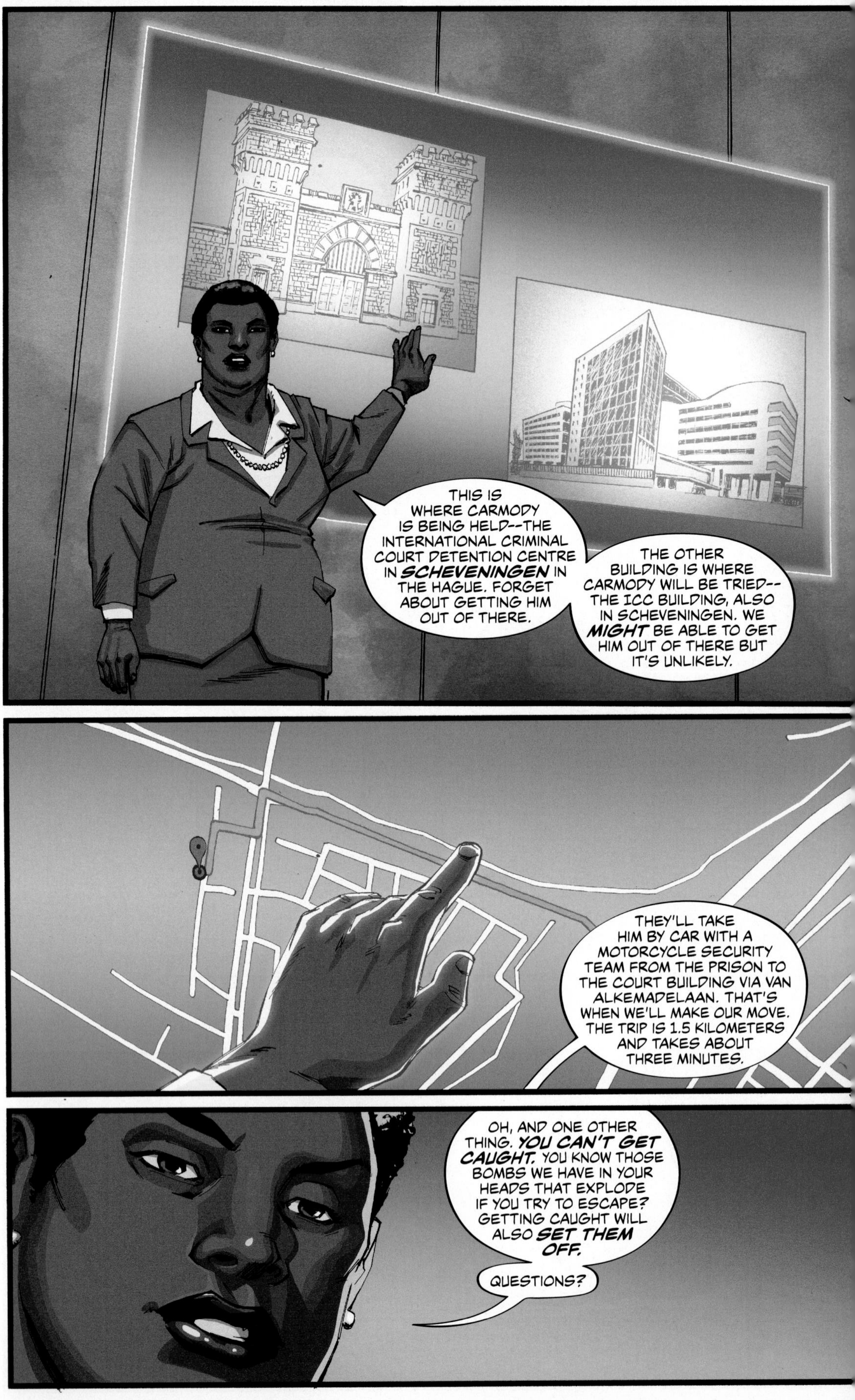
THIS IS WHERE CARMODY IS BEING HELD--THE INTERNATIONAL CRIMINAL COURT DETENTION CENTRE IN SCHEVENINGEN IN THE HAGUE. FORGET ABOUT GETTING HIM OUT OF THERE.
THE OTHER BUILDING IS WHERE CARMODY WILL BE TRIED--THE ICC BUILDING, ALSO IN SCHEVENINGEN. WE MIGHT BE ABLE TO GET HIM OUT OF THERE BUT IT'S UNLIKELY.
THEY'LL TAKE HIM BY CAR WITH A MOTORCYCLE SECURITY TEAM FROM THE PRISON TO THE COURT BUILDING VIA VAN ALKEMADELAAN. THAT'S WHEN WE'LL MAKE OUR MOVE. THE TRIP IS 1.5 KILOMETERS AND TAKES ABOUT THREE MINUTES.
OH, AND ONE OTHER THING. YOU CAN'T GET CAUGHT. YOU KNOW THOSE BOMBS WE HAVE IN YOUR HEADS THAT EXPLODE IF YOU TRY TO ESCAPE? GETTING CAUGHT WILL ALSO SET THEM OFF.
QUESTIONS?

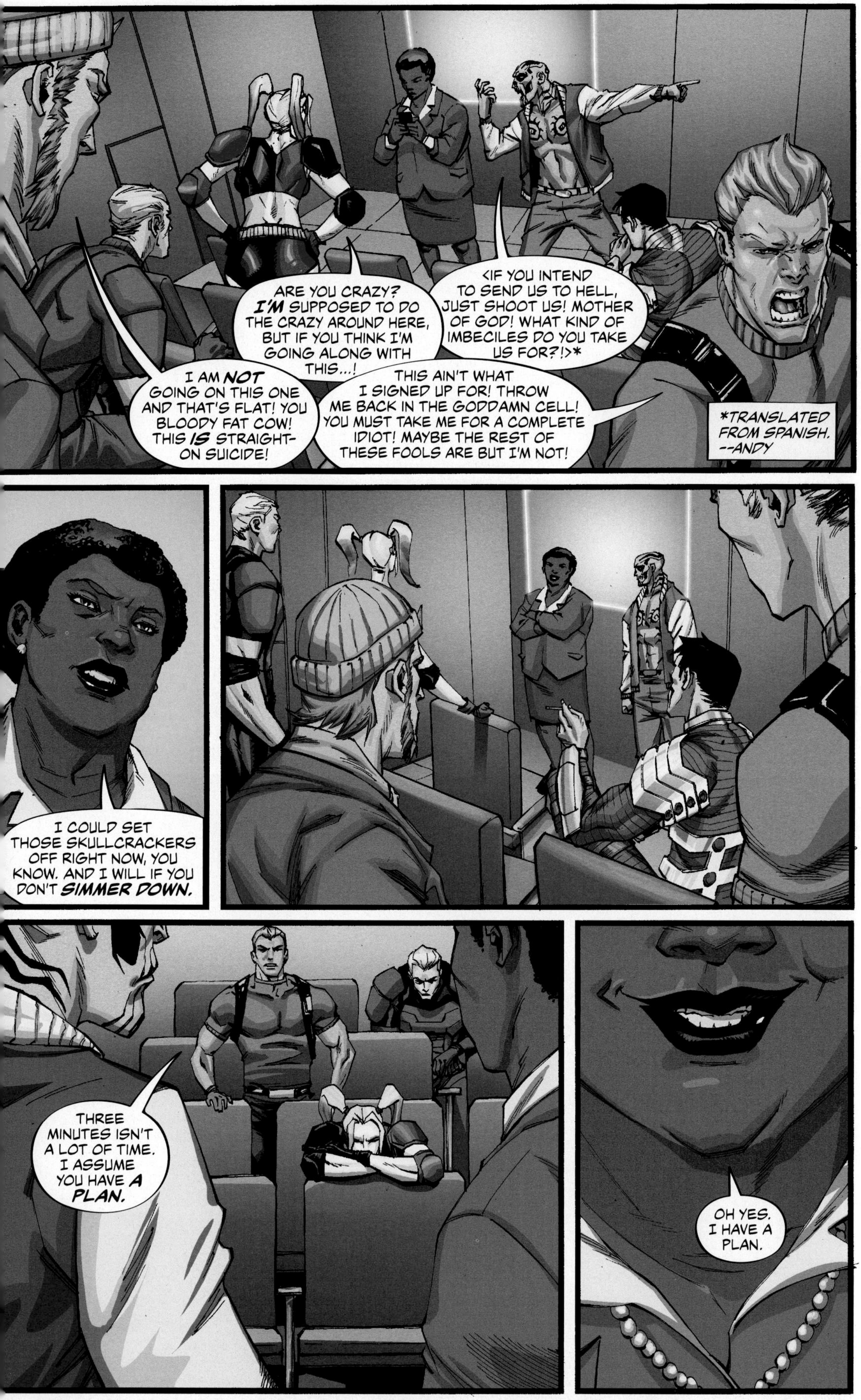
ARE YOU CRAZY? I'M SUPPOSED TO DO THE CRAZY AROUND HERE, BUT IF YOU THINK I'M GOING ALONG WITH THIS...!
<IF YOU INTEND TO SEND US TO HELL, JUST SHOOT US! MOTHER OF GOD! WHAT KIND OF IMBECILES DO YOU TAKE US FOR?!>*
I AM NOT GOING ON THIS ONE AND THAT'S FLAT! YOU BLOODY FAT COW! THIS IS STRAIGHT-ON SUICIDE!
THIS AIN'T WHAT I SIGNED UP FOR! THROW ME BACK IN THE GODDAMN CELL! YOU MUST TAKE ME FOR A COMPLETE IDIOT! MAYBE THE REST OF THESE FOOLS ARE BUT I'M NOT!
*TRANSLATED FROM SPANISH. --ANDY
I COULD SET THOSE SKULLCRACKERS OFF RIGHT NOW, YOU KNOW. AND I WILL IF YOU DON'T SIMMER DOWN.
THREE MINUTES ISN'T A LOT OF TIME. I ASSUME YOU HAVE A PLAN.
OH YES. I HAVE A PLAN.

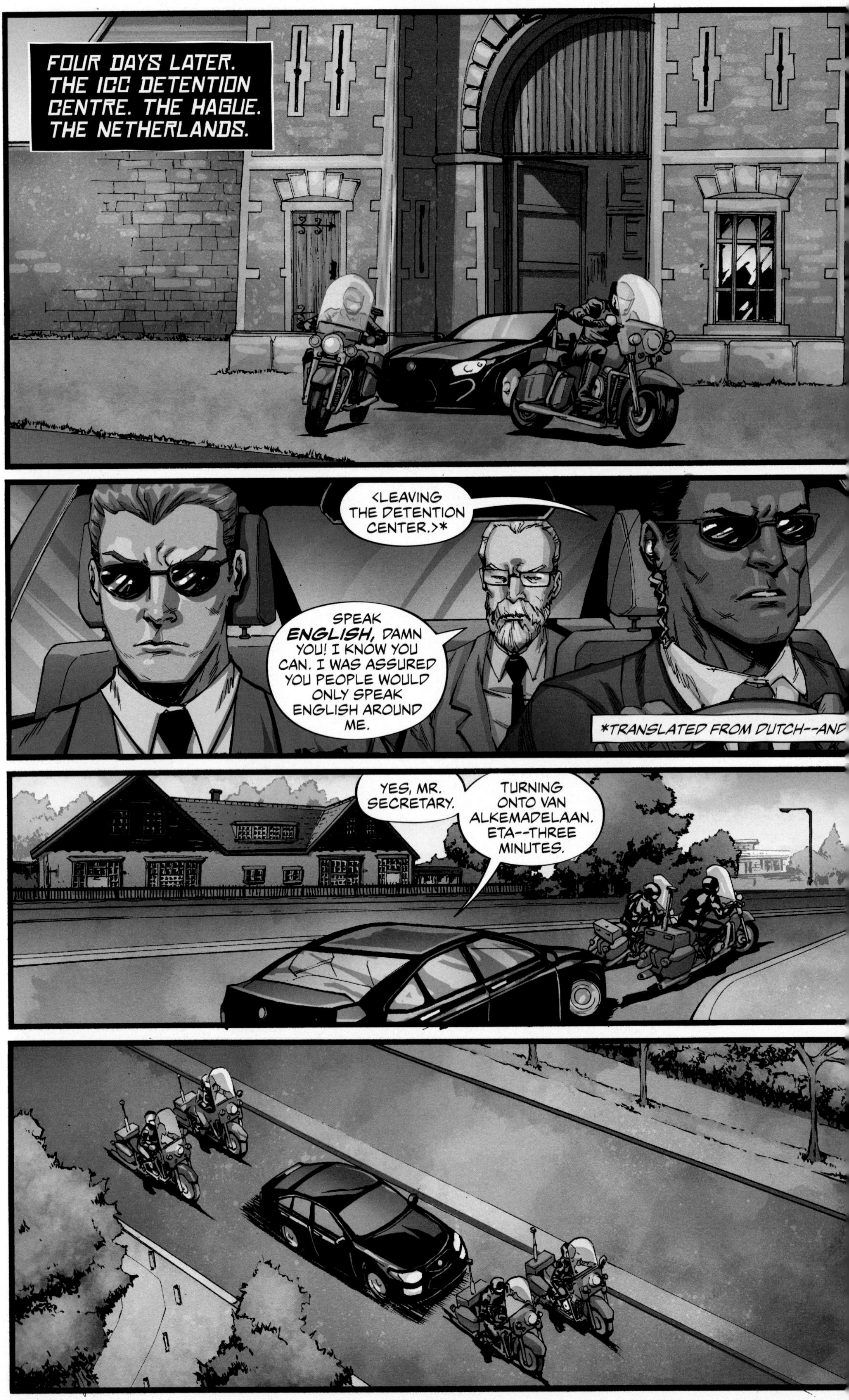
FOUR DAYS LATER. THE ICC DETENTION CENTRE. THE HAGUE. THE NETHERLANDS.
<LEAVING THE DETENTION CENTER.>*
SPEAK ENGLISH, DAMN YOU! I KNOW YOU CAN. I WAS ASSURED YOU PEOPLE WOULD ONLY SPEAK ENGLISH AROUND ME.
*TRANSLATED FROM DUTCH--AND
YES, MR. SECRETARY.
TURNING ONTO VAN ALKEMADELAAN. ETA--THREE MINUTES.

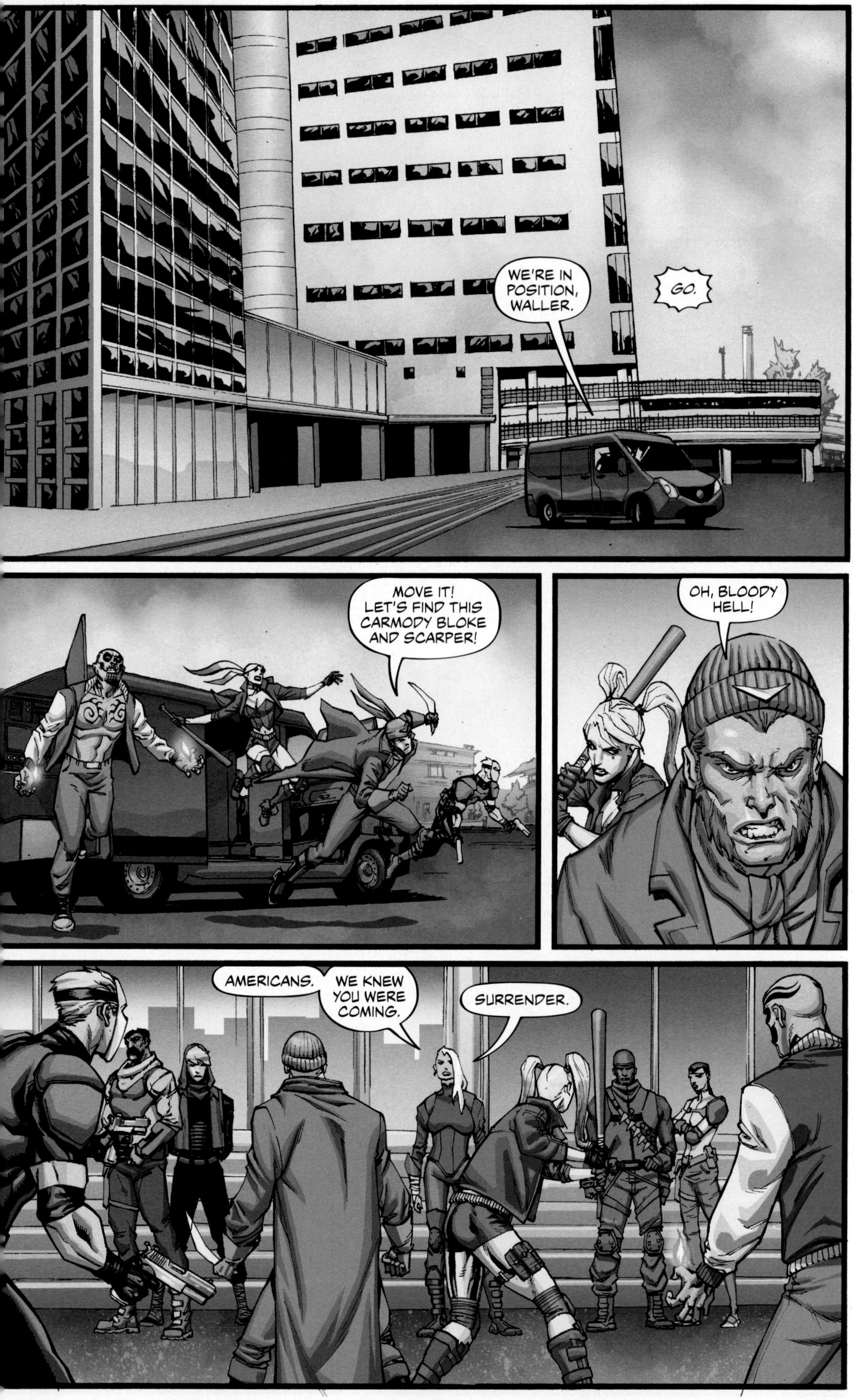
WE'RE IN POSITION, WALLER.
GO.
MOVE IT! LET'S FIND THIS CARMODY BLOKE AND SCARPER!
OH, BLOODY HELL!
AMERICANS.
WE KNEW YOU WERE COMING.
SURRENDER.

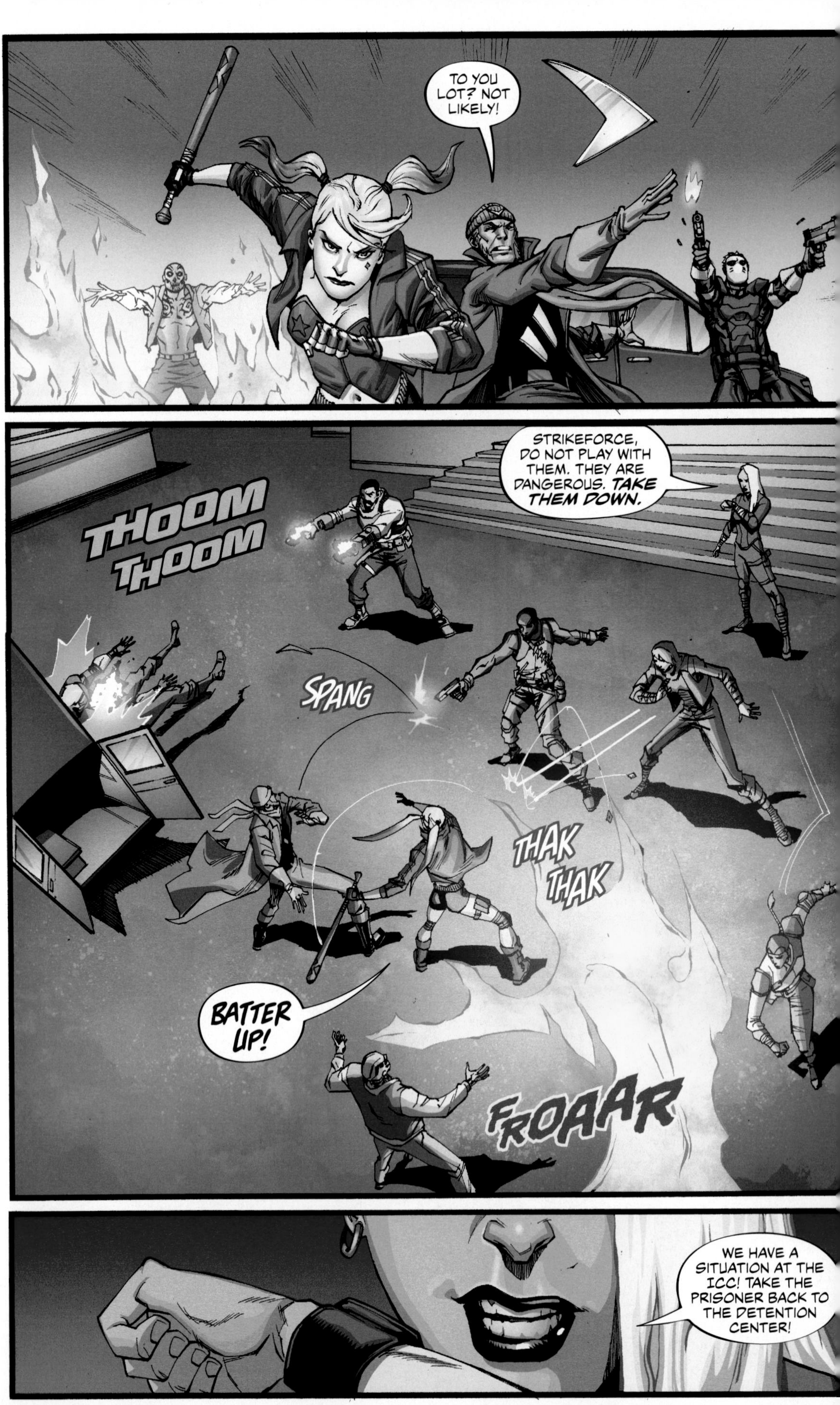
TO YOU LOT? NOT LIKELY!
STRIKEFORCE, DO NOT PLAY WITH THEM. THEY ARE DANGEROUS. TAKE THEM DOWN.
THOOM THOOM
SPANG
THAK THAK
BATTER UP!
FROAAR
WE HAVE A SITUATION AT THE ICC! TAKE THE PRISONER BACK TO THE DETENTION CENTER!

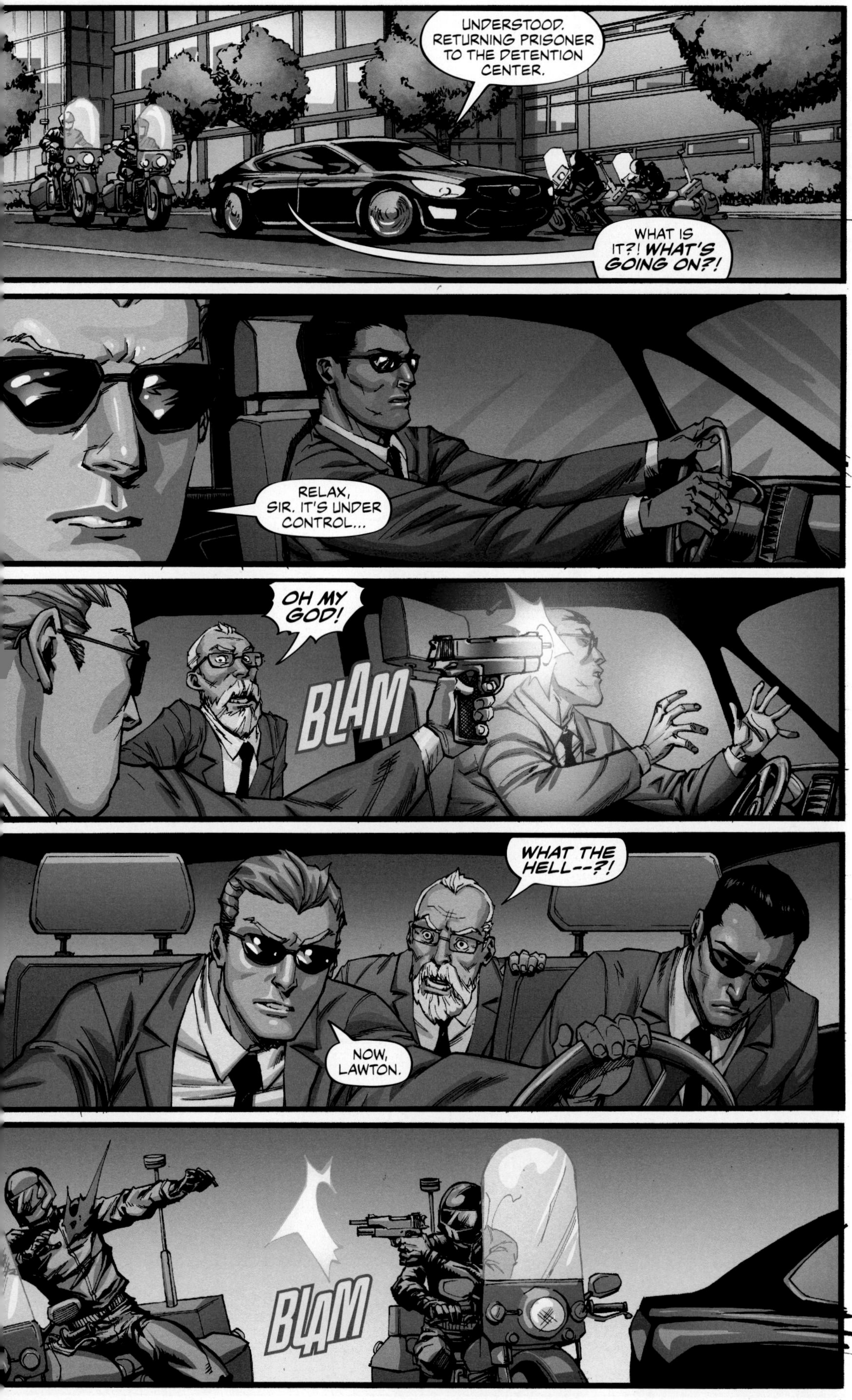

UNDERSTOOD. RETURNING PRISONER TO THE DETENTION CENTER.
WHAT IS IT?! WHAT'S GOING ON?!
RELAX, SIR. IT'S UNDER CONTROL...
OH MY GOD!
BLAM
WHAT THE HELL--?!
NOW, LAWTON.
BLAM

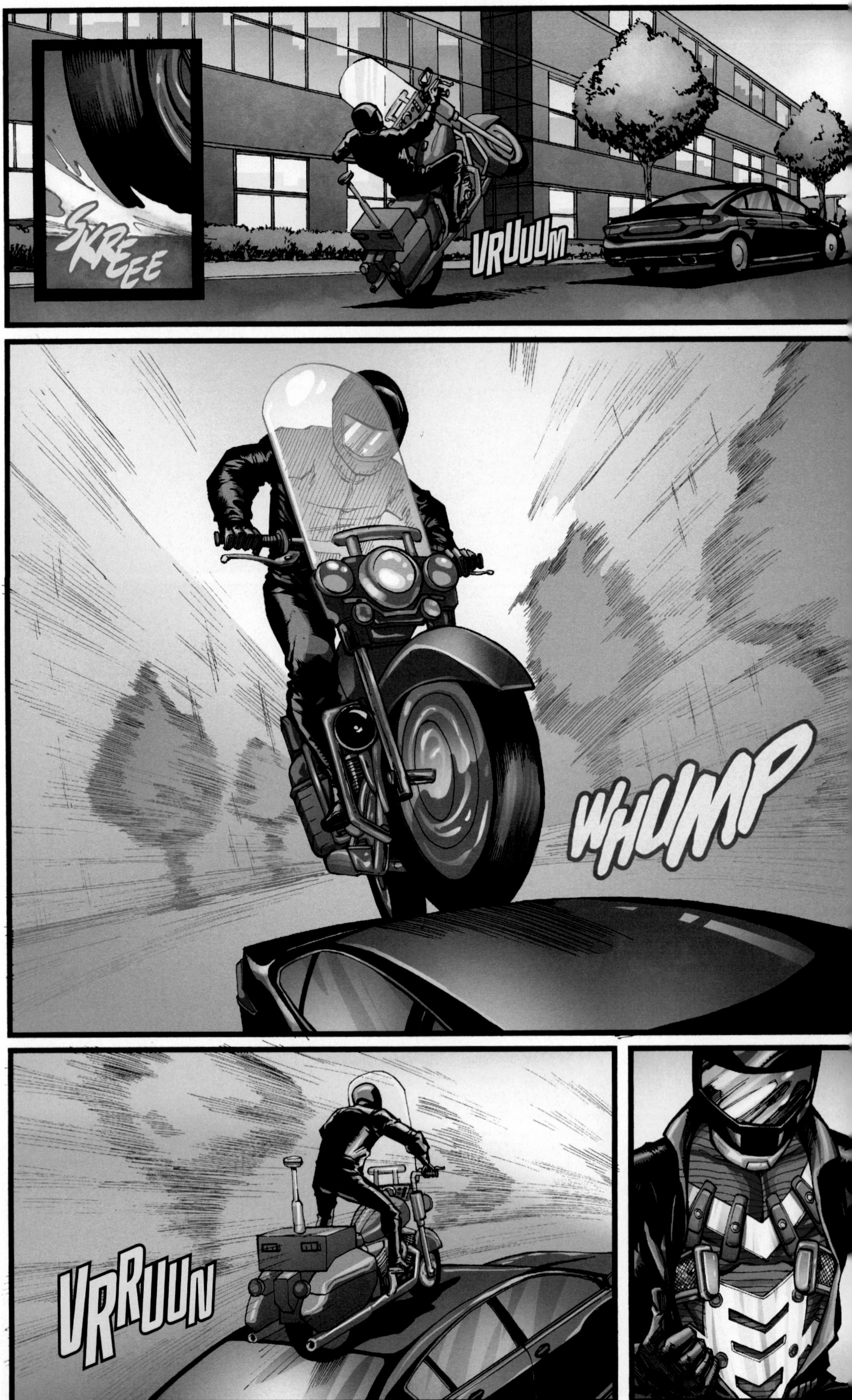
SKREEEE
VRUUUM
WHUMP
VRRUUN

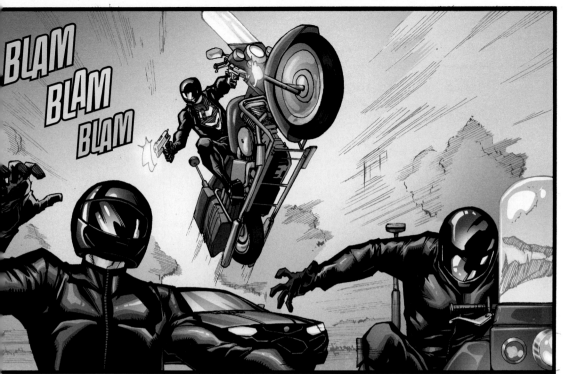

BLAM
BLAM
BLAM

VOOMP

I DEMAND TO KNOW WHAT'S GOING ON! WHO *ARE* YOU PEOPLE?!

WE'RE THE ONES GETTING YOU BACK TO THE STATES. NOW *SHUT UP.*

ALL UNITS, THIS IS *FLAG.* WITHDRAW AND GET TO THE RENDEZVOUS.

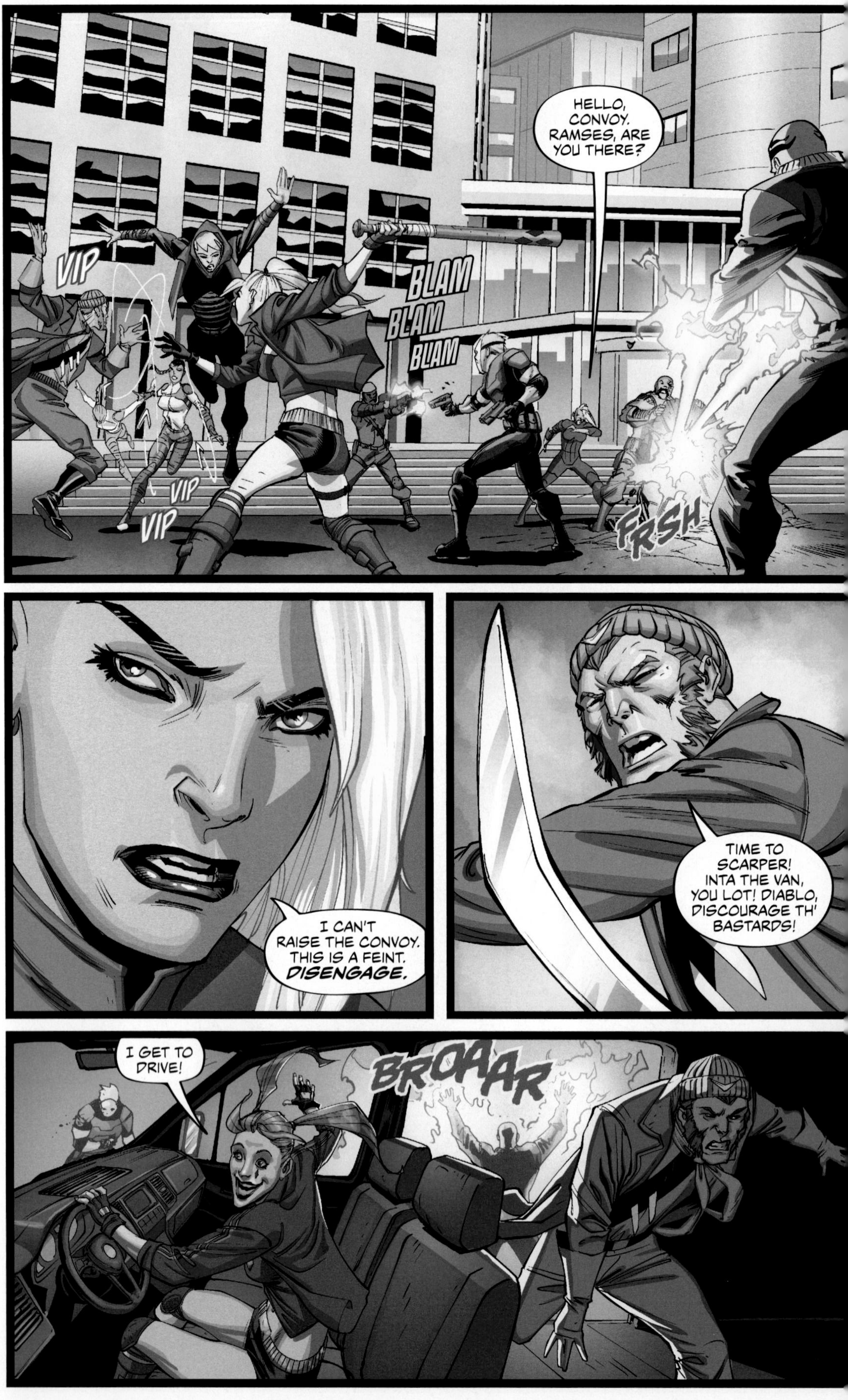

HELLO, CONVOY. RAMSES, ARE YOU THERE?
VIP
BLAM
BLAM
BLAM
VIP
VIP
FRSH
I CAN'T RAISE THE CONVOY. THIS IS A FEINT. DISENGAGE.
TIME TO SCARPER! INTA THE VAN, YOU LOT! DIABLO, DISCOURAGE TH' BASTARDS!
I GET TO DRIVE!
BROAAAR

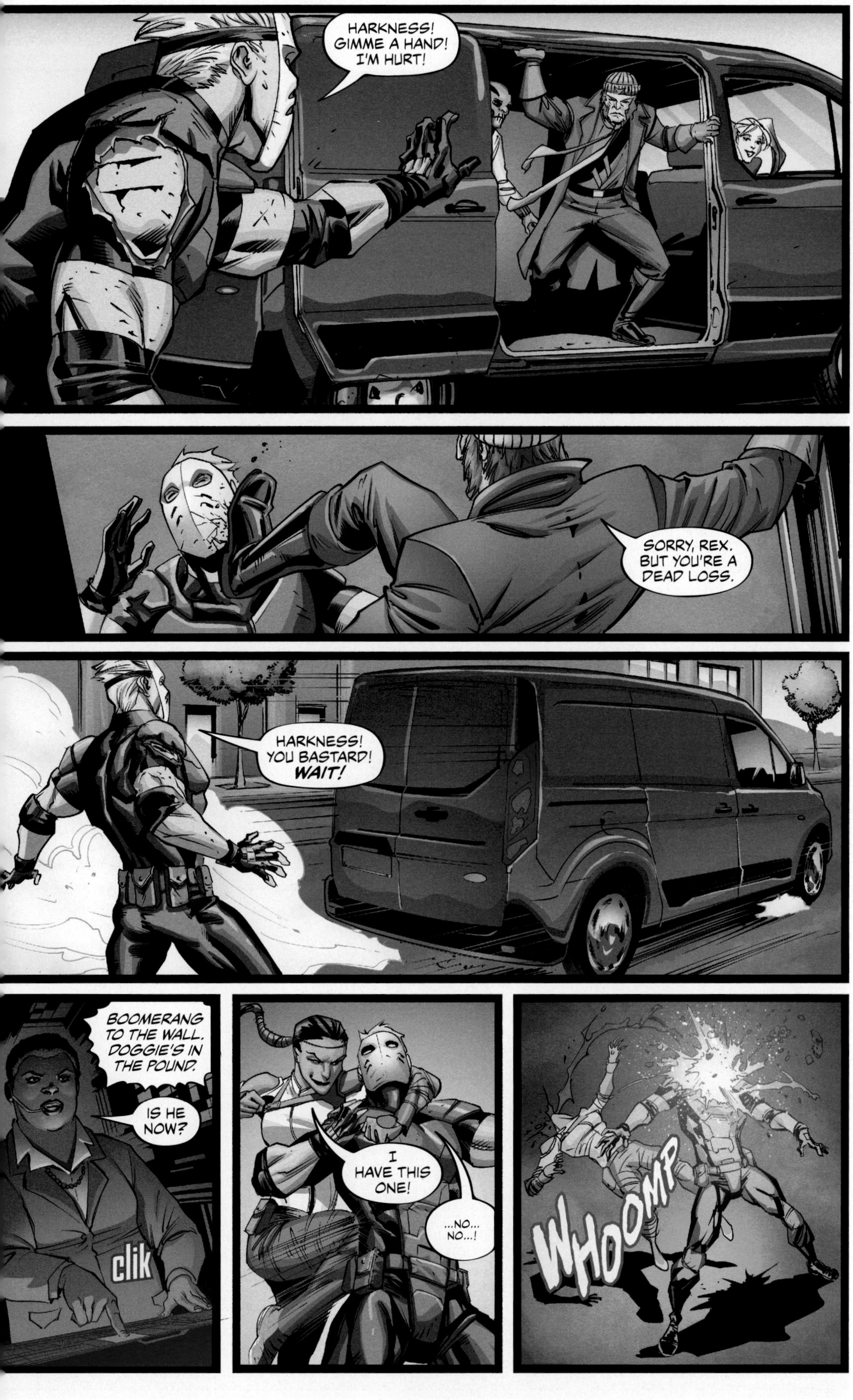
HARKNESS! GIMME A HAND! I'M HURT!
SORRY, REX. BUT YOU'RE A DEAD LOSS.
HARKNESS! YOU BASTARD! WAIT!
BOOMERANG TO THE WALL. DOGGIE'S IN THE POUND.
IS HE NOW?
clik
I HAVE THIS ONE!
...NO... NO...!
WHOOMP

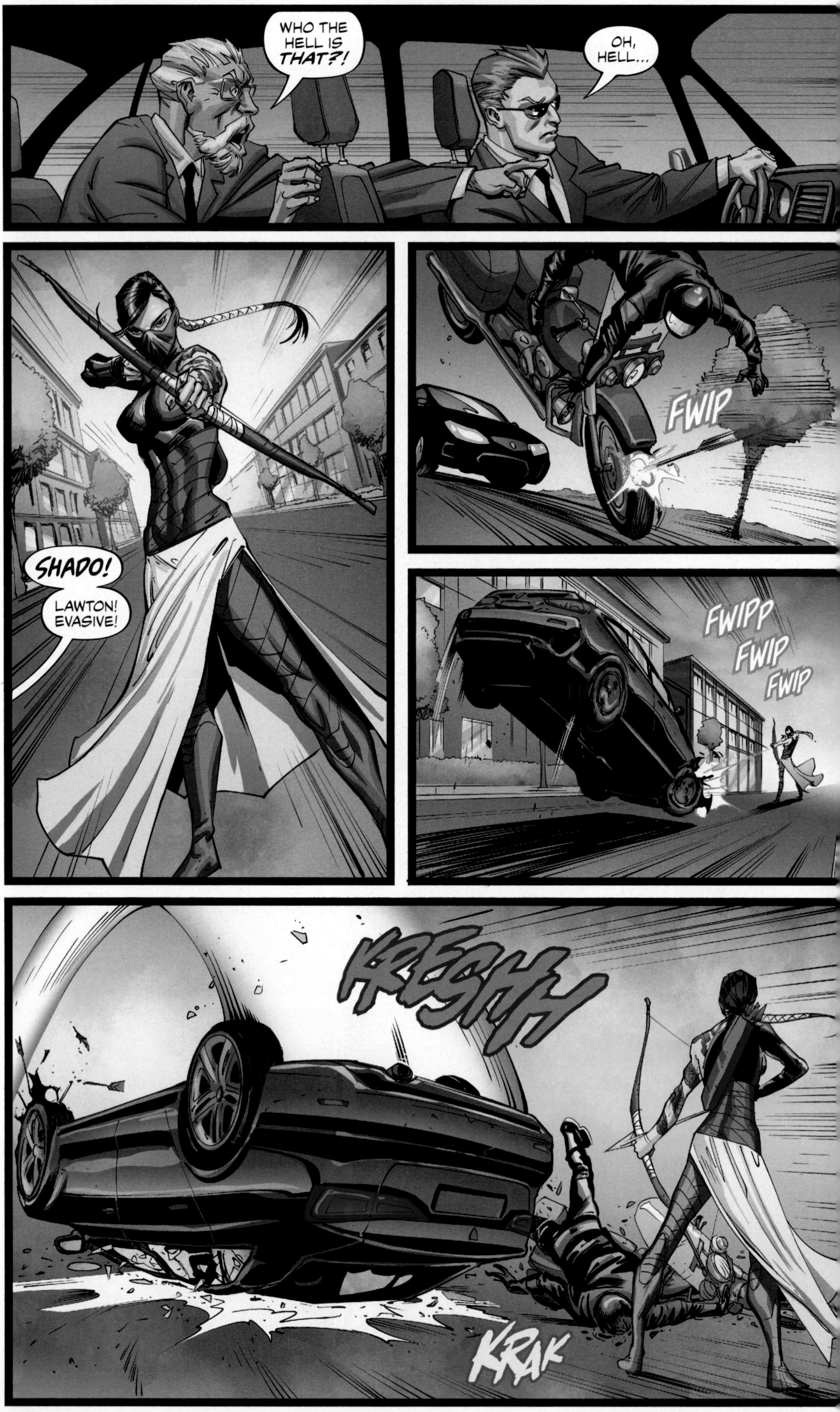

WHO THE HELL IS THAT?!
OH, HELL...
SHADO!
LAWTON! EVASIVE!
FWIP
FWIPP
FWIP
FWIP
KRESHH
KRAK

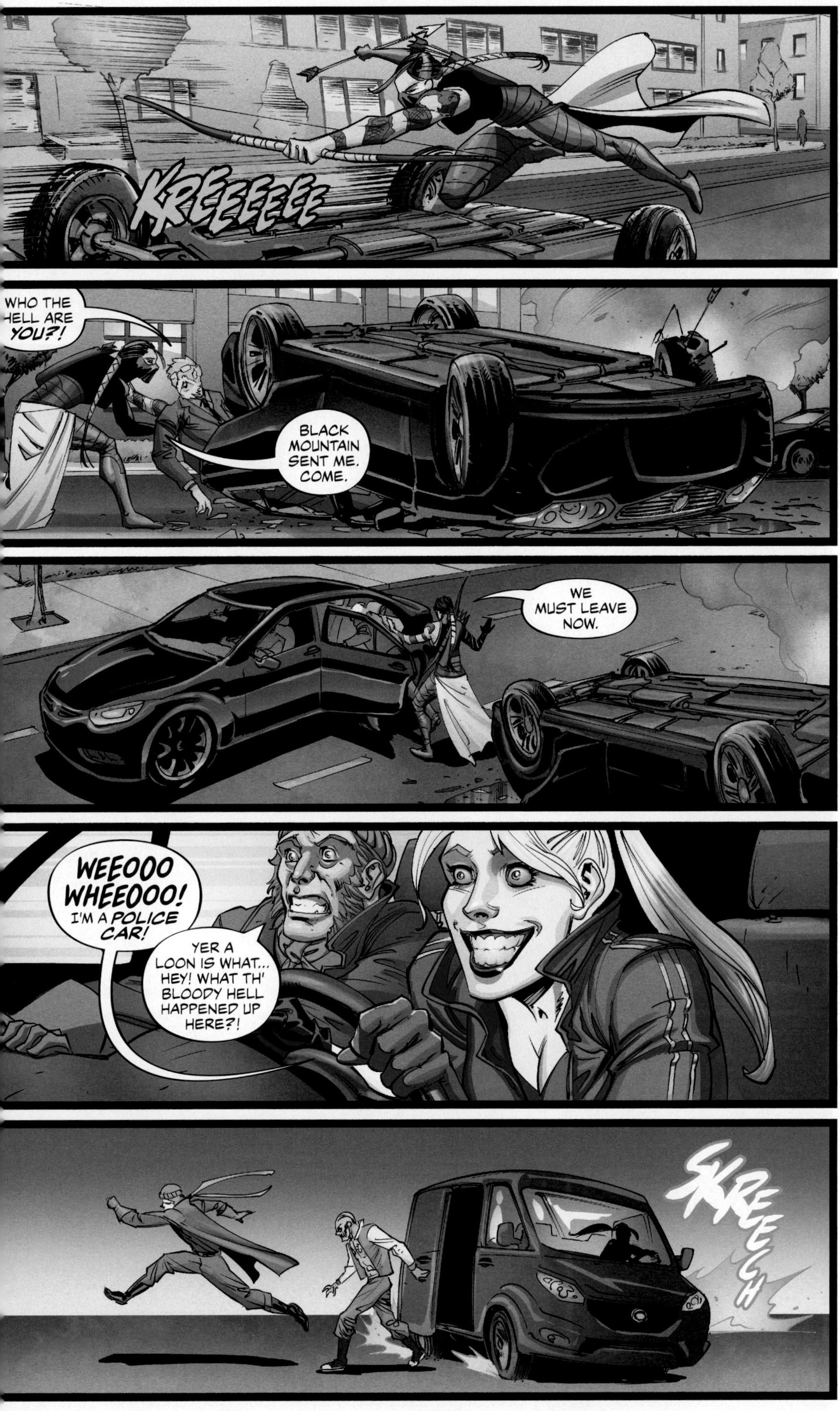
KREEEEEEE
WHO THE HELL ARE YOU?!
BLACK MOUNTAIN SENT ME. COME.
WE MUST LEAVE NOW.
WEEOOO WHEEOOO! I'M A POLICE CAR!
YER A LOON IS WHAT... HEY! WHAT TH' BLOODY HELL HAPPENED UP HERE?!
SKREECH

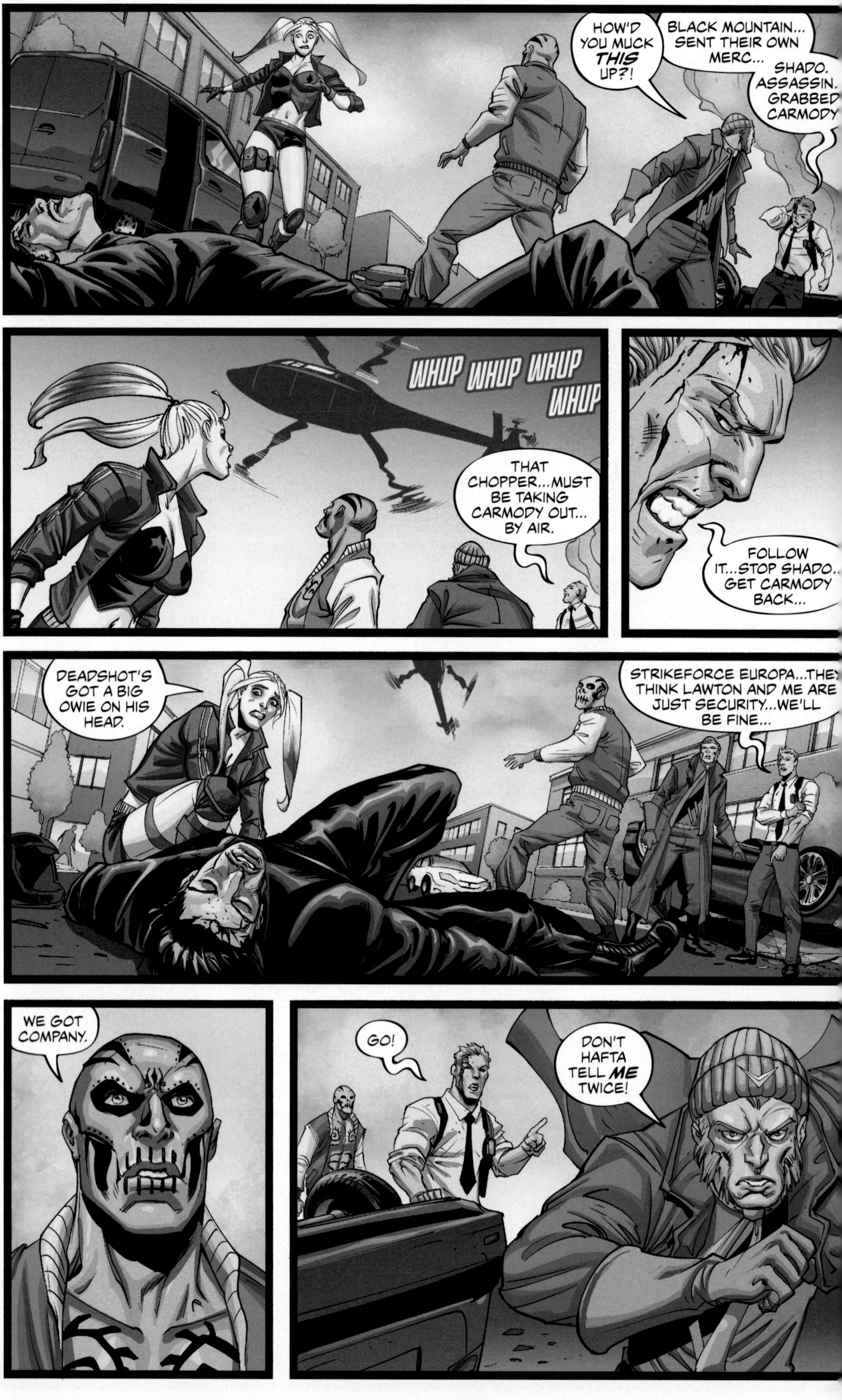
HOW'D YOU MUCK *THIS* UP?!
BLACK MOUNTAIN... SENT THEIR OWN MERC...
SHADO. ASSASSIN. GRABBED CARMODY
WHUP WHUP WHUP WHUP
THAT CHOPPER...MUST BE TAKING CARMODY OUT... BY AIR.
FOLLOW IT...STOP SHADO... GET CARMODY BACK...
DEADSHOT'S GOT A BIG OWIE ON HIS HEAD.
STRIKEFORCE EUROPA...THEY THINK LAWTON AND ME ARE JUST SECURITY...WE'LL BE FINE...
WE GOT COMPANY.
GO!
DON'T HAFTA TELL *ME* TWICE!

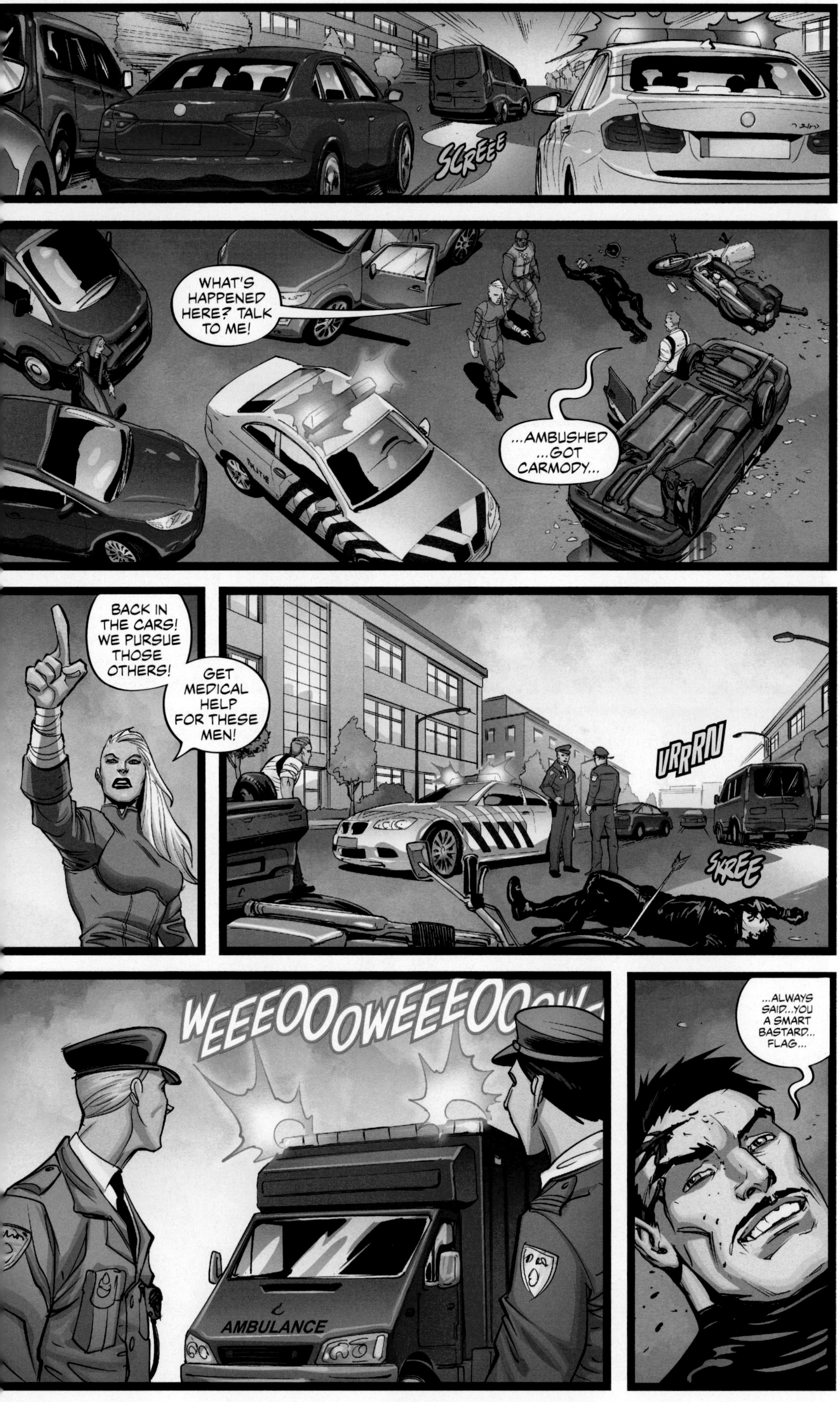
SCREEE
WHAT'S HAPPENED HERE? TALK TO ME!
...AMBUSHED ...GOT CARMODY...
BACK IN THE CARS! WE PURSUE THOSE OTHERS!
GET MEDICAL HELP FOR THESE MEN!
VRRRN
SKREE
WEEEOOOWEEEOOOW-
AMBULANCE
...ALWAYS SAID...YOU A SMART BASTARD... FLAG...

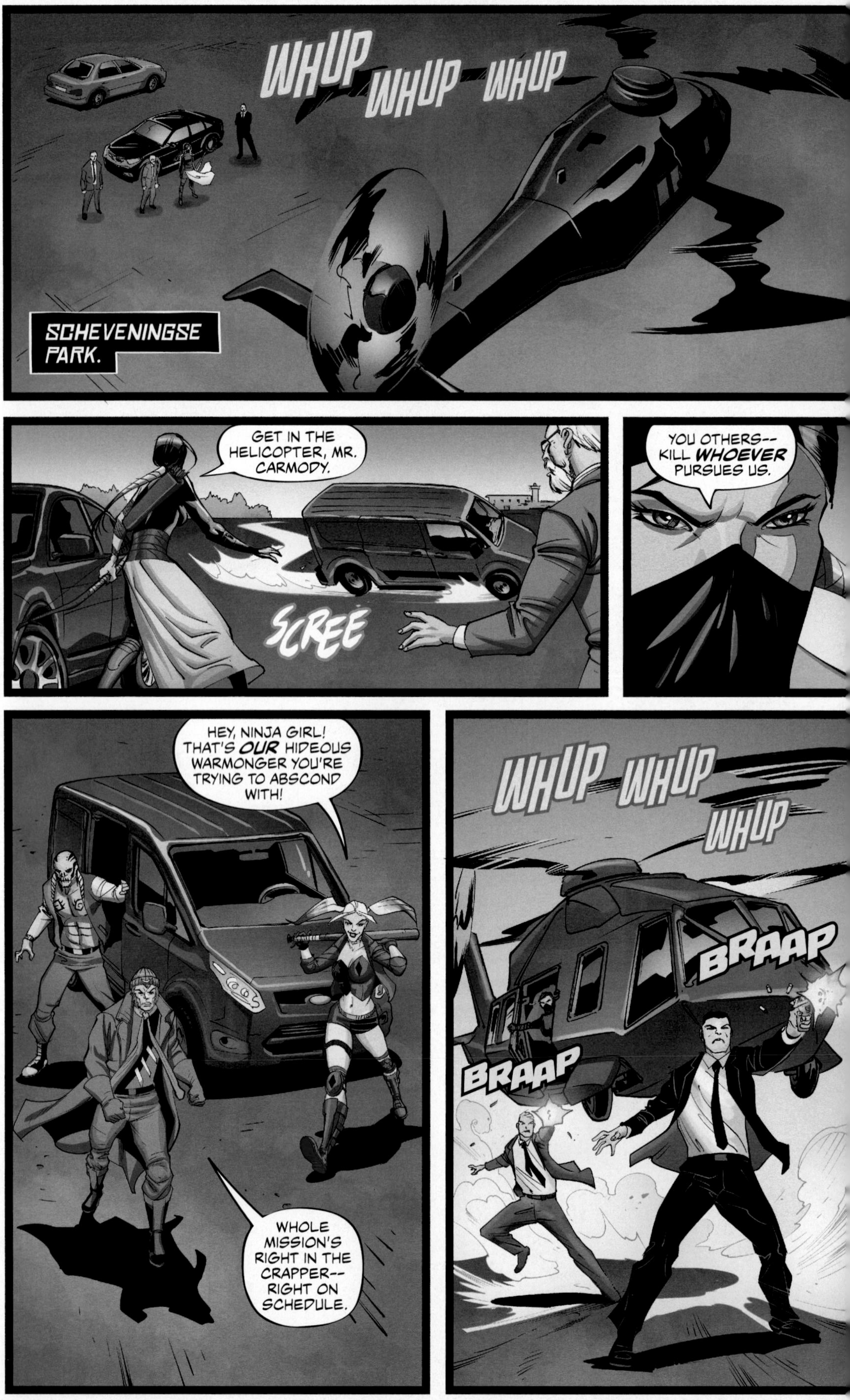
WHUP WHUP WHUP
SCHEVENINGSE PARK.
GET IN THE HELICOPTER, MR. CARMODY.
SCREE
YOU OTHERS-- KILL WHOEVER PURSUES US.
HEY, NINJA GIRL! THAT'S OUR HIDEOUS WARMONGER YOU'RE TRYING TO ABSCOND WITH!
WHOLE MISSION'S RIGHT IN THE CRAPPER-- RIGHT ON SCHEDULE.
WHUP WHUP WHUP
BRAAP
BRAAP

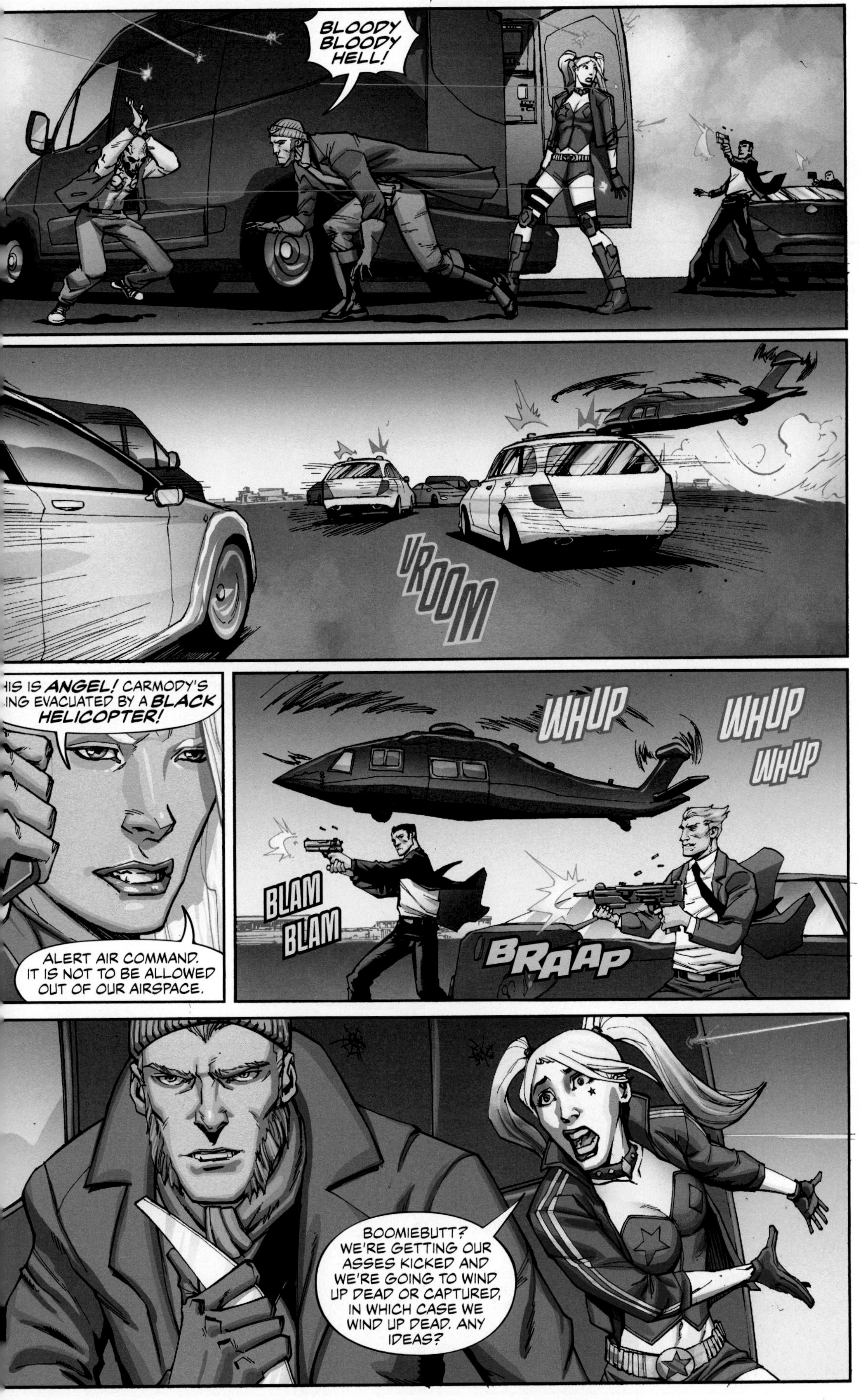
BLOODY BLOODY HELL!
VROOM
HIS IS ANGEL! CARMODY'S
ING EVACUATED BY A BLACK HELICOPTER!
ALERT AIR COMMAND. IT IS NOT TO BE ALLOWED OUT OF OUR AIRSPACE.
WHUP
WHUP
WHUP
BLAM
BLAM
BRAAP
BOOMIEBUTT? WE'RE GETTING OUR ASSES KICKED AND WE'RE GOING TO WIND UP DEAD OR CAPTURED, IN WHICH CASE WE WIND UP DEAD. ANY IDEAS?

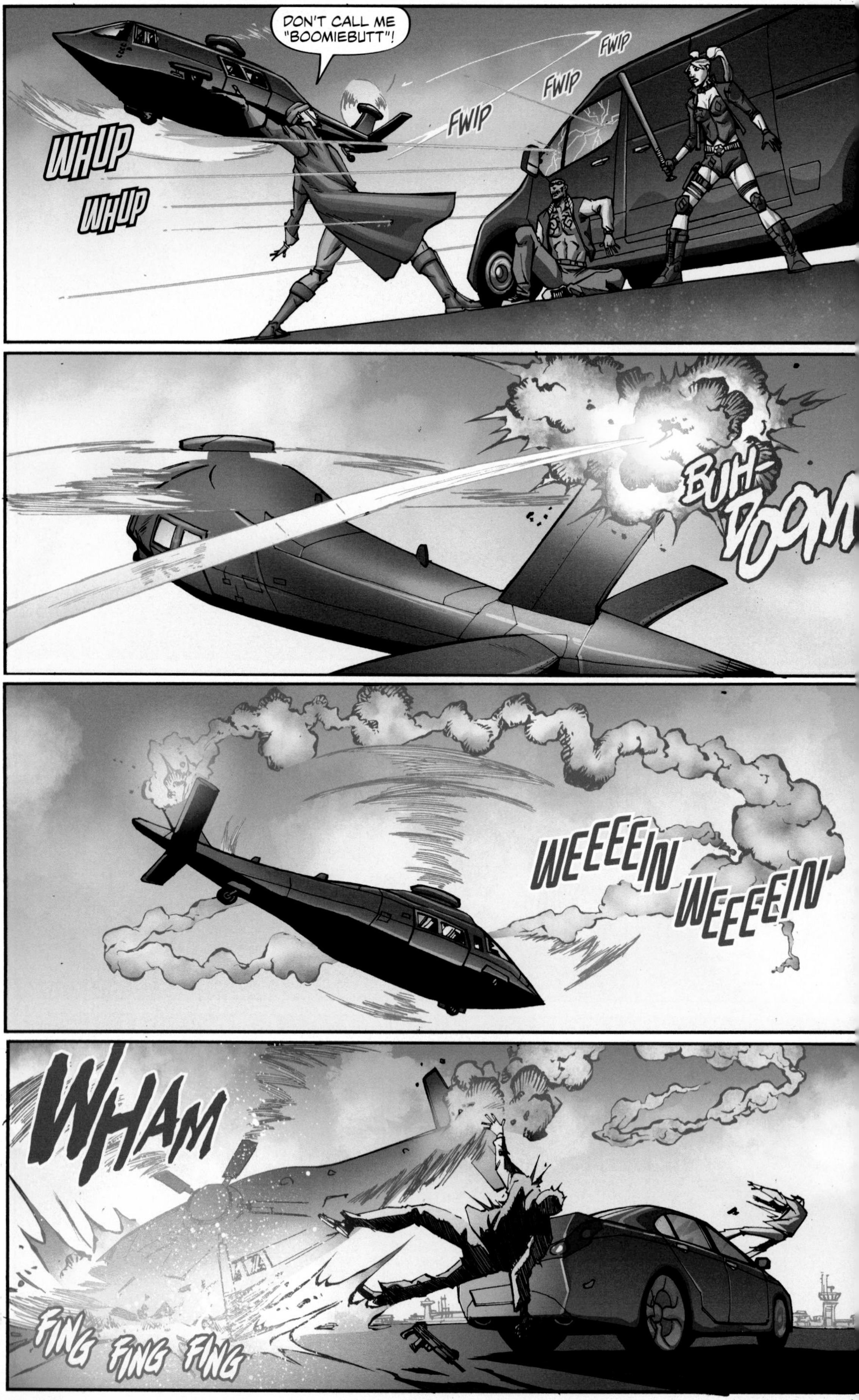
DON'T CALL ME "BOOMIEBUTT"!
WHUP
WHUP
FWIP
FWIP
FWIP
BUH-DOOM
WEEEEIN
WEEEEIN
WHAM
FING FING FING

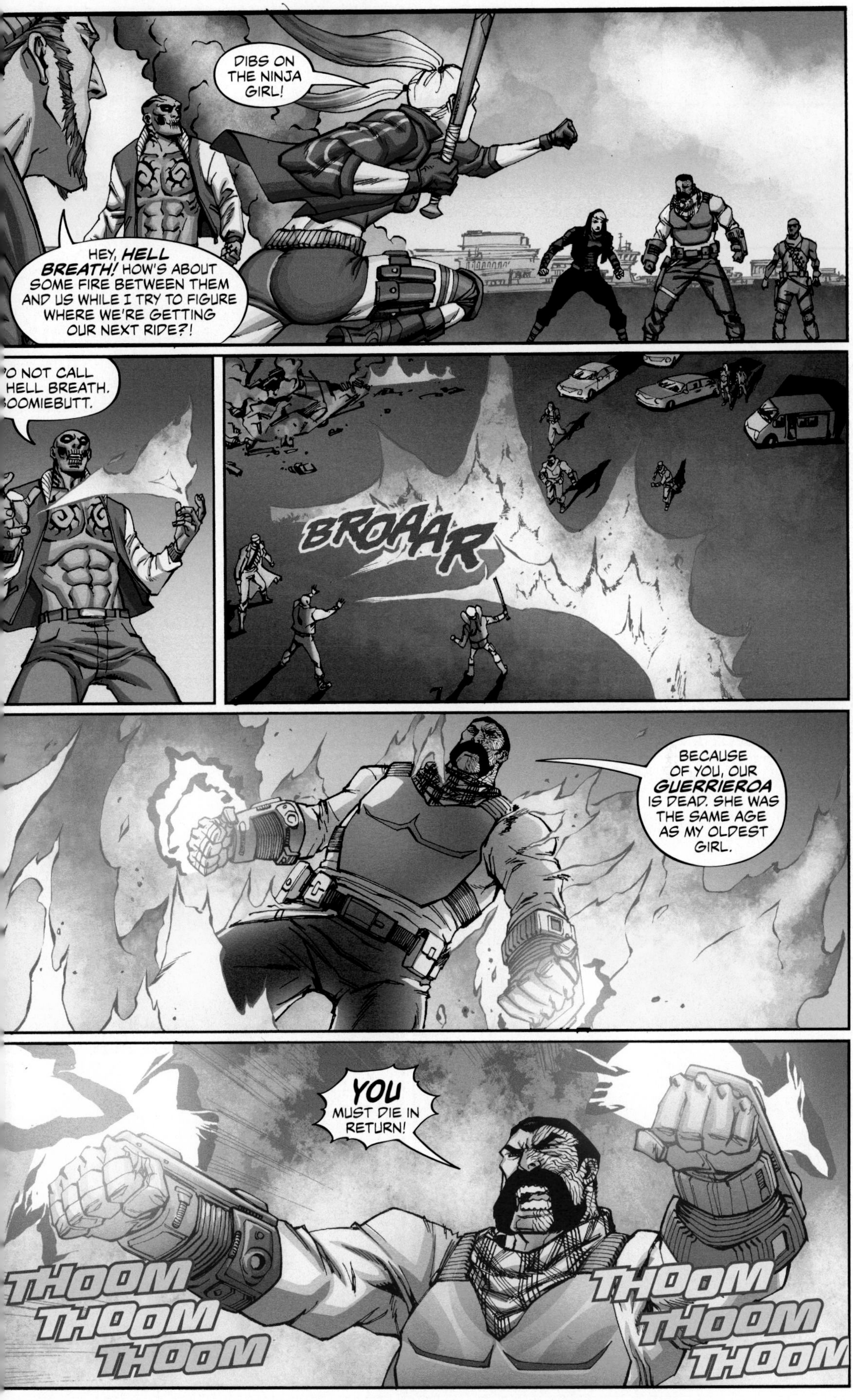
DIBS ON THE NINJA GIRL!
HEY, HELL BREATH! HOW'S ABOUT SOME FIRE BETWEEN THEM AND US WHILE I TRY TO FIGURE WHERE WE'RE GETTING OUR NEXT RIDE?!
O NOT CALL HELL BREATH. OOMIEBUTT.
BROAAR
BECAUSE OF YOU, OUR GUERRIEROA IS DEAD. SHE WAS THE SAME AGE AS MY OLDEST GIRL.
YOU MUST DIE IN RETURN!
THOOM THOOM THOOM
THOOM THOOM THOOM

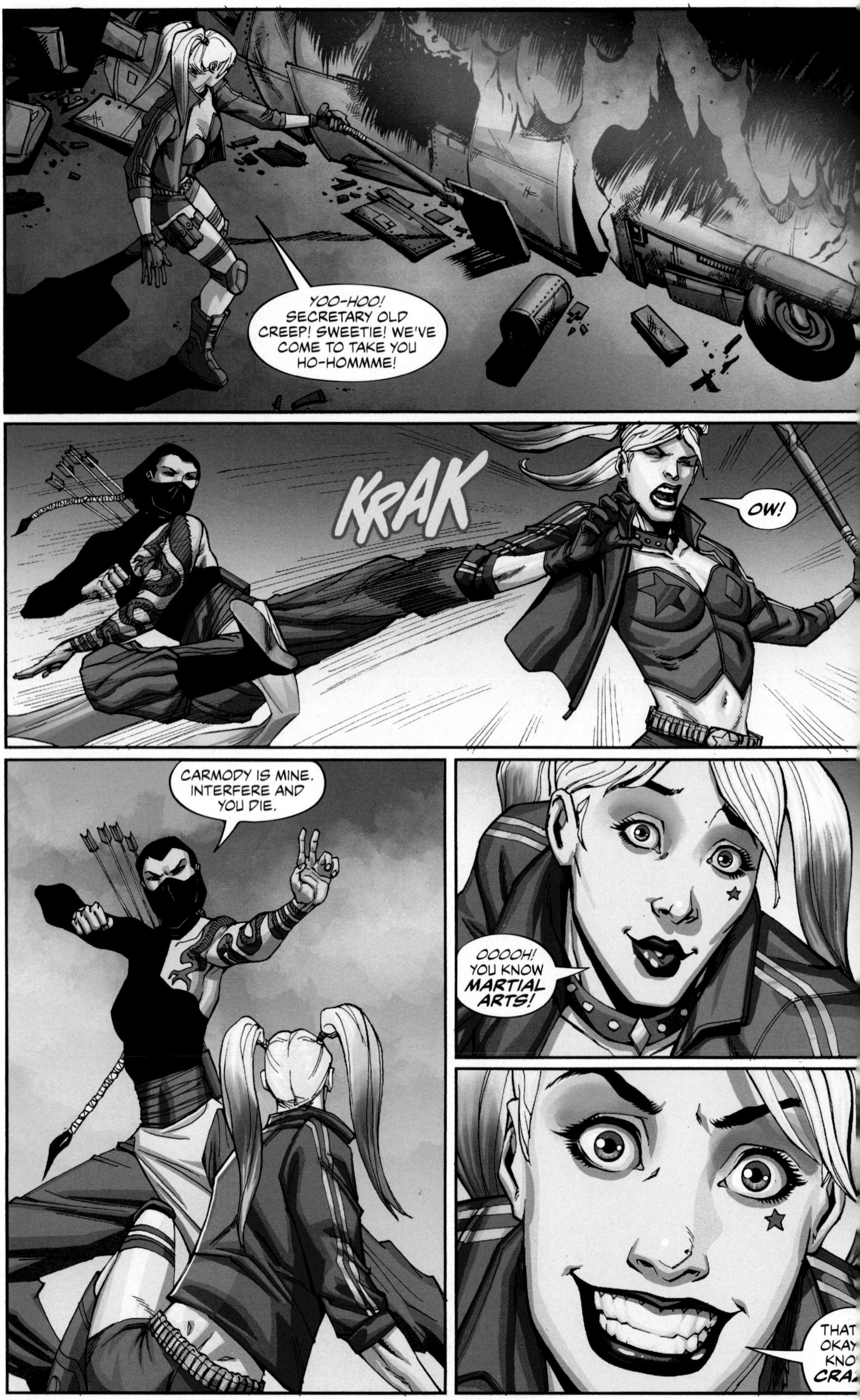
YOO-HOO! SECRETARY OLD CREEP! SWEETIE! WE'VE COME TO TAKE YOU HO-HOMMME!
KRAK
OW!
CARMODY IS MINE. INTERFERE AND YOU DIE.
OOOOH! YOU KNOW MARTIAL ARTS!
THAT OKAY KNO CRA

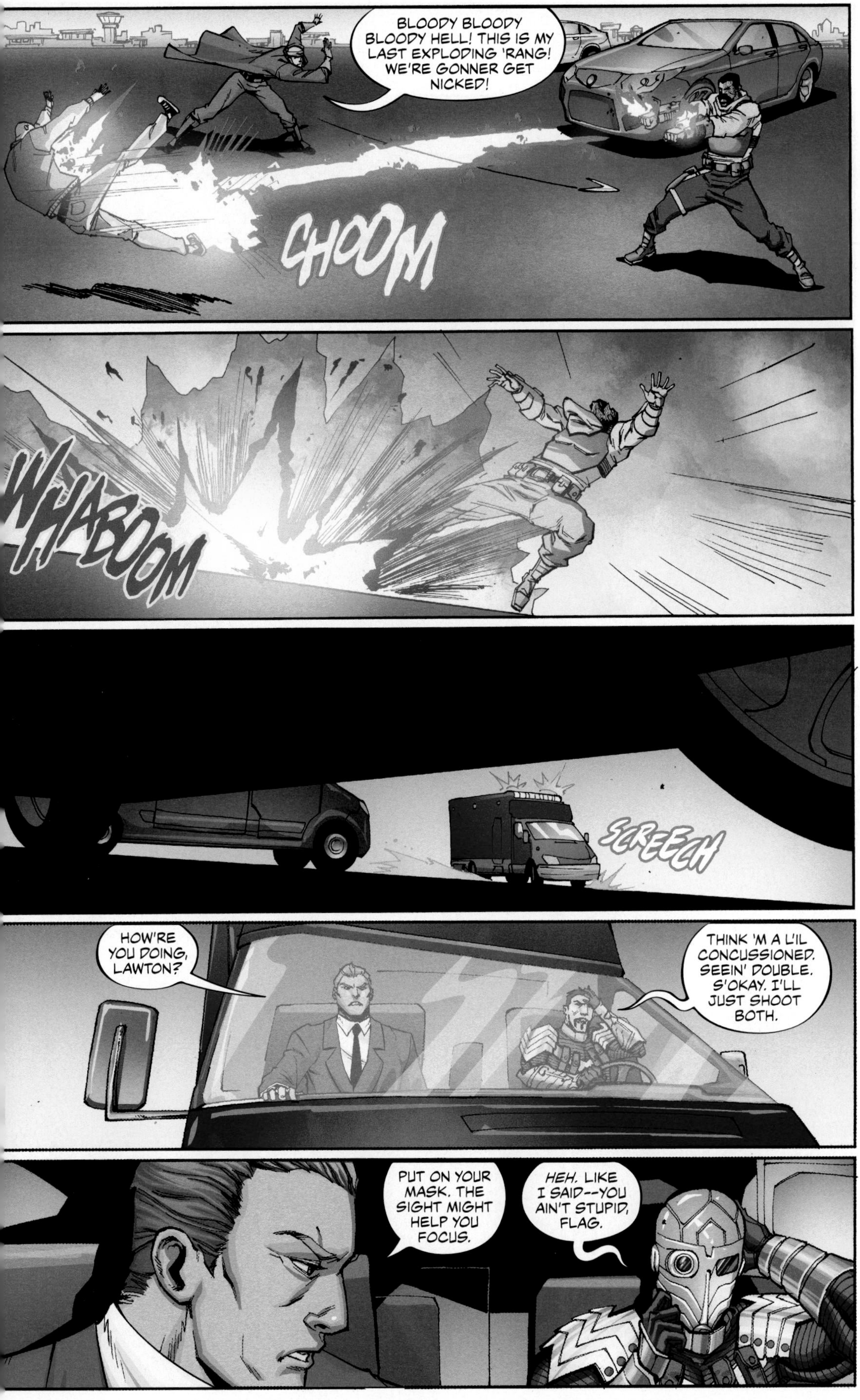
BLOODY BLOODY BLOODY HELL! THIS IS MY LAST EXPLODING 'RANG! WE'RE GONNER GET NICKED!
CHOOM
WHABOOM
SCREECH
HOW'RE YOU DOING, LAWTON?
THINK 'M A L'IL CONCUSSIONED. SEEIN' DOUBLE. S'OKAY. I'LL JUST SHOOT BOTH.
PUT ON YOUR MASK. THE SIGHT MIGHT HELP YOU FOCUS.
HEH. LIKE I SAID--YOU AIN'T STUPID, FLAG.

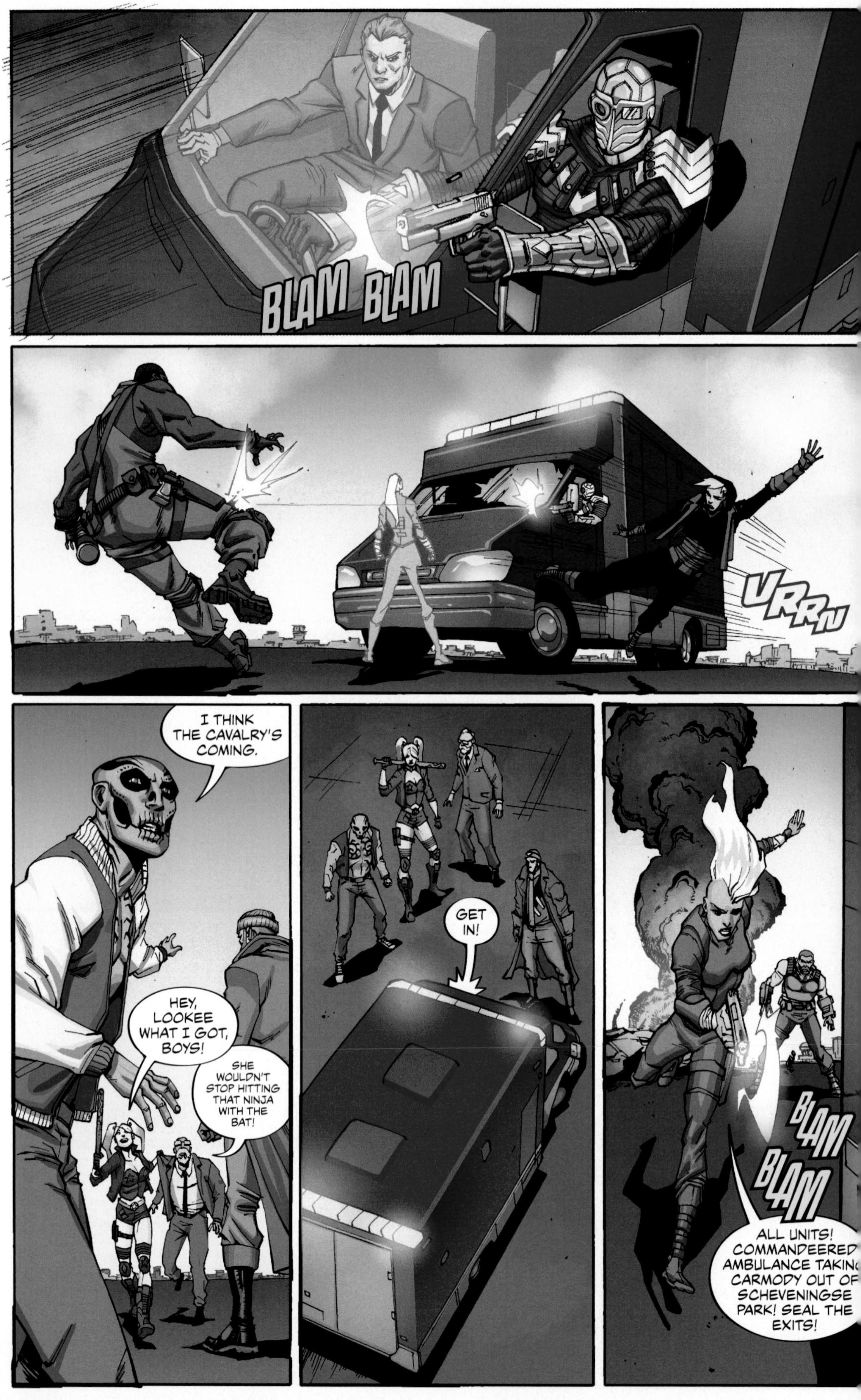
BLAM BLAM
URRN
I THINK THE CAVALRY'S COMING.
HEY, LOOKEE WHAT I GOT, BOYS!
SHE WOULDN'T STOP HITTING THAT NINJA WITH THE BAT!
GET IN!
BLAM
BLAM
ALL UNITS! COMMANDEERED AMBULANCE TAKING CARMODY OUT OF SCHEVENINGSE PARK! SEAL THE EXITS!

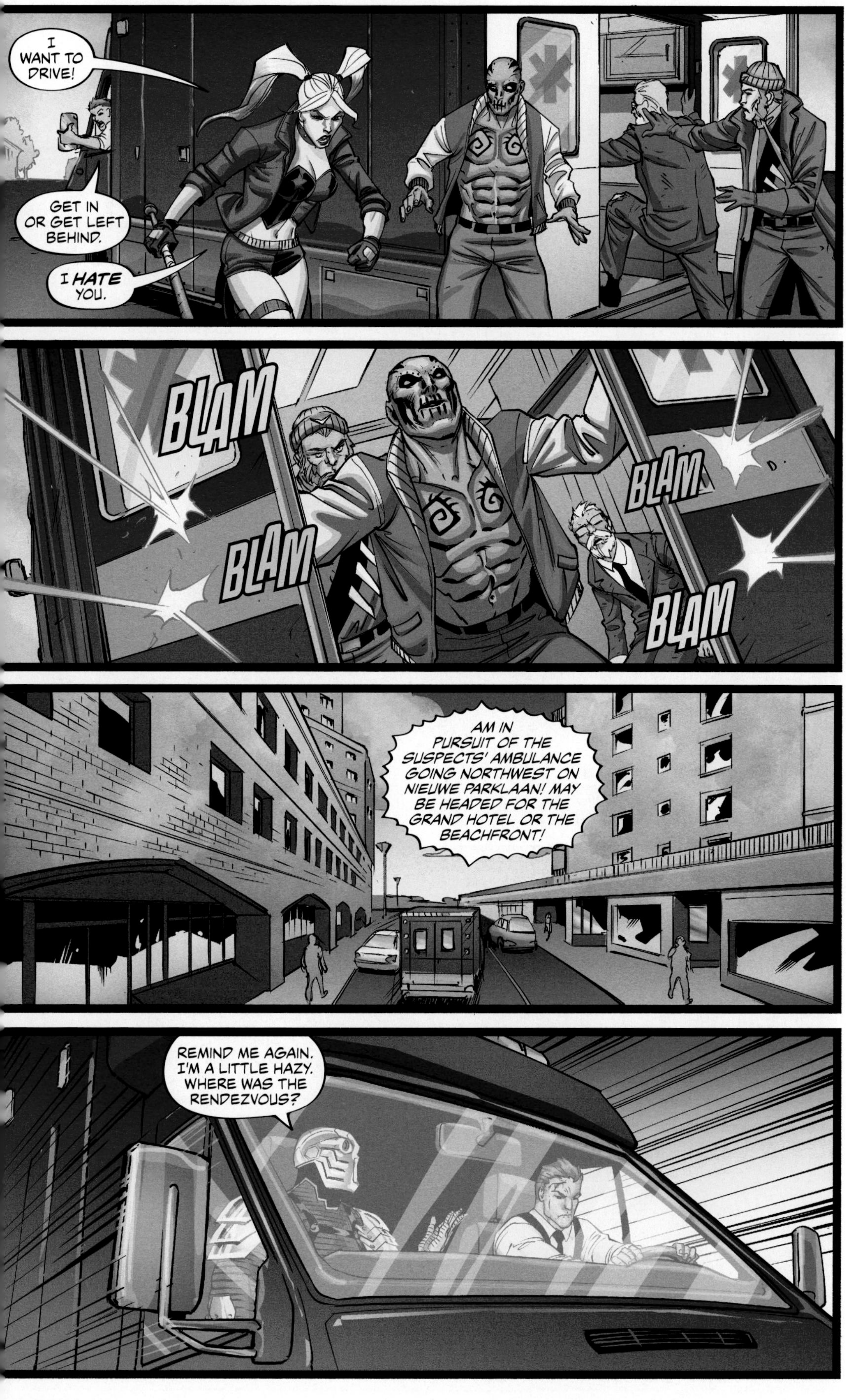
I WANT TO DRIVE!
GET IN OR GET LEFT BEHIND.
I HATE YOU.
BLAM
BLAM
BLAM
BLAM
AM IN PURSUIT OF THE SUSPECTS' AMBULANCE GOING NORTHWEST ON NIEUWE PARKLAAN! MAY BE HEADED FOR THE GRAND HOTEL OR THE BEACHFRONT!
REMIND ME AGAIN. I'M A LITTLE HAZY. WHERE WAS THE RENDEZVOUS?

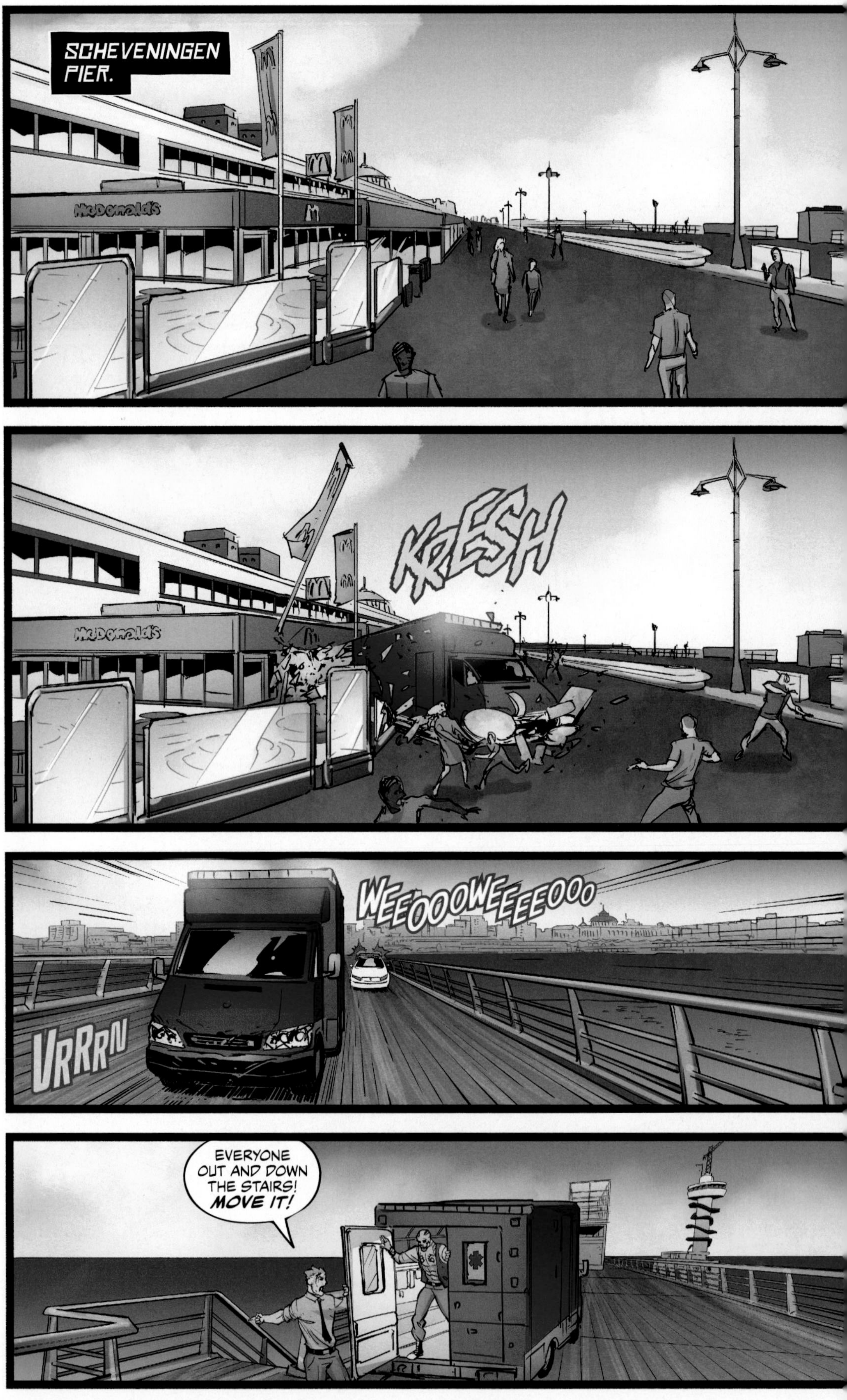
SCHEVENINGEN PIER.
McDonald's
KRESH
WEEOOOWEEEEOOO
VRRRN
EVERYONE OUT AND DOWN THE STAIRS! MOVE IT!

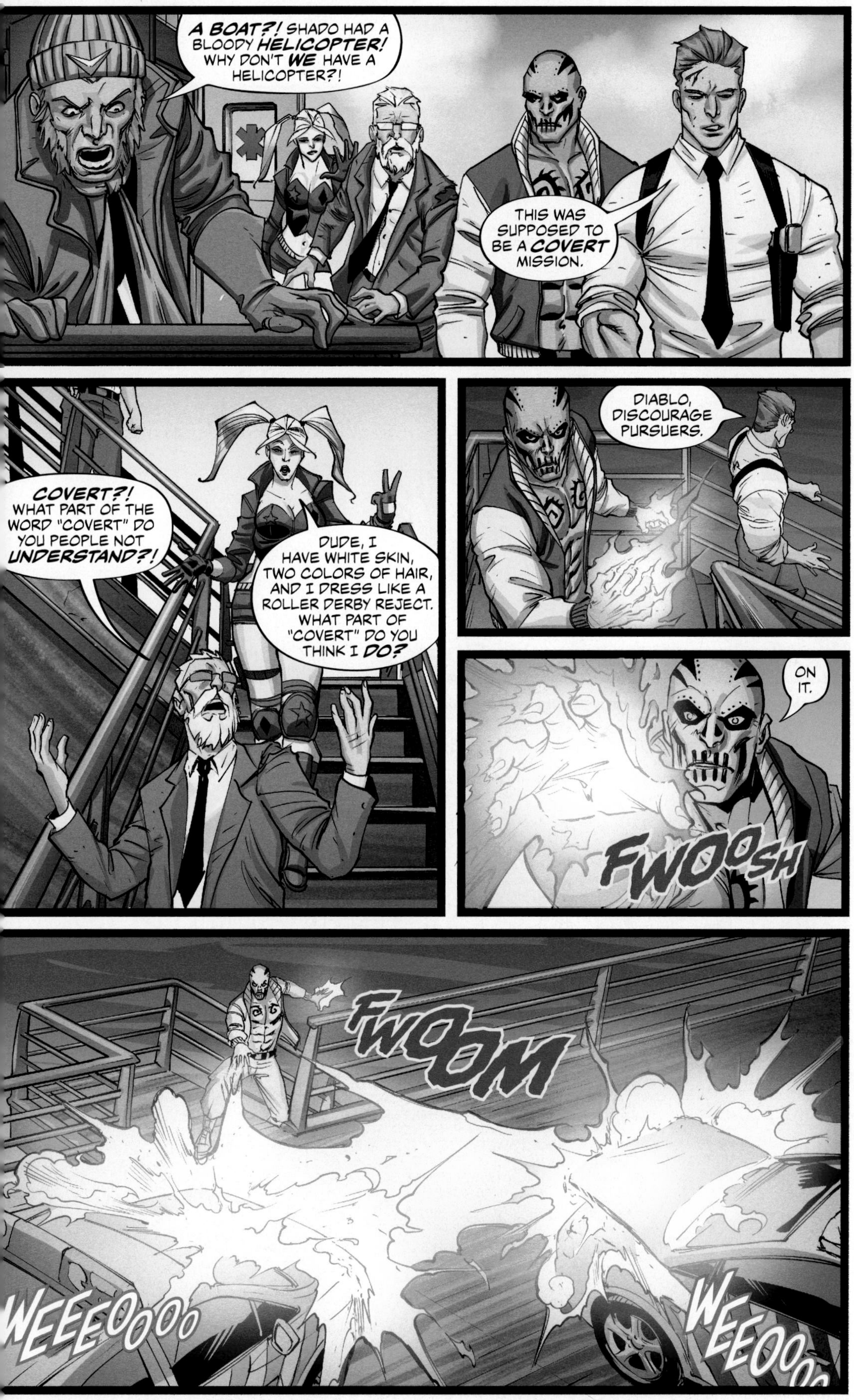

A BOAT?! SHADO HAD A BLOODY HELICOPTER! WHY DON'T WE HAVE A HELICOPTER?!
THIS WAS SUPPOSED TO BE A COVERT MISSION.
COVERT?! WHAT PART OF THE WORD "COVERT" DO YOU PEOPLE NOT UNDERSTAND?!
DUDE, I HAVE WHITE SKIN, TWO COLORS OF HAIR, AND I DRESS LIKE A ROLLER DERBY REJECT. WHAT PART OF "COVERT" DO YOU THINK I DO?
DIABLO, DISCOURAGE PURSUERS.
ON IT.
FWOOSH
FWOOM
WEEEOOOO
WEEOOO

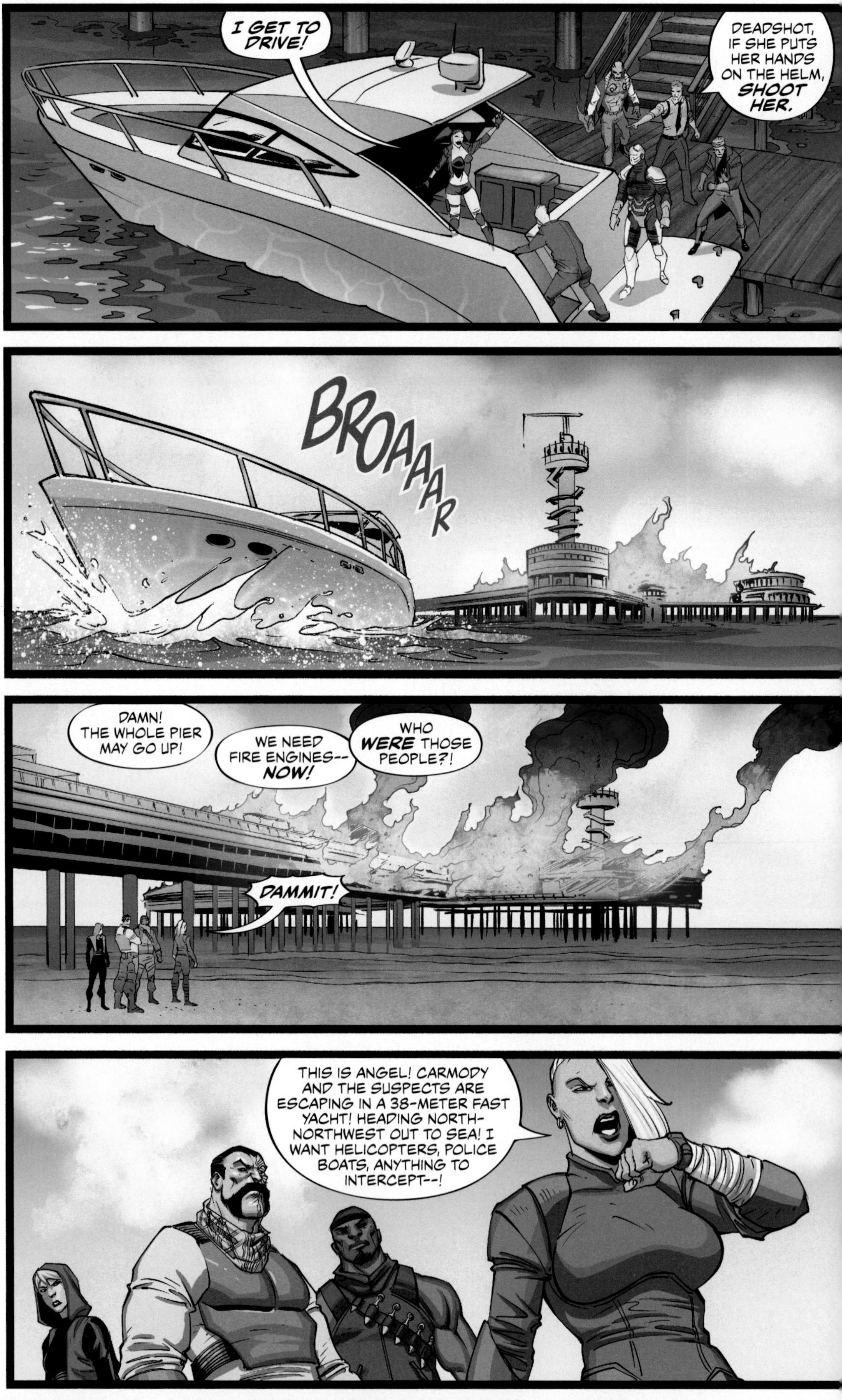
I GET TO DRIVE!
DEADSHOT, IF SHE PUTS HER HANDS ON THE HELM, SHOOT HER.
BROAAAAR
DAMN! THE WHOLE PIER MAY GO UP!
WE NEED FIRE ENGINES-- NOW!
WHO WERE THOSE PEOPLE?!
DAMMIT!
THIS IS ANGEL! CARMODY AND THE SUSPECTS ARE ESCAPING IN A 38-METER FAST YACHT! HEADING NORTH-NORTHWEST OUT TO SEA! I WANT HELICOPTERS, POLICE BOATS, ANYTHING TO INTERCEPT--!

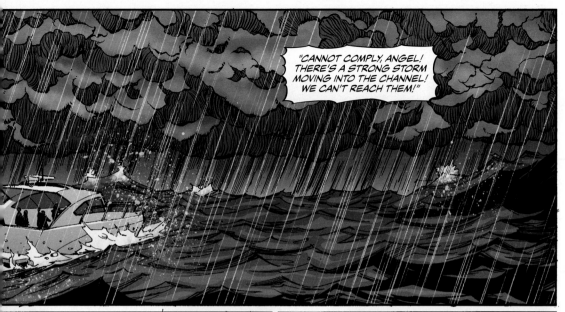

"CANNOT COMPLY, ANGEL! THERE'S A STRONG STORM MOVING INTO THE CHANNEL! WE CAN'T REACH THEM!"

HEY, JEFE! PLEASE TELL ME WE AREN'T CROSSING THE ATLANTIC IN THIS! I THINK MAYBE WE WON'T MAKE IT!

RALFF!

HARKNESS ESPECIALLY WILL NOT MAKE IT, AND HE MAY TAKE THE REST OF US WITH HIM.

THIS IS JUST THE FIRST STAGE. WE'RE HEADING FOR THE ENGLISH COAST.

"THERE'S A FORMER RAF BASE IN EAST ANGLIA NOW USED BY COVERT AGENCIES IN THE UK AND THE U.S.

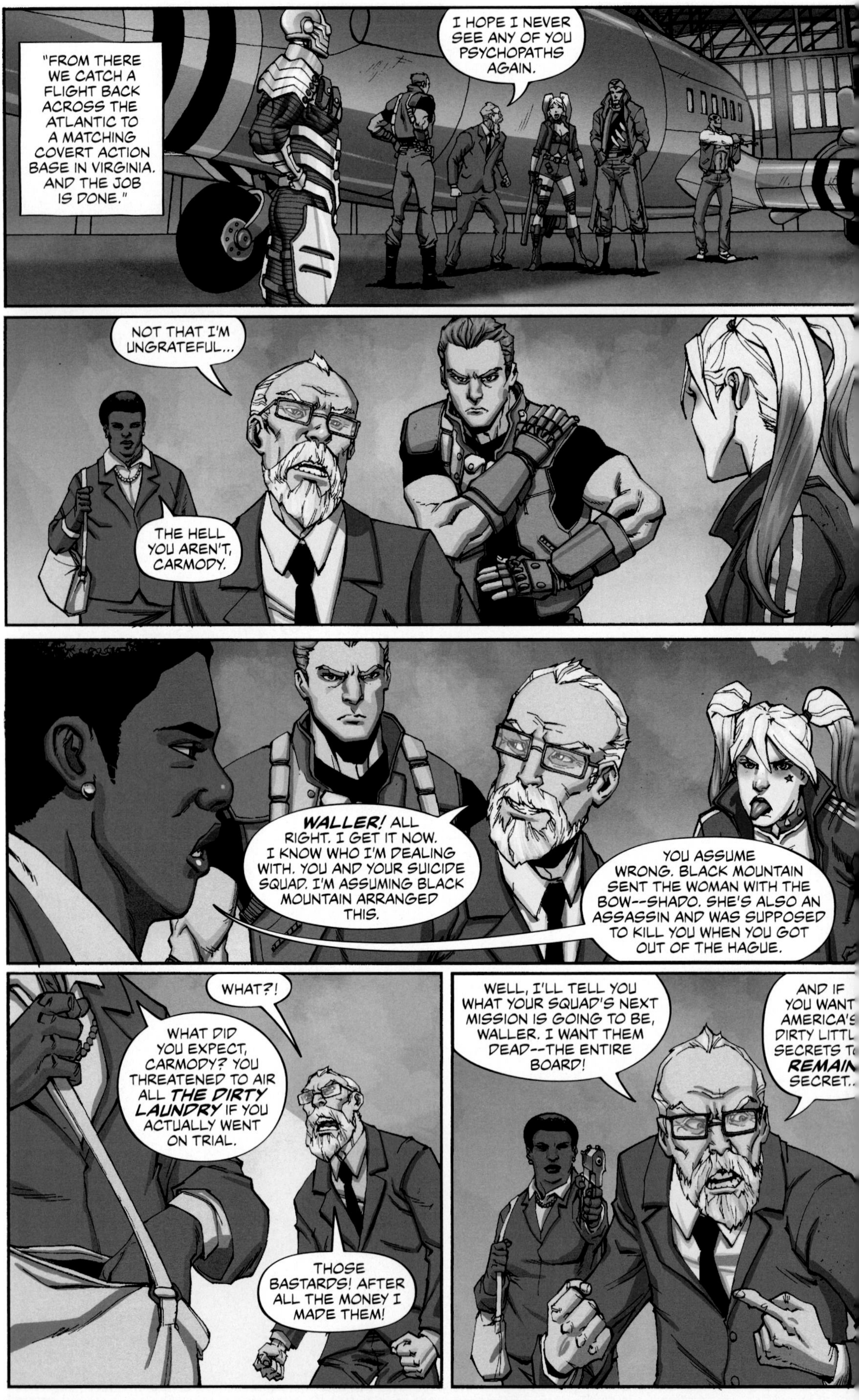
"FROM THERE WE CATCH A FLIGHT BACK ACROSS THE ATLANTIC TO A MATCHING COVERT ACTION BASE IN VIRGINIA. AND THE JOB IS DONE."
I HOPE I NEVER SEE ANY OF YOU PSYCHOPATHS AGAIN.
NOT THAT I'M UNGRATEFUL...
THE HELL YOU AREN'T, CARMODY.
WALLER! ALL RIGHT. I GET IT NOW. I KNOW WHO I'M DEALING WITH. YOU AND YOUR SUICIDE SQUAD. I'M ASSUMING BLACK MOUNTAIN ARRANGED THIS.
YOU ASSUME WRONG. BLACK MOUNTAIN SENT THE WOMAN WITH THE BOW--SHADO. SHE'S ALSO AN ASSASSIN AND WAS SUPPOSED TO KILL YOU WHEN YOU GOT OUT OF THE HAGUE.
WHAT?!
WHAT DID YOU EXPECT, CARMODY? YOU THREATENED TO AIR ALL THE DIRTY LAUNDRY IF YOU ACTUALLY WENT ON TRIAL.
THOSE BASTARDS! AFTER ALL THE MONEY I MADE THEM!
WELL, I'LL TELL YOU WHAT YOUR SQUAD'S NEXT MISSION IS GOING TO BE, WALLER. I WANT THEM DEAD--THE ENTIRE BOARD!
AND IF YOU WANT AMERICA'S DIRTY LITTL SECRETS T REMAIN SECRET...

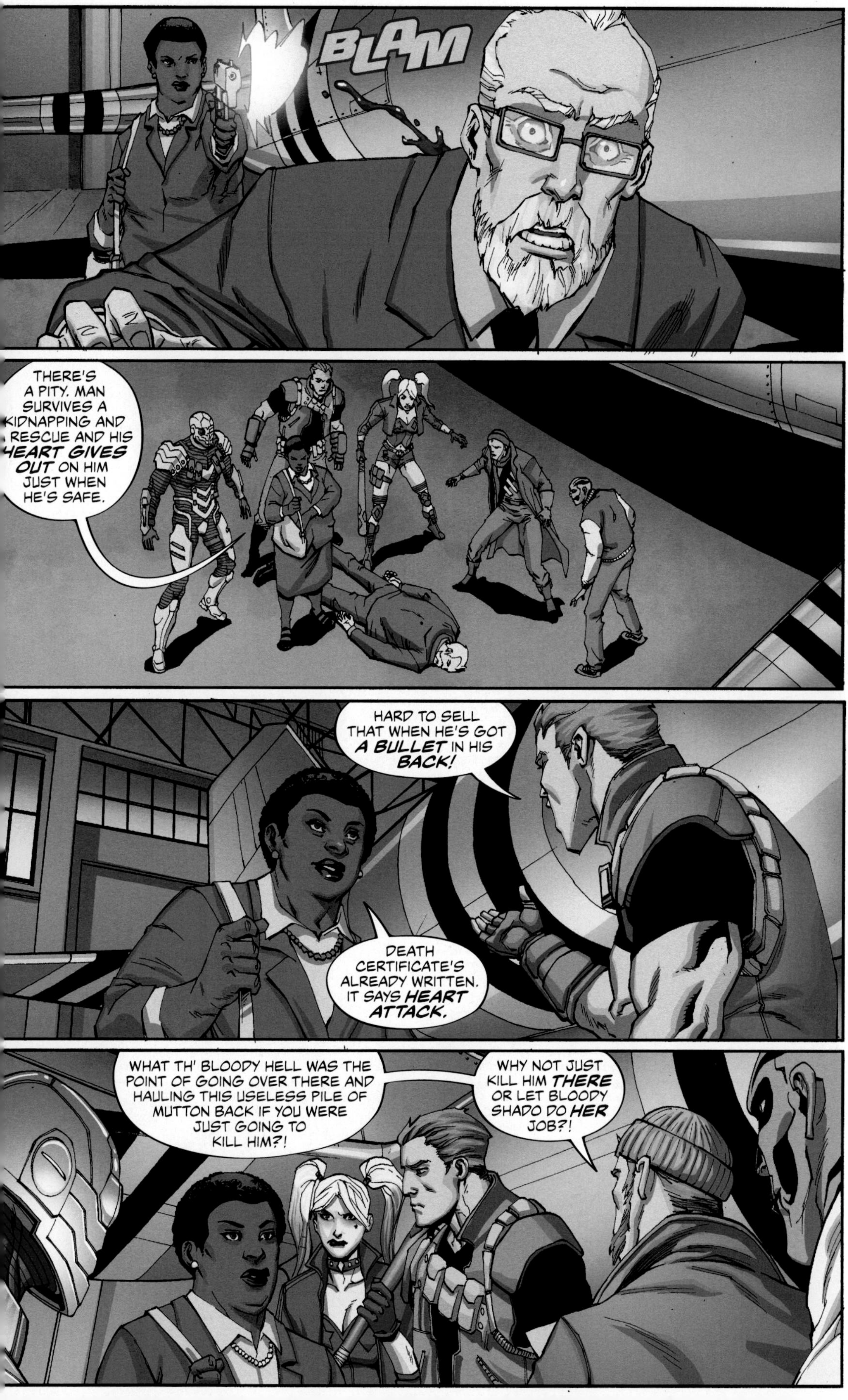
BLAM
THERE'S A PITY. MAN SURVIVES A KIDNAPPING AND A RESCUE AND HIS HEART GIVES OUT ON HIM JUST WHEN HE'S SAFE.
HARD TO SELL THAT WHEN HE'S GOT A BULLET IN HIS BACK!
DEATH CERTIFICATE'S ALREADY WRITTEN. IT SAYS HEART ATTACK.
WHAT TH' BLOODY HELL WAS THE POINT OF GOING OVER THERE AND HAULING THIS USELESS PILE OF MUTTON BACK IF YOU WERE JUST GOING TO KILL HIM?!
WHY NOT JUST KILL HIM THERE OR LET BLOODY SHADO DO HER JOB?!

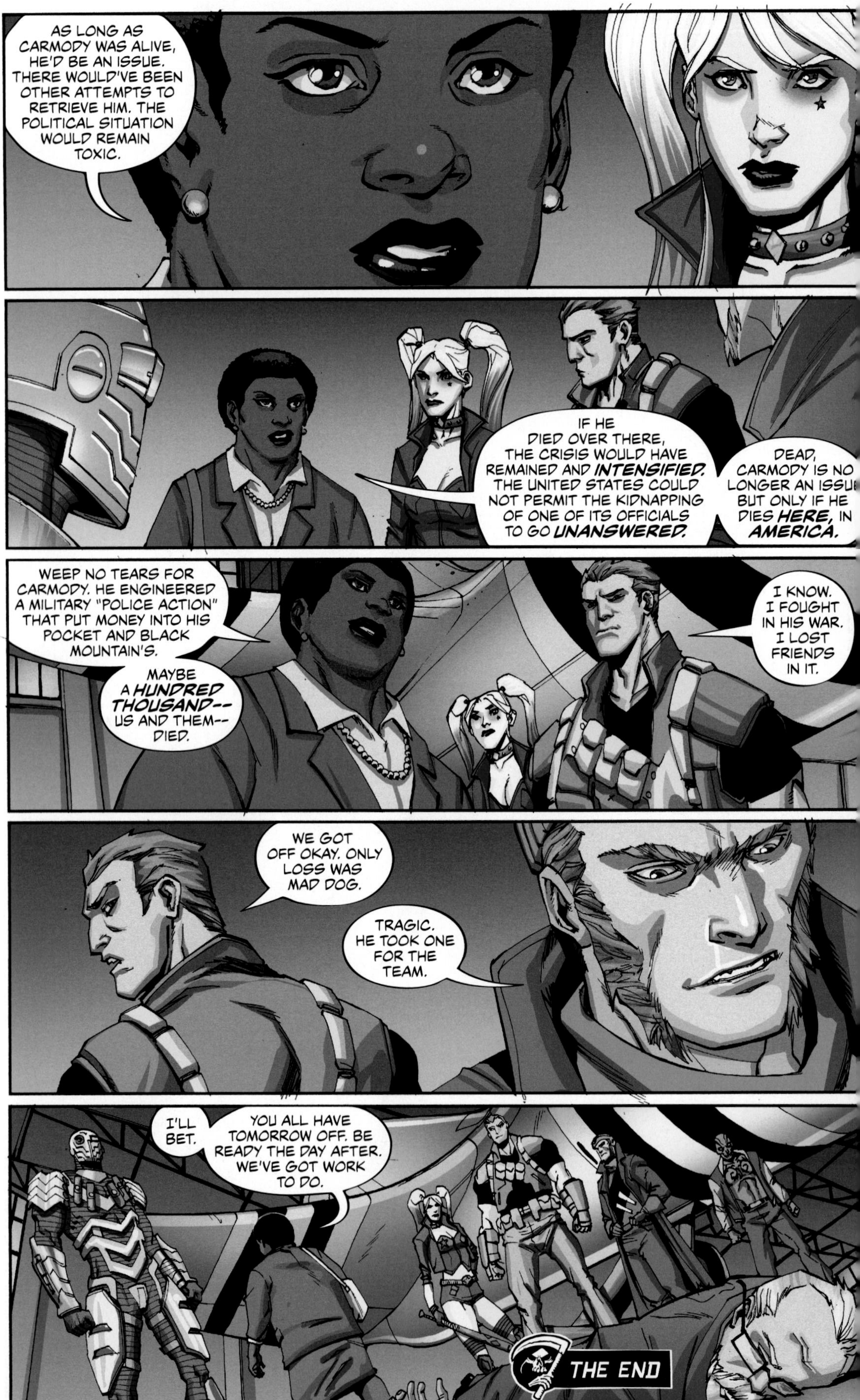
AS LONG AS CARMODY WAS ALIVE, HE'D BE AN ISSUE. THERE WOULD'VE BEEN OTHER ATTEMPTS TO RETRIEVE HIM. THE POLITICAL SITUATION WOULD REMAIN TOXIC.
IF HE DIED OVER THERE, THE CRISIS WOULD HAVE REMAINED AND INTENSIFIED. THE UNITED STATES COULD NOT PERMIT THE KIDNAPPING OF ONE OF ITS OFFICIALS TO GO UNANSWERED.
DEAD, CARMODY IS NO LONGER AN ISSUE BUT ONLY IF HE DIES HERE, IN AMERICA.
WEEP NO TEARS FOR CARMODY. HE ENGINEERED A MILITARY "POLICE ACTION" THAT PUT MONEY INTO HIS POCKET AND BLACK MOUNTAIN'S.
MAYBE A HUNDRED THOUSAND-- US AND THEM-- DIED.
I KNOW. I FOUGHT IN HIS WAR. I LOST FRIENDS IN IT.
WE GOT OFF OKAY. ONLY LOSS WAS MAD DOG.
TRAGIC. HE TOOK ONE FOR THE TEAM.
I'LL BET.
YOU ALL HAVE TOMORROW OFF. BE READY THE DAY AFTER. WE'VE GOT WORK TO DO.
THE END

Variant cover art for SUICIDE SQUAD #11 by LEE BERMEJO

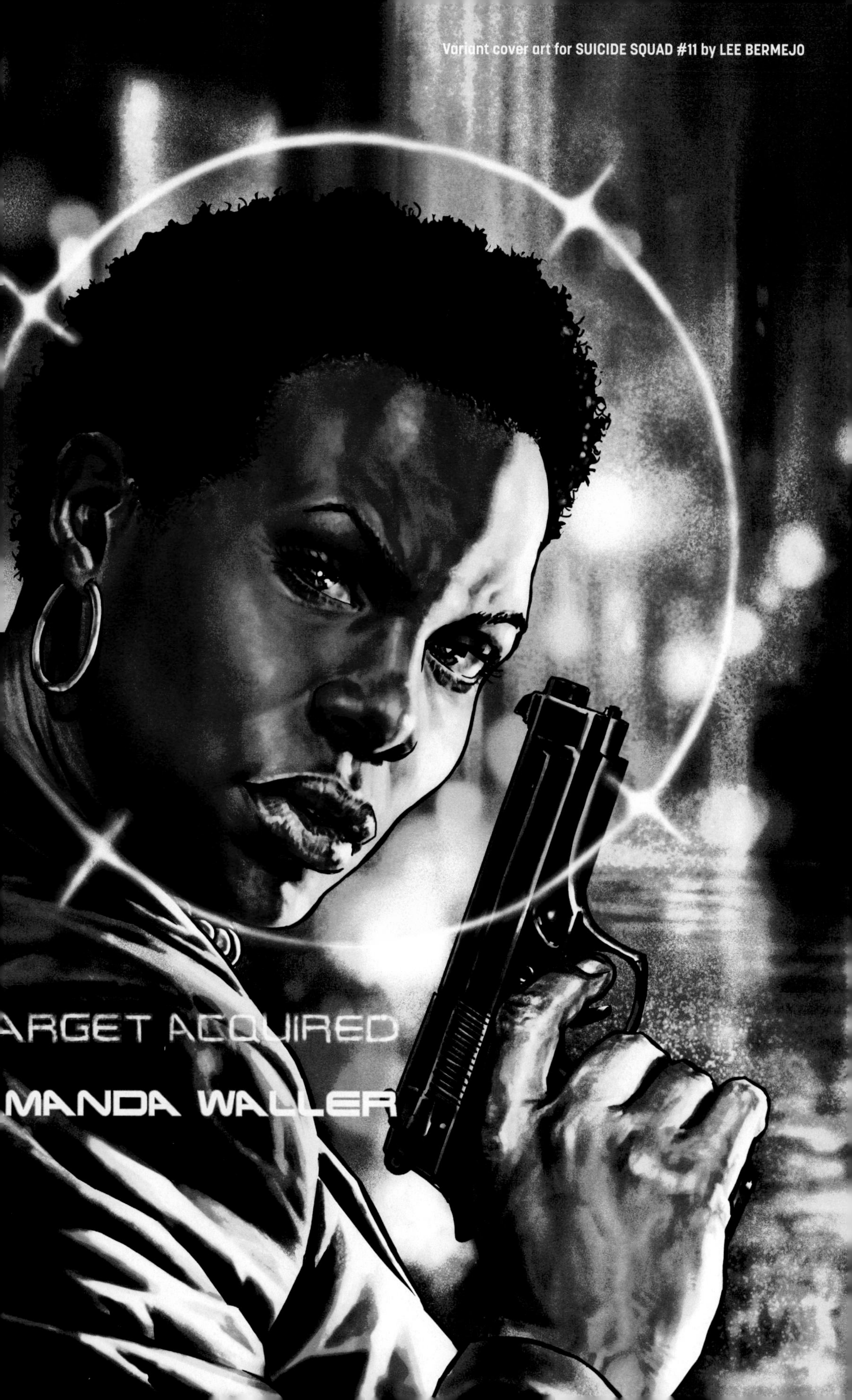
ARGET ACQUIRED
MANDA WALLER

Variant cover art for SUICIDE SQUAD #12
by WHILCE PORTACIO and ALEX SINCLAIR

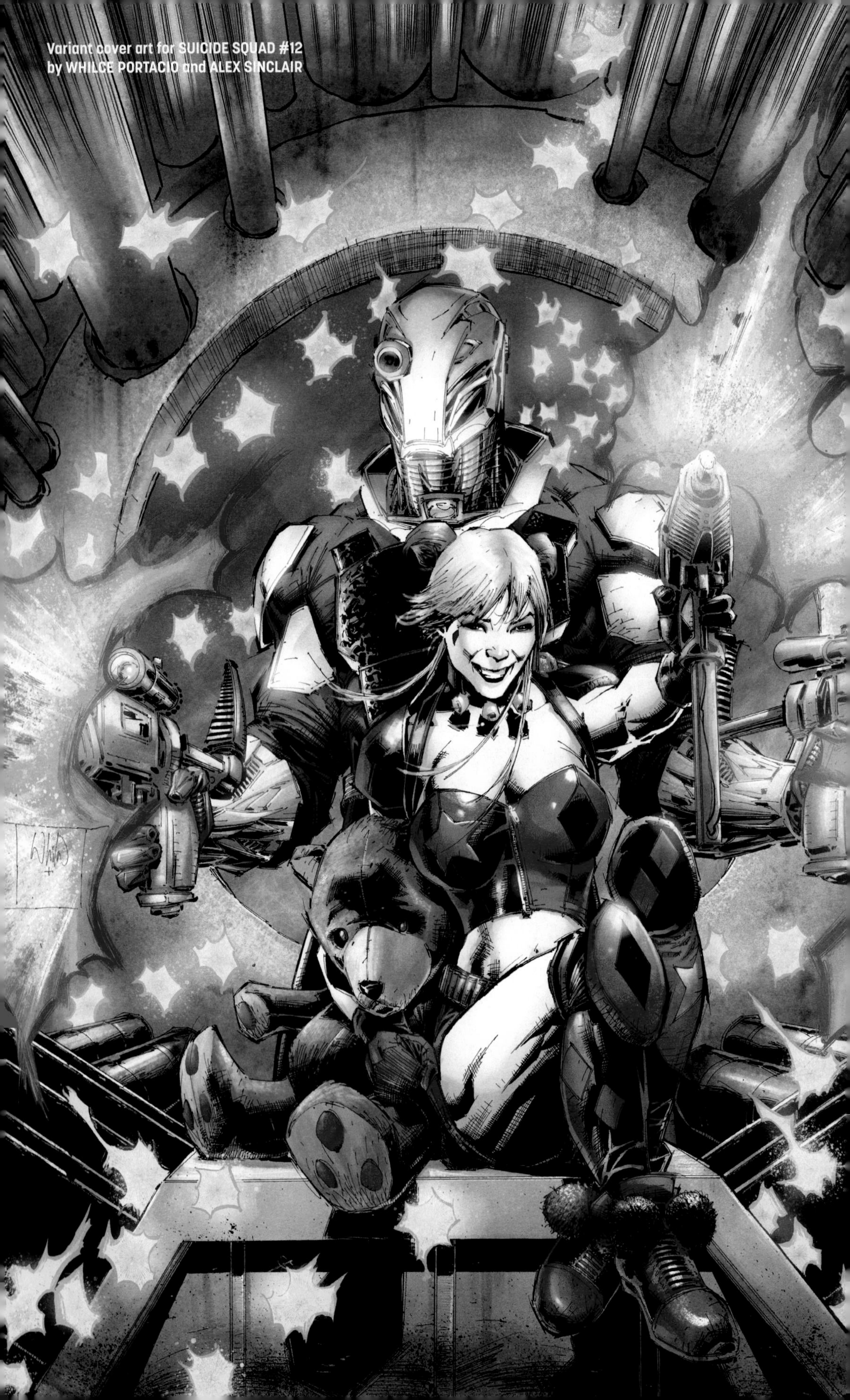

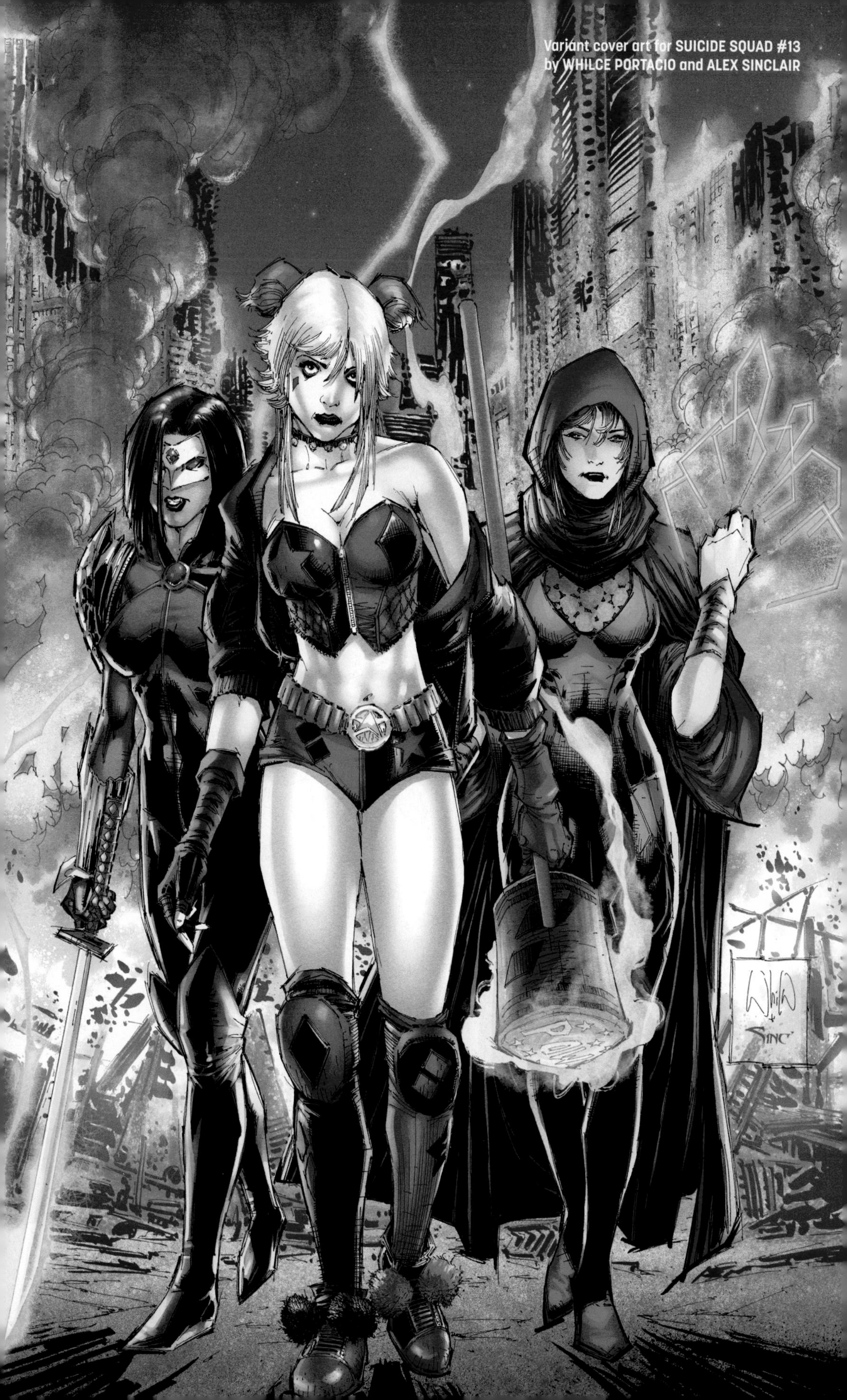

Variant cover art for SUICIDE SQUAD #13
by WHILCE PORTACIO and ALEX SINCLAIR

Variant cover art for SUICIDE SQUAD #14
by WHILCE PORTACIO and ALEX SINCLAIR

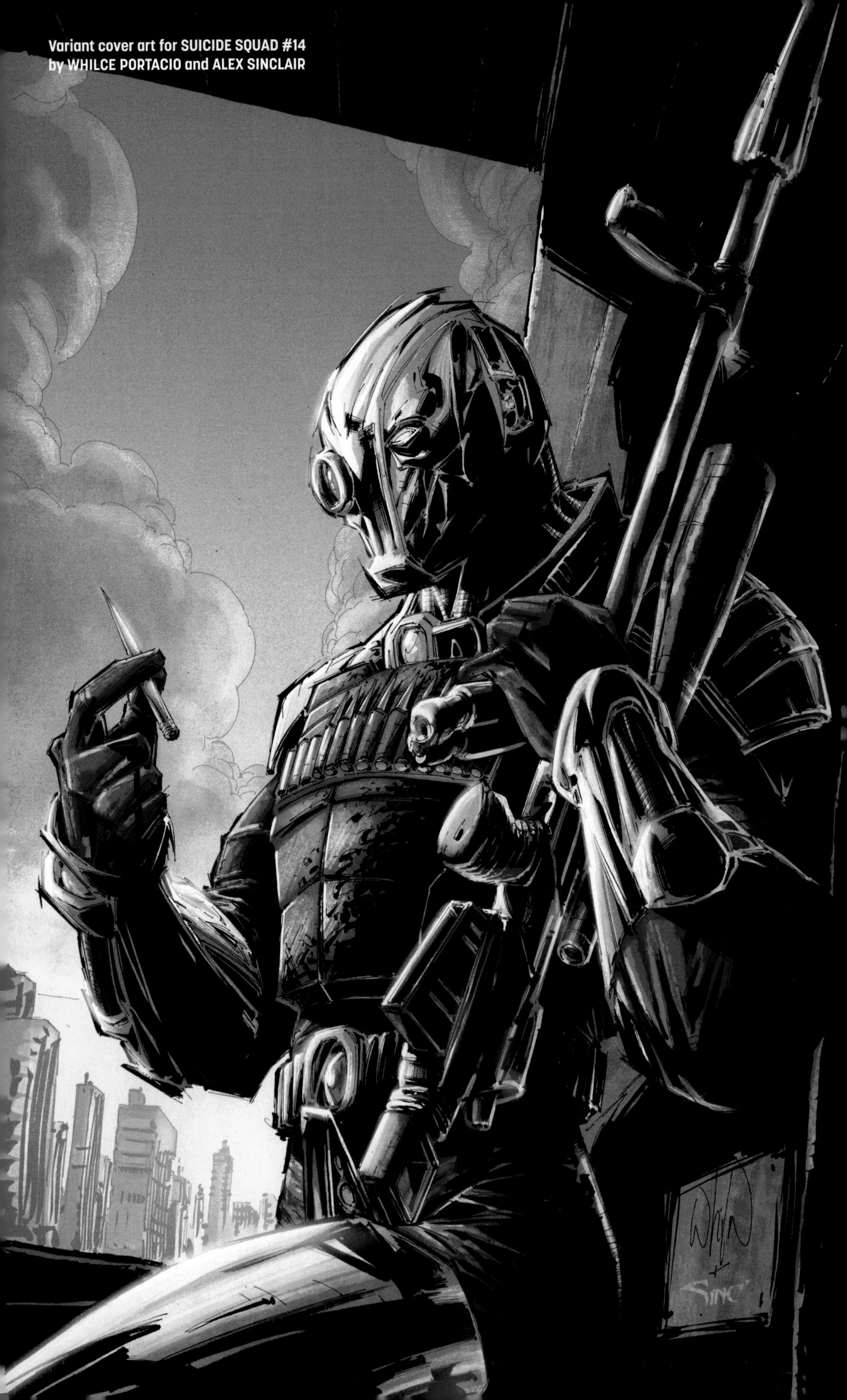

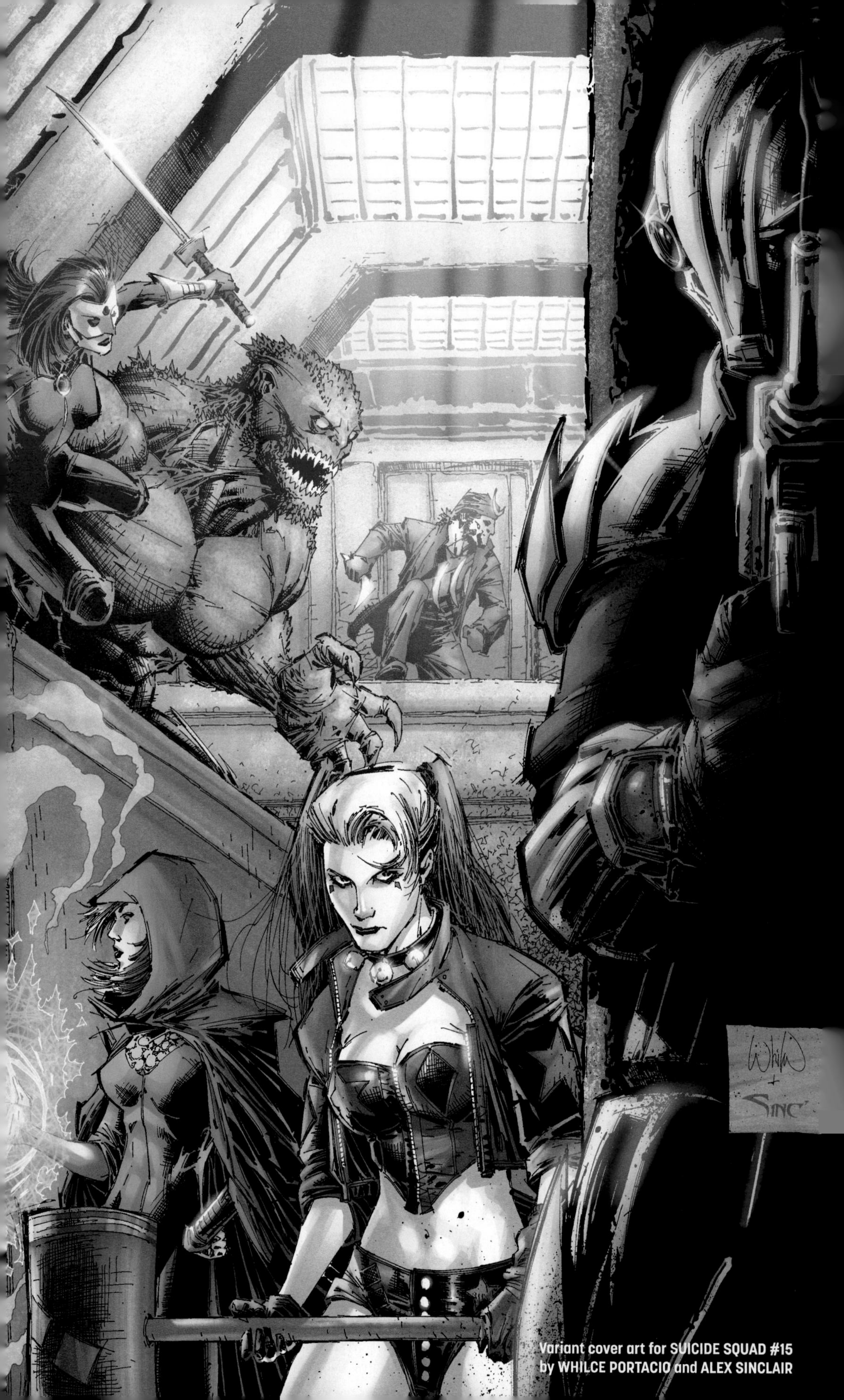

Variant cover art for SUICIDE SQUAD #15
by WHILCE PORTACIO and ALEX SINCLAIR

"It's nice to see one of the best comics of the late '80s return so strongly."
– **Comic Book Resources**

"It's high energy from page one through to the last page." – **BATMAN NEWS**

DC UNIVERSE REBIRTH
SUICIDE SQUAD

VOL. 1: THE BLACK VAULT

ROB WILLIAMS
with JIM LEE and others

VOL.1 THE BLACK VAULT
ROB WILLIAMS • JIM LEE • PHILIP TAN • JASON FABOK • IVAN REIS • GARY FRANK

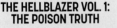

**THE HELLBLAZER VOL. 1:
THE POISON TRUTH**

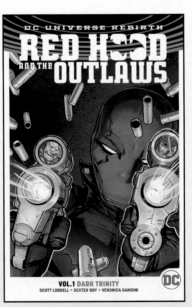

**RED HOOD AND THE OUTLAWS VOL. 1:
DARK TRINITY**

**HARLEY QUINN VOL. 1:
DIE LAUGHING**